NEW RESEARCH
CORPORATE FINANCE AN

Centre for Economic Policy Research

The Centre for Economic Policy Research is a network of over 530 Research Fellows and Affiliates, based primarily in European universities. The Centre coordinates the research activities of its Fellows and Affiliates and communicates the results to the public and private sectors. CEPR is an entrepreneur, developing research initiatives with the producers, consumers, and sponsors of research. Established in 1983, CEPR is a European economics research organization with uniquely wide-ranging scope and activities.

CEPR is a registered educational charity. Institutional (core) finance for the Centre is provided by major grants from the Economic and Social Research Council, under which an ESRC Resource Centre operates within CEPR; the Esmée Fairbairn Charitable Trust; and the Bank of England. The Centre is also supported by the European Central Bank; the Bank for International Settlements; 22 national central banks; and 45 companies. None of these organizations gives prior review to the Centre's publications, nor do they necessarily endorse the views expressed therein.

The Centre is pluralist and non-partisan, bringing economic research to bear on the analysis of medium- and long-run policy questions. CEPR research may include views on policy, but the Executive Committee of the Centre does not give prior review to its publications, and the Centre takes no institutional policy positions. The opinions expressed in this report are those of the authors and not those of the Centre for Economic Policy Research.

Centre for Economic Policy Research
90–98 Goswell Road
London EC1V 7RR
UK

Tel: (44 20) 7878 2900   Fax: (44 20) 7878 2999
Email: cepr@cepr.org   Website: www.cepr.org

New Research in Corporate Finance and Banking

Edited by

BRUNO BIAIS

and

MARCO PAGANO

OXFORD

UNIVERSITY PRESS

OXFORD
UNIVERSITY PRESS

Great Clarendon Street, Oxford OX2 6DP

Oxford University Press is a department of the University of Oxford.
It furthers the University's objective of excellence in research, scholarship,
and education by publishing worldwide in

Oxford New York

Auckland Bangkok Buenos Aires Cape Town Chennai
Dar es Salaam Delhi Hong Kong Istanbul Karachi Kolkata
Kuala Lumpur Madrid Melbourne Mexico City Mumbai Nairobi
São Paulo Shanghai Singapore Taipei Tokyo Toronto

with an associated company in Berlin

Oxford is a registered trade mark of Oxford University Press
in the UK and in certain other countries

Published in the United States
by Oxford University Press Inc., New York

British Library Cataloguing in Publication Data
Data available

Library of Congress Cataloging in Publication Data
Corporate finance and banking : selected readings / edited by Bruno Biais and Marco Pagano.
p. cm.
Includes bibliographical references.
1. Corporations—Finance.   2. Commercial credit.   3. Banks and banking.
I. Biais, B. (Bruno)   II. Pagano, Marco.
HG4028.F3 C67 2002   658.15–dc21   2001054553

ISBN 0-19-924323-9
ISBN 0-19-924324-7 (pbk.)

1 3 5 7 9 10 8 6 4 2

Typeset by Newgen Imaging Systems (P) Ltd., Chennai, India
Printed in Great Britain
on acid-free paper by
T.J. International Ltd., Padstow, Cornwall

Contents

Contents

Introduction

European financial systems differ considerably from each other: banks and securities markets play widely different roles, in some countries universal banks are dominant intermediaries and in others they hardly exist, and the pace of financial innovation is equally uneven. This startling diversity of experiences may partly explain why European research on the design of financial markets and contracts is particularly lively, in some cases posing novel questions and in others offering novel answers to old questions in corporate finance and banking. The chapters in this volume offer a sample of this research and of the various paths that it is treading. While on the surface the chapters may seem quite disparate and disconnected, upon careful consideration they are not. A number of important common themes and questions run across them, and similar methodologies are used in approaching them.

One of these common questions is why security markets have such different roles and importance relative to banks in different countries. A related issue is whether these different financial arrangements matter for the functioning of the real economy. Several studies approach these issues by focusing on the functioning of the primary equity market, or the process through which companies 'go public', which marks the transition from complete reliance on bank financing to partial reliance on security markets. Other studies approach the issue at a 'systemic' level, attempting to identify the comparative advantages of banks and security markets in solving the information problems involved in financing companies.

A further group of chapters shares another concern: explaining the variety in the design of contracts and institutions observed in credit markets. Why do some companies borrow from a single bank and others from several banks, or from a multitude of investors via bond markets? Why do some banks share information about their customers? Finally, two chapters consider whether credit market imperfections produce different real outcomes. Does the functioning of the credit market have independent effects on the ability of companies to compete and survive? And how does it affect the cyclical behaviour of the economy?

At a more fundamental level, all the studies in this book are bound together by the common idea that information and enforcement problems are the key obstacles to the provision of external finance to companies, and they all employ contract-theoretic tools to frame these problems and guide empirical work.

I. GOING PUBLIC

Several papers in this volume focus on the process through which companies list their shares on public equity markets. Understanding the motivations and design of initial public offerings (IPOs) is an important step towards answering the wider question of what is the function of the stock market. One of the main differences between the market-oriented financial system of Anglo-Saxon countries and the bank-based system of continental Europe lies precisely in the proportion of companies listed on the stock exchange. But, even in Great Britain and in the United States, some large companies are not public. So the decision to go public cannot be considered simply a 'natural' stage in the growth process of a company. These cross-country and cross-sectional differences indicate that going public is a *choice*.

Why Companies Go Public: Pagano, Panetta, and Zingales (1998)

The chapter by Pagano, Panetta, and Zingales explains what are the determinants of this choice, using data on accounting variables, interest rates, and bank loans for a large panel of Italian companies, a subset of which went public during the sample period. These data are used to analyse the determinants of IPOs as well as the consequences of this decision on the companies' investment, profitability, financial policies, ownership structure, and control.

They find that the main determinants of the probability of an IPO are the size of the company and the market-to-book price ratio in the relevant industry. The role of company size may indicate the presence of sizable fixed listing costs or may proxy for company age and associated reputation. The positive relationship with the market-to-book ratio may reflect a higher value of investment opportunities in the sector or rather these companies' ability in timing the market. The finding that investment, growth, and profitability decrease after the IPO lends credibility to the 'market timing' story. The new capital raised upon listing is not used to finance subsequent investment and growth, but rather to reduce leverage.

On the whole, these results suggest that in the Italian case the stock market has not catered mainly to small, young, and capital-thirsty companies, but to large and mature companies attempting to time the market and reduce leverage. The typical Italian IPO is eight times as large and six times as old as the typical IPO in the United States. This applies to most other European countries as well: the average age of firms going public in continental Europe is forty years (Rydquist and Hogholm, 1995), in contrast with the United States, where most IPOs are used to fund the early growth stages of start-up companies. This begs the question of why the stock market plays such different roles in continental Europe and the United States, an issue on which the chapters by Boot and Thakor on financial system design shed some light.

Another empirical finding reported by Pagano *et al.* (1998) is that going public permanently reduces the cost of bank credit. This effect is not fully explained by the reduction in leverage at the time of the IPO. It may partly reflect the improved quality of the accounting information concerning public companies and partly their greater bargaining power with banks. So another function of public equity markets in Europe may be to disenfranchise relatively mature companies from banks. This suggests that banks are unlikely to favour companies' access to public markets, a point again echoed in the chapters by Boot and Thakor.

Finally, IPOs are associated with some equity sales by controlling shareholders and by more frequent turnover of control than private companies. So the desire to divest from the company also plays a role in IPOs. The next three studies in this volume show that changes of share ownership and corporate control concerns also crucially affect the incentives to go public, as well as the design of IPOs.

The Role of Ownership and Control: Brennan and Franks (1997), Mello and Parsons (1998), Bulow, Huang, and Klemperer (1999), and Habib and Ljungqvist (2001)

The decision to go public is taken by the existing directors of the company. Therefore identifying their objectives and incentives is a prerequisite to understanding the decision to go public as well as the pricing and design of IPOs. For the existing directors of the company, the IPO is a key opportunity to design the subsequent share-ownership structure and control allocation. How will they exploit this opportunity? To the extent that they enjoy considerable private benefits of control, they will not want to be severely limited by the monitoring activity of large outside shareholders, or to expose their control benefits to the risk of a post-IPO takeover raid.

To protect their private benefits of control, the initial owner-manager will typically want a certain degree of dispersion, as shown by Pagano and Röell (1998). If he sells a minority stake (to finance new investment or to allow other owners to, divest), he will not sell the entire stake to a single shareholder, for fear of being 'excessively' monitored. If the desired degree of share-ownership dispersion is sufficiently large, going public is preferable to obtaining finance from many private shareholders. While the company stays private, each additional private shareholder must bear non-negligible costs to collect information about the company and trade its shares (due to the absence of a public market price), so that the company's cost of capital is increasing with the number of shareholders. Above a critical number of shareholders, it becomes preferable to pay the fixed listing cost and go public, thus avoiding altogether excessive monitoring by other shareholders. The incentive to go public is stronger, the larger the initial amount of external funding to be raised and the stricter the disclosure rules for public relative to private companies.

The incentive to disperse share ownership at the IPO stage is compounded by the danger of a post-IPO hostile takeover. This danger is greatly increased if an outside shareholder is allowed to accumulate a non-negligible toehold in the company. The chapter by Bulow, Huang, and Klemperer (1999) in this book shows that toeholds can have an enormous impact in takeover battles, such as those between two financial bidders. This is because a takeover contest can be seen as a 'common-value' auction. In this situation, the bidder who has a toehold can win very cheaply, because he has the incentive to bid aggressively: his bids do not just raise the price of the remaining shares but also the value of his own holdings. Expecting the toeholder to bid aggressively increases the other bidders' winner's curse and makes them less aggressive, which in turn reinforces the aggressiveness of the toeholder.

The empirical evidence confirms that a toehold greatly enhances its owner's chance of winning the control of a company and reduces the resistance of the incumbent management (Walkling, 1985; Stultz, Walkling, and Song, 1990; Jennings and Mazzeo, 1993; Betton and Eckbo, 1997). Conversely, a dispersed share ownership has two related benefits for incumbent management. On one hand, it avoids the danger of a future hostile takeover by a toeholder. On the other, it allows controlling shareholders to retain effective control via a stake considerably below 50 per cent, as the company's only toeholders.

Even if the initial controlling shareholders want to surrender control, it is efficient for them to sell the controlling stake separately after the IPO, as argued by Zingales (1995) and Mello and Parsons (1998). This two-stage sale allows the sale of the controlling stake at a different price, reflecting the private benefits (and costs) of control. In addition, as pointed out by Mello and Parsons, the IPO has a price discovery function, in that it enables the seller to elicit valuable information about the company's value and use it to set the terms for the sale of the controlling stake to a new controlling shareholder.

These theoretical predictions are supported by the evidence reported by Brennan and Franks (1997) in this volume. Using data from sixty-nine IPOs in Great Britain, they show that the IPO shares are underpriced in order to ensure oversubscription and allow existing directors of the company to discriminate among applicants for shares and disperse the shareholdings among a large number of investors. Rationing shares at the IPO enables directors to discriminate against investors who apply for large blocks, even at the cost of large under-pricing (which in fact appears to be positively related to subsequent share ownership-dispersion). This allows incumbent management to enjoy the private benefits of control without the hindrance of excessive monitoring by large non-controlling shareholders (as predicted by Pagano and Röell) or the danger of a hostile bid by a toeholder capable of taking control over the company (as highlighted by Bulow, Huang, and Klemperer). In fact, incumbent managers slept easily for many years after the IPO: Brennan and Franks report only three hostile takeover bids out of forty-three companies surviving up to 10 years after the IPO, only one of which was successful.

One may object that, through IPO underpricing, controlling shareholders themselves pay part of the cost associated with dispersion of non-controlling stake. But Brennan and Franks point out that controlling shareholders bear only a minor fraction of the cost of underpricing, since they sell very few shares at the IPO—most shares being sold by non-directors.

The same idea—that the distribution of the wealth losses associated with underpricing is central to the IPO design—is at the core of the study by Habib and Ljungqvist (2001) in this volume. They reckon that the initial shareholders' desire to avoid underpricing is crucially related to how many shares they plan to sell at the IPO stage: the more they sell, the less they want to underprice. But, Habib and Ljungqvist add, they can do so because they have another policy instrument to play with, besides underpricing. If they wish to limit underpricing, initial shareholders can spend more resources in promotion activities, such as hiring high-quality financial advisers or advertising the IPO. These promotion activities raise the demand by uninformed investors and thereby allow the initial share-holders to get a better price for their shares, other things being equal. Since at the margin promotion activities are more efficient for initial shareholders who plan to sell a large amount of shares, one would expect to see more promotion expenses and less underpricing when larger inside stakes are sold. These pre-dictions are supported by evidence based on a large sample of US IPOs floated on NASDAQ between 1991 and 1995.

II. FINANCIAL SYSTEM ARCHITECTURE

One of the reasons why companies go public is that banks and security markets are adept at solving different informational problems, and these problems typi-cally change as company characteristics change, as pointed out by Boot and Thakor in their two chapters in this volume. Companies perceived as low-quality on the basis of public information typically benefit by borrowing from banks, since bank monitoring is especially suited to solving the moral-hazard problems arising from borrowers' opportunistic behaviour. Companies that are perceived as high-quality instead gain more from accessing security markets, since the latter aggregate investors' diverse information and convey it to companies via prices. Security markets are not good monitors, but this matters less for companies of proven quality.

In the early stages of economic development, Boot and Thakor (1997*a*) argue, most firms tend to have low observable quality and therefore need to rely on bank finance and monitoring. As the financial system develops, successful borrowers acquire a better reputation and graduate to security-market financing, as in Diamond (1991). The attendant improvement in the average quality of compa-nies makes investment in security markets more attractive, so that a greater fraction of resources in the financial system is endogenously reallocated from bank lending and monitoring to investment and trade on security markets.

On this view of financial development, security markets tend to grow at the expense of bank financing. Therefore, to the extent that banks can collectively create some institutional impediment to the growth of financial markets, they will tend to do so. There is a collective action problem in doing so, however: unless banks coordinate their actions, they cannot defer or prevent the development of security markets. Such coordination will typically be more difficult if banks are competitive than in a credit market dominated by a few large players.

This insight is further refined in Boot and Thakor (1997*b*), which shows that the development of security markets does not only depend on the degree of banking competition, but also on the degree of functional separation between commercial and investment banking. In this study, Boot and Thakor distinguish between commercial banks, which specialize in lending and monitoring, and investment banks, which specialize in financial innovation via security design. Investment banks hold the key to security market access by companies, and thereby can reduce the scope of commercial banks' activity. Accordingly, commercial banks have all the incentives to restrain the activity of investment banks. They can do so by integrating them in their structure, if regulation allows the establishment of 'universal banks'. So the model predicts that in countries where universal banks dominate financial markets, financial innovation is less intense than in countries where commercial and investment banking cannot be joined within the same institution.

III. DESIGN OF CREDIT CONTRACTS AND INSTITUTIONS

Given the persistent prevalence of banks in financial intermediation (especially in Europe and Japan), it is natural to ask what is the economic function of the various contracts and institutions that appear to rule actual credit relationships. Some chapters in this volume illustrate this line of research, showing that the design of credit contracts and institutions can be regarded as an endogenous response to informational and incentive constraints.

Optimal Credit Contract Design: Bolton and Scharfstein (1996)

In some countries, companies tend to rely primarily on a single bank. In others, credit-seekers apply simultaneously for credit from several lenders and often manage to get loans and lines of credit from several institutions. As reported by Ongena and Smith (2000), in Norway, Sweden, Switzerland, and the United Kingdom, the median number of bank relationships is relatively low at less than three, and between three and four in Austria, Denmark, Finland, Ireland, Hungary, the Netherlands, and Poland. But it can be much larger in other countries: in France, Italy, and Portugal, the median number is nine or more.

The chapter by Bolton and Scharfstein in this volume analyses the choice of the number of a company's creditors as the result of an optimal contract. The starting point of the analysis, which is based on the theory of incomplete contracts, is that borrowers can default for liquidity reasons or as a result of opportunistic behaviour by the borrower. To avoid or reduce the occurrence of the latter, debt contracts must penalize default by entitling creditors of insolvent borrowers to liquidate the company's assets. But, to the extent that this right is enforced also when default is due to a liquidity shock, liquidation will occur inefficiently. The optimal contract will have to balance the disciplinary role of liquidation with the inefficiency ensuing from excessive liquidation of the company's assets.

The number of creditors is a key ingredient in designing the optimal contract, since it affects the ex-post liquidation incentives of creditors. Bolton and

Scharfstein show that with multiple creditors, the borrower ends up paying more than he would pay to a single creditor, in that the liquidation value of his assets is lower. Therefore, liquidation becomes more effective in penalizing strategic default, and also more costly in case of a liquidity default. Accordingly, multiple creditors should be preferred when liquidity default is unlikely, and a single creditor when the risk of liquidity default is high. By the same token, a single creditor is preferable when the firm's assets are worth substantially more together than apart: the higher the asset complementarity, the greater the cost of excessive liquidation.

Of course, borrowing from several creditors also has other costs and benefits besides those analysed by Bolton and Scharfstein. Multiple bank relationships discourage each bank from monitoring the borrower closely (since lenders free-ride on each others' monitoring efforts) and prevent the intertemporal sharing of rent surplus that would be possible within an exclusive bank–firm relationship (Petersen and Rajan, 1994). On the other hand, borrowing from several creditors may entail several additional benefits besides its disciplinary role against strategic default. First, it may help reduce the cost of credit by forcing lenders to compete. Second, by lending a small amount to each client, creditors can diversify their loan portfolios more than they would under exclusive lending. This can reduce interest rates by lowering the risk premium required by each lender. Third, a borrower who can obtain credit from several lenders is insured against the risk of having a loan or credit line withdrawn if a single lender suffers a liquidity shock (Detragiache, Garella, and Guiso, 2000).

Information Sharing Arrangements: Pagano and Jappelli (1993), Padilla and Pagano (1997)

Credit market performance is not only affected by the design of credit contracts but also by the design of institutions that shape information flows within the market, such as voluntary information sharing mechanisms ('credit bureaus') or mandatory ones ('public credit registers'). The paper by Pagano and Jappelli is the first to document the presence of information sharing agreements among lenders in the consumer credit market, and their differing importance across countries and over time.[1] The paper proposes an explanation for why lenders may find it worthwhile to share information about their customers. In the context of an adverse selection model, information sharing allows banks to target and price their loans more accurately, and thereby increase their profits—provided these are dissipated by competition, and the costs of the information sharing mechanism are not too high.

In the model, each bank has private information about the creditworthiness of credit applicants who reside in its market area but has no information about credit

---

[1] Jappelli and Pagano (2001) also document the pervasiveness of information sharing arrangements in other credit markets and for a larger set of countries.

applicants who have recently moved into its market area ('movers'). Therefore, banks face an adverse selection problem when lending to movers. However, another bank may have information about them. If they borrowed before moving, banks at their former location may know their creditworthiness. If all banks exchange private information about their clients, they can identify which of the movers who seek credit are creditworthy and can lend to them as safely as they do to long-standing clients. As a result, the default rate decreases.

The effect on lending, however, is ambiguous. The volume of lending may increase or decrease, because when banks exchange information about borrowers, the implied increase in lending to safe borrowers may fail to compensate for the reduction in lending to high-risk applicants. Banking competition strengthens the positive effect of information sharing on lending. When credit markets are contestable, information sharing reduces informational rents and increases banking competition, which in turn leads to greater lending.

The model also explores lenders' incentives to create a credit bureau. Lenders have a greater incentive to share information when the mobility of credit seekers is high and the potential demand for loans is large. Technical innovations that reduce the cost of filing, organizing, and distributing information should foster credit bureaus' activity. Banking competition, in contrast, may inhibit the appearance of credit bureaus; with free entry, a bank that supplies information about its customers to a credit bureau is in effect helping other lenders to compete more aggressively.

The exchange of information between banks can also increase borrowers' incentives to perform. Padilla and Pagano (1997) show that information sharing can generate this incentive effect by reducing the informational rents that banks can extract from their clients within lending relationships. They make this point in the context of a two-period model in which banks are endowed with private information about their borrowers. This informational advantage offers banks some market power over their customers and thereby generates a hold-up problem: anticipating that banks will charge predatory rates in the future, borrowers exert little effort to perform. This leads to high default and interest rates, and possibly to a collapse of the credit market.

If they commit to exchanging information about borrowers, however, banks restrain their own future ability to extract informational rents, and commit to leaving a larger portion of the surplus generated by the financed projects to entrepreneurs. As a result, these borrowers will have a greater incentive to ensure the success of their projects. This reduces the probability of default on their loans. The interest rate that banks charge will decline in step with the default rate, and total lending will be larger than in a regime without information sharing.

Exchanging information about borrowers can have other effects besides those analysed in these two studies. It can discipline borrowers by affecting their reputation: every borrower knows that if he defaults his reputation with all other potential lenders is damaged, and credit will become harder to get or more expensive for him. This disciplinary effect of information sharing has been analysed by Padilla and Pagano (2000). Moreover, borrowers have the incentive to become over indebted if they can draw credit simultaneously from many banks without the banks' realizing it. Information sharing mechanisms disclose to lenders the overall indebtedness of borrowers, thereby eliminating this incentive and the implied inefficiency in the provision of credit (Bennardo and Pagano, 2001).

IV. CREDIT-MARKET IMPERFECTIONS AND ECONOMIC ACTIVITY

The last two chapters in this volume show that the same informational frictions which explain the design of credit contracts and institutions can also affect real economic activity.

Credit Market Imperfections and Firm Survival: Zingales (1998)

When credit markets are imperfect, firms may be forced out of the market due to lack of liquidity, even though they are efficient. This applies particularly to firms that are already deeply in debt (though solvent), since these are most likely to be cut off from credit and forced to liquidate. The paper by Zingales (1998) tests this hypothesis by focusing on a 'natural experiment': the survival of trucking firms after the Carter deregulation of the US trucking industry. If capital markets were perfect, the deregulation should have led to the exit of the least-efficient firms, while the level of indebtedness should have played no role in firms' survival.

Instead, Zingales finds that highly leveraged trucking firms were less likely to survive the deregulation, even after controlling for various measures of efficiency and for the ex-ante risk of default. Under the pressure of indebtedness, these firms had to curtail investment and cut their prices more aggressively in order to generate the necessary liquidity, and therefore fewer of them managed to survive than deep-pocket (and possibly inefficient) firms. The effect of leverage on the prices charged by carriers during the price war induced by the deregulation is entirely concentrated in the imperfectly competitive segment of the industry. Accordingly, it is in this segment that the overall impact of leverage on subsequent survival is largest.

Credit Market Imperfections and the Business Cycle: Suarez and Sussman (1997)

Besides generating inefficiencies in the selection of firms and investments, credit market imperfections can have a role in macroeconomic fluctuations. There is a considerable literature in this area, both at the theoretical and the empirical level. Most of the theoretical work in this area, such as Bernanke and Gertler (1989) and Kiyotaki and Moore (1997), shows that credit market imperfections are a propagation mechanism. Given a real shock, they amplify its impact on the economy and in many cases generate an oscillatory reaction of real economic activity to the shock. The chapter by Suarez and Sussman (1997) in this book instead presents a model where financial-market imperfections create a pure reversion mechanism, in that they are capable of generating a two-period equilibrium cycle. They do so by extending the well-known Stiglitz–Weiss model of lending under moral hazard to a dynamic setting.

The moral hazard problem confers a central role to the liquidity position of entrepreneurs: the higher their liquidity, the less dependent they are on external finance and therefore the larger their effort and probability of success. But this increases the quantity produced in the subsequent period, and decreases prices and profits, and therefore the liquidity position of entrepreneurs. This generates two-period cobweb-like dynamics in production, prices, profits, and liquidity. This cycle can arise and persist even in the absence of any external shock, and is entirely driven by the moral hazard problem in the provision of external finance: it disappears if this problem is absent. Interestingly, while in Bernanke and Gertler (1989) and Kiyotaki and Moore (1997) external shocks are not anticipated, in the model by Suarez and Sussman agents anticipate future prices perfectly and can stipulate complete contracts, that is they can make them contingent on all relevant information. Therefore, the sole imperfection present in the model is the informational asymmetry in the credit market.

REFERENCES

Bennardo, Alberto, and Marco Pagano, 2001, 'Worthwhile Communication with Nonexclusive Lending', University of Salerno, unpublished manuscript.

Bernanke, Ben, and Mark Gertler, 1989, 'Agency Costs, Net Worth, and Business Fluctuations', *American Economic Review*, 79, 14–31.

Detragiache, E., P. G. Garella, and L. Guiso, 2000, 'Multiple versus Single Banking Relationships', *Journal of Finance*, 55(3), 1133–1161.

Diamond, Douglas W., 1991, 'Monitoring and Reputation: The Choice between Bank Loans and Privately Placed Debt', *Journal of Political Economy*, 99(4), August, 688–721.

Eckbo, B. Espen, and Herwig Langhor, 1989, 'Information Disclosure, Method of Payment, and Takeover Premiums: Public and Private Tender Offers in France', *Journal of Financial Economics*, 24, October, 363–403.

Jappelli, Tullio, and Marco Pagano, 2001, 'Information Sharing, Lending and Defaults: Cross-Country Evidence', *Journal of Banking and Finance*, forthcoming.

Jennings, Robert H., and Michael A. Mazzeo, 1993, 'Competing Bids, Target Management Resistance, and the Structure of Takeover Bids', *Review of Financial Studies* 6(4), Winter, 883–909.

Kiyotaki, Nobuhiro, and John Moore, 1997, 'Credit Cycles', *Journal of Political Economy*, 105(2), April, 211–248.

Ongena, S., and D. C. Smith, 2000, 'Bank Relationships: A Review', in P. Harker and S. A. Zenios (eds.), *The Performance of Financial Institutions*, Cambridge, UK: Cambridge University Press.

Padilla, A. Jorge, and Marco Pagano, 2000, 'Sharing Default Information as a Borrower Discipline Device', *European Economic Review* 44, December.

Pagano, Marco, and Ailsa Röell, 1998, 'The Choice of Stock Ownership Structure: Agency Costs, Monitoring and the Decision to Go Public', *Quarterly Journal of Economics*, 113(1), February, 187–225.

Petersen, M. A., and R. G. Rajan, 1994, 'The Benefits of Lending Relationships: Evidence from Small Business Data', *Journal of Finance*, 49(1), 3–37.

Stulz, René M., Ralph A. Walkling, and Moon H. Song, 1990, 'The Distribution of Target Ownership and the Division of Gains in Successful Takeovers', *Journal of Finance*, 45(3), July, 817–833.

Walkling, Ralph A., 1985, 'Predicting Tender Offer Success: A Logistic Analysis', *Journal of Financial and Quantitative Analysis*, 20, December, 461–478.

Zingales, Luigi, 1995, 'Insider Ownership and the Decision to Go Public', *Review of Economic Studies*, 62, 425–448.

PART I

GOING PUBLIC

1

Why Do Companies Go Public?
An Empirical Analysis

MARCO PAGANO, FABIO PANETTA, AND LUIGI ZINGALES

The decision to go public is one of the most important and least studied questions in corporate finance. Most corporate finance textbooks limit themselves to describing the institutional aspects of this decision, providing only a few remarks on its motivation. The conventional wisdom is that going public is simply a stage in the growth of a company. Although there is some truth in it, this 'theory' alone cannot explain the observed pattern of listings. Even in developed capital markets like the United States, some large companies—such as United Parcel Service or Bechtel—are not public.[1] In other countries, like Germany and Italy, publicly traded companies are the exceptions rather than the rule, and quite a few private companies are much larger than the average publicly traded company. These cross-sectional and cross-country differences indicate that going public is not a stage that all companies eventually reach, but is a choice. This begs the question of why some companies choose to use public equity markets and some don't.

The determinants of the decision to go public can be inferred both from the ex ante characteristics of the companies that go public and from the ex post consequences of this decision on a company's investment and financial policy.

This paper is part of the research project on 'The decision to go public and the stock market as a source of capital,' promoted by the Ente 'Luigi Einaudi' per gli studi monetari bancari e finanziari. The suggestions we received from Espen Eckbo, Tullio Jappelli, Mario Massari, Wayne Mikkelson, Marco Ratti, Jay Ritter, Andrei Shleifer, Jeremy Stein, Sheridan Titman, Guglielmo Weber, Oved Yosha, an anonymous referee, René Stulz (the editor), and particularly Steve Kaplan were very helpful. We also benefited from the comments of participants at the final conference of the research project in Rome, at the Nobel Symposium on Law and Finance, at the European Finance Association meetings in Milan, at the American Finance Association meetings in San Francisco, at the Maryland Finance Conference, at the Utah Winter Finance Conference, at the Journal of Financial Intermediation Conference in Amsterdam, and at seminars at the Milan Stock Exchange Council, the Italian Antitrust Authority, Columbia University, University of Florida, and University of Venice. Fulvio Coltorti and Luca Filippa kindly supplied data and crucial information, and Stefania De Mitri and Paolo Filippo Volpin provided truly outstanding research assistance. Pagano also acknowledges financial support from the Consiglio Nazionale delle Ricerche, and Zingales from the Center for Research on Security Prices at the University of Chicago and NSF grant #SBR-9423645.

[1] In 1992 UPS had $16.5 billion in sales and 267,000 employees. Bechtel group had $7.8 billion in sales and 31,000 employees.

In principle, if the relevant decision makers have rational expectations, the two methods should give consistent answers: the motives to go public uncovered on the basis of 'ex ante evidence' should square with the 'actual effects' of flotation. But in practice, rather than being redundant, ex post information is likely to complement the evidence based on the ex ante characteristics of the companies that go public, for two reasons. First, the importance of some variables can be assessed only by looking at ex post data; for example, the controlling shareholders' intention to divest after flotation can hardly be gauged from ex ante information. Second, in some cases the effects of the flotation may not be fully anticipated, so that only ex post information can uncover them. Thus, we attack the issue of why companies go public by using both ex ante and ex post information on their characteristics and performance.

The data needed to implement our approach are not generally available, but they turn out to be available for Italy. For this country, we have access to a unique data set that contains accounting information for a large sample of privately (and publicly) held firms, so that we observe companies that eventually go public many years before they do so. We also have data on the cost of bank credit for each firm, so that we can check if the cost of bank credit affects the choice to go public and, conversely, if going public affects the terms subsequently offered by banks. The availability of these unique data has prompted us to focus on Italy to study why companies choose to go public.

One could argue that Italy is not an ideal setting to study this issue, in light of the limited role of the stock market in the Italian economy. But in this respect Italy is not too different from many other industrial countries, where the equity market is underdeveloped relative to the scale of the economy. Germany, France, and all the Continental European countries are fairly similar both in terms of size of equity market to GDP and in terms of numbers of Initial Public Offerings (IPOs) per inhabitant (see La Porta et al. (1997)). Thus, understanding why few companies go public and many refrain from doing so in Italy can hopefully shed some light on the role of public equity markets in all these other countries as well.

We find that the main factor affecting the probability of an IPO is the market-to-book ratio at which firms in the same industry trade: a one-standard deviation increase in the market-to-book ratio raises the odds of an IPO by 25%. This positive relationship may reflect a higher investment need in sectors with high growth opportunities (and correspondingly high market-to-book ratios) or the entrepreneurs' attempt to time the market. Our finding that investment and profitability *decrease* after the IPO points to the latter explanation.

The second most important determinant is the size of the company: larger companies are more likely to go public. IPOs also tend to involve companies that before the IPO grew faster and were more profitable. It is remarkable that the typical newly listed company is much larger and older in Italy than in the United States. Because listing costs do not differ significantly between Italy and the United States, this raises the question of why in Italy firms need such a long track record before going public. One possible explanation is that the lack of enforcement of minority property rights makes it more difficult for young and small companies to capture the investors' trust.

We also identify some differences between the factors underlying the decision to list an independent company and a carve-out. The most striking is that size does not matter for the decision to list a subsidiary of a publicly traded company. Independent companies are also more likely to go public after major investments and abnormal growth, and to reduce their leverage and investment after the IPO. So their decision to go public can be interpreted as an attempt to rebalance their balance sheet after large investments and growth. By contrast, the main force behind carve-outs appears to be the desire to maximize the proceeds from selling shares in a subsidiary, as these IPOs are particularly sensitive to a 'window of opportunity.'

Among the post-IPO effects that we find is a reduction in profitability—a phenomenon consistent with findings by various authors in the United States (Degeorge and Zeckhauser (1993), Jain and Kini (1994), Mikkelson, Partch, and Shah (1995)). This effect survives, albeit its magnitude is smaller, even after controlling for the minimum profitability condition that companies must satisfy to list on Italian stock exchanges. We also find a reduction in investment and financial leverage. All these effects appear to persist beyond the first three years after the IPO.

We also document—for the first time, as far as we know—that independent companies experience a reduction in the cost of bank credit after the IPO. This effect is present even controlling for firms' characteristics and for the reduction in leverage experienced after going public. Moreover, after the IPO, these firms borrow from a larger number of banks and reduce the concentration of their borrowing. The reduced cost of credit may stem from the improved public information associated with stock exchange listing or from the stronger bargaining position vis-à-vis banks determined by the availability of an outside source of funds.

We find little evidence that portfolio diversification is important in the decision to go public. When an independent company undertakes an IPO the initial owners divest only 6 percent of the amount they hold in the company at that date and 1.3 percent more in the three subsequent years, retaining much more than a majority stake. Divestments are much larger (14.2 percent) for carve-outs. Finally, we find that in the three years after an IPO the turnover of the controlling group is larger than normal, which highlights the importance of looking at IPOs as a stage in the sale of a company, as suggested by Zingales (1995a).

The paper is organized as follows. Section I describes the data—a panel of 2,181 companies for the years 1982 through 1992. Section II surveys the main theories of why companies go public, highlighting their testable implications. Section III analyzes the determinants of the decision to go public on the basis of the companies' ex ante characteristics and behavior. Section IV reports the effects of an IPO on profitability, investment, financial policies, and the cost of bank credit. Section V studies the changes in ownership and control following an IPO. Finally,

Section VI discusses the results obtained while comparing them with those obtained for other countries.

I. DATA

A. Sources

We have three main sources of data. Balance sheet and income statement information come from the *Centrale dei Bilanci* database (Company Accounts Data Service). Information about interest rates, loan sizes, and lines of credit is drawn from the *Centrale dei Rischi* database (Central Credit Register). Data about ownership and control are drawn from IPO prospectuses and from the *Taccuino dell'azionista* (Stock Exchange Companies Handbook). Occasionally (see below), additional balance sheet data are drawn from companies' annual reports. Since the first two sources are quite novel, we provide some information on them below.

The *Centrale dei Bilanci* provides standardized data on the balance sheets and income statements of about 30,000 Italian nonfinancial firms. The data have been collected since 1982 by a consortium of banks interested in pooling information about their clients. A firm is included in the sample if it borrows from at least one of the banks in the consortium. The database is highly representative of the Italian nonfinancial sector: a recent report (Centrale dei Bilanci (1992)), based on a sample of 12,528 companies drawn from the database (including only the companies continuously present from 1982 through 1990 and with sales in excess of 1 billion lire in 1990), states that this sample covers 57 percent of the sales reported in national accounting data.

The *Centrale dei Rischi* is a department of the Bank of Italy in charge of collecting data on individual loans over 80 million lire (U.S. $52,000) granted by Italian banks to companies and individuals. These data are compulsorily filed by banks and are made available upon request to individual banks to monitor the total exposure of their customers. In addition, 79 banks (accounting for over 70 percent of total bank lending) have agreed to file detailed information about the interest rates charged on each loan. These data, which are collected for monitoring purposes, are highly confidential.

The third source of our data is the IPO prospectuses prepared for companies that undertook a public offering before being listed. The prospectuses are the only source that allows us to reconstruct the ownership structure of these companies *before* they went public. They are available for 62 of the 69 nonfinancial companies listed on the Milan Stock Exchange (MSE) from 1982 through 1992 and are present in our panel data set.[2] Information about ownership structure and control *after* these companies went public is drawn from the publication *Taccuino dell'azionista*.

---

[2] The remaining 7 companies were not required to file an IPO prospectus for a variety of reasons: the newly listed firm was a spin-off, it merged with an existing publicly traded firm, or it transferred from a minor regional exchange.

B. Sample

The sample is drawn from the Centrale dei Bilanci. In order to study the determinants of the decision to go public, we restrict our attention to companies that have at least a minimal probability of going public during the 11 years of our sample (1982–1992).

A 1975 law made the CONSOB (the Italian analogue of the SEC) responsible for establishing the listing requirements for Italian Stock Exchanges. But only in 1984 did the CONSOB explicitly specify two requirements. (i) book value of shareholders' equity in excess of 10 billion lire (U.S. $6.5 million); (ii) positive earnings in the three years before listing. Both these criteria, though, could be waived with the CONSOB's consent, at least until 1989. In that year the CONSOB strengthened its requirements, mandating that profitability measures be obtained irrespective of intragroup operations and extraordinary items. The new directive also dropped any mention of the possibility of waiving the shareholders' equity criterion, and the profitability criterion could be waived only in the presence of major and permanent changes in a company's structure. In such cases, however, at least the last income statement should show positive earnings.

The changing regulatory environment and its flexibility induced us to use a very mild criterion to extract our basic sample. We include all the companies that as of 1982 had at least 5 billion lire (U.S. $3.2 million) in shareholder's equity. This criterion reduces the Centrale dei Bilanci sample to 2,181 companies. The sample contains 89 percent of the nonfinancial companies that went public in the sample period. We apply this first screening to eliminate a large number of small firms whose accounting data are typically quite unreliable.[3] In the empirical analysis, though, we occasionally impose more restrictive criteria to test the robustness of our results to the selection bias induced by the listing eligibility requirements.

As Barca et al. (1994) have shown, most of Italian industry is organized around multicompany groups controlled by a single family via a holding company. This poses problems in establishing when a company can be considered as publicly traded: when the holding company is listed, all its subsidiaries might get some of the benefits and bear some of the costs of being public. For instance, they can indirectly access the public equity market to finance investments, and they must bear the cost of certified auditing as part of the parent company's disclosure requirements. This does not preclude these companies from seeking to be separately listed (in such case we would have a spin-off or a carve-out), but their reasons for doing so may be different from those of an independent company. Therefore, we create a separate category to account for subsidiaries of public companies, and distinguish between the listing of independent companies and

---

[3] We prefer a criterion based on shareholders' equity over one based on total assets for two reasons. First, it is directly linked to one of the listing requirements. Second, it eliminates many large government-owned firms with negative shareholders' equity (for example ENEL, the government-owned monopoly producer of electric power).

that of subsidiaries of publicly traded companies (which we collectively name carve-outs).[4]

A second problem arises in identifying when a company can be considered publicly traded. Besides the Milan Stock Exchange (MSE), by far the most important one, until 1991 there were nine other minor stock exchanges in different Italian cities, plus some informal markets, called 'Mercati Ristretti.' Because all of these other exchanges have very little volume and liquidity, we define as IPOs all the new listings on the MSE. Alternatively, we could have defined the date of new listing as the earliest date at which a company was listed in any of the above markets.[5] The samples obtained using the two definitions do not differ much and all the results are substantially unchanged, thus we report only the results using the first definition.

There were 139 new listings on the MSE from 1982 through 1992. Of these, 25 concerned banks and insurance companies, which are excluded from the sample because of intrinsic differences in the nature of their operations and accounting information. Of the remaining ones, 44 are classified as financial companies by *Indici e Dati*, a stock market handbook, but 6 of these are so closely identified with one industrial subsidiary that we simply use the accounting data of the industrial subsidiary.[6]

This leaves a total of 76 new nonfinancial listings. Of these, we lose 3 observations because the company was incorporated after 1982 and another observation because the company did not have 5 billion lire in shareholders' equity in 1982 and therefore is not included in our sample. Finally, we lose 5 companies because they were not reported in the Centrale dei Bilanci as of 1982. To these we add a company that went public by merging with a public company (Parmalat) and one that listed in New York instead of Milan (Luxottica).[7] So the final sample

---

[4] All new listings of subsidiaries of public companies except one are technically carve-outs. One case (Comau) is a spin-off.

[5] During our sample period we are aware of only one company that started to be listed in a foreign market before being listed in Italy. This is Luxottica, which listed on the NYSE in 1990.

[6] This is another problem created by the above-mentioned group structure. All the listed holding companies are, by definition, financial companies. In many cases this classification is misleading because some holding companies concentrate most of their assets in a single industrial company. For example, the Benetton family controls its industrial and commercial activities through Benetton Group SPA, a financial holding company listed on the Milan Stock Exchange since 1986, but 95 percent of the group's consolidated sales are due to Benetton SPA, a textile subsidiary. Even though Benetton SPA de facto coincides with Benetton Group SPA, formally it is not a listed company. We overcome this problem by classifying Benetton Group as a textile company. Because the Centrale dei Bilanci only provides accounting data for industrial companies, we replace the missing data from the consolidated accounts of Benetton Group with the accounting data of its textile subsidiary. We follow this procedure only if a listed holding company owes more than 75 percent of its consolidated sales to a single subsidiary. This happens in six cases: Benetton Group, Boero Bartolomeo, Pininfarina, Raggio di Sole Finanziaria, SISA, and Tripcovich.

[7] In 1990 Parmalat merged into a listed financial company (Finanziaria Centro Nord) and reorganized completely under the name of Parmalat. We take this to be equivalent to a new listing. Luxottica went public on the New York Stock Exchange in 1990. We assume that the effects of this choice are comparable to those of listing on the MSE.

contains 69 companies, of which 40 are new listings of independent companies, and 29 are carve-outs.

These IPOs are evenly distributed over the decade, except for a clustering in 1986 and 1987 when 45 percent of the listings took place. This clustering of IPOs is a well-established phenomenon both in the United States and other countries (Loughran, Ritter and Rydqvist (1994), Ljungqvist (1995)). Note that, unlike most stock exchanges, the MSE peaked in May 1986, so that the IPO 'hot market' followed the stock market boom with a small time lag.

C. Summary Statistics

Table I contains some summary statistics on our entire sample. The sample contains 19,817 firm-years. The median firm in the sample has 51 billion lire (U.S. $33 million) in sales, a return on assets of 11 percent, a debt to capital ratio of 38 percent, capital expenditures of 21 percent of net property plant and equipment, and pays no dividend. Retained earnings represent the main source of finance for the median firm: external equity plays no role, and external debt only adds 2 percent to capital every year.[8] The number reported for industry market-to-book value is the median market-to-book value of equity for publicly traded companies in the same industry in each year.[9]

In evaluating the determinants and the effects of new listing, one must take into account that every year only certain companies meet the listing require-ments. Therefore, the appropriate benchmark against which the newly listed firms are to be compared is not the entire sample, but the sample of firms that did not list despite meeting the listing requirements. As previously mentioned, the listing requirements changed during the same period.

In Table I Panel B we report the summary statistics for all the company-years that satisfy the listing requirements as of that year. Not surprisingly, the median company in the sample is larger (60 billion lire in sales), more profitable (the median return on assets is 14 percent), less leveraged (the median ratio of debt to capital is 33 percent), and invests more (24 percent). The median company in our sample is about four times as large as the typical IPO in the United States in terms of sales (Ritter (1991)).

Table I Panel C reports the summary statistics of the newly listed companies as of the year they went public. It is interesting to note that the median IPO is twice as large as the median potential IPO in terms of sales, employees, and total assets. By contrast, the median IPO is not more profitable than the median potential IPO and is more highly levered.

Finally, Table I Panel D reports some statistics on the age of new public companies and on the difference between their age and that of similar companies

---

[8] The average inflation rate, measured by the percentage change of the consumer price index, is 8.3 percent in the sample period.

[9] Companies are divided into 23 industries according to the classification made by the Centrale dei Rischi. This roughly follows the SIC two-digit classification.

Table I. *Summary statistics*

Variable	Mean	Median	Std. Dev.	Min	Max	Obs.
Panel A: The Whole Sample						
Total assets (billions of lire)	190	50.4	1,113	2.0	57,000	19,817
Shareholders' equity (billions of lire)	50.3	14.7	296.6	−169	14,000	19,817
Sales (billions of lire)	1,741	50.7	768.5	0.036	27,300	19,817
Employees	737	258	3,251	0	108,662	19,817
ROA	0.12	0.11	0.11	−1.0	1.21	19,817
ROS	0.12	0.11	0.20	−2.49	2.23	19,817
Leverage	0.39	0.38	0.25	0	1	19,816
Coverage	8.19	2.77	17.15	0	100	19,766
Taxes	0.18	0.13	0.17	0	1	18,103
Industry market-to-book	1.39	1.29	0.62	0.34	5.85	18,268
CAPEX	0.25	0.21	0.20	0	1	18,263
Investments	0.023	0.008	0.09	−0.99	0.93	19,808
Equity financing	0.023	0	0.16	−0.47	16.26	19,814
Debt financing	0.039	0.018	0.181	−1.00	0.99	19,710
Payout	0.26	0	3.77	0	336.5	17,679
Loan rate (%)	15.88	15.00	3.81	3.78	30.43	15,048
Concentration credit	0.19	0.13	0.18	0.02	1	19,118
Number of banks	13.9	11	11.3	0.0	134	19,274
Panel B: Sample Eligible to Go Public						
Total assets (billions of lire)	222.5	59.9	1,350.3	5.8	57,000	12,391
Shareholders' equity (billions of lire)	62.9	18.8	363.6	−33.7	14,000	12,391
Sales (billions of lire)	1,935	61.1	835.9	0.036	27,300	12,391
Employees	865	307	3,772	0	108,662	12,391
ROA	0.14	0.13	0.10	−0.93	1.21	12,391
ROS	0.14	0.12	0.17	−2.48	2.23	12,391
Leverage	0.35	0.33	0.23	0	1	12,391
Coverage	9.56	3.28	18.76	0	100	12,352
Taxes	0.20	0.18	0.17	0	1.00	11,632
Industry market-to-book	1.35	1.25	0.62	0.34	5.85	11,365
CAPEX	0.28	0.24	0.21	0	0.99	10,937
Investments	0.03	0.01	0.09	−0.96	0.93	12,388
Equity financing	0.02	0	0.06	−0.47	1.30	12,391
Debt financing	0.04	0.016	0.17	−1.00	0.99	12,345
Payout	0.31	0.06	4.56	0	336.5	10,621
Loan rate (%)	16.42	15.59	4.23	3.78	30.44	9,285
Concentration credit	0.19	0.13	0.18	0.02	1	12,040
Number of banks	14.6	12	11.86	0.0	134	12,148
Panel C: The IPO Sample						
Total assets (billions of lire)	440.8	163.3	888.0	11.6	6,234.7	66
Shareholders' equity (billions of lire)	138.3	48.2	360.5	7.5	2,790.0	66
Sales (billions of lire)	257.2	123.5	352.7	3.5	1,737	66

Table I. (*Continued*)

Variable	Mean	Median	Std. Dev.	Min	Max	Obs.
Employees	1,447.7	759.5	2,190	3	12,906	66
ROA	0.14	0.13	0.85	0.002	0.40	66
ROS	0.19	0.15	0.12	0.01	0.52	66
Leverage	0.38	0.40	0.24	0	0.81	66
Coverage	10.24	3.80	18.51	1	100	66
Taxes	0.21	0.21	0.13	0.01	0.60	65
Industry market-to-book	1.66	1.25	0.55	0.75	2.89	66
CAPEX	0.35	0.31	0.21	0.00	0.87	64
Investments	0.09	0.05	0.12	−0.15	0.49	66
Equity financing	0.09	0.003	0.16	0.00	0.68	66
Debt financing	0.06	0.032	0.20	−0.38	0.79	66
Payout	0.30	0.22	0.37	0.00	2.79	65
Loan rate (%)	14.25	13.00	3.18	8.99	21.76	60
Concentration credit	0.11	0.08	0.13	0.03	1	63
Number of banks	23.4	23	13.5	0.0	59	65
Panel D: Age of IPOs						
Age	33.43	26	28.31	3	144	68
Age difference	10.38	3	29.54	−57	93	68

Note: In Panel A, the summary statistics refer to the entire sample, in Panel B to the company-years that satisfy the official requirements for listing as of that year, in Panel C to the companies that went public between 1982 and 1992, as of the year of the Initial Public Offering (IPO). Until 1984 there were no listing requirements. Between 1985 and 1989 the requirements were: (i) shareholders' equity in excess of 10 billion lire and (ii) positive earnings in the previous three years. After 1989 the second requirement became positive earnings net of extraordinary items. In Panel C we lose three observations because the IPO-year contain some outliers (2 observations) and because the information for that company-year is not available from our dataset (1 observation). Panel D reports the age since incorporation of IPOs and its difference with respect to a matching company, defined as the closest company in size (net sales) which belongs to the same industry. ROA is EBITDA (earnings before interest, taxes, depreciation, and amortization) over total assets at the end of the previous year. ROS is EBITDA over revenues. Leverage is book value of short plus long term debt divided by book value of short plus long term debt plus book value of equity. Coverage is EBITDA divided by interest expenses (values above 100 are truncated at 100, values below zero are truncated at zero). Taxes is taxes paid divided by operating income. The MTB is the median market-to-book value of equity of firms in the same industry which traded on the Milan Stock Exchange. CAPEX is capital expenditures over end of the year net property plant and equipment. Investment is financial investment divided by total assets. Equity financing is the equity issued divided by total capital (total debt plus equity). Debt financing is debt issues divided by total capital. Payout is dividends paid divided by net income plus depreciation. The loan rate is the median interest rate paid by a firm on its lines of credit outstanding. The concentration of credit is the Herfindahl index of the credit lines outstanding. All the figures are in Italian lire. In the text the exchange rate used to convert figures to U.S. dollars is $1 = 1560$ lire. In the 1982–92 interval the exchange rate ranged between 1198 lire in 1990 and 1910 lire in 1985 (yearly averages).

that stayed private (matched by sector, and within the sector by size).[10] The average age of companies that went public from 1982 through 1992 is 33 years.

[10] Our data set does not contain the year of incorporation of a company. For this reason, we hand-collect the year of incorporation for the companies that did go public and for a sample of privately held firms matched by sector and size.

These figures are roughly in line with the European average value of 40 years reported by Rydqvist and Högholm (1995), and much higher than the corresponding values for U.S. new public companies: 5 years for venture-backed firms (Gompers (1996)). Moreover, companies that go public appear to be significantly older than those that stay private: they were 10.4 years older in the 1980s.[11]

II. COMPETING THEORIES

The decision to go public is so complex that no single model can hope to capture all of the relevant costs and benefits. But almost all of the effects of this decision have been evaluated in one model or another. Although these theories can hardly be nested in a single model, one can derive a set of (not mutually exclusive) testable predictions from them. In Table II and in the rest of this section we summarize the predictions of the main models.

A. The Costs of Going Public

A.1. *Adverse Selection*
In general, investors are less informed than the issuers about the true value of the companies going public. This informational asymmetry adversely affects the average quality of the companies seeking a new listing and thus the price at which their shares can be sold (Leland and Pyle (1977)), and also determines the magnitude of the underpricing needed to sell them (Rock (1986) and many others).

As highlighted by Chemmanur and Fulghieri (1995), this adverse selection cost is a more serious obstacle to the listing of young and small companies, which have little track record and low visibility, than for old and large companies. So in the presence of adverse selection, the probability of going public should be positively correlated with the age and/or the size of a company. Unfortunately, our data do not contain the date of incorporation, so that we shall only focus on company size, defined as the logarithm of a company's sales (SIZE).

A.2. *Administrative Expenses and Fees*
Beside the initial underpricing, going public implies considerable direct costs: underwriting fees, registration fees, etc. On top of the initial expenses, there are the yearly layouts on auditing, certification, and dissemination of accounting information, stock exchange fees, etc. Since many of these expenses do not increase proportionally with the size of the IPO, they weigh relatively more on small companies. Ritter (1987) has estimated that in the United States the fixed costs equal approximately $250,000 and the variable costs are about 7 percent of

---

[11] This figure is not specific to the sample period investigated. To check this we collect the data for the age of companies which went public in the period 1968 to 1981: the average IPO is even older (52.4 years), and significantly older than a matching company (+17 years).

Table II. *Empirical predictions of the main theories concerning the decision to go public*

		Empirical predictions	
	Model	Effects on the probability of IPO	Consequences after IPO
Panel A: Costs of Going Public			
Adverse selection and moral hazard	Leland and Pyle (1977), Chemmanur and Fulghieri (1995)	Smaller and younger companies less likely to go public	Negative relation between operating performance and ownership
Fixed costs	Ritter (1987)	Smaller companies less likely to go public	
Loss of confidentiality	Campbell (1979), Yosha (1995)	High-tech companies less likely to go public	
Panel B: Benefits of Going Public			
Overcome borrowing constraints		IPO more likely for high-debt/ high-investment companies	Deleveraging/ high investment
Diversification	Pagano (1993)	Riskier companies more likely to go public	Controlling shareholder decreases his stake
Liquidity	Market microstructure models	Smaller companies less likely to go public	Diffuse stock ownership
Stock market monitoring	Holmström and Tirole (1993), Pagano and Röell (1998)	High-investment companies more likely to go public	Large use of stock-based incentive contracts / Diffuse stock ownership
Enlarge set of potential investors	Merton (1987)		Decrease in borrowing rates
Increase bargaining power with banks	Rajan (1992)	IPO more likely for companies paying higher rates	
Optimal way to transfer control	Zingales (1995a)	High market-to-book values in the relevant industry	Higher turnover of control
Exploit mispricing	Ritter (1991)		Underperformance of IPOs; no increase in investments

Note: The table illustrates the main costs (Panel A) and benefits (Panel B) of the decision to go public. Each cost or benefit (first column) is associated with the most representative models capturing it (second column) and with the empirical predictions of these models on the variables affecting the probability of an Initial Public Offering (IPO) (third column) and the likely consequences of the IPO (fourth column).

the gross proceeds of the IPO. In Italy the fixed costs are about the same as in the United States and the variable costs are 3.5 percent of the gross proceeds, so that the total direct costs of an IPO of comparable size are lower than in the United States.[12]

As for adverse selection, the existence of fixed costs of listing suggests that the likelihood of an IPO should be positively correlated with company size.

A.3. Loss of Confidentiality

The disclosure rules of stock exchanges force companies to unveil information whose secrecy may be crucial for their competitive advantage, such as data about ongoing Research & Development (R&D) projects or future marketing strategies. They also expose them to close scrutiny from tax authorities, reducing their scope for tax elusion and evasion relative to private companies. Campbell (1979) was first to point to confidentiality as a deterrent from getting funding in public markets. Yosha (1995) has shown that in equilibrium those firms with more sensitive information are deterred from going public if the costs of a public offering are sufficiently high.

This would suggest a negative correlation between the R&D intensity of an industry and the probability of an IPO. Because we lack R&D data, we cannot test this hypothesis. But we shall examine the effect of listing on corporate taxes as an alternative source of evidence on the role of confidentiality in the choice to go public.

B. The Benefits of Going Public

B.1. Overcoming Borrowing Constraints

Gaining access to a source of finance alternative to banks (and, in the United States, to venture capital) is probably the most cited benefit of going public, which is explicitly or implicitly present in most models. The opportunity to tap public markets for funds should be particularly appealing for companies with large current and future investments, high leverage, and high growth. All these factors should be positively related with the likelihood of an IPO. We measure current investment as capital expenditure over property plant and equipment (CAPEX). As a proxy for future investment opportunities we use the median ratio of the market-to-book value of equity of public companies in the same industry (MTB).[13] We measure leverage as the lagged value of total debt plus equity (LEVERAGE), and growth as the rate of growth in sales (GROWTH).

Other implications of the financial constraint hypothesis, which can be tested using ex post data, are: (i) newly listed companies should increase their

---

[12] In Italy, the direct costs of an IPO are approximately 380 million lire (administrative costs) plus 3.5 percent of the gross proceeds (underwriting fees). Source: *Il Sole 24 Ore*, Special Insert 'Guida alla quotazione,' 29 July 1994, p. 24, based on estimates of the Stock Exchange Council.

[13] The data are from *Indici e Dati*, published by Mediobanca.

investment or reduce their debt exposure after the IPO; (ii) they are not likely to increase their payout ratio after the IPO.

B.2. *Greater Bargaining Power with Banks*

Another potential problem with bank loans is that banks can extract rents from their privileged information about the credit worthiness of their customers. By gaining access to the stock market and disseminating information to the generality of investors, a company elicits outside competition to its lender and ensures a lower cost of credit, a larger supply of external finance, or both, as highlighted by Rajan (1992).

The prediction here is that companies facing higher interest rates and more concentrated credit sources are more likely to go public, and credit will become cheaper and more readily available after an IPO, controlling for profitability and leverage. We measure the relative cost of credit to company i by $RCC_{it} = (1 + r_{it})/(1 + \bar{r}_t)$, i.e., the ratio between the interest factor charged to company i at time t, $1 + r_{it}$, and the average interest factor, $1 + \bar{r}_t$.[14] The concentration of the company's credit is measured by the Herfindahl index of the lines of credit granted to it by all banks (HERFINDAHL).

B.3. *Liquidity and Portfolio Diversification*

The decision to go public affects the liquidity of a company's stock as well as the scope for diversification by the initial holders of the company. Shares of private companies can be traded only by informal searching for a counterpart, at considerable cost for the initiating party. Share trading on an organized exchange is cheaper, especially for small shareholders who want to trade on short notice. As a result, if the initial owners raise money from dispersed investors, they factor in the liquidity benefit provided by being listed on an exchange. As shown by many market microstructure models, the liquidity of a company's shares is an increasing function of their trading volume, so that this liquidity benefit may be effectively reaped only by sufficiently large companies. This creates another reason to expect a positive relationship between size and the likelihood of an IPO.[15] Similarly, taking a company public provides to its owners opportunities for diversification. This can be achieved directly, by divesting from the company and reinvesting in other assets, or indirectly, by having the company raise fresh equity capital after the IPO and acquire stakes in other companies. If diversification is an important motive in the decision to go public, as in Pagano (1993), we should expect riskier companies to be more likely to go public, and controlling shareholders to sell a large portion of their shares at the time of the IPO or soon afterward.

---

[14] A justification for this definition is provided in Section IV.*B*.

[15] Bhide (1993) and Bolton and von Thadden (1998) point to a possible cost of liquidity, i.e., the decreased incentive to monitor associated with more dispersed ownership. Maug (1998), however, argues that liquidity increases the incentives to monitor because in a more liquid market large investors will hold larger positions in companies and will benefit more from monitoring through purchases of additional shares in the market.

B.4. *Monitoring*

The stock market also provides a managerial discipline device, both by creating the danger of hostile takeovers and by exposing the market's assessment of managerial decisions. Moreover, the shareholders of a public company can use the information embodied in stock prices to design more efficient compensation schemes for their managers, for instance by indexing their salaries to the stock price or by offering them stock options, as argued by Holmström and Tirole (1993) and documented by Schipper and Smith (1986). Unfortunately, we cannot test this hypothesis because Italian companies do not disclose data on the structure of managerial compensation.

By contrast, Pagano and Röell (1998) argue that private companies owned by more than one shareholder may be overmonitored. If the scale of a planned expansion is very large, and thus needs to be financed by many investors, the cost of this overmonitoring becomes so large that it is preferable to go public. So this model predicts a positive correlation between the probability of an IPO and the scale of the subsequent investment.

B.5. *Investor Recognition*

It is well known that most investors hold portfolios that contain a small fraction of the existing securities, often because they simply ignore that a certain company exists. Listing on a major exchange can help to overcome this problem, by acting as an advertisement for the company. Merton (1987) has captured this point in a capital asset pricing model with incomplete information, showing that stock prices are higher the greater the number of investors aware of the company's securities.

This theory finds indirect support in the fact that when companies already listed elsewhere announce their decision to list also in New York, their stock yields a 5 percent abnormal return on average (Kadlec and McConnell (1994)).[16] However, we cannot think of a clean way to test this hypothesis with our data.

B.6. *Change of Control*

In Zingales (1995a) the decision of a firm to go public is the result of a value maximizing decision made by an initial owner who wants to eventually sell his company. By going public, the initial owner can change the proportion of cash flow rights and control rights which he will retain when he bargains with a potential buyer. If the market for corporate control is not perfectly competitive, but the market for individual shares is, this proportion will affect the total surplus he can extract from a potential buyer of the company. By selling cash flow rights to disperse shareholders and still retaining control, the incumbent succeeds in extracting the surplus that derives from the buyer's increased cash flow, avoiding the need to bargain over it with the buyer. However, by retaining control, the

---

[16] Dharan and Ikenberry (1995), however, document a post-listing negative drift.

incumbent succeeds in extracting some of the surplus deriving from the buyer's larger private benefits in a direct negotiation. So the initial owner uses the IPO as a step to achieve the structure of ownership in the company that will maximize his total proceeds from its eventual sale. If this is an important motivation behind IPOs, we expect a high incidence of control transfers after listing.

B.7. *Windows of Opportunity*

If there are periods in which stocks are mispriced, as suggested by Ritter (1991), companies recognizing that other companies in their industry are overvalued have an incentive to go public.[17] To the extent that entrepreneurs manage to exploit the overvaluation of their companies by investors, one would also expect a company to be more likely to go public when the market for comparable companies is particularly buoyant. We measure the buoyancy of the relevant market by the median market-to-book ratio of public companies in the same industry (MTB).

As noted above, however, a high market-to-book ratio may alternatively indicate that rational investors place a high valuation on the future growth opportunities in the industry. If these growth opportunities require large investments, companies will be induced to go public in order to raise the necessary funding.

We shall try to discriminate between these two hypotheses mainly by relying on ex post evidence: if newly listed companies invest at an abnormal rate and earn large profits, then the relationship between market-to-book and IPOs is likely to be driven by expectations of future growth opportunities; otherwise, it is likely to reflect the desire to exploit a window of opportunity. But an indirect test can also be based on ex ante evidence: if raising funds for future investment is the main reason to go public, the likelihood of carve-outs should not be affected by the market-to-book ratio, because in that case the parent company already has access to the stock market.

III. ANALYSIS OF THE EX ANTE DETERMINANTS

The predictions derived in the previous section are of two types: predictions on the variables that should affect the likelihood of an IPO and predictions on the likely consequences of an IPO. We follow the same distinction in testing them. In this section we estimate a probit model of the probability of going public; in the next section we study the effects of this decision on performance, financing, and cost of credit by comparing newly listed firms with similar firms that remained private even though they met the listing requirements.

---

[17] This 'window of opportunity' hypothesis, modeled and tested by Rajan and Servaes (1997), is consistent with international time-series evidence in the 1980s (Loughran et al. (1994)). It is also consistent with the cross-sectional clustering of IPOs near sectoral stock price peaks (Ritter (1984), Lerner (1994)) and low long-run returns (Ritter (1991), Loughran and Ritter (1995)).

On the basis of the above discussion, we estimate the following model of the probability of going public:

$$Pr(\text{IPO}_{it} = 1) = F(\alpha_1 \text{SIZE}_{it} + \alpha_2 \text{CAPEX}_{it} + \alpha_3 \text{GROWTH}_{it} + \alpha_4 \text{ROA}_{it}$$
$$+ \alpha_5 \text{LEVERAGE}_{it} + \alpha_6 \text{MTB}_{it} + \alpha_7 \text{RCC}_{it}$$
$$+ \alpha_8 \text{HERFINDAHL}_{it} + \gamma_t \text{YEAR}_t), \tag{1}$$

where IPO_{it} is a variable that equals 0 if company i stays private in period t and equals 1 if it goes public, $F(\cdot)$ is the cumulative distribution function of a standard normal variable, and YEAR_t is a calendar year dummy. At any time t the sample includes all the private companies that satisfy the listing requirements in that year as described in Section I.B.[18] Of course, after a company goes public we drop it from the sample. We also exclude from the sample the Italian subsidiaries of foreign corporations (14 percent of the sample), because no such company has ever gone public in Italy.[19]

The only explanatory variable that needs further discussion is profitability, which we measure as the lagged return on assets (ROA: earnings before interest, taxes, depreciation, and amortization—hereafter EBITDA—divided by total assets). Profitability may affect the likelihood of an IPO in many different ways. First, profits are bound to be positively correlated with the likelihood of an IPO because of the effect of the listing requirements (see Section I.B). To avoid the distortion induced by this sample selection, we restrict our estimates to company-years that satisfy the listing requirements. But, even after controlling for this sample selection problem, the predicted effect of profitability remains ambiguous. On the one hand, a more profitable company needs less external equity, suggesting a negative impact of profitability on the probability of an IPO. On the other hand, a company experiencing a temporary surge in profits may list, hoping that investors will mistakenly perceive its high profitability as permanent and will over-value its shares. In the latter case, one would expect profitability to increase the probability of going public.

A. Results on the Entire Sample

Table III reports the maximum likelihood estimates of this probit model, as well as their standard errors. The 'Whole Sample' column of Table III reports the estimates obtained by pooling independent companies and subsidiaries of listed companies. In other words, we do not distinguish between the IPOs of independent companies and carve-outs.

---

[18] Before 1989 the listing requirements could have been waived at the discretion of the CONSOB and we have no way to tell which companies could have obtained a waiver from the CONSOB. In our sample only two companies list without satisfying the requirements. Our qualitative results do not change if we include all the companies in the estimation.

[19] Including these companies does not materially affect our estimates.

Table III. *Determinants of the decision to go public*

Variable	Whole sample	Independent IPOs	Carve-outs
Sales	0.202^a (0.044)	0.230^a (0.055)	-0.070 (0.088)
CAPEX	0.167 (0.180)	0.343^b (0.169)	-0.770 (0.528)
Growth	0.234^c (0.131)	0.322^b (0.150)	-0.428 (0.415)
ROA	0.791^c (0.449)	1.170^b (0.485)	1.768^c (1.045)
Leverage	-0.032 (0.277)	0.183 (0.317)	-0.596 (0.492)
Bank rate	-4.093 (5.535)	5.070 (4.460)	-16.156 (12.424)
Concentration of borrowing	0.151 (0.575)	-0.668 (0.832)	-0.193 (0.731)
Industry MTB	0.241^a (0.065)	0.206^b (0.081)	0.333^b (0.174)
No. of observations	5,350	4,919	431
Pseudo-R^2	0.100	0.143	0.131
Tax effect	0.511	0.854	0.176
F-test (p-value)	0.050	0.011	0.500

[a]Coefficient significantly different from 0 at the 1 percent level or less.
[b]Coefficient significantly different from 0 at the 5 percent level.
[c]Coefficient significantly different from 0 at the 10 percent level.

Note: The effect of the variables listed on the probability to go public is estimated by a probit model. The estimation method is maximum likelihood. The dependent variable is 0 if the company is not listed and 1 on the year of listing (observations for public companies are dropped from the sample). The sample is restricted to all company-years that satisfy the listing requirement as of that year. Subsidiaries of foreign corporations are excluded from the sample. The independent-IPO sample excludes all subsidiaries of publicly traded companies from the sample; the carve-out sample is restricted to subsidiaries of publicly traded companies. Sales is the lagged value of the logarithm of revenues. CAPEX is the lagged value of capital expenditures over Property Plant and Equipment. Growth is the rate of growth of sales in that year. ROA is the lagged value of EBITDA over total assets. Leverage is the lagged value of the ratio of the book value of short plus long term debt divided by book value of short plus long term debt plus book value of equity the year before. Bank rate is the lagged value of the relative cost of borrowing for firm i relative to the average borrowing rate of all the firms in the sample. The concentration of borrowing is the lagged value of the Herfindahl index of the lines of credit granted by different banks. The industry MTB is the median market-to-book value of equity of firms in the same industry which traded on the Milan Stock Exchange. The regression also includes a constant term and calendar year dummies (not reported). Standard errors are in parentheses. The tax effect is the average value of the calendar year dummies in the three years when there was a tax incentive to go public. The p-value of an F-test for the hypothesis that the joint effect of these three variables equals zero is also reported.

Not surprisingly, a company's size is an important determinant of an IPO. A one standard deviation increase in the logarithm of sales increases the probability of an IPO by one-third of a percentage point. This corresponds to a 40 percent increase in the sample average probability of going public. This effect is statistically significant at the 1 percent level.

Both the variables that measure a firm's financing needs—i.e., investment and growth—increase the probability of listing, as expected. But the coefficient of investment is not statistically significant, and that of growth is only significant at the 10 percent level.

The proxies for the cost and availability of credit do not have much explanatory power either. Contrary to expectations, both the relative cost of bank credit and a firm's leverage have a negative impact on the likelihood of an IPO, but neither is statistically significant at the 10 percent level. By contrast, consistent with expectations, the concentration of bank credit appears to increase the likelihood of an IPO, but this effect also is not statistically significant.

Even when we restrict the sample to companies eligible to go public, profitability has a positive impact on the probability of going public, significant at the 10 percent level. A one standard deviation increase in profitability increases the probability of going public by one-tenth of a percentage point (roughly a 12 percent increase in the sample average probability of an IPO).

Finally, beside size, the industry market-to-book ratio appears to be the most significant determinant of the probability of listing. We find that a one standard deviation increase in the market-to-book ratio raises the probability of listing of a firm in the same sector by one-fifth of a percentage point, corresponding to a 25 percent increase in the sample average probability of going public. In our sample this translates into 16 more companies going public a year.

The 1984 through 1986 new listings were given a temporary tax incentive in Italy. We analyze the effect of this tax incentive by testing if, after controlling for other factors, IPOs are more likely in those three years. In the pooled sample, the probability of an IPO is 1.4 percentage points bigger in the 1984–1986 period, and this effect is statistically significant at the 5 percent level. At face value, the impact of this tax incentive appears huge, especially if compared with the other estimated effects. But we feel uncomfortable in attributing the entire effect of these year dummies to the tax incentive because they may be capturing a time clustering of IPOs such as those identified by Ritter (1984). This alternative hypothesis is supported by the fact that the 'hot market' also persists in 1987, despite the end of the tax incentive (the 1987 dummy is not significantly different from that of the preceding triennium).

One possible source of concern for the specification we adopt is that it ignores the possible existence of unobservable firm-specific effects, which might be correlated with our regressors. For example, practitioners talk about a 'cultural resistance' of many entrepreneurs to take their companies public. If this entrepreneurial resistance is more widespread in traditional businesses, which happen to be associated with low market-to-book value, then this cultural bias might account for the observed correlation between market-to-book and probability to go public. For this reason, we also estimate a linear probability model with firm-specific effects. The results (not reported) largely confirm our findings. In particular, the industry market-to-book ratio and the company's size remain the two most important determinants of an IPO. We also estimate (not reported) a proportional hazard ratio model of the probability of a private firm going public for the 11 years at our disposition. It remains the case that the industry market-to-book ratio and the company's size are the two most significant factors underlying the probability of an IPO, while the level of profitability and the rate of growth lose statistical significance.

B. Differences between Independent IPOs and Carve-Outs

Further insights on the determinants of IPOs can be obtained by dividing the sample between independent IPOs and carve-outs. The factors underlying the decision of an independent company to go public are likely to differ from those driving the decision of a subsidiary of public company. This hypothesis is supported by the data. A likelihood ratio test rejects at the 1 percent level the equality of the coefficients in the two subsamples.

The first striking fact is that size does not matter for carve-outs.[20] The usual explanation for the importance of size is that fixed flotation costs can be recovered only by firms above a certain threshold or, equivalently, that the liquidity benefits of listing only accrue above a critical level of trading volume and capitalization. A possible reason why size matters only for independent companies is that for subsidiaries the fixed costs of listing are partly sunk, being already borne by the parent company. This applies not only to the overhead costs of certification and dissemination of accounting information, but also to the implicit listing costs deriving from greater visibility to the tax and legal authorities. Another—possibly complementary—interpretation is that size acts as a proxy for reputation. As in Chemmanur and Fulghieri (1995), small independent companies find it hard to become known to the investing public, and thus incur a large adverse selection cost in selling equity on public markets. In contrast, small subsidiaries of established public companies can exploit the reputation of their parent company.

A second difference is that both the estimated effects of profitability and of the market-to-book ratio of traded firms in the same industry appear approximately 50 percent bigger for carve-outs than for independent companies, though the difference is not statistically significant. Because these subsidiaries could already raise external equity via their parent company, the estimated effect of the market-to-book ratio on the likelihood of carve-outs already lends some support to the window of opportunity hypothesis. A third difference concerns the role of leverage. More indebted companies are more likely to list if they are independent and less likely to list if they are subsidiaries, but neither effect is statistically significant.

A final difference regards investment and growth. Independent IPOs are companies that invested and grew more than the rest of the sample (both effects are statistically significant). By contrast, carve-outs are subsidiaries that invested *less* than the rest and grew less (albeit this effect is not statistically significant).

These findings may help identify the different motives behind a carve-out and a normal IPO. A subsidiary of a publicly traded company has already incurred most of the costs (in terms of accounting and disclosure) of going public. It is also

---

[20] One may suspect that the lack of statistical significance of size in the carve-out sample is due simply to all the subsidiaries of public companies being above the minimum size required for listing. Their average size is indeed larger, but its range is not much different. To check that the different effect of size in carve-outs is not merely due to a different size distribution, the regression is reestimated dropping smaller firms from the sample of independent companies: size remains a significant determinant.

less likely to be forced to go public to raise new funds. It follows that its management has a greater freedom to time the IPO to take advantage of a favorable market valuation in its particular sector. This hypothesis is consistent with the much stronger impact of the industry market-to-book value on the probability of a carve-out.[21] Given this greater freedom, a subsidiary of a publicly traded company will be taken public only if it is in sound economic and financial condition. This might explain why in carve-outs we observe a higher coefficient of profitability and MTB and a negative coefficient of leverage. An independent company may instead want to go public for need of equity capital, and this is more likely to be the case if the company is highly levered. The picture that emerges so far is that carve-outs are driven by financial rather than real factors. This finding is consistent with evidence by Michaely and Shaw (1995), for the United States. Public companies carve out their most profitable subsidiaries in industries that trade at a premium relative to their book value, irrespective of their size. By contrast, for independent companies, size is the most important determinant of the choice to go public and IPOs are more likely for high-growth firms that invested a lot.

IV. ANALYSIS OF THE EX POST CONSEQUENCES OF AN IPO

An alternative strategy for uncovering the determinants of the decision to go public is to compare the ex post performance of the companies that went public relative to otherwise identical firms that remained private. We investigate this by estimating fixed-effects regressions in which the effect of the decision to go public is captured by dummy variables for the year of the IPO and the three subsequent years. In estimating these regressions we face two sample selection problems.

First, only companies that meet the listing requirements can go public. The performance of newly listed companies may differ from that of private companies simply because they had to meet a profitability criterion before listing (for instance, their expected profitability will be higher if profits are positively autocorrelated). To correct for this sample selection problem, our regressors must include variables that capture the effect of meeting the listing requirements. To this purpose, we create four dummy variables, which at time t equal 1 only if a company met the listing requirement at times t, $t-1$, $t-2$, and $t-3$ respectively. This presupposes that the effect of having met the listing requirement does not extend beyond three years.

Second, in estimating the ex post consequences of IPOs, we face a potential endogenous selection problem: the companies that went public have chosen to do so. In principle this problem could be solved via a two-stage procedure, where the first stage involves estimating a model of the decision to go public such as

---

[21] It is interesting that when we estimate a proportional hazard model (not reported) the market-to-book ratio is not statistically significant at the 5 percent level for independent companies, but it is significant at the 1 percent level for carve-outs.

equation (1) estimated in the previous section. Unfortunately, the very limited explanatory power of equation (1) eliminates the practical relevance of this procedure.

A. Accounting Measures of Performance

Table IV reports the estimates of the effects of the IPOs on some operating and financial variables. For all the variables we use the following specification:

$$y_{it} = \alpha + \sum_{j=0}^{3} \beta_j IPO_{t-j} + \beta_4 IPO_{t-n} + \sum_{j=0}^{3} \gamma_j QUOT_{t-j} + u_i + d_t + \epsilon_{it}, \qquad (2)$$

where u_i and d_t are, respectively, a firm-specific and calendar year specific effect, IPO_{t-j} are dummy variables equal to one if year $t - j$ was the IPO year, IPO_{t-n} is a dummy variable equal to one if the IPO took place more than three years before, and $QUOT_{t-j}$ are dummy variables equal to one if company i satisfied the listing requirements in year $t - j$.

By using a fixed-effect model we are using a firm before the IPO as a control for itself after the IPO. The table only reports the coefficients on the IPO and post-IPO dummy variables.

Before presenting the results, it is worthwhile to discuss an obvious objection to our specification. Changes in accounting measures of performance may not hinge only on the decision to go public but also on other variables: for instance, profitability may depend also on lagged profitability, sales, investment, and so on. To control for these other variables, we have also estimated richer reduced-form models where the list of regressors also includes lagged values of the dependent variable and of other accounting variables that might be relevant a priori. In most cases the results of these richer dynamic models are found to be qualitatively similar to those reported in Table IV; therefore, we do not report their estimates in a separate table, but we discuss them in what follows. We will make an exception only for the results on the cost of credit.

A.1. *Profitability*

The first row of the table shows that the profitability declines after the IPO. The effect increases gradually but steadily, rising from 1.5 percent less in the first year after the IPO to 3 percent in the third year and in subsequent years. The fall in profitability is statistically significant at the 1 percent level in each individual year. The permanent effect is even stronger for carve-outs (−5%). This is consistent with the finding of Jain and Kini (1994) and Mikkelson, Partch, and Shah (1997).[22]

---

[22] The standard errors reported do not control for possible serial correlation. Following one of the referee's suggestions, we run further regressions (not reported) to check whether our results depend on first-order or second-order serial correlation in the residuals. The results are substantially unchanged.

Table IV. *Effects of the decision to go public*

	Sample used	Year 0	Year 1	Year +2	Year +3	Year >3	F-test
ROA	Whole sample 19,804	-0.008 (0.006)	-0.015^a (0.006)	-0.020^a (0.007)	-0.028^a (0.007)	-0.031^a (0.005)	0.000
	Independent 18,425	-0.009 (0.008)	-0.010 (0.007)	-0.029^a (0.009)	-0.036^a (0.010)	-0.027^a (0.008)	0.000
	Carve-outs 1,379	-0.009 (0.010)	-0.029^a (0.010)	-0.018^b (0.010)	-0.029^a (0.009)	-0.048^a (0.009)	0.000
CAPEX	Whole sample 18,251	0.023 (0.018)	0.016 (0.017)	-0.017 (0.018)	-0.041^a (0.016)	-0.042^a (0.016)	0.304
	Independent 16,929	-0.010 (0.023)	-0.009 (0.023)	-0.027 (0.027)	-0.091^a (0.022)	-0.070^a (0.022)	0.017
	Carve-outs 1,322	0.064^a (0.027)	0.028 (0.027)	0.002 (0.023)	0.032 (0.024)	0.010 (0.024)	0.136
Leverage	Whole sample 19,803	-0.051^b (0.021)	-0.031 (0.022)	-0.054^a (0.018)	-0.064^a (0.018)	-0.116^a (0.014)	0.000
	Independent 18,424	-0.070^a (0.027)	-0.047^b (0.026)	-0.048^a (0.024)	-0.050^a (0.025)	-0.094^a (0.019)	0.000
	Carve-outs 1,379	-0.002 (0.033)	0.022 (0.037)	-0.015 (0.027)	-0.036 (0.026)	-0.095^a (0.224)	0.016
Financial investments	Whole sample 19,796	0.024^b (0.015)	0.002 (0.015)	-0.007 (0.012)	-0.015 (0.013)	-0.006 (0.011)	0.949
	Independent 18,417	0.013 (0.016)	-0.001 (0.015)	0.003 (0.014)	-0.032^a (0.012)	0.001 (0.014)	0.704
	Carve-outs 1,379	0.039 (0.026)	0.010 (0.030)	-0.019 (0.021)	-0.004 (0.026)	-0.027 (0.021)	0.999
Equity financing	Whole sample 19,801	0.062^a (0.019)	0.010 (0.010)	0.004 (0.012)	0.005 (0.013)	-0.004 (0.010)	0.063
	Independent 18,422	0.067^a (0.022)	0.004 (0.013)	0.007 (0.014)	-0.002 (0.015)	0.002 (0.014)	0.136
	Carve-outs 1,379	0.048 (0.034)	0.018 (0.019)	-0.002 (0.022)	0.014 (0.024)	-0.010 (0.015)	0.320
Debt financing	Whole sample 19,698	0.003 (0.027)	0.014 (0.025)	-0.001 (0.025)	-0.007 (0.022)	-0.021 (0.018)	0.886
	Independent 18,325	0.016 (0.038)	0.019 (0.031)	0.031 (0.032)	-0.022 (0.024)	-0.030 (0.024)	0.892
	Carve-outs 1,373	-0.024 (0.037)	0.005 (0.044)	-0.042 (0.040)	-0.008 (0.034)	-0.032 (0.033)	0.457
Payout	Whole sample 17,667	-0.001 (0.085)	-0.053 (0.085)	-0.055 (0.077)	-0.041 (0.098)	-0.052 (0.131)	0.609
	Independent 16,374	-0.060 (0.111)	-0.009 (0.119)	-0.106 (0.090)	-0.020 (0.135)	-0.184 (0.146)	0.382
	Carve-outs 1,293	-0.097 (0.192)	-0.212 (0.237)	0.013 (0.184)	-0.094 (0.319)	0.069 (0.438)	0.757
Taxes	Whole sample 18,096	0.021^b (0.012)	0.018 (0.017)	0.025 (0.019)	0.014 (0.021)	0.018 (0.014)	0.050
	Independent 16,902	0.014 (0.015)	0.009 (0.024)	0.014 (0.024)	-0.034 (0.025)	0.018 (0.020)	0.736
	Carve-outs 1,194	0.027 (0.021)	0.022 (0.025)	0.029 (0.029)	0.057 (0.035)	0.005 (0.024)	0.101
Growth	Whole sample 17,347	0.031 (0.023)	0.029 (0.021)	-0.003 (0.022)	0.015 (0.026)	0.005 (0.019)	0.282
	Independent 16,137	0.016 (0.036)	0.017 (0.029)	-0.040 (0.031)	-0.023 (0.036)	0.016 (0.027)	0.898
	Carve-outs 1,210	0.038 (0.029)	0.038 (0.031)	0.045 (0.031)	0.051 (0.037)	-0.046 (0.032)	0.260

Interest rate						
Whole sample 11,797	−0.0023ᵃ (0.0011)	−0.0016 (0.0012)	−0.0038ᵃ (0.0014)	−0.0034ᵃ (0.0013)	−0.0016 (0.0011)	0.005
Independent 11,017	−0.0035ᵃ (0.0015)	−0.0035ᵃ (0.0018)	−0.0060ᵃ (0.0020)	−0.0062ᵃ (0.0019)	−0.0025 (0.0016)	0.001
Carve-outs 780	−0.0006 (0.0017)	−0.0003 (0.0017)	−0.0021 (0.0018)	−0.0001 (0.0016)	−0.0009 (0.0017)	0.535
Concentration of credit						
whole sample 19,099	−0.002 (0.008)	−0.006 (0.011)	−0.013 (0.016)	−0.025ᵇ (0.009)	0.010 (0.011)	0.372
Independent 17,751	−0.005 (0.010)	−0.025ᵃ (0.006)	−0.040ᵃ (0.008)	−0.043ᵃ (0.010)	−0.026ᵃ (0.009)	0.000
Carve-outs 1,348	0.006 (0.014)	0.022 (0.025)	0.026 (0.038)	−0.005 (0.020)	0.031 (0.026)	0.370
Number of banks						
Whole sample 19,254	1.47ᵃ (0.578)	2.28ᵃ (0.636)	3.16ᵃ (0.685)	3.25ᵇ (0.777)	−0.002 (0.597)	0.000
Independent 17,844	2.13ᵃ (0.610)	3.67ᵃ (0.780)	4.92ᵃ (0.879)	4.77ᵃ (1.003)	1.92ᵃ (0.629)	0.000
Carve-outs 1,410	0.654 (1.082)	0.944 (1.054)	1.637 (1.073)	2.488ᵃ (1.234)	−0.349 (1.113)	0.149

ᵃCoefficient is significantly different from 0 at the 5 percent level or less.

ᵇCoefficient is significantly different from 0 at the 10 percent level.

Note: For each of the variables listed we estimate the following specification:

$$y_{it} = \alpha + \sum_{j=0}^{3} \beta_j IPO_{t-j} + \beta_4 IPO_{t,-n} + \sum_{j=0}^{3} \gamma_j QUOT_{t-j} + u_i + d_t + \epsilon_{it},$$

where u_i, and d_t are respectively a firm-specific and calendar year-specific effect, IPO_{t-j} are dummy variables equal to one if year $t-j$ was the IPO year, $IPO_{t,-n}$ is a dummy variable equal to one if the IPO took place more than three years before, and $QUOT_{t-j}$ are dummy variables equal to one if company i satisfied the listing requirements in year $t-j$. By using a fixed effect model we are using each company before the IPO as a control for itself after the IPO. The table only reports the coefficients on the IPO and post-IPO dummy variables. The independent sample excludes subsidiaries of publicly traded companies, and the carve-out sample is restricted to subsidiaries of publicly traded companies. The number of observations is reported beside the definition of each sample and may vary slightly because of data availability. ROA is EBITDA over total assets at the end of the previous year. CAPEX is capital expenditures over property plant and equipment. Financial investment is divided by total assets. Leverage is book value of short plus long term debt divided by book value of short plus long term debt plus book value of equity. Equity financing is the equity issued divided by total capital (total debt plus equity). Debt financing is debt issues divided by total capital. Payout is dividends paid divided by net income plus depreciation. Taxes is taxes paid divided by operating income. Growth is the rate of growth of sales in that year. Interest rate is the relative cost of credit of firm i measured as one plus the median rate paid on all the outstanding credit lines divided by one plus the average rate paid by all firms in the sample during that year. The concentration of credit is the Herfindahl index of the credit lines outstanding. The number of banks is the number of banks with a credit line outstanding. Heteroskedasticity robust standard errors are reported in parentheses. The last column reports the *p*-value of an *F*-test of the hypothesis that the sum of the coefficients of all the post-IPO dummies are equal to zero.

As Degeorge and Zeckhauser (1993) point out, this result may be not all that surprising: entrepreneurs may time their issues to coincide with unusually high profitability or they may engage in 'window-dressing' of their corporate accounts at the time of the IPO. According to this view this result is simply due to a normal regression to the mean. We have already partly addressed this potential criticism by inserting dummies when a company satisfied the listing requirements in previous years. These dummies, which are all negative and highly statistically significant, suggest that only a third of the observed 3 percent drop in profitability of IPOs can be explained by a normal regression to the mean.

We try to probe this issue deeper, by adding to the list of regressors the first lag of profitability and the profitability in the year before the IPO. The first lag of profitability turns out to be very significant (with an estimated coefficient of 0.438 and a standard error of 0.14) but the coefficient of the profitability in the year before the IPO is small and imprecisely estimated. In this specification, the impact coefficient of the IPO dummy decreases further to -0.011 and becomes significant at the 5 percent level, and those of the post-IPO dummies remain negative and significant at conventional levels. The long-run impact of each dummy is approximately equal to the respective coefficient in the first row of Table IV. The same is true if the regressors also include lagged investment and the log of lagged sales, which both enter the regression with significant coefficients. We conclude that the fall in profitability is really associated with the IPO and does not result only from regression to the mean or from the effect of some other variable on profitability. This post-IPO fall in profitability, as well as the decline in investment for independent IPOs (see below), lends further support to the window of opportunity hypothesis.[23]

One possible explanation for this permanent drop in profitability has to do with the accounting changes brought by the decision to go public. In preparing their accounts for the IPO, companies try to provide a fair (or even inflated) picture of the value of their assets, whereas private companies are more concerned about hiding their value from tax authorities.[24] As a result, the value of assets may be less undervalued (or more overvalued) in public companies than in private ones, correspondingly deflating the observed profitability.[25]

Other, more fundamental, explanations of the decline in profitability, are based on adverse selection (companies go public when profitability is about to decline permanently) or moral hazard (controlling shareholders have a greater incentive

---

[23] An alternative hypothesis would be that our measure of profitability falls immediately after the IPO because the cash infusion is largely invested in interest-earning assets. However, this hypothesis would predict a subsequent recovery in profitability as this excess liquidity is depleted to finance real investment, contrary to our finding of a permanent fall in profitability.

[24] The same reason, though, suggests that private companies are more likely to underreport profits, biasing the results against our finding.

[25] This problem might be particularly severe in Italy, where the high inflation rate of the 1970s and early 1980s distorted the valuation of assets based on historical cost and where fiscal authorities periodically concede tax benefits to companies that voluntarily step up the book value of assets.

to extract private benefits at the expense of minority shareholders). In both cases, the relevant models predict that the fall in profitability will be larger for companies where the original owners retain less equity: In the adverse selection model of Leland and Pyle (1977), lower equity retention is a signal of bad quality, and in the moral hazard model by Jensen and Meckling (1976) it heightens the agency problem.

We can distinguish between the accounting and the two more fundamental explanations for post-IPO performance by examining the effect of the size of the incumbent's stake on a company's profitability after the IPO. If the accounting explanation is right, then there should be no relationship between the two. By contrast, if either the moral hazard or the adverse selection explanations are correct, then we expect a negative relationship. Consistent with the second hypothesis, in an unreported regression we find that the post-IPO decline in profitability is negatively related to the change of the incumbent's stake at the IPO.

A.2. *Investment and Leverage*

Surprisingly, for independent companies the decision to go public has a negative impact on capital expenditures, as shown in the second row of Table IV (CAPEX). The decline in investment becomes significant only two years after the IPO but is large and permanent (a 7 percent reduction of the capital stock). In contrast, carve-outs exhibit a significant temporary increase in investment at the time of the IPO (6 percent of the capital stock). These estimated effects persist when the regressors also include current profitability, external debt, external equity, and lagged investment, sales and profitability (all of which have positive and significant coefficients, except for lagged investment and sales).

Independent companies and carve-outs also differ markedly in the change of their leverage after the IPO, as illustrated by the third row of the table. Independent companies deleverage immediately, substantially (between 5 and 7 percent in the first four years) and permanently (by 9 percent), while carve-outs do so only in the long run (also by 9 percent). One may suspect that the finding that independent IPOs reduce their leverage after going public derives from their high profitability before the IPO (recall that there is a strong negative correlation between leverage and profitability; see, for example, Rajan and Zingales (1995)). But the result persists when one controls for lagged leverage, for current and lagged profitability (all highly significant), and for profitability in the year before the IPO (not significant).

If we consider these results together with those arising from our ex ante analysis in Section III, a consistent story emerges. Recall that before the IPO, independent companies tend to display abnormally high investment and growth, but carve-outs have abnormally low investment and leverage. The ex post evidence adds that after the IPO the independent companies reduce their leverage and—with a lag—investment; carve-outs step up investment temporarily at the time of the IPO and reduce leverage only later on. So independent companies tend to go public to rebalance their capital structure after implementing substantial investment plans, while carve-outs occur to raise resources to finance current investment and, as we shall see later, to allow the controlling shareholder to divest partly from the company.

A.3. *Other Accounting Variables*

The results concerning the other accounting variables in Table IV are less striking. Investment in financial assets rises temporarily at the time of the IPO, probably because the new public companies temporarily 'park' the lumpy inflow of cash from the IPO in financial assets. Moreover, as one would expect, equity financing rises sharply (by 6 percent) in the year of the IPO. There is no significant change in debt financing, payout, and growth. The result for growth is at odds with the prototype of the IPO as a means to finance corporate growth, but squares with the above-reported results about investment (at least for the independent companies).

An interesting result is that new public companies appear to be subject to a permanent increase in tax pressure after the IPO: as a fraction of their operating income, they pay about 2 percent more taxes per year than before, although the effect is imprecisely estimated. This provides some basis for the argument that the greater accounting transparency associated with listing prevents companies from eluding or evading taxes, and that this represents one of the costs of going public.[26]

B. Cost of Credit

One of the often claimed advantages of going public is that access to security markets may reduce the cost of credit (Basile (1988)), possibly because of the firm's improved bargaining position with banks, as pointed out by Rajan (1992). This hypothesis can be tested using our data on the rates offered by the largest 79 Italian banks to their clients.

In measuring changes in the cost of credit we face two problems. First, we need to define properly what we mean by a change in the relative cost of credit during a period when the level of bank rates was extremely variable (the average annual rate oscillated between 12.95 and 22.76 percent). We choose to define the relative cost of credit of firm i with respect to the average cost of credit as the ratio between the interest factor charged to company i at time $t(1 + r_{it})$ divided by the average interest factor charged to all the companies in the sample at that time $(1 + \bar{r}_{it})$.[27] The appealing feature of this definition is that it is invariant to

---

[26] We find another piece of evidence in favor of the view that tighter accounting standards entail greater tax pressure: if the regression is reestimated after adding a dummy for Italian subsidiaries of foreign companies, which are presumably forced by their parent company to keep to strict accounting rules, one finds that these companies pay 2 percent more taxes than domestic companies.

[27] This is the appropriate definition in a risk neutral world where differences in loan rates are solely determined by default risk. For instance, if company i has a probability π_i to default (and in default it does not pay anything back), then $1 + r_{it}$ equals $(1 + r_{ft})/(1 - \pi_i)$, where r_{ft} is the risk free rate at time t.

changes in the general level of interest rates. We also use (in unreported regressions) the difference between a firm's rate and the average rate as a measure of the relative cost of credit and we obtain results that are economically and statistically similar.

A second issue regards which interest rate we should use, given that all companies have a credit relationship with several banks. We choose to use the median rate charged to firm i at time t (defined as the last quarter of the year), because of its robustness to reporting errors.[28] We also try a weighted average of the rates charged to each firm by its banks on all the outstanding credit lines, without significant changes in the results.

The estimates reported in Table IV indicate a drop in the relative cost of credit of IPOs. This effect is statistically and economically significant in the IPO year and in the three subsequent years, but it weakens afterwards. The effect appears to be entirely concentrated among independent IPOs, and for these firms we can reject the hypothesis that there are no changes in the cost of credit after an IPO at the 1 percent level, but we cannot reject it for carve-outs.

The observed drop corresponds to a reduction in the rate of between 40 and 70 basis points.[29] Considering that the average IPO has debt equal to 99 billion lire (U.S. $64.3 million), this reduction, if it applies to all debt, would produce 495 million lire (U.S. $321,000) of savings per year. If permanent, this would imply a present value of savings of 3.1 billion lire (U.S. $2 million)—a sum larger than the direct costs of going public.[30]

There are at least three (possibly complementary) reasons why rates may fall after an IPO. First, upon listing, companies may become safer borrowers because they reduce their leverage, as shown in Table IV. Second, more information becomes publicly available about them, so that lenders spend less to collect information about their creditworthiness. Because by its very nature this information cannot be appropriated by any lender, banking competition will ensure that the lower information costs are rebated to borrowers in the form of lower interest rates. Third, being listed on the stock market offers to the company an outside financing option that curtails the bargaining power of banks (as in Rajan (1992)).

In Table V we analyze the post-IPO changes in the cost of credit while controlling for the changes in the fundamental risk characteristics of a company. As proxies for risk we use a company's size, its leverage, and its

---

[28] The raw data report the quarterly payment (interest plus fixed fees) made by a firm to the bank and its quarterly average balance. Of course, using these data to compute the average interest rate will overestimate the rates of banks with a small average balance. For this reason, we eliminate the rates referring to credit lines with less than 50 million lire (U.S. $32,500) in average daily balance.

[29] This is obtained by multiplying the coefficients (ranging between 0.0035 and 0.0062) by 1 *plus* the average bank rate during the period (0.16).

[30] As explained earlier, in Italy, the direct costs of going public equal approximately U.S. $250,000 plus 3.5 percent of the gross proceeds, so that an IPO worth 50 billion lire costs about 2.13 billion lire, that is, 4.3 percent of the gross proceeds.

Table V. *The effect of an IPO on bank rates*

	Whole sample	Independent	Carve-outs
ROA	0.0010 (0.0019)	0.0015 (0.0020)	−0.0087 (0.0054)
Leverage	0.0041[a] (0.0008)	0.0049[a] (0.0009)	−0.0044 (0.0024)
Size	−0.0022[a] (0.0003)	−0.0021[a] (0.0003)	−0.0043[a] (0.0010)
IPO year	−0.0017 (0.0011)	−0.0028[c] (0.0015)	−0.0001 (0.0016)
IPO year +1	−0.0010 (0.0012)	−0.0029[c] (0.0018)	0.0008 (0.0018)
IPO year +2	−0.0022 (0.0014)	−0.0047[b] (0.0020)	0.0005 (0.0018)
IPO year +3	−0.0018 (0.0013)	−0.0047[a] (0.0018)	0.0023 (0.0023)
IPO year > +3	−0.0016 (0.0011)	−0.0021 (0.0017)	−0.0016 (0.0019)
Number of observations	11,880	11,073	807
R^2	0.54	0.61	0.58
p-Value of F-test for total effect equal to zero	0.066	0.008	0.783

[a]Coefficient significantly different from 0 at the 1 percent level or less.
[b]Coefficient significantly different from 0 at the 5 percent level.
[c]Coefficient significantly different from 0 at the 10 percent level.

Note: We estimate the effect of an IPO on the cost of credit with a within estimator. The cost of credit is defined as $(1 + r_{it})/(1 + \bar{r}_t)$, where r_{it} is the median rate across all banks paid by firm i in year t and $\bar{r}_t$ is the cross sectional average of rates charged to the firms in the sample in year t. A separate dummy is inserted in the IPO year and the following three years. We then have a dummy which equals 1 in all the firm-years following the third year after the IPO, and 0 otherwise. We control for the selection bias generated by the listing requirements by inserting four analogous dummies (not reported) if a company satisfied the listing requirements respectively that year, the year before, two years before, and three years before. We also insert calendar year dummies (not reported). Besides these dummies we include as a regressor the level of profitability (ROA is EBITDA over total assets), leverage (book value of short plus long term debt divided by book value of short plus long term debt plus book value of equity) and the company's size (logarithm of sales). Heteroskedasticity robust standard errors are reported in parentheses.

profitability.[31] The estimated drop in the rates is only marginally reduced in this more complete specification. It remains true that independent IPOs exhibit an economically and statistically significant drop (30–55 basis points) in their cost of credit in the IPO year and in the three years afterward. The effect is weaker (25 basis points) and imprecisely estimated after the third year following an IPO and is absent for carve-outs.

Overall, Table V suggests that the drop in the cost of credit should not simply be attributed to an improvement in the creditworthiness of newly listed firms. Although we cannot exclude that an unobservable improvement in credit quality (not captured by our regressors) causes the drop, we regard this possibility as unlikely.

[31] The estimates reported use the current level of profitability and leverage. We choose contemporaneous values because, as we previously show, both profitability and leverage change significantly after the IPO and the rates we use refer to the last quarter, when most of these changes have probably already occurred. We also try using lagged values of profitability and leverage, with no material changes in the results.

To support this view, there are also the data on the concentration of credit (measured as the Herfindahl index of the lines of credit granted to a company by all its banks) and the number of banks with an outstanding line of credit toward an IPO firm. As the last two rows of Table IV indicate, independent IPOs experience a reduction in the concentration of credit and an increase in the number of banks. The second effect is common to both sub-samples, but is larger and statistically significant only for independent IPOs; the first one is present only in independent IPOs. Moreover, this effect appears mostly concentrated in the first three years after the IPO, along with the reduction in rates.

In sum, these results suggest that there is more occurring around the IPO than a simple change in the credit quality of newly listed firms. At this stage, however, it is not possible to distinguish between the two other explanations—information and bargaining.

V. OWNERSHIP AND CONTROL

The change in the structure of ownership and in the controlling shareholder can offer important insights into the motives to go public. In particular, if the IPO is accompanied or followed by substantial divestment by the controlling share-holders or by surrender of control to outsiders, the likely motivation of the IPO is to allow the controlling shareholders to diversify their portfolio or increase consumption, rather than to tap fresh sources of finance for company investment.

Table VI reports ownership changes for the IPOs in our sample. The figures in the first entry (Holdings of the control group) show that the median percentage stake of voting rights held by the controlling group falls by 30 points at the time of the IPO and by 5 more points in the three subsequent years (23 and 2 percent respectively if one looks at mean values). The initial owners, though, still retain a stake much larger than the one that would ensure their control (i.e., 50 percent). The stake retained by the controlling shareholders is larger than what Mikkelson et al. (1997) find in the United States (44 percent) and Brennan and Franks (1997) find for Britain (35 percent).

To determine if controlling shareholders have divested from the company, however, we need to factor in the amount of capital raised at the IPO and in the three subsequent years. This is accomplished in the second and third rows. There are no reporting requirements for non-voting shares, so we can only approximate the exact fraction of cash flow rights retained by controlling shareholders. The figures in the second row are obtained assuming that controlling shareholders underwrite pro quota any new equity issue of non-voting shares. By contrast, the third entry assumes that they do not buy any newly issued non-voting stock. The results are substantially the same under the two assumptions, and they indicate that controlling shareholders divest very little of their holdings in the company at the IPO (−3.2 percent) and they even slightly increase their holdings in the three subsequent years (+0.2 percent).

Table VI. *Changes in the ownership structure*

Variable	All IPOs			Independent IPOs			Carve-outs		
	Before IPO	At IPO	3 Years after	Before IPO	At IPO	3 Years after	Before IPO	At IPO	3 years after
Holdings of the control group	99.1	69.2	64.4	90.1	70.0	64.2	100	67.9	67.5
	87.8 (16.7)	65.2[b] (13.6)	63.2[a] (14.3)	84.0 (18.2)	65.7[b] (14.9)	62.5 (13.9)	92.7 (13.3)	64.7[b] (12.0)	64.2 (14.4)
Purchase (sale) of common stock		-3.2	0.2		0.0	0.0		-11.8	1.1
		-8.7[a] (12.9)	7.6[a] (26.5)		-6.0[a] (9.1)	1.3 (15.9)		-14.2[a] (15.6)	15.8 (34.5)
Purchase (sale) of voting stock		-3.2	0.4		0.0	1.1		-11.6	0.3
		-8.7[a] (13.3)	12.7[a] (38.2)		-5.3[a] (8.6)	5.3[a] (17.7)		-13.2[a] (16.7)	22.4 (53.3)
Issues of voting shares		7.2	0.0		10.2	0.0		0.0	0.0
		12.0[a] (14.2)	9.9[a] (35.9)		12.5[a] (13.3)	6.3[a] (11.1)		11.5[a] (15.5)	14.6 (31.3)
Total equity issues (voting and non-voting)		7.4	0.0		10.2	0.0		0.2	0.0
		12.9[a] (14.9)	16.2[a] (35.9)		12.7[a] (13.7)	11.5[a] (18.9)		13.1[a] (16.7)	22.2 (49.8)
Number of shareholders	3	3,325	1,900	4	2,800	1,800	2	4,600	2,040
	34 (127)	8,449[b] (12,624)	4,906[c] (7,945)	44 (159)	7,969[b] (13,940)	3,987[c] (8,131)	22 (69)	9,057[b] (10,934)	6,110[c] (7,665)
Turnover in control			13.6			10.5			17.9
Number of observations	62	69	69	35	39	39	27	30	30

[a]Significantly different from 0 at the 1 percent level.
[b]Significantly different from the value *before* the IPO at the 1 percent level.
[c]Significantly different from the value *at* the IPO at the 1 percent level.

Note: This table reports the changes in the ownership structure at the time of the IPO and in the three subsequent years. The time of the IPO is defined as the end of the year in which the company became listed on the Milan Stock Exchange. The holdings of the control group is the percentage of voting shares held by the largest shareholder, by members of his/her family, and by any other holder who signed a binding voting trust with him/her, provided this trust is mentioned in the prospectus. The purchase (sale) of equities is the fraction of total market value of equity bought (sold) by the control group at the IPO. The purchase (sale) of equities in the following three years is the fraction of total market value of equity (as measured at the IPO) bought (sold) by the control group, where sales and purchases are computed at the IPO price (this figure is meant to capture the effective fraction divested, independent of the price at which it is divested). The figures regarding common stock are based on the assumption that the control group underwrites non-voting equity issues pro quota. The figures regarding voting stock are based on the assumption that the control group does not underwrite any non-voting equity issue. Issues of voting and non-voting shares is the amount of capital raised respectively through the issue of voting and non-voting stock as a fraction of the market capitalization at the IPO in the 6 months before and after the IPO. (Saving shares that are convertible into voting shares are treated as voting shares.) The turnover in control is defined as the change in the identity of the major shareholder. The numbers reported are respectively the median, the mean, and the standard deviation (in parentheses).

These two facts suggest that controlling shareholders do not seem to plan the IPO to diversify their equity holdings. This seems to rule out the diversification motive. But the reduction of the riskiness of the controlling group's holdings may still be an important determinant of IPOs, because newly listed companies significantly decrease their leverage with the funds raised at the IPO.

But these descriptive statistics conceal who is doing what: the data reveal that in 40.6 percent of the cases the company raises new equity and the control group does not sell its equity at the time of the IPO, and in another 40.6 percent the company does not raise new equity and the control group sells some equity. Only in 11.6 percent of the cases does the company issue new equity while the control group decumulates.[32] In fact, the correlation between the issue of new equity and the reduction of the control group's stake is −0.35, and is significant at the 1 percent confidence level. So there are two quite distinct groups of companies in the sample: those in which the control group keeps a strong financial commitment and demands new funds from outside investors, and those in which it divests and does not raise new equity.

The fourth row of Table VI shows the amount of new equity raised through issues of voting shares, and the fifth row shows the total amount of new equity issues. Newly quoted companies raise a substantial amount of fresh equity capital, mostly at the time of the IPO (7.2 percent of their market value for the median company).

The sixth row indicates that the number of shareholders increases more than 1,000 times if one looks at median values. However, in contrast to the United States, the median IPO has only 3 shareholders, and there is a substantial reduction in the number of shareholders in the subsequent three years (more than one-third of the shareholders exit).[33]

In the three years after the IPO, the control group sells out the controlling stake to an outsider in 13.6 percent of the cases (next row). This figure shows that the turnover of control in newly quoted companies is about twice as high as in the Italian economy at large: employing a sample of 973 manufacturing firms used in the study by Barca et al. (1994), the probability of a change in control over a horizon of three years is estimated to have been 7 percent in the 1980 to 1983 period and 5.5 percent in the 1986 to 1990 period.[34] A chi-square test rejects at the 1 percent level the hypothesis that in privately held companies control is as likely to change hands as in new IPOs. This suggests that going public makes a

---

[32] In 28 cases the control group sells equity and the company does not issue new equity. In another 28 cases the control group does not sell equity and the company issues new equity. In 5 cases the control group sells equity while the company issues new equity, while in 6 companies a noncontrol group cashes out.

[33] In an exploratory analysis of the U.S. evidence, we look at the first ten firm–commitment IPOs in 1985. In all cases but one, three years after the IPO the number of shareholders had increased (median increase: 158 percent).

[34] Riccardo Cesari, one of the authors of that study, has kindly estimated this probability at our request, using the INVIND sample, which is well representative of the Italian manufacturing sector and contains a negligible number of public companies (34 out of 973).

change in control much more likely than it is for private companies. This may reflect the greater ease of transferring control of a public company or the greater incidence of control transfers associated with bad performance of the company (recall that our IPOs feature substandard profitability). An alternative explanation is that listing is chosen by controlling shareholders who want to sell out. This is consistent with Zingales (1995a), who sees the transfer of control as a key factor underlying the decision to go public.

Table VI also distinguishes between independent IPOs and carve-outs. The significant differences are that in independent companies (i) the control group starts out with a lower percentage stake than in carve-outs, (ii) controlling shareholders are less likely to divest at the time of the IPO (42 percent of the companies versus 63 percent for carve-outs) and they divest less on average (6 percent of the value of the company, compared with 14 percent for carve-outs), and (iii) controlling shareholders surrender control to outsiders less frequently (in only 10.5 percent of the cases versus 17.9 percent for carve-outs). So divestment and reallocation of control play much more important roles in the decision to carve out a subsidiary than in the decision to list an independent company. This is consistent with the view that public holding companies act more strategically in their decision to list their subsidiaries than independent private companies in their choice to go public: public holding companies appear to list their profitable, low-debt subsidiaries with superior market timing, and they often do this before transferring ownership and control over the subsidiary to a third party.

VI. DISCUSSION AND CONCLUSIONS

As is well known (e.g., Pagano (1993)), the Italian stock market is very small relative to the size of its economy. The limited number of IPOs in the last decade confirms this peculiarity. One may then wonder to what extent our results can be generalized outside this country. In this section we try to address this question while reviewing our main results.

To start with, it is important to realize that even though the Italian case appears as an anomaly compared to the United States, it is far from unique in the European context. Rather, it typifies in an extreme form the differences between the stock markets of Continental Europe and those of Anglo–Saxon countries, both in terms of market capitalization relative to GDP and in terms of number of IPOs. This suggests that some of our qualitative results on the motivations of IPOs and the role of the stock market in Italy may extend to other European equity markets. As we shall see below, there is some evidence pointing in this direction.

Our first finding is that the probability of an IPO is positively affected by the stock market valuation of firms in the same industry. This result is neither surprising nor unique to our sample. The clustering of IPOs is a well-established regularity both in the United States (Ritter (1984)) and other countries (Loughran et al. (1994), Ljungqvist (1995)). But our approach allows us to distinguish whether this positive relationship reflects a higher investment need in sectors with good growth opportunities (and correspondingly high market-to-book ratio) or the owners' attempt to exploit sectoral mispricing. In the Italian case, investment and profitability *decrease* after IPOs—making the explanation based on mispricing appear more appropriate.

Second, we find that a company's size is significantly correlated with the probability of listing. Again, this result is not so surprising. What is more surprising is how large an Italian company must be before it considers going public. The typical Italian IPO is 8 times as large and 6 times as old as the typical IPO in the United States. As the fixed component of the direct listing costs does not differ significantly, this raises the question of why in Italy firms need such a long track record before going public. One possible argument is that Italian companies need higher reputational capital to go public because the lack of enforcement of minority property rights makes the magnitude of the potential agency problem much bigger. This is consistent with independent evidence that Italian companies can more easily dilute the value of minority shareholdings, and with the much larger value of control compared to the United States (Zingales (1994, 1995b)). That size may act as a proxy of reputation in our data also squares with the fact that it does not affect the likelihood of carve-outs: subsidiaries of publicly listed companies can presumably draw upon the reputational capital of their parent company.

An alternative explanation of this finding turns on another—often ignored— fixed cost of listing, the implicit costs of a higher visibility to the tax and legal authorities. As the *Financial Times* (1994) puts it, 'In Italy it is common knowledge most companies keep two sets of books and that tax evasion is widespread' (December 30, p. 4). Upon listing, a company must have its accounts certified externally, which increases the cost of keeping a parallel accounting system. Smaller independent firms may find it prohibitively expensive to set up such systems and so avoid tapping public equity markets. Under this explanation, the likelihood of carve-outs is unaffected by size because in their case the 'visibility cost' is already borne by the parent company.

But the lack of young-company IPOs cannot be explained only by features specific to Italy: the average age of firms going public in Continental Europe is 40 years (Rydqvist and Högholm (1995)), in contrast with United States where many startup companies go public to finance their expansion.

This leads us to our third finding, that is, the contribution of the stock market to investment and growth. Here, our results are again strikingly similar to the evidence for other European countries—and stand in a related contrast to the United States. We find that companies do *not* go public to finance subsequent investment and growth, but rather to rebalance their accounts after a period of high investment and growth. IPOs also do not appear to finance subsequent investment and growth in Spain (see Planell (1995)) and in Sweden (see Rydqvist and Högholm (1995)). In contrast, in the United States newly listed companies feature phenomenal growth (see Mikkelson et al. (1995)). Again, this difference may reflect the more mature age of European IPOs: Mikkelson et al. (1997) also find that in the United States older firms are more likely to use the funds raised to pay down debt than to finance growth.

In addition, our evidence indicated that going public provides benefits not examined in previous studies: it enables companies to borrow more cheaply. Around the IPO date the interest rate on their short-term credit falls and the number of banks willing to lend to them rises. It is an open question how widely this result generalizes to other countries.[35]

Finally, our data reveal that IPOs are followed by an abnormally high turnover in control. This occurs even though the controlling group always retains a large controlling block after the IPO. This finding is consistent with Zingales' (1995a) argument that IPOs are undertaken to maximize the incumbent's proceeds from an eventual sale of the company. This is not necessarily unique to Italy: in the Swedish data analyzed by Rydqvist and Högholm (1995) the eventual surrender of control over the company emerges as a key motivation of IPOs.

One important question this study raises and that only future research will be able to address is why in Continental European countries the stock market mainly caters to large, mature companies with little need to finance investment, while the opposite is true of the United States. Does this reflect the ability of small companies to find other, more efficient channels to finance their investments or rather the inability of small companies to access public equity markets? And in the latter case, which are the main obstacles obstructing their access to the stock market? As suggested earlier, one such obstacle may be the greater visibility of listed companies to tax and legal authorities, especially considering the higher tax pressure and more intrusive regulation featured by Europe compared to the United States. In a recent article, *The Economist* (January 25, 1997) identifies two other possible obstacles: the lack of institutional investors specialized in venture capital and the absence of a liquid stock market dedicated to small firms. The absence of these institutions, however, may itself be a reflection of the paucity of European companies interested in going public.

REFERENCES

Barca, Fabrizo, Madga Bianco, Luigi Cannari, Riccardo Cesari, Carlo Gola, Giuseppe Manitta, Giorigio Salvo, and Luigi Signorini, 1994, Proprietà, modelli di controllo e riallocazione nelle imprese industriali italiane (Il Mulino, Bologna).
Basile, Ignazio, 1998, Gli intermediari creditizi e la quotazione di Borsa, in M. Cattaneo et al. eds.: *L'ammissione alla quotazione di Borsa: un' analisi interdisciplinare* (Vita e Pensiero, Milano).

[35] Planell (1995) finds some evidence that newly listed Spanish companies face a comparatively high cost of credit before the IPO, but enjoy no significant decrease in interest rates after the IPO.

Bhide, Amar, 1993, The hidden cost of stock market liquidity, *Journal of Financial Economics* 34, 31–52.

Bolton, Patrick, and Ernst-Ludwig von Thadden, 1998, Blocks, liquidity, and corporate control, *Journal of Finance* 53, 1–26.

Brennan, Mark, and Julian Franks, 1997, Underpricing, ownership, and control in initial public offerings of equity securities in the UK, *Journal of Financial Economics* 45, 391–414.

Campbell, Tim, 1979, Optimal investment financing decisions and the value of confidentiality, *Journal of Financial and Quantitative Analysis* 14, 913–924.

Centrale dei Bilanci, 1992, *Economia e finanza delle imprese italiane (1982–1990)* (Il Sole 24 Ore Libri, Milano).

Chemmanur, Thomas, and Paolo Fulghieri, 1995, Information production, private equity financing, and the going public decision, Working paper, Columbia University.

Degeorge, François, and Richard Zeckhauser, 1993, The reverse LBO decision and firm performance: Theory and evidence, *Journal of Finance* 48, 1323–1348.

Dharan, Bala G., and David L. Ikenberry, 1995, The long-run negative drift of post-listing stock returns, *Journal of Finance* 50, 1547–1574.

The Economist, 1997, Adventures with Capital, January 25, 15–16.

The Financial Times, 1994, A year of corruption: Corruption had become so pervasive the practice carries no stigma, December 30, 4.

Gompers, Paul, 1996, Grandstanding in the venture capital industry, *Journal of Financial Economics* 42, 133–156.

Holmström, Bengt, and Jean Tirole, 1993, Market liquidity and performance monitoring, *Journal of Political Economy* 101, 678–709.

Il Sole 24 Ore, 1994, Guida alla quotazione, 29 July, 24.

Jain, Bharat A., and Omesh Kini, 1994, The post-issue operating performance of IPO firms, *Journal of Finance* 49, 1699–1726.

Jensen, Michael C., and William H. Meckling, 1976, Theory of the firm: Managerial behavior, agency costs, and ownership structure, *Journal of Financial Economics* 4, 305–350.

Kadlec, Gregory B., and John J. McConnell, 1994, The effect of market segmentation and illiquidity on asset prices, *Journal of Finance* 49, 611–636.

La Porta, Rafael, Florencio Lopez-de-Silanes, Andrei Shleifer, and Robert Vishny, 1997, Legal determinants of external finance, *Journal of Finance* 52, 1131–1150.

Leland, Hayne E., and David H. Pyle, 1977, Informational asymmetries, financial structure, and financial intermediation, *Journal of Finance* 32, 371–387.

Lerner, Joshua, 1994, Venture capitalists and the decision to go public, *Journal of Financial Economics* 35, 293–316.

Ljungqvist, Alexander P., 1995, When do firms go public? Poisson evidence from Germany, Working paper, University of Oxford.

Loughran, Tim, and Jay R. Ritter, 1995, The new issues puzzle, *Journal of Finance* 50, 23–52.

—, and Kristian Rydqvist, 1994, Initial public offerings: International insights, *Pacific-Basin Finance Journal* 2, 165–199.

Massari, Mario, 1992, *Le imprese che possono accedere alla Borsa Valori in Italia* (Il Sole 24 Ore Libri, Milano).

Maug, Ernst, 1998, Large shareholders as monitors: Is there a trade-off between liquidity and control? *Journal of Finance* 42, 483–510.

Merton, Robert C., 1987, Presidential address: A simple model of capital market equilibrium, *Journal of Finance* 42, 483–510.

Michaely, Roni, and Wayne H. Shaw, 1995, The choice of going public: Spin-offs vs. carve-outs, Working paper, Cornell University.

Mikkelson, Wayne H., Megan Partch, and Ken Shah, 1997, Ownership and operating performance of companies that go public, *Journal of Financial Economics* 44, 281–308.

Pagano, Marco, 1993, The flotation of companies on the stock market: A coordination failure model, *European Economic Review* 37, 1101–1125.

—, and Ailsa Röell, 1996, The choice of stock ownership structure: Agency costs, monitoring and the decision to go public, *Quarterly Journal of Economics*, forthcoming.

Planell, Sergio Bermejo, 1995, Determinantes y efectos de la salida a Bolsa en Espana: Un analisis empirico, Working paper, Centro de Estudios Monetarios y Financieros.

Rajan, Raghuram G., 1992, Insiders and outsiders: The choice between informed and arm's-length debt, *Journal of Finance* 47, 1367–1400.

—, and Henri Servaes, 1997, The effect of market conditions on initial public offerings, *Journal of Finance* 52, 507–529.

—, and Luigi Zingales, 1995, What do we know about capital structure: Some evidence from international data, *Journal of Finance* 50, 1421–1460.

Ritter, Jay R., 1984, The hot issue market of 1980, *Journal of Business* 32, 215–240.

—, 1987, The costs of going public, *Journal of Financial Economics* 19, 269–281.

—, 1991, The long-run performance of initial public offerings, *Journal of Finance* 46, 3–27.

Rock, Kevin, 1986, Why new issues are underpriced, *Journal of Financial Economics* 15, 187–212.

Rydqvist, Kristian, and Kenneth Högholm, 1995, Going public in the 1980s: Evidence from Sweden, *European Financial Management* 1, 287–315.

Schipper, Katherine, and Abbie Smith, 1986, A comparison of equity carve-outs and seasoned equity offerings, *Journal of Financial Economics* 15, 153–186.

Yosha, Oved, 1995, Information disclosure costs and the choice of financing source, *Journal of Financial Intermediation* 4, 3–20.

Zingales, Luigi, 1994, The value of the voting right: A study of the Milan Stock Exchange, *The Review of Financial Studies* 7, 125–148.

—, 1995a, Insider ownership and the decision to go public, *The Review of Economic Studies* 62, 425–448.

—, 1995b, What determines the value of corporate votes? *Quarterly Journal of Economics* 110, 1047–1073.

2

Underpricing, Ownership and Control in Initial Public Offerings of Equity Securities in the UK

M. J. BRENNAN AND J. FRANKS

1. INTRODUCTION

The underpricing of Initial Public Offerings (IPO) of common stock has been confirmed by researchers in many different countries. A plethora of theoretical explanations have been advanced to explain why the owners of a company would rationally sell shares to outsiders for less than the apparent maximum price achievable (see, Loughran et al., 1994, for a review of the evidence and the possible causes of underpricing).

In this paper, we cast new light on the underpricing phenomenon by analyzing the costs and benefits to the different contracting parties. On the cost side, we relate the magnitude of the underpricing costs to the value of pre-IPO shareholdings and allocate these costs between directors and other pre-IPO shareholders. We argue that this allocation is important because directors, together with the investment bankers, set the issue price. We find that, for the median issue, over 75% of underpricing costs are borne by non-directors and that costs to directors amount to only 0.77% of the value as a proportion of their pre-IPO holdings.

We thank Maria Carapeto, Luc Renneboog and Aneel Keswani for valuable research assistance and helpful comments. We thank Leslie Warman and Peter Grodzinski for helpful discussions on the new issue process. We are grateful to the National Westminster Bank and Morgan Grenfell for providing some of the data. We thank Dick Brealey, Mark Britten-Jones, Bhagwan Chowdhry, Phillipe Henrotte, Anthony Neuberger, Henri Servaes, and Kyeongwoo Wee for comments on an earlier draft of the paper. The paper has been presented at the Fifth and Seventh Centre Economic Policy Research European Summer Symposium on Financial Markets in Gerzensee, Switzerland, at the 1995 Annual Meeting of the American Finance Association held in Washington, and at the Universities of North Carolina at Chapel Hill, Bologna, Florence, and the Sloan School at MIT. We are grateful to our discussants Claudio Loderer, Ron Anderson and Jay Ritter for their insights and also to participants including James Dow, Francois de George, Mark Grinblatt, Michel Habib, Colin Mayer, Antonio Mello, Narayan Naik, Kristian Rydqvist, Walter Torous, Ivo Welch and Marc Zenner. We thank the referee, Jay Ritter, for many valuable comments on previous drafts of the manuscript.

It is predominantly non-directors, who may not have private benefits of control, that take advantage of the IPO and the post-IPO secondary market to dispose of their shareholdings. In contrast, directors' holdings remain substantially intact. We argue that one benefit of underpricing in the IPO is that the resulting oversubscription allows the issuer both to ration the allocation of shares and to discriminate between applicants so as to reduce the individual size of new blockholdings post-IPO. The greater dispersion of outside holdings reduces incentives for the new shareholders to monitor the current management. We call this the reduced monitoring hypothesis.

Booth and Chua (1996) point out that there is another advantage to diffuse ownership. Diffuse ownership may improve liquidity, and this strategy would tend to make for a lower rate of return required by investors and thus a higher equilibrium price for the firm's shares. This result will be important as insiders dispose of additional shares after the IPO. Maug (1996) provides a model that links underpricing to market liquidity, rationing, and discrimination against large investors in the IPO. Holmstrom and Tirole (1993) argue that an additional advantage of a diffuse shareholding is that it will lead to greater noise trading which, in turn, will encourage more information collection by speculators. Thus, the share price will be more informative permitting more efficient contracting with managers. In contrast, Stoughton and Zechner (1995) provide a model where rationing in the IPO is used to favor large rather than small shareholders so as to obtain an ownership structure that improves monitoring of the firm by outsiders and thereby raises firm value.

This paper is based upon a data set of IPOs made in the UK. The advantage of this data set, compared with that of IPOs made in the US, for example, is that the UK new issue process allows explicit observation of rationing and discrimination between investors in the allocation of shares in the offering. Part of this data set has been provided by two investment banks and is not publicly available.

In Section 2 of the paper we develop the hypotheses and describe the data. In Section 3, we analyze how the costs of underpricing are borne by different groups of pre-IPO shareholders, including directors and non-directors, and show how underpricing is used to discriminate against large subscribers to prevent the formation of large blocks. In Section 4, we track the evolution of ownership for several years following the IPO, distinguishing between the shareholdings of directors and those of other pre-IPO investors. In Section 5, we test the implications of the reduced monitoring hypothesis by regressing the size of large blocks held by new investors on the level of underpricing, and by relating underpricing to the marginal cost of underpricing borne by directors. In Section 6, we summarize our results.

2. HYPOTHESES AND DATA

In this section, we examine the hypotheses, the data set and the process of going public in the UK.

2.1. Hypotheses

We presuppose that directors of the IPO firm wish to maintain control of the firm after the IPO, to avoid the possibility of a hostile takeover (see, Shleifer and Vishny, 1986). Underpricing the issue could reduce the risks of a takeover since underpricing will lead to oversubscription. Oversubscription allows the directors to achieve a more dispersed pattern of ownership by permitting discrimination against large applications. The more dispersed ownership reduces incentives for outside investors to monitor the firm.

Despite the ex post incentive of the owner to allocate shares in full to the smallest subscribers until the issue is fully allocated, it may be more efficient to commit to allocate shares to large subscribers in advance, even if the issue will be oversubscribed. Without such a precommitment, large subscribers will face a significant adverse selection problem and disappear from the market, thereby reducing the probability of a successful issue. This provides a role for the investment banker who can precommit to an allocation rule for large subscribers on account of his repeated appearance in the market (see, Benveniste and Spindt, 1989). Chowdhry and Sherman (1995) argue that under certain assumptions discrimination against larger applications may be revenue maximizing, since it reduces the winner's curse or adverse selection problem found by small uninformed investors.

Reduced monitoring resulting from dispersed ownership, then, will tend to lead to lower efficiency. Lower efficiency will reduce the share value and the resulting cost will fall on all pre-IPO shareholders. However, the costs of underpricing which are intended to generate oversubscription in the IPO will fall more heavily on those pre-IPO investors who sell shares in the IPO, and less on those who retain their shares. In our sample, we find that selling shareholders tend to be non-directors rather than directors.

It may be argued that if large shareholders can buy shares in the secondary market after the offering, then large blocks can be assembled which will nullify the effects of discriminatory allocation at the IPO stage. However, if a change in ownership and control is expected, the price will rise to anticipate the gains, thereby eliminating any abnormal returns from such purchases of large blocks. As Shleifer and Vishny (1986) argue, 'If ownership structure is very diffuse and trading is public it is not profitable to assemble a large block of shares'.

Zingales (1995) provides a theoretical model of insider ownership and the decision to go public. In his model, the entrepreneur seeks a diffuse ownership structure by selling stock so as to maximize his total proceeds from the sale of his company. That is, diffuse ownership with insiders controlling a block of shares is intended to extract more surplus from a potential future buyer. Clearly, if blocks can be assembled with ease, the reduced monitoring motive for underpricing would not be relevant. Therefore, the reduced monitoring hypothesis has the following testable implications.

H1. *In the event of oversubscription, rationing will occur and will tend to discriminate against large applicants.*

H2. *The greater the degree of underpricing, the smaller the block holdings of outsiders.*

The benefits of reduced monitoring are enjoyed by the incumbent management. In choosing the level of underpricing, directors will trade off the expected benefits of reduced monitoring against their expected marginal cost of underpricing. Directors will also take account of the size of their holdings post-IPO. The smaller their holdings, the more vulnerable directors are to the loss of private benefits and the greater the incentive to underprice. Therefore, we expect that, holding the benefits of control constant,

H3. *The level of underpricing will be negatively related to the marginal cost of underpricing borne by directors in relation to their pre-IPO holdings, and will be negatively related to their expected post-IPO holdings.*

We might also expect to observe that when pre-IPO investors wish to sell stock they will prefer to sell shares in the secondary market after the IPO in order to avoid the costs of underpricing in the offering. An absence of hostile changes in control would also be expected if the protection of control benefits is effective.

The improved liquidity hypothesis of Booth and Chua (1996) implies that directors, in choosing the level of underpricing, will trade off two effects on their wealth that arise from underpricing: first, the immediate cost of underpricing, and, second, the later benefit of being able to sell shares at a price that is higher because of the greater liquidity brought about by a more diffuse shareholding. This tradeoff suggests that the level of underpricing will be negatively related to directors' sales at the time of the IPO and positively related to post-IPO sales of stock by directors. We report below the results of empirical tests that bear on these hypotheses.

2.2. IPO Process and the Data Set

Until recently, there have been three dominant types of initial public offerings in the U.K. (i) a *fixed price offering* is an underwritten sale of shares at a fixed price. (ii) an *offer for sale by tender* requires investors to place bids for the shares specifying both quantity and price, and (iii) *placings*, where shares are allocated to institutions and individuals informally through underwriters. For fixed price offerings, the offering is advertised by prospectus to the general public, giving investors an average of 10 days to apply for shares. With offerings made by the second type, offers for sale by tender, the shares are underwritten at a price which is usually the minimum tender price, and a single issue price is struck. Although the issue price could be struck at the market clearing level so that all applicants who apply for shares at or above this price receive their tender in full, it is typically set below this level, and applicants are rationed. However, the underpricing is smaller than in fixed price issues (see, Merrett et al., 1967; Levis, 1993).

There are, in addition, *mixed offerings*, in which an initial tender is followed by an offer for sale. In all cases, a London Stock Exchange rule requires that a minimum of 25% of the company's post-IPO shares must be in the hands of the general public (see, The London Stock Exchange, 1996).

An alternative to underpricing as a means of protecting insiders' control is to issue non-voting shares. However, investing institutions and the London Stock Exchange have discouraged the issuance of non-voting shares and other devices for discriminating against different shareholders. This sanction is confirmed by the sample used in the paper. None of the IPOs included the issuance of dual-class shares, nor did any prospectus provide super priority rights to a particular group of shareholders, or other constraints on the control rights of a particular class of shareholders.

In contrast, NYSE, AMEX, and Nasdaq permit dual-class voting shares to be issued in the IPO and allow restrictions on control changes to be included in the corporate charter. For example, in the 1989 IPO of American Capital and Research, dual class shares were issued. One class of shares, owned by management and employees, represented 97% of the votes. In the 1988 IPO of US West New Vector Group, the corporate charter required an 80% majority to approve a merger and a similar majority for a change to this article. Lastly, in the 1988 IPO of Franklin First National Corporation, the prospectus stipulated that no new shareholder could acquire more than 198,000 shares, comprising about 4% of the share capital, in the offering, and that within 5 years of the IPO no shareholder could amass more than a 10% stake. In a sample of 752 IPOs for the period 1988–1992, 29% contained such specific restrictions.[1] In addition, we have been informed by investment bankers that rationing and discrimination can also occur in US IPOs to deter a hostile change of control. Thus, we might expect IPO underpricing to vary both within and across capital markets because of different mechanisms for protecting insiders against control changes in the IPO process. Chowdhry and Sherman (1996) show that differences in national IPO underwriting practices are associated with differences in average underpricing across countries. IPO underpricing may also vary because private benefits of control are larger in one market than in another.

The original sample of initial public offerings analyzed in this study consists of all UK offers for sale by tender or fixed price offerings reported in The Quality of Markets Quarterly, published by the London Stock Exchange for the years 1986–89. Placings were excluded where data was missing. Offers for sale by investment trusts, or closed-end mutual funds, were also excluded on the grounds that private benefits and control problems were of relatively small importance. For a contrary view of the control problems of investment trusts, see Barclay et al. (1993). Data collected from the prospectus included the size of offering, the names and stakes of existing owners, share sales by existing owners and by the

[1] We are grateful to Laura Field of Pennsylvania State University for providing these statistics and for supplying us with the IPO documents in the cases cited above.

Table 1. *Summary of initial public offerings (IPOs) by type, for 1986–1989*

Type of offer	1986	1987	1988	1989	Total
Tender	4	0	0	0	4
Fixed price	38	12	10	4	64
Mixed	0	1	0	0	1
Total	42	13	10	4	69

Note: The sample includes 69 IPOs. Fixed price offerings are shares sold at a fixed price, tender offers require investors to place bids for shares, and mixed offerings involve an initial tender offer followed by an offer for sale.

company, and the price at which the shares were sold, or the minimum tender price, where appropriate. Data were also collected from The Financial Times on the level of over- or undersubscription and the share allocations to applicants of different numbers of shares.

The published details of the allocation schemes used for oversubscribed offers do not include the number of applications or the total number of shares allocated to a given size category. However, complete details of the rationing scheme were obtained from two investment banks for a subset of the sample.

Ownership data in the years subsequent to the IPO were taken from the Jordan and Extel data bases. For Jordan, the name and size of holdings for individual shareholders were available for companies for the year ending 1990. For Extel, the same information was available for either 1993 or 1992.

Table 1 shows the number of IPOs in our sample partitioned by the three offering methods. Of the 69 observations, the large majority are offers for sale at a fixed price, only four are by tender, and one is a mixed offering. As a result, the empirical analysis will focus on offers for sale at a fixed price. Since ownership data is available for only 43 companies in our sample, several of the subsequent tables will relate to this subsample. Table 2 provides summary statistics for the subsample of fixed price offerings, including size of company, size of issue, proportion of firm sold, oversubscription rate, and underpricing. The table shows that the average value of the company post-IPO is almost 76 million pounds, and the average size of offering in the IPO is 24 million pounds. The average rate of oversubscription in the IPO is 18.8 times and the average level of underpricing is 9.5%.

3. UNDERPRICING AND RATIONING

In this section we report the extent of underpricing in our sample of IPOs and analyze the allocation of the costs of underpricing between directors and other shareholders, and between those who sell their shares in the offering and those who do not. We also analyze the allocation of shares in oversubscribed offers and document a general policy of rationing and discrimination against large applicants.

Table 2. *Characteristics of a subsample of initial public offerings (IPOs)*
offered for sale at a fixed price

	Size of company post-IPO (£)	Size of offering (£)	Percentage of firm sold as a proportion of pre-IPO value	Oversubscription	Underpricing %
Mean	75 785 141	23 671 336	52.35%	18.77	9.52
Maximum	752 962 000	177 663 950	233.33%	95.00	48.12
Minimum	11 865 000	3 955 000	24.97%	−0.95	−43.24
Standard deviation	1 36 918 525	37 972 273	34.65%	24.85	16.43

Note: The subsample includes 64 fixed price offerings. The table reports the value of the company post-IPO, the size of the offering in pounds sterling, the percentage of the firm sold, expressed as a proportion of the pre-IPO value, the rate of oversubscription, where zero is defined as fully subscribed, and the size of underpricing measured as the difference between the issue price and the price at the end of the first 5 days of dealings, adjusted for market movements. Statistics reported are the mean, maximum, minimum, and standard deviation for the subsample.

3.1. The Degree of Underpricing

The first line of Table 3 reports the distribution of underpricing in the sub-sample of 43 fixed-price IPOs from 1986–1989, as measured by the return from the offering price to the close on the fifth day of trading, adjusted by the market return. One week underpricing of 9.52% compares with 9.42% at the end of the first day of trading. The mean underpricing of 9.52% compares with 11.5% found by Levis (1993) for UK IPOs over the period 1980–1988, and 9.87% reported by Miller and Reilly (1987) for the US. Levis (1993) also reports mean long run overpricing of IPOs in the UK, as does Ritter (1991) for the US. The mean underpricing is only 5.02% of the company's pre-issue value computed at the offer price, which reflects the fact that the size of the new issue is considerably smaller than the pre-IPO size of the company (see Table 2).

Since, on average, about 10 trading days elapse between the time the issue is advertized, when the offer price is set, and the first day's trading, movements in the market and specific information about the company during the 10-day window may produce a difference between the expected and actual level of underpricing. For our sample, the Financial Times Actuaries Index moved, on average, 1.22% over the period of the window. However, movements in the market cannot be the only explanation for the difference between expected and actual underpricing for our sample. An extreme case is Richmond Oil and Gas which suffered a loss of 43% by the end of the first day of trading. Overpricing was anticipated by investors since they applied for only 12% of the issue.

This level of market movement contrasts with the US where price changes between the preliminary and final offer price averaged −4.3%, and were accompanied by significant changes in the size of the issue (see, Hanley, 1993).

Table 3. *Amount and allocation of underpricing costs between directors and other pre-Initial Public Offerings (IPO) investors for a subsample of 43 firms, for 1986–1989*

	Mean	Q1	Median	Q3	Maximum
1 week underpricing: u	9.52	−2.34	10.01	19.08	48.12
Underpricing as % of the value of old shares: u_p	5.02	−1.07	4.03	10.52	44.27
Costs borne by retainers as % of pre-IPO holdings: u_r	2.60	−0.02	0.69	3.33	4.43
Costs borne by disposers as % of pre-IPO holdings: u_d	12.12	−2.57	1.09	25.80	69.56
Sterling costs of underpricing directors: (C_D)	368 034	0.00	57 912	793 059	4 063 525
Sterling costs of underpricing others: (C_O)	22 264 926	0.00	100 643	2 867 159	410 040 981
Costs borne by directors as % of their pre-issue holdings: c_D	3.13	0.00	0.77	5.49	44.27
Costs borne by outsiders as % of their pre-issue holdings: c_O	3.83	0.00	1.35	10.58	25.96
Fraction of total costs borne by directors: f_D	39.73	4.66	23.98	80.08	100.00

Note: The table reports (i) the size of underpricing as the difference between the issue price and the price at the end of the first 5 days of trading, adjusting for market movements (u), (ii) underpricing expressed as a percentage of the value of the firm's pre-IPO capitalized value, using the price at the end of the fifth day for the valuation (u_p), (iii) the proportion of the costs of underpricing borne by pre-IPO investors who retained their shares at the time of the IPO (u_r), (iv) the costs of underpricing borne by those investors disposing of their shares, (u_d), (v) the sterling costs of underpricing incurred by directors (C_D) and non-directors (C_O) respectively, (vi) the costs of underpricing borne by directors as a proportion of the value of their pre-IPO holdings (c_D), (vii) the costs of underpricing borne by other investors as a proportion of their pre-IPO holdings (c_O), and (viii) the fraction of total underpricing costs borne by directors (f_D). The column labeled Q1 reports the value of the statistic at the 25th percentile, the column labeled median reports the statistic at the 50th percentile, and the column labeled Q3 reports the value of the statistic at the 75th percentile. The subsample includes 43 IPOs for which ownership data is available.

For UK issues, there were no changes in the issue price or the size of the issue after it had been publicly advertized.

3.2. The Allocation of the Costs of Underpricing

Barry (1989) recognized how the costs of underpricing might fall differentially on pre-IPO investors who sell shares in the IPO and those investors who retain their holdings. In this section we rewrite Barry's equation in terms of holdings by directors and non-directors.

We define the proportionate underpricing, u:

$$u = \frac{P_s - P_0}{P_0},$$

where P_0 is the offer price of a share, and P_s is the market-adjusted secondary market price at the close of the first day or the first week of trading. The total cost of underpricing to the company and selling shareholders, TC, is referred to by practitioners as the 'amount of money left on the table.' TC is equal to the gains of purchasers of newly issued shares sold by the company and of shares sold by pre-IPO investors at the issue price P_0:

$$\text{TC} = uP_0(n_\text{N} + n_\text{d}) = uP_0 n_\text{I},$$

where n_N is the total number of new shares issued by the company, n_d is the number of secondary shares sold by old shareholders, and n_I is the total number of shares sold in the issue, such that $n_\text{I} = n_\text{N} + n_\text{d}$. Since only a fraction of the firm is typically sold in the IPO, the cost of underpricing is a smaller fraction of total firm value than implied by u. Therefore, we define u_p, the cost of underpricing as a proportion of the pre-IPO firm value at the offering price:

$$u_\text{p} = \frac{\text{TC}}{n_0 P_0} = u\frac{n_\text{I}}{n_0},$$

where n_0 is the pre-issue number of shares. Next, we calculate the cost of underpricing per share for those retaining and for those disposing of shares in the offering. In the absence of sales of newly issued shares, the cost of underpricing is borne solely by those insiders who sell shares in the offering. However, newly issued shares sold at a discount dilute the value of those retaining shares. The cost of underpricing on the newly issued shares borne by each pre-issue share is

$$\frac{un_\text{N} P_0}{n_0}.$$

Then the cost of underpricing borne per dollar of old shares held, valued at P_0, by pre-IPO investors who do not sell in the offering (retainers), u_r, is obtained by dividing the above expression by P_0:

$$u_\text{r} = \frac{un_\text{N}}{n_0}.$$

The cost of underpricing for those pre-IPO investors who sell shares in the offering (disposers), u_d, is more complex since the secondary market price P_s is reduced by the underpricing of the issue. In the absence of that underpricing, the shares would be valued at an amount greater than P_s, i.e., $P_s + un_\text{N}(P_0/n_0)$. The latter term is the dilution effect of issuing new shares at a discount. This implies that u_d, the cost of underpricing borne per dollar of shares sold, valued at the offer price P_0, for an individual who disposes of his shares is given by

$$u_\text{d} = \frac{P_s + (un_\text{N}(P_0/n_0)) - P_0}{P_0}$$

$$= \frac{P_s - P_0}{P_0} + \frac{un_\text{N}}{n_0} = u + u_\text{r}.$$

We denote the total costs of underpricing borne by directors by C_D, and the total costs borne by other shareholders by C_O, where

$$C_D = [n_{Dr}u_r + n_{Dd}u_d]P_0$$
$$C_O = [n_{Or}u_r + n_{Od}u_d]P_0,$$

where n_{Dr}, and n_{Dd} are the numbers of shares retained and disposed of by the directors and n_{Or} and n_{Od} are the corresponding figures for other, old investors. Note that $TC = C_D + C_O$. Taking the derivative of C_D with respect to the underpricing variable u, yields

$$\frac{dC_D}{du} = \left(\frac{n_N}{n_0} + \frac{n_{Dd}}{n_D}\right)n_D P_0,$$

where n_D is the total number of shares owned by directors. We see that the marginal cost of underpricing for directors is higher the greater is the ratio of new shares issued to shares outstanding (n_N/n_0), and the greater the fraction of directors' shares disposed of (n_{Dd}/n_D).

In Table 3, the median cost of underpricing expressed as a proportion of the value of the old shares held, valued at the offer price, is 0.69% for those who retain their shares (u_r) and 1.09% for those who dispose of their shares (u_d), although the means are substantially higher at 2.6% and 12.12%, respectively. Thus, u, the average rate of return from the offering price, which is the standard measure of underpricing, substantially overstates the average cost of under- pricing for those who retain their shares and substantially understates it for those who dispose of their shares in the offer. Taking account of the size of the holdings disposed of and retained, the median total costs of underpricing for directors and others, C_D and C_O, are £57 912 and £100 643, respectively. This result implies that the costs of underpricing fall more heavily upon other shareholders than direc- tors. The difference in costs borne by directors and other investors results for two reasons: directors typically own less than one half of the stock, and they are less likely to sell in the IPO. The disparity between the means is larger because particular issues, such as Wellcome, were very large and sales of shares in the IPO were solely made by non-directors, and directors had no significant shareholdings.

When the costs of underpricing for directors and others are expressed as a proportion of the value of their respective pre-issue holdings, $c_D = C_D/(n_{Dd} + n_{Dr})P_0$, $c_O = C_O/(n_{Od} + n_{Or})P_0$, the medians are 0.77% for directors and 1.35% for others. The means are substantially higher at 3.13% and 3.83%, respectively, although if one outlier is excluded in which the proportion of new shares issued to pre-issue shares sold is 233%, the means are 2.15% for directors and 3.88% for others. The value-weighted average of c_D and c_O equals 5.02% as in line 2 of Table 3; the means are shown because they represent values for the typical company. Thus, for a typical firm making an IPO, the costs of underpricing may be regarded as modest when compared with the total value of the firm, and the costs borne by directors as a proportion of the value of their shareholdings is approximately half as much as for other shareholders, because directors dispose of relatively few shares in our sample.

3.3. Underpricing, Oversubscription and Rationing

Just as underpricing represents a cost to the shareholders in the issuing company, so it represents a gain to those who purchase shares in the offer. It is not surprising, therefore, to find that IPOs that are underpriced tend to be over-subscribed, so that the issues must be rationed. Table 4 describes the relation between the level of underpricing, u, measured by the one-week market-adjusted returns, and the level of oversubscription for a sub-sample of 68 firms. The level of oversubscription increases monotonically with underpricing up to a level of 40%, and the average number of applicants for each issue increases with underpricing up to a level of 30%. The regression results reported in the table suggest that for each 1% change in underpricing there is a 0.64 change in oversubscription, a result that is consistent with Levis (1990). For the smaller sample of 43 IPOs used in the paper, the pattern is almost identical.

For oversubscribed offers the underpricing gains must be allocated by rationing the shares awarded to applicants. In the UK, the investment bank must publish the basis for allocation and, subject to some exceptions, the London Stock Exchange requires that the allocation rule discriminates only on the basis of the size of application and not according to the identity of the applicant. However, the allocation rule is published after the applications have been received, so the

Table 4. *The relation between underpricing and the level of oversubscription for a subsample of 68 firms*

Underpricing levels u	Average level of oversubscription OS	Average number of applicants	N
$u < 0$	0.49	24 255	20
$0 < u < 5\%$	6.84	42 693	11
$5\% < u < 10\%$	16.34	111 433	7
$10\% < u < 20\%$	18.55	230 598	17
$20\% < u < 30\%$	23.75	1 036 435	7
$30\% < u < 40\%$	50.59	209 000	3
$40\% < u < 50\%$	34.58	58 087	3
Regression	$OS = 0.088 + 0.64u$	$(t = 4.58)$	$R^2 = 0.24, N = 68$

Note: The subsample includes 68 initial public offerings (IPOs) from the period 1986–1989. The table partitions the sample by different levels of underpricing (u), measured by one-week market-adjusted returns, the level of oversubscription (OS), the average number of applicants for each issue, and the number of IPOs at each level. If the issue is fully subscribed, the level of oversubscription is defined as 0. The table also reports regression equation results using the data for this sample.

rule may reflect discrimination against particular applicants. This rule does not prevent the issuing firm from allocating shares to preferential investors prior to the issue. Such allocations are disclosed in the prospectus. Also, the allocation rule is devised after application lists have been closed and therefore will reflect the size and identity of the applicants.

The reduced monitoring hypothesis implies that the scheme used to allocate shares will be designed where possible to prevent the emergence of large shareholders. However, a cost of discriminating against large applicants in successful offerings is that the resultant adverse selection imposed on them will discourage them from subscribing, increasing the probability that the investment bank will be left with unsuccessful offerings. See Rock (1986) for a model of adverse selection in IPOs. Therefore, we expect that the issuing company will not discriminate against large applicants unless it is necessary to do so to prevent the emergence of large shareholders.

As an example, consider the actual share allocation scheme used by a company to ration shares in an oversubscribed offer described in Table 4. For this company there were 480051 applications for nearly 693 million shares, and the issue was oversubscribed 8.5 times. Almost 45% of the applications were small, with applicants requesting between 400 and 2000 shares, and they totaled about three times the number of shares on offer. There was substantial discrimination for this issue. For example, applicants for between 400 and 1000 shares received 150 shares each, and this category in aggregate received 70% of the total issue compared with its share of 32% of applications, yielding a ratio of allocations to applications of 2.2 to 1 (as shown in the final column of Table 5). For applicants of 15 000 shares, the ratio of allocations to applications falls to 0.24, and for investors applying for between 150 000 and 10 000 000 shares no allocations were made at all. The largest new shareholding was 0.003% of the offering and the five largest shareholders combined held only 0.02% of the issue.

For the 13 companies where we have the detailed allocations data as described in Table 5, we have used two criteria to measure discrimination. The first reports results of individual company regressions relating the percentage of the issue applied for by an individual applicant within a size category (e.g. 400–2000) to the ratio of the percentage allocation to the percentage application as reported in the last column of Table 5. Where there is discrimination in favor of small and against large applicants, we would expect declining values as reported in the last column and therefore a negative slope coefficient. We find that in nine out of 13 cases, the slope coefficient is negative and in six cases it is significantly so at the 5% level or better. In only one case is it significantly positive. The second criterion measures the percentage of the issue sold to the largest applicant and the five largest applicants, respectively. For the sample of 13 companies, on average, the largest applicant receives 2.39% of the issue, and the five largest applicants receive 6.96% in aggregate. However, as a proportion of the post-IPO size, these proportions fall to about 0.8% and 2.3%, respectively. These are relatively small holdings for new investors who wish to exercise control through greater monitoring.

Table 5. *The size pattern of share applications and allocations for a single Initial Public Offering from the sample of IPOs for 1986–1989*

Size of application category (Number of applications)	Total number of shares applied for	Proportion of total shares applied for (%)	Allocation rule (no. of shares)	Number of shares allocated	Proportion of total shares allocated (%)	Ratio of proportion of shares allocated to proportion applied for
400–1000 (381 282)	221 000 000	31.89	150	57 192 300	70.08	2.20
1500–2000 (54 718)	96 929 000	13.99	200	10 943 600	13.41	0.96
3000–5000 (29 200)	110 681 000	15.97	250	7 300 000	8.94	0.55
6000–7000 (5889)	36 102 000	5.21	300	1 766 700	2.16	0.41
8000–10 000 (5893)	57 136 000	8.25	350	2 062 000	2.53	0.31
10 000–15 000 (927)	13 905 000	2.01	425	393 975	0.48	0.24
15 000–20 000 (730)	14 600 000	2.11	500	365 000	0.45	0.21
20 000–25 000 (247)	6 175 000	0.89	625	154 375	0.19	0.21
25 000–30 000 (184)	5 520 000	0.80	750	138 000	0.17	0.21
30 000–35 000 (62)	2 170 000	0.31	875	54 250	0.07	0.22
35 000–40 000 (80)	3 200 000	0.46	1000	80 000	0.01	0.02
40 000–45 000 (23)	1 035 000	0.15	1125	25 875	0.03	0.20
45 000–50 000 (326)	16 300 000	2.35	1250	407 500	0.50	0.21
50 000–60 000 (80)	4 800 000	0.69	1500	120 000	0.15	0.22
60 000–70 000 (25)	1 750 000	0.25	1750	43 750	0.05	0.20
70 000–80 000 (42)	3 360 000	0.48	2000	84 000	0.01	0.21
80 000–90 000 (21)	1 890 000	0.27	2250	47 250	0.06	0.22
90 000–100 000 (173)	17 300 000	2.50	2500	432 500	0.53	0.21
150 000–10 000 000 (149)	79 000 000	11.40	0	0	0.00	0.00

Note: The table reports the number of applications for different sizes of share application categories in the IPO, the proportion of shares applied for in each category, the number of shares allocated per applicant in each category (allocation rule), and the number and proportion of the IPO allocated to each size application category. The final column of the table reports the ratio of shares allocated to the proportion applied for.

A third measure of discrimination reports the extent to which the issuing firm places a limit on the number of shares allocated to the largest applicants in the IPO. This criterion was applied to 29 firms where we have these data. For these 29 firms, one-third of the firms have a cap which takes the form of an absolute number of shares. The cap ranges from 25 000 to 250 000 shares, except for one case where it is zero. In another third of cases, the level of oversubscription was less than twice the number of shares available in the IPO, and as a consequence discrimination was difficult to practice. In some of the remaining cases, the level of oversubscription was so great that discrimination was unnecessary to create small post-IPO holdings; for example, Tip Top was oversubscribed 66 times and Golden Greenless, 59 times.

We conclude that, consistent with our hypothesis H1, rationing and discrimination against large applicants is a significant feature of the allocation scheme for the sample of IPOs. The results for this sample are typically not consistent with the hypothesis of Stoughton and Zechner (1995) that large outside holdings are created to increase monitoring activities by external investors. It may be that share allocations are made to new investors prior to the IPO and those investors become non-executive directors and perform the monitoring function described by Stoughton and Zechner (1995). We do not distinguish in our sample between shareholdings of executive and non-executive directors.

In the next section, we examine how the ownership of pre-IPO investors evolves both at the time of the IPO and in years subsequent to it. These data will allow an examination of the extent to which underpricing is related to the changing patterns of ownership of pre-IPO investors, and the need to safeguard the private benefits of control.

4. THE EVOLUTION OF OWNERSHIP AND CONTROL AROUND IPOs

Private companies and large public corporations represent opposite extremes of the relation between ownership and control. The initial public offering is a crucial step in the evolution of a management-owned firm into a public corporation and the development of a separation between ownership and control. Tables 6 and 7 document the changes in ownership stakes that take place around the IPO and in subsequent years.

In Table 6, all share amounts are expressed as a percent of the number of shares outstanding before the issue. Prior to the IPO, the mean proportional ownership of the firm by directors is 42% while the median is 24%. The remainder of the firm is owned by other investors who include both institutional and private investors. Private investors who are not directors frequently have the same name as that of some of the directors, and the indications are that they are often related to the founding families. The number of shares sold in the IPO averages 52.4% of the pre-issue number of shares outstanding. The latter consists of 28.4% of newly

Table 6. *Ownership of shares prior to the Initial Public Offering (IPO), number of shares offered in the IPO, and ownership data immediately following the IPO for a subsample of 43 firms for the period 1986–1989*

	Mean	Q1	Median	Q3	Maximum
Panel A: Share ownership prior to the IPO					
Shares owned by directors	41.97	6.20	23.99	78.85	100.00
Shares owned by others	58.03	21.62	75.99	93.92	100.00
Total	100.00				
Panel B: Shares sold in the IPO					
New issues by company	28.39	7.18	17.81	33.41	233.33
Shares sold by directors	6.67	0.00	1.88	9.79	40.00
Shares sold by others	17.29	0.00	3.50	23.41	100.00
Total sales in IPO	52.35				
Panel C: Share ownership after the IPO					
Shares owned by directors	35.30	5.53	20.13	65.92	100.00
Shares owned by other old shareholders	40.74	7.53	41.00	76.33	100.00
Shares owned by new shareholders	52.35	33.53	42.81	53.97	233.33
Total shares outstanding	128.39				

Note: All holdings presented in the table are expressed as a percentage of the pre-IPO number of shares outstanding. The subsample includes 43 IPOs for which ownership data is available. The column labeled Q1 reports the value of the statistic at the 25th percentile, the column labeled Median reports the value at the 50th percentile, and the column labeled Q3 reports the value at the 75th percentile.

Table 7. *Ownership by different categories of pre-IPO shareholders for four different periods: pre-IPO, immediately after the IPO, 1990 and 1993*

Type of investor	Pre-IPO	Post-IPO	Shareholdings in: 1990	1993
Directors	41.97 (43)	35.30 (43)	27.89 (30)	28.89 (40)
Vendors	43.60 (43)	27.94 (43)	10.12 (35)	2.95 (38)
Others	14.43 (43)	12.79 (43)	0.96 (31)	4.73 (36)

Note: Numbers are expressed as a proportion of the total number of shares prior to the IPO. The sample size for each item is given in parentheses. The table represents a sample of 43 IPOs from 1986–1989 for which ownership data is available, which includes 15 companies where small amounts of pre-IPO holdings are not identified with any particular shareholding. As a result, those particular shareholdings are assumed to be zero in 1990 and 1993. Directors include the holdings of directors and their family trusts. Vendors are private investors who are closely related to the members of the board of directors, but are not directors themselves. Other investors are institutional investors such as venture capital firms and insurance companies. Shareholdings in 1990 are taken from The Jordan's Data Base of shareholdings and in 1993 from The Extel Company.

issued shares, 6.7% shares sold by directors, and the remaining 17.3% shares sold by other pre-IPO investors. Thus, the company increases its number of shares outstanding by an average of only 28.4%, and the corresponding figure for the median is less than 18%. On average, almost as many shares in the offering come from pre-IPO holders as from the company itself, and almost three quarters of sales by pre-IPO investors are from non-directors. Immediately following the IPO, new shareholders own about 52.4% of the company, with the remainder being split between directors and other old investors. The medians give significantly lower ownership for directors pre-IPO and a smaller issue size.

Table 7 describes the evolution of ownership following the IPO. We partition holdings by directors and their family trusts, private investors who are typically members of the family but are not members of the board of directors (and are referred to as vendors in the prospectus) and other investors, who are typically institutional investors such as venture capital funds and insurance companies. The sizes of their shareholdings are given both before and immediately after the offering and in 1990 (Jordan's data) and 1993 (Extel's data). The table provides data for the sample of 43 companies analyzed in Table 6. For 15 companies there are small amounts of missing ownership data about pre-IPO holdings. If we exclude these companies, the results in Table 7 barely change.

Table 7 shows that holdings of directors are reduced by about a third, from 42% of the pre-issue number of shares outstanding prior to the IPO to 29% in 1993. In contrast, holdings of vendors are virtually eliminated over the same period, declining from 43.6% of the pre-issue number of shares to less than 3%. In the IPO itself, vendors sell on average about 36% of their holdings. Holdings of other investors are little changed at the IPO, but fall almost as dramatically as the holdings of vendors in the post-IPO period. In contrast, in German IPOs, the old shareholders retain holdings that are 50% larger than in the UK (see, Goergen, 1996). The analysis also compares with that of Barry et al. (1990) who find substantially larger pre-IPO holdings of venture capitalists and greater stability of ownership post-IPO.

The pattern of ownership post-IPO is consistent with the view that 'going public' is a vehicle for the disposal of shares by non-directors. Holdings sold in the IPO may be necessary to meet the 25% rule of the Stock Exchange to ensure a liquid after-market. For example, the sale by vendors of about two thirds of their shares after the IPO is consistent with vendors wishing to avoid the costs of underpricing in the IPO. Also, we found a strongly negative relation at better than the 1% level ($t = 6.06$) between sales made by all pre-IPO shareholders in the IPO and newly issued shares by the company. This negative relation suggests that the greater the number of new shares issued in the IPO the smaller the sales of existing shares.

If discrimination in the allocation process is effective in protecting insiders against monitoring or a change in control, we would expect discrimination to limit the size of stakes assembled in the secondary market after the IPO. Table 8 provides details in a subsample of 29 companies of the size of large share stakes, other than those held by insiders, reported by Extel in 1993. A large stake is defined as at least 3% of the outstanding share capital. The maximum number of individual large stakes for any company is 6. On average, the large share stakes total almost 21% of the outstanding shares. In the second column we have subtracted from the

Table 8. *Average size of large share stakes of outsiders disclosed in 1993 by Extel for 29 companies in the subsample of 43 IPOs from 1986–1989, for which ownership data is available*

Average of the sum of the large share stakes	Average of the sum of the large share stakes excluding nominee holdings	Average of the largest share stake in each company
20.59%	18.74%	10.0%

Note: The percentages are based upon the number of shares in the most recent financial year. A large stake is defined as at least 3% of the company's outstanding shares. The second column excludes nominee holdings which are held by investment banks or brokerage firms on behalf of groups of investors.

data in column 1 nominee or non-beneficial holdings where there is evidence that they are held by an institution, such as a bank, acting as custodians on behalf of a number of shareholders. In this case the average total large share stake falls to 18.74%. The third column reports the size of the largest stake in each company, which averages 10%. In the next section, we shall investigate the extent to which the size of these outside stakes are related to underpricing.

5. ADDITIONAL TESTS OF THE REDUCED MONITORING HYPOTHESIS

The evidence reported above shows that underpricing is related to over-subscription, and oversubscription is frequently related to discrimination against large shareholders in the allocation process. In this section, we provide two additional tests of the reduced monitoring hypothesis. H2 predicts that the block holdings of outsiders will tend to be smaller the greater is the degree of under-pricing. To test this hypothesis, the aggregate size of all large outside holdings expressed as a proportion of all outside holdings is regressed on the one-week market-adjusted returns. The shareholding data were taken from Extel for 1993, and were available for a limited sample. The results are reported in Table 9. The slope coefficient is negative as predicted, and significant at the 5% level $(t = -2.37)$. That is, for every 1% increase in underpricing the aggregate size of large stakes falls by 0.77%. The analysis was repeated using the size of the single largest outside shareholding as a proportion of total outside shareholdings as the dependent variable. This largest relative block size measure was again negatively and significantly associated with the measure of underpricing, despite the fact that the IPOs for some companies had occurred as many as 7 years previously. Thus, consistent with the reduced monitoring hypothesis, there is evidence that underpricing tends to be related to the reduced size of large blocks of shares in the hands of outside shareholders. This result together with the previous evidence that there is discrimination in the allocation process in the IPO against large shareholders, provides support for Shleifer and Vishny's (1986) proposition that, if ownership is diffuse, it is difficult to assemble large blocks.

Table 9. *Regression results for the reduced monitoring hypothesis, using a subsample of IPOs for 1986–1989*

	Regression 1	Regression 2	Regression 3	Regression 4
Variables:				
Dependent	Total of large outside stakes in 1993 as a fraction of all outside holdings	Single largest outside shareholding in 1993 as a fraction of all outside holdings	Level of underpricing (one week abnormal returns)	Level of underpricing (one week abnormal returns)
Independent	1 week abnormal returns	1 week abnormal returns	(i) Relative marginal costs of underpricing for directors (ii) Log size (value of new shares issued) (iii) Post-IPO holdings of directors	(i) Sales by directors at IPO (ii) Sales by directors post-IPO
Results:			(i) (ii) (iii)	(i) (ii)
Slope coefficient	−0.77	−0.34	0.02 −0.13 −0.04	−0.08 0.06
t value	−2.37	−2.24	0.19 −1.23 −0.26	−0.53 0.79
R^2	0.20	0.19	0.06	0.02
No. of observations	24	24	34	34

Note: The first regression relates the total of all large share stakes to the size of underpricing. Large holdings are defined as those in excess of 3% as of 1993. The second regression relates the largest outside shareholdings to the size of underpricing. The third regression relates the level of underpricing to the relative marginal costs of underpricing borne by directors, the size of the issue, and the post-IPO holdings of directors. The fourth regression relates underpricing to sales by directors at the IPO and sales by directors post-IPO.

H3 predicts that the level of underpricing will be negatively related to the marginal cost of underpricing for directors. We also control for their expected holdings post-IPO since the lower these holdings the more vulnerable directors are to the accumulation of outside shareholdings. In order to test H3, the level of underpricing was regressed on the marginal cost of underpricing by directors divided by the value of their initial holdings, $n_D P_0$. The results for Regression 3 in Table 9 show that the coefficient for the marginal cost variable is positive and not significant and the coefficient for post-IPO holdings of directors is negative and also not significant. This lack of significance may reflect the relatively low costs of underpricing borne by directors and the fact that the private benefits of control may vary across companies.

An important implication of the data shown earlier in Table 7 is that by 1993, the pre-IPO shareholders, on average, no longer have a controlling interest in the company and therefore may be vulnerable to a takeover and change in managerial control. As a result, we examined the fate of all 43 companies in our sample up to June 1996 to determine which ones had been acquired and the extent to which there had been a hostile change of control. Out of 43 companies, 11 had been acquired and 1 had been taken private by pre-IPO shareholders. Of the 11 acquired, there was only one case of a successful hostile bid where hostility was defined as opposition by target management and the incidence of revised bids (definitions used by Franks and Mayer, 1996). In two other cases hostile takeovers failed. In one case the target accepted a bid two years later and in another a white knight was found. In Glaxo's successful hostile takeover of Wellcome, the management opposed the bid but it was immediately accepted by the main shareholder, the Wellcome Foundation, which had a controlling shareholding; management owned virtually no shares. We also examined the incidence of revised bids, which Franks and Mayer (1996) contend are indications of auctions and potential hostility; we found none. This pattern contrasts to aggregate UK takeover activity where almost a quarter of takeovers are hostile and half of those takeovers include revised bids.

The last test concerns the Booth–Chua hypothesis that underpricing will be negatively related to the proportion of director holdings disposed of in the IPO, and positively related to the proportion disposed of in the after market. The results for Regression 4 are reported in Table 9, and we find that although the signs of the coefficients were consistent with the Booth and Chua hypothesis, the size of the coefficients were not significant.

6. CONCLUSION

This paper provides a study of how the separation of ownership and control evolves in British companies. An important finding is that, on average, a large majority of shares owned by pre-IPO shareholders are sold at the IPO or in subsequent years. The shares sold subsequent to the IPO are consistent with pre-IPO investors wishing to avoid some of the costs of underpricing associated with the IPO. Significantly, these sales derive substantially from those insiders who are not directors of the company, which we interpret as evidence that directors derive private benefits of control that are not available to non-directors.

The paper finds that underpricing is typically associated with oversubscription and is followed by substantial rationing and discrimination in the allocation of shares. The discrimination is usually against large applicants and in favor of smaller applicants as predicted by the reduced monitoring hypothesis. In addition, the results show that the size of the underpricing is negatively related to the size of large blocks assembled after the IPO, which is consistent with underpricing being an effective mechanism to secure a diffuse outside shareholding. Furthermore, even though we find a high incidence of acquisition among the sample, there is only one case of a successful hostile change of control, and in that case pre-IPO shareholders recommended the takeover over the objections of management who had virtually no shareholdings. However, we do not find evidence that underpricing is related to the marginal costs of underpricing borne by directors. It may be that the size of underpricing is more a function of differences in private benefits than differences in relative marginal costs.

REFERENCES

Barclay, M. J., Holderness, C. G., Pontiff, J., 1993. Private benefits from block ownership and discounts on closed-end funds. Journal of Financial Economics 33, 263–291.

Barry, C. B., 1989. Initial public offering underpricing: The issuer's view–a comment. Journal of Finance 44, 1099–1103.

—, Muscarella, C. J., Peavy III, J. W., Vetsuypens, M. R., 1990. The role of venture capital in the creation of public companies: Evidence from the going-public process. Journal of Financial Economics 27, 447–471.

Benveniste, L. M., Spindt, P.A., 1989. How investment bankers determine the offer price and allocation of new issues. Journal of Financial Economics 24, 213–232.

Booth, J. R., Chua, L., 1996. Ownership, dispersion, costly information and IPO underpricing. Journal of Financial Economics 41, 291–310.

Chowdhry, B., Sherman, A., 1995. The winner's curse and international methods of allocating initial public offerings. Pacific-Basin Finance Journal 4, 15–30.

—, —, 1996. International differences in oversubscription and underpricing of IPO's. Journal of Corporate Finance 2, 359–368.

Franks, J., Mayer, C., 1996. Hostile takeovers and the correction of managerial failure. Journal of Financial Economics 40, 163–181.

Goergen, M. G. J., 1996. The transfer of control in British and German IPOs. Working paper, University of Oxford, Oxford, UK.

Hanley, K. W., 1993. The underpricing of initial public offerings and the partial adjustment phenomenon. Journal of Financial Economics 34, 231–250.

Holmstrom, B., Tirole, J., 1993. Market liquidity and performance monitoring. Journal of Political Economy 101, 678–709.

Levis, M., 1990. The winner's curse problem, interest costs and the underpricing of initial public offerings. Economic Journal 100, 76–89.

—, 1993. The long-run performance of initial public offerings: the UK experience 1980–1988. Financial Management 22, 28–41.

The London Stock Exchange, 1996. Report of the Committee on Private Share Ownership, July.

Loughran, T., Ritter, J. R., Rydqvist, K., 1994. International public offerings: international insights. Pacific–Basin Finance Journal 2, 165–199.

Maug, E., 1996. Ownership structure at a determinant of IPO underpricing: a theory of the decision to go public for venture capital backed companies. Working paper, London Business School, London, UK.

Merrett, A. J., Howe, M., Newbould, G. D., 1967. Equity Issues and the London Capital Market. Longman Press, London, UK.

Miller, R. E., Reilly, F. K., 1987. An examination of mispricing, returns, and uncertainty for initial public offerings. Financial Management 16, 33–37.

Quarterly Review: Quality of Markets, The London Stock Exchange, 1986–1989.

Ritter, J. R., 1991. The long run performance of initial public offerings. Journal of Finance 32, 1151–1168.

Rock, K., 1986. Why new issues are underpriced. Journal of Financial Economics 17, 187–212.

Shleifer, A., Vishny, R. W., 1986. Large stakeholders and corporate control. Journal of Political Economy 94, 461–488.

Stoughton, N., Zechner, J., 1995. IPO mechanisms, monitoring, and ownership structure. Working paper, University of California at Irvine, Irvine, CA.

Zingales, L., 1995. Insider ownership and the decision to go public. Review of Economic Studies 62, 425–448.

3

Going Public and the Ownership Structure of the Firm

ANTONIO S. MELLO AND JOHN E. PARSONS

1. INTRODUCTION

That ownership structure is an important determinant of firm value is now well established in the finance literature. Large, active investors often play a monitoring role that raises the value of all shares. The presence of large shareholders also improves the efficiency of the market for corporate control. How does the significance of ownership structure shape the process for issuing equity?

When a firm goes public, the large volume of new shares sold, as well as the large volume of existing shares transferred to new owners, lastingly shapes the firm's ownership structure and thereby influences the firm's value. To maximize the revenue raised from the shares sold in the public offering, it is important to design the sale of new shares with the final ownership structure in mind. Most investors will remain relatively small and passive holders of the firm's shares, while others will seek a large block of shares and are prepared to actively shape the firm's management, either as monitors of the current management or as proponents of an alternative strategy or management team (see Mikkelson and Ruback, 1985; Shleifer and Vishny, 1986; and Barclay and Holderness, 1989). The market for dispersed shareholdings is distinct from the market for potentially influential blocks; Hanley and Wilhelm (1995) provide evidence that the market for shares is segmented. Is it possible to ignore the heterogeneity among investors and design a sale of shares uniformly addressed to all buyers? If not, how should this heterogeneity shape the firm's strategy for selling shares?

We establish that the optimal strategy involves a staged process of financing beginning with an IPO for small investors, then selling a controlling block (possibly at a discount), and concluding with a contingent sale of additional shares. Our results highlight the fact that going public is a complex and extended process. The IPO is particularly suited for the sale of dispersed shareholdings to small and passive investors but is not a good method for selling control. The marketing of potentially controlling blocks of shares to active investors should occur separately and, perhaps as important, after the IPO has taken place.

If securities regulators prohibit price discrimination among different investors, then we show that the optimal strategy is to sell a controlling block subsequent to the IPO.

We show that favorable treatment for investors seeking potentially controlling blocks maximizes the revenue raised in the aggregate sale of shares. Because an active investor with a controlling block can benefit all shareholders, discriminating in favor of the active investor by offering the controlling block at a discount assures an efficient ownership structure and raises the market value of the firm. On the other hand, insofar as the active investor can use the controlling block to extract private benefits, the seller can raise the price at which a controlling block is offered. Consequently, whether the controlling block is offered at a discount or a premium depends upon the relative significance of the public and private benefits associated with the controlling block.

It is also necessary that active investors seeking controlling blocks be put into competition with small, passive investors seeking the same shares in dispersed allotments. This can be done, for example, by initially selling a portion of the shares to passive investors and then later putting a controlling block up for sale on terms determined in part by the price for the outstanding shares. This highlights the importance of treating the issuance of shares as a process incorporating transactions over time, instead of as a single event independent of the firm's plans for subsequent financing as has often been the case. The results of each sale affect the terms of later sales, and the terms of earlier sales are determined in part by the beneficial impact on ownership structure and the terms of later sales. One contribution of our paper is to explain why some privately held firms go public instead of selling control exclusively to another set of private investors, despite the apparent value loss associated with the free rider problem (Weston et al., 1990, p. 663).

A great deal of recent empirical evidence establishes that going public is an extended process and that, as its name implies, the IPO is but the first stage in this process. This literature shows that questions of ownership structure and control are at the center of this process and also seems to indicate that the IPO is not a good way of selling control. Rydqvist and Högholm (1994) present evidence that often the decision to go public cannot simply be explained by the growth experienced by the firm. According to Barry et al. (1990), venture capitalists have mechanisms to ensure that in many instances firms go public before any controlling blocks are sold. Indeed, in most of the cases analyzed, Barry et al. report that none of the venture capitalists sold shares during the IPO, although their ownership stakes gradually declined over time thereafter. Mikkelson et al. (1995) also find that initial owners rarely dispense controlling blocks at the IPO. Brennan and Franks (1995) provide evidence that firms manage the sale of shares with the purpose of discriminating between passive investors and applicants for large blocks and that the timing of the sale of large blocks is carefully chosen: most blocks remain intact during the IPO, but almost one-half of the offering company's shares are sold subsequently. Indeed, the strategy of going public followed by a transfer of control seems to be a more frequent strategy in the sale of firms than it might appear at first. Evidence of control turnover after IPOs is documented by Holderness and Sheehan (1988) for the U.S., by Rydqvist and Högholm (1994) for Sweden and the U.K., and by Pagano et al. (1996) for Italy.

Although much of this literature deals with stand-alone firms, divisions of public corporations are sometimes also sold through a public offer of shares. The importance of seeing the sale as an extended process arises here as well. For example, Schipper and Smith (1986) and Klein et al. (1991) report that the initial public offering of shares in a wholly owned unit—an 'equity carve-out'—is frequently followed by the sale of the remaining interest by the parent corporation. Recent examples in which flotation has been proposed as the first stage of a complete ownership transfer are Agfa, currently owned by Bayer, Suburban Propane, a U.S. subsidiary of Hanson, the U.K. industrial conglomerate, and Thermo King, the transport refrigeration unit of Westinghouse (see the Financial Times, 11/8/95, 12/21/95; the New York Times, 11/14/96).

Other researchers have also begun to call attention to the important relationship between ownership structure and the process of going public. The papers most closely related to this one are Zingales (1995) and Stoughton and Zechner (1998). Both of these papers analyze how the decision to go public is affected by considerations of corporate control and suggest that the sale of the company should proceed in stages. In a model with perfect information but in which the seller has better bargaining power against passive investors than against an investor seeking control, Zingales shows that first selling a portion of the firm's shares to the passive investors and then selling a controlling block maximizes the seller's revenue. Zingales also explores how the separation of control rights and cash flow rights can raise the seller's revenue even more. Uncertainty about the value added by the active investor and uncertainty about the demand of small investors play a role in our setting that is not present in Zingales'. In our model the seller obtains valuable information from the sale of shares to small investors that is useful in negotiating the terms of a sale to an active investor. We interpret the IPO as a mechanism that provides the seller valuable information to set the conditions under which the controlling block will be sold.

Stoughton and Zechner (1998) emphasize as well the importance of favoring large investors. But because they abstract from the effects of asymmetric information among investors, their suggested optimal method is quite the opposite of ours—they suggest first selling shares to the large investor and then selling to small investors at the same price. This order of events does not seem to be supported by the empirical evidence. Stoughton and Zechner explain underpricing and rationing in an IPO as a second-best response to regulatory constraints on price discrimination which make implementation of the optimum ownership structure difficult, while we, on the other hand, argue that an IPO should be seen as the first step in a process of a staged financing used to implement an efficient ownership structure. To our knowledge this paper is the first that analyzes the discovery role of the IPO in models of the sale of control blocks when investors have different information. Indeed, in Zingales the IPO stage may not even be optimal when the value of the cash flow rights under the management of the new large investor is less than the value under the initial owner. In our case the IPO is always a good choice, because it helps to reveal information about the demand for dispersed shares and the market's assessment of the value of the firm under the management of a potential new large investor. If this value is low, the current owner can then decide not to sell to the large investor, but that decision can only be made after the IPO.

The paper proceeds as follows. The next section describes the model and illustrates the relation between the allocation made in the public offering and the final ownership structure when investors are given the opportunity to trade in the firm's shares. In Section 3 we develop a framework for analyzing strategies for going public, and in Section 4 we use this framework to evaluate alternative strategies, comparing the outcomes of methods of sale that have been most frequently used. In Section 5 we discuss some possible variations that will help obtain an optimal solution. The concluding section summarizes the major findings.

2. A MODEL OF THE SALE OF SHARES WITH A SECONDARY MARKET

In this section we describe the basic framework of analysis and the fundamental assumptions. We model an initial sale together with a sequence of aftermarkets in which shares can be traded and out of which is established a final ownership structure. We then close the model with a concluding period in which all holdings are liquidated and any anticipated cash flows are actually realized. Finally, we present a numerical example that illustrates the relation between the allocation made in the public offering and the final ownership structure.

2.1. The Population of Investors

Investors are assumed to be risk neutral and to differ in their demands for the shares of the firm as well as in their degree of influence on the firm once they become shareholders. There is a population of small investors for whom the value of a share in the firm is the sum of several components. One component, y, captures the value calculated under a common metric and about which there is no uncertainty. Added to this common component is an idiosyncratic component, w, which is private information to each investor. For example, the small investor's tax status or liquidity preference might affect his or her valuation of the firm's expected cash flows. Diversity in the population of small investors is described by the distribution $G(w \mid \alpha)$ on the range $[w_{\min}(\alpha), w_{\max}(\alpha)] \subseteq R^+$ with $\int_{w_{\min}}^{w_{\max}} dG(w \mid \alpha) = 1$. The parameter α is a random variable in R^+ that captures variation in the aggregate valuation of small investors, and has the distribution

$H(\alpha)$. We assume that $\partial G/\partial \alpha > 0$ everywhere that $H(\alpha) \in (0, 1)$. Each small investor knows its own type, w, but does not directly observe the population parameter α and is therefore uncertain about aggregate demand. We normalize each small investor's demand for a share with the condition that aggregate demand at any fixed price, p, is given by $\int_{p-y}^{w_{\max}} dG(w|\alpha) = 1 - G(p - y|\alpha)$.

In addition, there is a large, active investor denoted by 'a' who seeks a controlling block in order to actively influence future management's decisions. This investor might be interested in acquiring control because of information about a strategy for using the assets of the firm that could increase the value of the firm's cash flows. Control is reached with 50% of the shares, although a lower proportion can be used to illustrate the problem. Upon achieving control of the firm, the large shareholder can implement changes in the operations of the firm that will increase the value of the firm's expected future cash flows by an amount z. Initially, the value of z is private information to the active investor. The seller and the small investors view the active investor's control premium as a random variable drawn from a distribution $F(z)$. The large investor's idiosyncratic component of the value is w_a. The model can be extended to include multiple active investors without changing the essential dynamics of the problem, but it is necessary that the active investors not be atomless—size matters. According to Wruck (1989, p. 10), the most common case is indeed that of one large buyer per sale.

Since the efficiency of the allocation of shares plays a central role in this paper, it is useful to characterize the efficient allocation. Consider first the allocation among the class of small shareholders. For an arbitrary quantity of shares for the class as a whole, the optimal allocation is to assign the shares first to those with the highest private valuation and then to shareholders with lower and lower private valuations until the quantity available is exhausted. The last small investor to receive a share is the marginal small investor, given the quantity to be allocated. Consider next the allocation of shares either to the active investor or to the pool of small investors. It will either be efficient to allocate a controlling block or not. Efficiency requires that we allocate the controlling block to the active investor whenever the per unit value of the shares in the active investor's hands, $w_a + z$, is greater than the average per unit value of the shares in the hands of the small investors displaced, $\int_{\bar{w}_0(\alpha)}^{\bar{w}_{1/2}(\alpha)} w \, dG(w|\alpha)$, where $\bar{w}_{1/2}(\alpha)$ denotes the marginal small investor when the active investor has received exactly a controlling stake and $\bar{w}_0(\alpha)$ denotes the marginal small investor when the active investor has received zero shares. Note that the efficient decision of whether to allocate the controlling block to the active investor is contingent upon the parameter α, which measures the aggregate demand of small investors. We can summarize these results in formal notation as follows. Denote by $q_a^*(\alpha, z, w_a)$ the efficient allocation to the active investor contingent on all realizations of the two parameters α and z, for a given value of w_a. Then $q_a^* = \frac{1}{2}$ whenever $w_a + z \geq \bar{z}(\alpha) = \int_{\bar{w}_0(\alpha)}^{\bar{w}_{1/2}(\alpha)} w \, dG(w|\alpha)$. Denote by $q_s^*(w, \alpha, z)$ the efficient allocation among small investors. If $q_a^* = 1/2$, then $q_s^*(w, \alpha, z) = 1/2$ for $w \geq \bar{w}_{1/2}(\alpha)$ and zero otherwise, and if $q_a^* = 0$, then $q_s^*(w, \alpha, z) = 1$ for all $w \geq \bar{w}_0(\alpha)$.

2.2. The Sequence of Markets

Consider a firm that is for sale by its owner(s). There are many reasons that could explain this exit decision, including the benefits of diversification, liquidity preferences, the realization of gains from selling to better-positioned parties, exploiting favorable market conditions, gains from focus, etc. In this paper we take the decision to sell as given and concentrate on the issues surrounding the implementation of the sale.

The full sequence of events is broken down into six periods, $\tau = 0, \ldots, 5$, as shown in Figure 1. At $\tau = 0$, the risk neutral seller makes public the choice of method used in the initial sale. The sale is open to all interested investors. At $\tau = 1$, the initial sale of shares takes place according to the rules established by the seller, the resulting allocation, $q_a^1(w_a, \alpha, z), q_s^1(w, \alpha, z)$, is made public, and all investors update their beliefs about the unknown parameters α and z based upon this information.

At $\tau = 2$, small investors trade shares in a secondary market at a competitive, rational expectations equilibrium price, p^2. This price can be informative about the unknown parameters. The active investor cannot trade anonymously in the secondary market at $\tau = 2$ and must instead make all trades in a tender offer market at $\tau = 3$. The active investor can use the tender offer market to buy any quantity of shares or to sell some or all of any holdings accumulated in the initial offering. The active investor's decision to make a tender offer at the price p^3 can be also informative about the unknown parameters. The results of the tender offer are public information. At $\tau = 4$, competitive trading among the small investors resumes at a rational expectations equilibrium price p^4. At $\tau = 5$, the firm is liquidated and shareholders receive their prorated share of the firm's cash flows, valued as described earlier.

Variations on this sequencing are also possible. For example, the initial sale can take place in stages within period $\tau = 1$, and in Section 4 we consider a sale in which some of the shares are distributed at $\tau = 1$ and a second portion is distributed after a secondary market price is established.

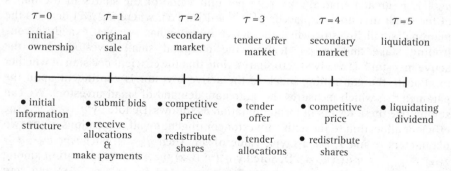

Figure 1. *The sequence of events*

2.3. Trade and Information in the Secondary Market

Investors can buy shares in the primary market as well as later when the secondary market opens for trading. One question that immediately arises is whether the extended trading opportunities effectively provide for an optimal ownership structure in the firm. For example, is it always possible for the active investor to accumulate a block in the secondary market when the optimal outcome includes block ownership by an active investor? If so, then naturally that will reshape the equilibrium bidding in the initial sale. Also, why should the seller worry about designing a method of sale if investors can revise their allocations in the secondary market? If a passive investor can buy shares in the secondary market at a competitive price, then it would appear impossible to design the initial sale to raise any more than the expected value of a share in the secondary market. Faced with the secondary market as a constraint on the price paid by the passive investor, it would seem that rules of sale that strategically invite the participation of specific groups of investors are relatively innocuous and ultimately implemented at the expense of the seller.

We show that the markets for shares cannot ensure an optimal ownership structure in the firm all the time, and therefore the choice of the method of sale is an important consideration. Suppose that in equilibrium the initial sale always establishes the efficient ownership of the firm. At the start of period $\tau = 2$, passive investors know whether the active investor has been allocated a controlling block and therefore whether the ultimate value of a share to them incorporates a control premium. Moreover, small investors infer from the active investor's allocation in the initial sale whether $z \geq \bar{z}(\alpha)$. When $q_a^1 = 0$, a small investor demands a share if and only if $p^2 < y + w$. The market-clearing price is therefore $p^2 = y + \bar{w}_0(\alpha)$. When $q_a^1 = \frac{1}{2}$, a small investor must make an estimate of the size of the control premium, z. The small investor's own private valuation provides information about the likely values for α and therefore for z. The active investor's allocation tells the small investor that $z \geq \bar{z}(\alpha)$. Finally, the equilibrium price can itself provide additional information about the likely values for α and z. The small investor demands a share if and only if $p^2 < y + w + \mathcal{E}(z \mid w_a, z \geq \bar{z}(\alpha), p^2)$. The rational expectations equilibrium price function $p^2 = y + \bar{w}_{1/2}(\alpha) + \mathcal{E}(z \mid w_a, \alpha, z \geq \bar{z}(\alpha))$ fully reveals α, making each small investor's own private valuation entirely superfluous in conditioning the posterior distribution on z, and clears the market.

We can summarize the results of the competitive market with the following characterization of the market price as a function of the underlying parameters:

$$
p^*(\alpha, z) = \begin{cases} y + \bar{w}_0(\alpha), & z < \bar{z}(\alpha), \\ y + \bar{w}_{1/2}(\alpha) + \mathcal{E}(z \mid w_a, z \geq \alpha, \bar{z}(\alpha)), & z \geq \bar{z}(\alpha). \end{cases}
$$

This market price acts as an important constraint on the original terms of sale that can be imposed on small investors. Knowing that it is always possible to obtain a share in the competitive market on these terms, each small investor puts a limit on the price he or she is willing to pay in the initial sale. We discuss these issues in detail in the next section, but first it is necessary to complete our discussion of the secondary market.

In the analysis above we assume that the initial sale of shares always establishes an efficient ownership structure for the firm. However, the derivations of the equilibrium price function actually only rely upon the assumption that the initial sale establishes a controlling block whenever that is efficient. Consequently, the same equilibrium price function will obtain regardless of the allocation of shares among small investors. Small investors with private valuations greater than the marginal valuation impounded into the price, $w \geq \bar{w}(\alpha)$, will purchase a share if they do not own one, and small investors with a private valuation below the marginal valuation, $w < \bar{w}(\alpha)$, will sell a share if they have one. The secondary market can be relied upon to establish the efficient allocation of shares among small investors, even when the initial sale does not.

However, the tender offer market cannot be relied upon to the same degree. An active investor seeking to obtain a controlling stake makes a single tender offer at a take-it-or-leave-it price p^3, for the specified number of shares, $1/2 - q_a^1$. If the tender is successful, the active investor's net profits are $1/2(y + w_a + z) - (1/2 - q_a^1)p^3$. Alternatively, the active investor can sell his or her stake, which must be done at the price $y + w_0(\alpha)$, netting profits of $q_a^1(y + w_0(\alpha))$. A tender offer to buy at the price p^3 is optimal for the active investor only if $1/2(y + w_a + z) - (1/2 - q_a^1)p^3 \geq q_a^1(y + w_0(\alpha))$. For convenience we restate this condition as $z \geq d$ where $d = (1 - 2q_a^1)(p^3 - y) - 2(1/2w_a - q_a^1 w_0(\alpha))$. In other words, if the active investor does not receive a controlling block in the secondary market, even when that would be efficient, it is not always possible to acquire one in the tender offer market.

Lemma 1. *The tender offer market does not always allow a controlling stake to be accumulated.*

Proof. For a tender offer to succeed, a sufficient number of the small investors currently owning a share must be willing to tender, i.e., all $w \leq \bar{w}_{1/2}(\alpha)$, or

$$\frac{\frac{1}{2}(y + w_a + z) - q_a^1(y + w_0(\alpha))}{\frac{1}{2} - q_a^1} \geq p^3 \geq y + \bar{w}_{1/2}(\alpha) + \mathscr{E}(z \mid z > d).$$

The marginal small investor accepts the tender if the offered price is greater than his or her valuation of a share incorporating the information that $z \geq d$: $p^3 \geq y + \bar{w}_{1/2} + \mathscr{E}(z \mid z \geq d)$. Whenever $q_a^1 = 0$ we have $d = p^3 - (y + w_a)$. This condition implies the impossible result that $p^3 - (y + w_a) > \mathscr{E}(z \mid z \geq p^3 - (y + w_a))$, and consequently a successful tender offer is not possible whenever $w_a < \bar{w}_{1/2}$, regardless of the value of z. This is due to the free rider problem first demonstrated by Grossman and Hart (1980). When $q_a^1 > 0$, as Shleifer and

Vishny (1986) and Hirshleifer and Titman (1990) point out, a successful tender offer will be possible for sufficiently large z. However, a tender offer might not succeed for all values of z for which a controlling allocation is efficient. Indeed, it is always possible to choose reasonable parameter values for which the final allocation is everywhere efficient only if the previous allocation that results from the original sale is everywhere efficient. To see this, let $\bar{w}_0 \approx \bar{w}_{1/2}$, in which case $q_a^*(\alpha, z) = 1/2$ for all $w_a + z > \frac{1}{2}\bar{w} + \varepsilon$, with ε arbitrarily close to zero. Then, for an active investor with $z = \frac{1}{2}\bar{w} - w_a + \varepsilon + \delta$, with δ arbitrarily close to zero, the feasibility condition for a successful tender offer is certainly violated, and unless the sale efficiently allocates one-half of the shares, the active investor being unable to buy enough shares from the passive investors who demand too high a price, chooses instead to sell the original allocation: $\{q_a^1 < \frac{1}{2}\} = \{q_a^3 = 0\}$. $\quad\square$

2.4. A Numerical Example

The following example illustrates the relation between the allocation made in the original sale and the result of the tender offer market. It also illustrates the relation between the price prevailing in the secondary market at $\tau = 2$ and the tender offer price at $\tau = 3$.

Let $H(\alpha)$ be the uniform distribution over $[0, 1]$, let $G(w \,|\, \alpha)$ be the uniform distribution over $[\alpha, \alpha + 1]$, and let $F(z)$ be the uniform distribution over $[0, 1]$. For simplicity, assume $w_a = 0$. Then, efficiency requires that $q_a^*(\alpha, z) = \frac{1}{2}$ whenever $z \geq 1/2\alpha + 1/8$, and zero otherwise. Figure 2 shows the parameter space $[\alpha, z]$. In region I it is efficient for all of the shares to go to the small investors and for no controlling block to be allocated. In all other regions it is

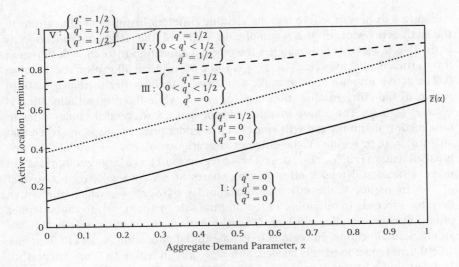

Figure 2.

efficient to allocate the active investor a controlling block. Since our focus is on whether the secondary and tender offer markets assure efficiency in the final allocation, we assume an inefficient but otherwise arbitrary result from the original sale and explore what happens in the secondary and tender offer markets that follow.

Suppose, for example, that the equilibrium allocation from the original sale yields

$$
q_a^1(\alpha, z) = \begin{cases} 0, & z < \frac{1}{2}\alpha + \frac{3}{8}, \\ z - (\frac{1}{2}\alpha + \frac{3}{8}), & \frac{1}{2}\alpha + \frac{3}{8} < z \frac{1}{2}\alpha + \frac{7}{8}, \\ \frac{1}{2}, & \frac{1}{2}\alpha + \frac{7}{8} \leq z. \end{cases}
$$

This allocation is inefficient whenever $\frac{1}{2}\alpha + \frac{7}{8} > z \geq \frac{1}{2}\alpha + \frac{1}{8}$ since the active investor should have obtained control but in fact only obtains $q_a^1(\alpha, z) < 1/2$. The competitive market-clearing price at $\tau = 2$ reveals α and, given the allocation at $\tau = 1$, also reveals z. A successful tender offer at $\tau = 3$ is feasible whenever

$$
z \geq \frac{\alpha + \frac{1}{2}}{2q_a^1(\alpha, z)} - \frac{1}{2},
$$

which, for the relevant values of $q_a^1(\alpha, z)$, is equivalent to

$$
z \geq -\tfrac{1}{4}(\alpha - \tfrac{1}{4}) + \tfrac{1}{4}\sqrt{\alpha^2 + \tfrac{23}{2}\alpha + 7\tfrac{1}{16}}.
$$

Otherwise, the tender offer will not succeed. So the original sale fails to generate an efficient final allocation whenever

$$
\tfrac{1}{2}\alpha + \tfrac{1}{8} < z < -\tfrac{1}{4}(\alpha - \tfrac{1}{4}) + \tfrac{1}{4}\sqrt{\alpha^2 + \tfrac{23}{2}\alpha + 7\tfrac{1}{16}}.
$$

Figure 2 displays the five regions yielding different histories of allocations to the active investor in this example. In region I the efficient allocation is $q_a^*(\alpha, z) = 0$, and this also matches the original allocation $q_a^1(\alpha, z) = 0$. In region II the efficient allocation is $q_a^*(\alpha, z) = \frac{1}{2}$, while the original allocation is $q_a^1(\alpha, z) = 0$. The active investor fails to make a successful tender offer so that $q_a^3 = 0$. In region III the efficient allocation is $q_a^*(\alpha, z) = \frac{1}{2}$, while the original allocation is $q_a^1(\alpha, z) \in (0, \frac{1}{2})$. The active investor cannot make a successful tender offer to obtain control and instead sells shares at the tender price $p^3 = y + w_0(\alpha)$ so that again $q_a^3 = 0$. In region IV the efficient allocation is $q_a^*(\alpha, z) = \frac{1}{2}$, while the original allocation is $q_a^1(\alpha, z) \in (0, \frac{1}{2})$. The active investor has a large enough stake to make a successful tender offer, buying shares at $p^3 = y + \bar{w}_{1/2}(\alpha) + z$ so that $q_a^3 = \frac{1}{2}$. In region V the efficient allocation is $q_a^*(\alpha, z) = \frac{1}{2}$, which the active investor succeeds in obtaining in the original sale, $q_a^1(\alpha, z) = \frac{1}{2}$, so that a tender offer is unnecessary. Regions I and V are those in which the initial sale establishes an efficient allocation. In regions II–IV, the initial allocation is not efficient and an efficient tender market is needed, although only in region IV is one successful. The outcome in region II is like that described in Grossman and Hart (1980): it is not possible for an investor without an initial stake in the firm to make a successful tender offer because of the free rider problem. The outcome in region IV is like that described by Shleifer and Vishny (1986): the investor who begins with a large enough stake is able to make a credible tender offer. Region III contains those allocations in which an investor has some initial stake but it is not large enough to make a successful tender offer credible.

It is interesting to take note of the equilibrium price for our example in the different regions. In regions I–III, the competitive secondary market price is $p^2 = p^4 = y + \bar{w}_0(\alpha)$. In region III the active investor sells shares in a tender offer at this price, $p^3 = p^2$. In regions IV and V the competitive market price is $p^2 = p^4 = y + \bar{w}_{1/2}(\alpha) + z$. In region IV the active investor purchases the shares necessary for a controlling stake in a tender offer with the price $p^3 = p^2$.

Of course, for higher values of w_a an efficient allocation of the controlling block will easily result. Indeed, large buyers with $w_a > w_{max}(\alpha)$ will always be able to obtain control independent of the number of shares sold in the public offering. Therefore, the problem is only interesting when $w_a < w_{max}(\alpha)$, and the large shareholder's idiosyncratic component of value is not absolutely bigger than that of the population of small investors.

Having shown that the tender offer market does not always allow a controlling stake to be accumulated, we now turn to the question of how the tender offer market functions in allowing an active investor to sell excess shares received in the initial sale.

Lemma 2. *The active investor does not always use the tender offer market to sell excess shares.*

Proof. When $q_a^1 > \frac{1}{2}$ the large investor wishes to sell $q_a^1 - \frac{1}{2}$. A tender offer to sell is optimal for the active investor at $p^3 \geq y + w_a + z$. Faced with a tender offer to sell, the marginal passive investor is only willing to buy if $y + \bar{w}_{1/2} + \mathscr{E}(z \mid w_a, z \leq p^3 - (y + w_a)) \geq p^3$, which can be rewritten as $\bar{w}_{1/2} + \mathscr{E}(z \mid w_a, z \leq p^3 - (y + w_a)) \geq p^3 - y$. If $\bar{w}_{1/2}$ is close to zero, then this is impossible. That is, if the passive investors are uncertain about the value of z, then $z - \mathscr{E}(z \mid w_a, z < p^3 - (y + w_a))$ could be large enough to violate the necessary conditions for a successful sale of the block to occur. The active investor is frustrated by the familiar adverse selection or lemons problem.[1] □

---

[1] In our model, the active investor's private valuation, w_a, is proportional to his or her ownership stake. That may not be the case. The private benefits can flow from control and be independent of the number of shares in excess of the minimum required for control. The proof given above need be only modestly revised. A tender offer to sell excess shares is optimal for the active investor at $p^3 \geq y + z$. Faced with a tender offer to sell, the marginal passive investor is only willing to buy if $y + \bar{w}_{1/2} + \mathscr{E}(z \mid w_a, z \leq p^3 - y) \geq p^3$ which can be rewritten as $\bar{w}_{1/2} + \mathscr{E}(z \mid w_a, z \leq p^3 - y) \geq p^3 - y$. If $\bar{w}_{1/2}$ is close to zero, then this is impossible. That is, if the passive investors are uncertain about the value of z, then $z - \mathscr{E}(z \mid w_a, z < p^3 - y)$ could be large enough to violate the necessary conditions for a successful sale of the block to occur.

From the above lemmas the tender offer market is doubly disadvantaged in assuring an efficient ownership structure: it neither assures the accumulation of a controlling block where useful, nor assures the liquidation of an inefficiently large block.

Lemma 3. *Whenever the original allocation to the active investor is efficient, the final allocation of shares is everywhere efficient.*

Proof. As noted above, the competitive market always assures an efficient allocation of that portion of shares allocated to the passive investors. Here we note that in equilibrium the active investor does not use the tender offer market to trade away from the efficient allocation, regardless of the expectations and information going into the tender offer market. The assumption that the active investor cannot trade anonymously is important for this and previous results. Of course, the more the large shareholder is able to internalize the gains by trading shares prior to being identified, the more closely will the final equilibrium allocation match the efficient allocation regardless of the allocation made in the initial sale. As an example, it can arise that $q_a^1 = \frac{1}{2}$ and that $p^2 = y + \bar{w}(\alpha) + \mathscr{E}^2(z) < y + w_a + z$, so that the active investor would like to offer to buy additional shares at the prevailing competitive market price. However, to try and do so would alter the expectations of the passive investors so that the necessary tender offer price would be higher than the active investor would be willing to pay. Consequently no trade would take place (see Milgrom and Stokey, 1982).

So although the competitive secondary market assures an efficient allocation among passive investors, the tender offer market does not always assure an efficient allocation of shares to the active investor. Relying upon the secondary market to determine whether a controlling block is assembled does not guarantee the same result as the establishment of a controlling block in the original sale whenever that is best. Consequently, the method of sale can have a profound impact on both the ultimate ownership structure of the firm and the seller's expected revenue. The importance of the share allocation in our model contrasts sharply with other models of IPOs in which the distribution of shares among investors is essentially a zero sum game, despite the differences in information that characterize the set of investors (see for example, Allen and Faulhaber, 1989; Grinblatt and Hwang, 1989; and Welch, 1989).

3. OPTIMAL DESIGN FOR THE SALE OF SHARES WITH ASYMMETRIC INVESTORS

The results in the previous section show that the choice of method of sale influences whether a transfer of control will take place, which in turn affects the proceeds from the sale and how the surplus is divided between the seller and the various interested buyers. In this section we evaluate a wide variety of alternative strategies for going public. One research option is to analyze each alternative individually, solving for the equilibrium secondary market price and for equilibrium investor strategies and then calculating the revenue raised by the firm. Unfortunately, the enormous range of alternatives available for the sale of shares makes this option impractical. The majority of papers on IPOs and staged equity financing resolve this predicament by restricting consideration to a pair of alternative financing strategies and establishing the relative benefits of one over the other. As a result, only a restricted number of financing strategies are considered and the optimal choice in the class is derived. We overcome this limitation by utilizing the methods employed in the mechanism design literature, in particular, the revelation principle. The advantage of using this approach is that it allows us to characterize the maximum revenue that can be raised from *any* alternative financing strategy, given the informational assumptions of our model. After characterizing the maximum revenue raised from any financing strategy, we can compare and evaluate specific alternatives and identify the optimal strategy. In this section we provide the general characterization, while the next section provides an analysis of specific alternatives.

In brief, the mechanism design approach analyzes the subset of all possible rules for sale that are direct mechanisms, i.e., those in which the strategy space is a simple reporting of each investor's type, $\hat{w}$ (which yields an $\hat{\alpha}$) and $\hat{z}$, and the outcome is an allocation of shares, $[q_s^1(\hat{w}, \hat{\alpha}, \hat{z}), q_a^1(w_a, \hat{\alpha}, \hat{z})]$, and payments to the seller, $[x_s^1(\hat{w}, \hat{\alpha}, \hat{z}), x_a^1(w_a, \hat{\alpha}, \hat{z})]$. Without loss of generality, we can restrict attention further to the set of incentive-compatible mechanisms in which it is optimal for each investor to truthfully report his or her type, $\hat{w} = w$ (and therefore $\hat{\alpha} = \alpha$) and $\hat{z} = z$. This limited focus is admissible since the revelation principle establishes that each strategy for sale from the complete set of available strategies is equivalent in equilibrium to some incentive-compatible direct mechanism. Consequently, the maximum revenue attainable in the set of incentive compatible direct mechanisms is also the maximum revenue attainable in the full set of available strategies for the sale of shares.

Lemmas 4 and 5 describe the maximum revenue that can be raised from the passive and active investors, respectively. Proposition 1 then establishes that the revenue-maximizing strategy for the sale of shares involves a discount to the active investor that is contingent on the amount by which the investor's control raises the firm's value. All proofs are contained in the Appendix.

Lemma 4. *For any efficient allocation $q^1 = q^*$, the maximum average revenue received from a small investor, $X_s^*(w)$, satisfies the following condition:*

$$X_s^*(w) = \int_z \int_\alpha p^*(\alpha, z) q_s^*(w, \alpha, z)\, dH(\alpha \mid w)\, dF(z).$$

The lemma says that the maximum price paid by any small investor is the secondary market price in a fully revealing rational expectations equilibrium with the efficient allocation, $p^*(\alpha, z)$. It is not possible to price discriminate among small investors with different information: all small investors buying a share pay the same fixed price. Small investors are unable to capture any economic rents on the private information they originally have about the value of the firm. The information possessed by any individual small investor and reflected in his or her demand has zero marginal value, since the demands of the other small investors are sufficient to fully reveal the unknown parameter, determining aggregate demand. In the language of Milgrom and Weber (1982), the information of an individual small investor is completely substitutable. It is important to note that both the inability of the small investors to capture information rents and the inability of the seller to discriminate among small investors are consequences of the future existence of a competitive secondary market in the shares of the firm. The price paid by any small investor is always the value of the share to the marginal small investor.

Lemma 5. *For any efficient allocation $q^1 = q_a^*$, the maximum average revenue received from an active investor, $X_a^*(z, w_a)$, satisfies the following condition:*

$$X_a^*(z, w_a) = \int_\alpha (y + w_a + z) q_a^*(w_a, \alpha, z) \, dH(\alpha)$$

$$- \int_\alpha \int_{z_{min}}^z q_a^*(w_a, \alpha, s) \, ds \, dH(\alpha).$$

The lemma says that the maximum price charged to the active investor can be divided into two parts. The first part is the value of the shares received in the efficient allocation. This would be the price if the seller had full information on the active investor's valuation and so could extract all of the value of the shares. However, lacking full information on the active investor's valuation, the seller must set a price that is discounted from the full valuation. The active investor is thereby able to capture a portion of the surplus. The second part of the price is this discount from the full valuation. The discount depends upon the seller's uncertainty about the active investor's type, z, relative to the demand by small investors, $H(\alpha)$, and upon the contingent probability of obtaining the controlling block at various types, $q_a^*(w_a, \alpha, s)$. This is the usual basis for the division of surplus when the seller has incomplete information about the buyer's valuation (see Myerson, 1981). If there were multiple active investors competing for the controlling block, then the informational advantage would be partially dissipated and the seller would be able to capture a greater portion of the surplus: i.e., the significance of the second part of the equation would decline.

Both the price and the discount, measured as a percent of the full valuation, increase with the parameter z, the active investor's contribution to value through control. Note that the price also increases with the active investor's private benefits, w_a. The price charged to the active investor is discounted from the full valuation inclusive of the private benefits. Note also that the price paid by the active investor is contingent on the parameter of aggregate demand, α. Although unable to extract everything from the large buyer's valuation, the seller is able to increase his or her share of the surplus by making the allocation to the active investor a function of α. The commitment to sell a fraction of the shares to small investors is an effective way of putting pressure on active investors to compete more aggressively.

The optimal method of sale must ensure that the efficient allocation of shares maximizes the expected value of the proceeds from the sale. Lemmas 1–3 imply that $q^1 = q^*$ and Lemmas 4 and 5 yield the conditions on the payment rule. This establishes the following proposition:

Proposition 1. *A method of sale is optimal if and only if $q^1 = q^*$ and X^1 satisfies the conditions of Lemmas 4 and 5.*

Lemma 4 does not directly compare the price paid by the active investor with the price paid by the small, passive investors. This is done in the following proposition.

Proposition 2. *Maximizing revenue from a sale that establishes an efficient ownership structure requires giving the active shareholder a discount whenever the expected external benefits derived from large block ownership are larger than the private benefits from control.*

Among the optimal pricing rules satisfying Lemma 4 is the rule in which $x_s^*(w, \alpha, z) = p(\alpha, z) q_s^*(w, \alpha, z)$. Using Lemma 5, an optimal pricing rule for the active investor is given by $x_a^*(\alpha, z, w_a) = (p_s(\alpha, z) - \pi(\alpha, z, w_a)) q_a^*(w_a, \alpha, z)$, where

$$\pi(\alpha, z, w_a) = (\bar{w}_{1/2}(\alpha) - w_a) + \int_{z_{min}}^{z} q_a^*(w_a, \alpha, s) \, ds.$$

Whenever $w_a < \bar{w}_{1/2}(\alpha) + \int_{z_{min}}^{z} q_a^*(w_a, \alpha, s) \, ds$, the price paid by the active investor is discounted, and when the inequality is reversed, the price paid contains a premium. The discount or premium, π, has a straightforward interpretation in terms of its two components. The first component, $(\bar{w}_{1/2}(\alpha) - w_a)$, is the typical discount given in a monopolist's price discrimination problem when the ex ante expected valuation of two classes of buyers differs. The current owner behaves as a monopolist who discriminates by setting a higher price for that class of buyers with the higher expected valuation. If the active investor's private benefits from control are significant, then this component is negative and potentially transforms the discount into a premium. The second component, the one central to this paper, is the discount given specifically due to the public benefit of the active investor's ownership in the firm. Although the large shareholder receives a discount relative to the price paid by small shareholders, giving this relative discount benefits the seller by raising the expected value of the firm and therefore the average price of the shares.

Proposition 2 also helps us understand the optimal method of sale when there exist private benefits from control (see Barclay and Holderness, 1989). When the private benefits to the large shareholder are expected to be large, i.e., $w_a > \bar{w}_{1/2}(\alpha) + \int_{z_{min}}^{z} q_a^*(w_a, \alpha, s)\,ds$, then the first component is negative and dominates the second component, so that the large shareholder would actually pay a premium.[2] This seems to be the case analyzed in Brennan and Franks (1995) when they conjecture that discriminatory pricing is strategically used to screen applicants for shares and increase the price for acquiring a block.

In Lemmas 4 and 5 and Propositions 1 and 2 we restrict ourselves to mechanisms that yield efficient allocations and characterize the revenue-maximizing payment rules for this class. It is a well known and general result that in a sale to buyers with private information, introducing the right kind of inefficiency in the allocation can allow a seller to raise the revenue extracted. In a few cases when it is efficient to allocate shares to an active investor who has a low valuation, the seller may be better off by denying the active investor the controlling block. This is because reducing the allocation to active investors with low valuations raises the price the seller can charge to active investors with high valuations. Bebchuk and Zingales (1995) illustrate this possibility in another model of the sale of shares. In a model with private information and a secondary and tender offer market, the problem is more complicated because the seller's allocation in the initial sale is not the final allocation. The seller must determine the right amount of inefficiency to induce in the final allocation as well as the allocation in the initial sale that induces the right allocation in the final sale. While these considerations can modify the allocation that is optimal from the seller's point of view, the tradeoffs in pricing the shares sold to different classes of investors documented in the propositions above remain.

4. AN EVALUATION OF ALTERNATIVE STRATEGIES FOR GOING PUBLIC

The previous section develops a framework for analyzing methods for going public. In this section we apply this framework to evaluate and compare the methods that have been most used in countries with developed capital markets.

The best strategy is to design a method of sale that satisfies a number of conditions: (i) investors differ in their size and role in the firm; (ii) value is contributed by active investors; (iii) all investors are in competition with one another; and (iv) trading opportunities are provided by the opening of a secondary market in the shares of the firm. The third condition arises out of the desire of the seller to extract surplus from active investors potentially interested in obtaining control. This condition is of particular importance, for example, in setting the price of the initial public offering. Indeed, the inability of the seller to

---

[2] There exist optimal payment rules which, for a particular realization of the parameters α and z, have the active investor paying more per share.

discriminate among small investors makes an IPO consisting of just a portion of the shares of the firm and sold at a fixed price an optimal choice. This establishes a market in the firm's shares and a public price that reflects the information and demands of the small investors. Subsequently, the firm markets a controlling block to an interested active investor. The firm negotiates a price for the block that is based upon the market price, but with a discount that reflects the perceived contribution to value by the large investor. If the active investor does not purchase the block, then the firm organizes a seasoned public offer to sell the shares to the passive shareholders at a new market-clearing price. This result is formalized as follows:

Corollary 1. *A sequential sale beginning with an initial public offering of dispersed shares, followed first by a negotiated sale of a controlling block and then by a seasoned offering, is optimal:*

(i) *with a partial sale of $q = \frac{1}{2}$ unit at a rational expectations equilibrium or clearing price equal to*

$$p^1 = y + \bar{w}_0(\alpha)F(\bar{z}(\alpha)) + (\bar{w}_{1/2}(\alpha) + \mathcal{E}(z \mid w_a, \alpha, z \geq \bar{z}(\alpha)))(1 - F(\bar{z}(\alpha)))$$

(ii) *with the seller making a take-it-or-leave-it offer to the active investor at $\tau = 3$ contingent on the revelation of α from this initial public offer and the secondary market price at $\tau = 2$ and at the price*

$$p^3 = y + w_a + \bar{z}(\alpha),$$

(iii) *and, should the active investor reject the offer, with the seller then making a seasoned public offering at $\tau = 4$ and at the secondary market price*

$$p^4 = y + \bar{w}_0(\alpha).$$

This view that the initial public offering of shares is not an isolated step but part of a more elaborate process for selling shares seems to be confirmed by the existing empirical evidence. Barry et al. (1990) report that IPOs represent the most frequently used method of selling a fraction of the shares by venture capital firms and that during this first transaction the equity holdings of venture capital investors do not change much. Later on these investors sell a significant portion of their stakes, either to another investor or to another company or through a follow-on offering. Control turnover subsequent to the IPO is also found by Holderness and Sheehan (1988) for the U.S., Rydqvist and Högholm (1994) for Sweden and the U.K., and Pagano et al. (1996) for Italy. This also seems to be the case in many equity carve-outs, according to Schipper and Smith (1986) and Klein et al. (1991). The findings on the transfer of control raise certain doubts about Barry et al.'s interpretation of the decision not to sell during the IPO as reflecting the venture capitalists' willingness to bind themselves to the value of new issues by maintaining their holdings beyond the IPO. Our view is that an immediate exit strategy may not be optimal, so that temporarily retaining a stake can tell small investors participating in the IPO that a block is reserved for a possible future sale. Also important, by selling the block afterwards, the owner can make the price of the block dependent on the conditions prevailing in the market for dispersed shares.

Partial sales have been advocated by other authors studying IPOs, for a different reason. This branch of the literature highlights the opportunity to signal the quality of the seller, in contrast to the signal on the demand described here.[3] We believe that both supply and demand aspects are important to a better understanding of the pricing and method for selling equity stakes, especially in IPOs.[4]

The sequential sales suggested above can be contrasted, for example, to a public offering of all shares at a single fixed price. In the offer for sale by tender, employed both in the U.K. and in France, investors place bids for the shares indicating both quantity and price. After the bids have been received, a single sale price is set and all buyers pay that price. It is possible to show, however, that issuing all shares at a single price is not an optimal strategy.

Corollary 2. *A public offering of all shares at a uniform price is not optimal.*

This result is a direct implication of Proposition 2. The active investor must receive a discount that reflects the expected contribution of block ownership to the firm's value. The discount gives the large investor an incentive to bid competitively for the controlling block. Without this the resulting proceeds from the sale are not maximized.

Consider now a sale in which investors tender bids and those bidding the highest pay the price bid, i.e., the traditional sealed-bid, discriminatory auction. Discrimination can be accomplished in a number of ways. Even in the U.S., for example, where shares in an IPO must be offered at a uniform price, there is evidence that discrimination among buyers occurs through the allocation of oversubscribed issues and the expectation that buyers will sometimes accept allotments of undersubscribed issues (see Hanley and Wilhelm, 1995). Brennan and Franks (1995) also present evidence of discrimination in the U.K. market. Although it is not possible to evaluate specific discriminatory practices without more detailed information on the allocation rules, we find that the standard discriminatory sale is not optimal.

---

[3] See Leland and Pyle (1977), Allen and Faulhaber (1989), Grinblatt and Hwang (1989), Welch (1989), and Chemmanur (1993).

[4] There may be some additional advantages to another sort of partial sale in which the size of the controlling block is contingent on the bidding of the active investor or investors due to the additional surplus that can be extracted when the investor's valuation is ex post observable through the realized income of the firm. For example, in a privatization it may be possible for the seller to extract a larger amount of surplus by reserving for the state a portion of the non-controlling shares and having the size of this reserve determined by the active investor bidding for control. Similarly, in acquisitions payment can be in cash or various securities, and an auction in terms of shares can possibly extract greater surplus from bidders than an auction in cash payments (see Riley, 1988; Hansen, 1985).

Corollary 3. *A discriminatory auction in which each bidder pays the amount bid is not optimal.*

Consider next a sequential sale in which a controlling block is first sold to the active investor, after which there follows a public offering to small investors. At times this method has been used by some private companies, as well as by governments in privatizations. In mixed offers, as they are also called, a tender offer is first made to large shareholders and the resulting tender price is then used to set the fixed price for the sale to small investors of the remaining shares. Besides violating the optimality condition that prescribes some form of contingent discriminatory rule, the mixed offer does not follow the right sequence, as shown next.

Corollary 4. *Selling the controlling block before the IPO is, in general, not optimal.*

Selling the controlling block first avoids the free rider problem (see Grossman and Hart, 1980), and it can also help reduce the winner's curse problem faced by small investors (see Rock, 1986). However, by selling the controlling block first, the active investor's allocation cannot be contingent on the parameter of aggregate demand by small investors, α. Furthermore, if the active investor is assured a controlling block, then it is impossible to extract the maximum revenue from most types of active investors. Since large investors with low valuations are assured shares, there is no leverage with which to force a higher price from those with higher valuations. As a result, conducting the sale sequentially assures them an even greater discount than the optimal method. However, in the special case in which $w_a \geq w_{max}(\alpha_{max})$, it is obvious that the block should go to the active investor and negotiating this sale first is not disadvantageous.

Corollary 4 shows that it is not optimal to sell shares using a mixed offer in which a tender offer is made first to large investors and the tender price is then used to set the fixed price in the offer for sale to small investors. This conclusion is not shared by Stoughton and Zechner (1998), who advocate a mixed offer as their main prescription. In their model there is no uncertainty about the demand of small investors, and so there is no loss from selling to the active investor prior to learning about aggregate demand and estimates of value. This result highlights that simply selling a fraction of the company in an IPO is not always an optimal mechanism, but with the addition of some clauses and by following the right sequence of offerings the seller can adjust the ownership structure to obtain a higher sale price.

Selling some amount of non-controlling shares allows the seller to obtain information about the aggregate demand of small investors on which the price of the controlling block can be made contingent. Although the sale occurs in stages and the active investor never directly bids against the small investors, competition between them arises through the conditions imposed on the sale to the large investor based on the results of the first sale to small investors. If the model included more than one potential large shareholder, then it would be necessary to run an auction or contest among them. However, the advantage of selling some shares to the public ahead of time remains. We should note here that the expression for X_a^* derived in Lemma 2 would be slightly more involved with multiple active investors, but in form it would remain very much the same.

The same result can potentially be achieved in some single-period offerings by making the allocations to different classes of investors contingent on the orders received.

Corollary 5. *There is an optimal single-period discriminatory pricing rule. The large investor gets control only with a bid that is higher than the average bid of the marginal small investors competing for the shares of the controlling block. Upon the successful sale of the block, small investors pay a uniform price equal to the marginal small investor's bid for one-half of the shares plus a control premium. The large investor receives a reduction from the price paid by small investors based upon the public benefits of control and pays a premium over the price paid by small investors based upon the private benefits of control. If the large investor does not obtain control, all shares are sold to the small investors at the clearing bid.*

Perhaps because of the elaborate procedures it involves, a simultaneous sale of shares with a discriminatory allocation of a potentially controlling block is not very common. However, Brennan and Franks (1995) refer to a method that has recently been experimented with in the U.K. and Australia and has features similar to those just described. This method combines a private placement, targeting large investors, with a simultaneous public offering. It could be an optimal method depending on the allocation and pricing rules used for investors of different types. It is worth noting that whenever it has been used, this method usually includes a clawback provision. According to our model, perhaps this is done intentionally, because the clawback provision makes the allocation to large investors dependent on the demand by small investors, therefore creating competition among investors of different types.

Although we have focused only on comparing various methods of sale, there are other mechanisms that could be used to help reduce the uncertainty surrounding both the demand and the valuation of different investors. For example, if it were possible to open a when-issued market in the new stock, then the price in this market would provide crucial information to the seller that would make it possible to extract the maximum surplus given the need to assure a successful sale. Another alternative would be to ask investors to submit indications of interest, just as they do under 'book-building', knowing that some bidders would be eliminated from the subsequent sale. Although the NASD Rules of Fair Practice require that all investors pay a uniform price in the offering, the seller can always discriminate in the allocation of shares. Alternatively, and recognizing that a sale of control should not be carried out through the IPO, the seller can use a simultaneous public and private offer, as in Corollary 5, or follow the sequence in

Corollary 1 and choose an allocation in the IPO that is influenced by the prospect of a future sale of the controlling block. In both cases, however, the book-building effort will provide the seller with information about the aggregate demand of passive investors on which the price of the controlling block can be made contingent.

5. OTHER DETERMINANTS OF THE OWNERSHIP STRUCTURE

This paper indicates that the design of the sale increases the value of the firm. It emphasizes that the choice of method of sale is important because the capital market does not establish an optimal ownership structure for the firm. The idea that the process of going public cannot be left to the capital market to achieve an efficient outcome goes back to Berle and Means (1932) and has also been recently analyzed, among others, by Kahan (1993), Bebchuk (1994), and Bebchuk and Zingales (1995). Bebchuk discusses how voting arrangements and freeze-out schemes improve the transfer of ownership, while Bebchuk and Zingales discuss deviations from one vote per share that allow the seller to obtain greater revenue. Given that control considerations are also the focus of these papers, it is important to see how the ideas proposed in our model relate to the legal arrangements suggested in this literature.

Bebchuk evaluates two rules governing sale of control transactions: the market rule, followed in the U.S., and the equal opportunity rule, followed in many European countries and to be adopted by the European Union. In the market rule (MR), a control block can be transferred without the participation of minority shareholders. Under the equal opportunity rule (EOR), minority shareholders are entitled to participate in the transaction on the same terms as the control seller. Bebchuk shows that when the buyers' private benefits are significant, the MR might not avoid inefficient transfers, while the EOR prevents all inefficient transfers. However, the EOR fares worse in facilitating efficient transfers. As Bebchuk points out, neither of the rules dominates the other in all instances. But how about a mixture of the two rules? From the previous section, it is easy to see that a suitable combination of the two rules is what is implicit in the optimal method of sale proposed in this paper. First, all investors are entitled to participate in the primary market, so in that sense the first stage of the ownership transfer is equivalent to the EOR. Recognizing, however, that the EOR might discourage efficient transfers, the terms of the sale are set in a way that favors large share-holders who contribute to the firm. The discriminating clause, which depends on the characteristics of the large shareholder, appropriately modifies the rules governing the transfer of the controlling block and, in so doing, retains the good features of the MR.

This conclusion is also clear from Bebchuk's discussion of legal arrangements that improve the outcomes of the MR and the EOR, such as voting arrangements and freeze-out clauses. In order to facilitate efficient transfers, Bebchuk claims that voting arrangements would have to be strengthened to enable small shareholders to approve a payment to the large investor. In the same vein, he contends that a freeze-out prior to the sale of the block would move the transfer of control close to the first best, although this would deny small shareholders the gain from selling their shares at the market price. Again, the legal arrangements suggested by Bebchuk are simply alternative forms of benefiting the large shareholder, the outcome of our Proposition 2. Although they have merit in theory, it is questionable whether in practice a sale of shares organized without recognizing that investors are different, combined with strengthened voting and freeze-out provisions, if allowed, would be easier to implement. Most probably, asymmetric information and problems of moral hazard would make it difficult to determine the right compensation involved. The advantage of making the allocation and the price of the controlling block contingent on demands by small investors is that it helps to determine the compensation to be attributed to the large shareholder with greater transparency and without costly haggling between shareholders.

So far we have assumed that the firm issues equity with corresponding voting power. However, given that the market for control cannot always establish an efficient ownership structure, it is important to consider the possibility of issuing dual class shares, or equity with differential voting rights. More specifically, the seller could allocate a disproportional voting power to the active shareholder, while selling shares that give the right to future cash flows to passive investors. This would, in principle, seem a revenue-maximizing solution, since it would apparently minimize the number of shares that would have to be offered at a discount to a potential controller. In the context of our model, however, all the value-enhancing activities performed by the large shareholder are reflected in higher cash flows, not in private benefits of control. Thus, in the limiting case in which all cash flow rights would be sold to small shareholders, the large shareholder would gain nothing from contributing to the firm's value and there would thus be no reason to bid for control. Without the ability to attract a control buyer, the seller would not expect to capture any surplus from selling cash flow rights to passive shareholders, who would not value the firm as highly as if it were under the control of a large shareholder. Of course, with a disproportionately large fraction of the votes the controller could always try later on to dilute the rights of small shareholders. But if this type of action were admissible, rational small shareholders would discount the negative effects in the price of the shares. Thus, there seems to be no obvious way for the seller to profit from deviating from the rule of one vote per share.

The discussion above seems to point out that the discount per share offered to the control buyer presumably depends on the size of the allocated block, q_a^1. A larger block requires a smaller discount per share and a smaller block requires a larger discount per share, so that the total discount, pq_a^1, is always approximately the same amount.

It is interesting to contrast these results with those in Bebchuk and Zingales (1995), who advocate a deviation from the rule of one vote per share as a way to increase the expected revenue of the seller. Their suggestion, however, relies on the complete separation of cash flow rights and private rights to control. Even if the seller disperses cash flow rights so as to extract more surplus from the large investor, the large investor will still be interested in obtaining control to realize his or her private benefits. Interestingly, in their model the private benefits of control are assumed to increase with the fraction of the cash flow rights sold to small shareholders, and therefore include an implicit form of dilution that makes these benefits even more attractive to a controller. Whether the valuation of the company to a large shareholder essentially comes from the private benefits of control or from improved future expected cash flows is an empirical question that is still to be resolved. What our results, on the one hand, and Bebchuk and Zingales's, on the other hand, seem to imply is that when private benefits of control are significant and voting rights can be isolated from cash flow rights it may be best for the seller to deviate from one vote per share, but not otherwise.

6. CONCLUSIONS

It is clear that ownership structure matters for the value of a corporation and its future performance. We address how different methods for the sale of shares fare in establishing the appropriate ownership and maximizing revenue. Our results are an important contribution to the ongoing debate over the importance of treating controlling blocks distinctively in selling a firm. Does it matter that the sale disperses the shares when interested parties can trade in a secondary market that includes a tender offer market? Or is it better to pass on a block to someone who wants a controlling stake? And if this alternative is advantageous, then how should the firm design a sale of shares to maximize expected revenue?

Because large shareholders can provide the public good associated with monitoring activity, it is always better to make sure that they participate in the sale, and if this depends on their chances of getting control, the sale should be designed to benefit them. The seller can always recover part of the added value of having a large investor through the higher bids posted by small investors who profit from the monitoring activities of the large investor. But guaranteeing the large shareholder a controlling stake would eliminate the competitive pressure to bid aggressively. Therefore, it is crucial that the method of sale promote the participation of potential large shareholders and at the same time make their allocations and payments contingent on the demands of the small investors. This is necessary because in many instances the large shareholder will be unable to assemble a controlling block later in the secondary market, due to the free rider problem. But an active secondary market also prevents the seller from extracting higher payments that would make investors turn to this market, instead of buying the shares in the original sale.

We provide an analysis of the problem and show that commonly used methods of sale are in general not optimal. We characterize various optimal selling strategies, which have features of some existing methods. We are able to explain why some privately held firms go public despite the apparent value loss associated with the free rider problem. Viewing the IPO as a step in a more complete process of selling the firm is the result of considering the inherent asymmetry of investors together with the strategic behavior on the part of the seller. By taking into account the fact that firms manage the sale of shares with the purpose of discriminating between small investors and applicants for large blocks, it is possible to improve our understanding of the pricing and method of selling companies.

Appendix A. Proofs

Proof of Lemma 4: The utility of a small investor of type w and who reports that type to be $\hat{w}$, given a mechanism with allocation rule q^* and payment rule x, is given by

$$U_s(w, \hat{w} \mid q^*, x) = \int_\alpha \int_z v(w, z, q_a^*) q_s^*(\hat{w}, \alpha, z) - x_s(\hat{w}, \alpha, z) \, dF(z) \, dH(\alpha \mid w).$$

Notice that the investor's valuation, v, is a function of the investor's actual valuation and not of the reported valuation, while the investor's allocation and payment, q_s^* and x_s, are a function of the investor's reported valuation and not the actual valuation. Notice also that the seller is always able to infer correctly α, regardless of this investor's report. The population of small investors is atomless and the distribution of reports by the other investors is sufficient to identify α. The report of a single small investor is immaterial to this inference. This fact is central to the results of the model—in the competitive market rational expectations equilibrium as well as here in the incentive compatibility design—since it effectively determines that the small investor's information has no market value and does not earn the small investor any return.

The set of truthful direct revelation mechanisms with allocation q^* is defined by three constraints on the payment x_s extracted from the small investors. First, the mechanism must be incentive compatible, i.e., the small investor's utility is maximized with a truthful report. Second, the mechanism must be individually rational, i.e., the small investor's utility must be at least as great as if he or she simply withdrew and did not participate in the sale of shares. Third, the mechanism must be dynamically rational, i.e., the small investor's utility must be at least as great as if the shares were purchased instead in the secondary market. We show that setting the payment equal to the maximum allowed under the third constraint yields the expected revenue shown in the statement of the lemma, and also satisfies the other constraints.

The third constraint is written

$$\forall w U_s(w, w \mid q, x) \geq \int_\alpha \int_z (v(w, z, q_a^*) - p^*(\alpha, z)) q_s^*(w, \alpha, z) \, dF(z) \, dH(\alpha \mid w),$$

which can be rearranged to yield

$$\int_\alpha \int_z p^*(\alpha, z) q_s^*(w, \alpha, z)\, dF(z)\, dH(\alpha \mid w) \geq \int_\alpha \int_z x_s(\hat{w}, \alpha, z)\, dF(z)\, dH(\alpha \mid w).$$

The left-hand side is the upper bound which appears in the statement of the lemma, $X_s^*(w)$. Clearly, setting $x_s(\bar{w}, \alpha, z) = p^*(\hat{w}, \alpha, z) q_s^*(\hat{w}, \alpha, z)$ satisfies the constraint with equality. It also clearly satisfies the individual rationality constraint, $U_s(w, w \mid q_s^*, x) \geq 0$. It remains to be shown that it satisfies the incentive-compatibility constraint:

$$\forall w \text{ and } \forall \hat{w} \neq w \quad U_s(w, w \mid q_s^*, x) \geq U_s(w, \hat{w} \mid q_s^*, x).$$

The two sides of the inequality can be expanded as follows:

$$\int_\alpha \int_z v(w, z, q_a^*) q_s^*(w, \alpha, z) - x_s(w, \alpha, z)\, dF(z)\, dH(\alpha \mid w)$$

$$\geq \int_\alpha \int_z v(w, z, q_a^*) q_s^*(\hat{w}, \alpha, z) - x_s(\hat{w}, \alpha, z)\, dF(z)\, dH(\alpha \mid w).$$

which, upon rewriting $x_s(\hat{w}, \alpha, z) = p^*(\alpha, z) q_s^*(\hat{w}, \alpha, z)$, become

$$\int_\alpha \int_z v(w, z, q_a^*) q_s^*(w, \alpha, z) - p^*(\alpha, z) q_s^*(w, \alpha, z)\, dF(z)\, dH(\alpha \mid w)$$

$$\geq \int_\alpha \int_z v(w, z, q_a^*) q_s^*(\hat{w}, \alpha, z) - p^*(\alpha, z) q_s^*(\hat{w}, \alpha, z)\, dF(z)\, dH(\alpha \mid w).$$

Rearranging, we have

$$\int_\alpha \int_z (v(w, z, q_a^*) - p^*(\alpha, z))(q_s^*(w, \alpha, z) - q_s^*(\hat{w}, \alpha, z))\, dF(z)\, dH(\alpha \mid w) \geq 0.$$

Clearly, it is sufficient to show that $\forall \alpha$

$$\int_z (v(w, z, q_a^*) - p^*(\alpha, z))(q_s^*(w, \alpha, z) - q_s^*(\hat{w}, \alpha, z))\, dF(z) \geq 0.$$

Conducting the integration over two discrete regions, the condition is again rewritten as follows:

$$\int_{z < \bar{z}(\alpha)} (v(w, z, q_a^*) - p^*(\alpha, z))(q_s^*(w, \alpha, z) - q_s^*(\hat{w}, \alpha, z))\, dF(z)$$

$$+ \int_{z \geq \bar{z}(\alpha)} (v(w, z, q_a^*) - p^*(\alpha, z))(q_s^*(w, \alpha, z) - q_s^*(\hat{w}, \alpha, z))\, dF(z) \geq 0.$$

Solving for $v - p^*$ within each region of integration yields

$$\int_{z < \bar{z}(\alpha)} (w - \bar{w}_0(\alpha))\, \mathrm{d}F(z)(q_s^*(w, \alpha, z) - q_s^*(\hat{w}, \alpha, z))_{z < \bar{z}(\alpha)}$$

$$+ \int_{z \geq \bar{z}(\alpha)} (w - \bar{w}_{1/2}(\alpha) + z - \mathcal{E}(z \mid z \geq \bar{z}(\alpha))\, \mathrm{d}F(z)$$

$$\times (q_s^*(w, \alpha, z) - q_s^*(\hat{w}, \alpha, z))_{z \geq \bar{z}(\alpha)} \geq 0.$$

And finally,

$$(w - \bar{w}_0(\alpha)) \int_{z < \bar{z}(\alpha)} \mathrm{d}F(z)(q_s^*(w, \alpha, z) - q_s^*(\hat{w}, \alpha, z))_{z < \bar{z}(\alpha)}$$

$$+ (w - \bar{w}_{1/2}(\alpha)) \int_{z \geq \bar{z}(\alpha)} \mathrm{d}F(z)(q_s^*(w, \alpha, z) - q_s^*(\hat{w}, \alpha, z))_{z \geq \bar{z}(\alpha)} \geq 0.$$

To see that this condition is satisfied, consider for example $w \in (\bar{w}_0(\alpha), \bar{w}_{1/2}(\alpha))$. The allocation given a truthful report is $q_s^*(w, \alpha, z) = 1$ when $z < \bar{z}(\alpha)$ and $q_s^*(w, \alpha, z) = \frac{1}{2}$ when $z \geq \bar{z}(\alpha)$. A report of $\underline{\hat{w}} > \bar{w}_{1/2}(\alpha)$ would increase the allocation whenever $z \geq \bar{z}(\alpha)$, but this would only lower utility since in those events $w < \bar{w}_{1/2}(\alpha)$. $\qquad\square$

Proof of Lemma 5. The incentive compatibility of a mechanism $[q_a^*, x]$ for the active investor requires that $\forall z$ and $\forall \hat{z}$,

$$U_a(z, z \mid q_a^*, x) \geq U_a(z, \hat{z} \mid q_a^*, x).$$

Having a control component of an investor's allocation is, in the setting of Myerson (1981), like having a revision function where the nth player is the active investor. Unlike in Myerson, this component of the valuation is allocation contingent. By the same steps found in Myerson's Lemma 2, then, incentive compatibility requires

$$U_a(z, z \mid q_a^*, x) = U_a(z_{\min}, z_{\min} \mid q_a^*, x) + \int_{z_{\min}}^{z} \int_{\alpha} q_a^*(w_a, \alpha, s)\, \mathrm{d}H(\alpha)\, \mathrm{d}s.$$

Expanding the left-hand side and rearranging yields

$$\int_{\alpha} x_a(\alpha, z)\, \mathrm{d}H(\alpha) = \int_{\alpha} \left((y + w_a + z)q_a(\alpha, z) - \int_{z_{\min}}^{z} q_a^*(\alpha, s)\, \mathrm{d}s \right) \mathrm{d}H(\alpha)$$

$$- U_a(z_{\min}, z_{\min} \mid q_a^*, x).$$

The last equality says that given an allocation rule, q_a^*, the average payment for any type other than the lowest type, $x_a(z + w_a \neq z_{\min} + w_a)$ is completely determined by the utility afforded to the lowest type and the incentive-compatibility constraints. Since the average payment for any type of active investor increases with the payment of the lowest type, the revenue-maximizing rule sets this at the largest possible amount as determined by the individual rationality constraint for the lowest-type active investor, i.e., so that $U_a(z_{min}, z_{min} \mid q_a^*, x) = 0$. Then, the average payment made by any type of active investor is as given in the statement of the lemma. $\square$

Proof of Proposition 2. As mentioned in the discussion of Lemma 4, the revenue-maximizing payment function $X_s^*(w)$ is equivalent to charging the single price $p^*(\alpha, z)$ to all small investors. The revenue-maximizing payment function for the active investor $X_a^*(z, w_a)$ can be decomposed into the price charged the small investors, $p^*(\alpha, z)$, and a discount $\pi(\alpha, z, w_a)$, where $\pi(\alpha, z, w_a) = (\bar{w}_{1/2}(\alpha) - w_a) + \int_{z_{min}}^z q_a^*(w_a, \alpha, s) \, ds$. The price paid by the active investor is discounted if $\pi(\alpha, z, w_a) > 0$. By Lemmas 4 and 5, any other pricing rule that maximizes revenue is equivalent in expected revenue to this pricing rule and so must yield in expectation an equivalent contingent discount to the active investor. $\square$

Proof of Corollary 3. For the equilibrium bidding functions of the active investor, $b_a(z, w_a)$, and of the passive investors, $b_s(w)$, to yield $X_a^*(z, w_a)$ and $X_s^*(w)$ as each investor's average payment, the bidding functions would have to satisfy $b_a(z) = X_a^*(z, w_a)/Q_a^*(z)$ and $b_s(z) = X_s^*(w)/Q_s^*(w)$, where $Q_a^*(z) = \int_\alpha q_a^*(\alpha, z) \, dH(\alpha)$ and $Q_s^*(w) = \int_\alpha \int_z q_s^*(\alpha, z) \, dF(z) \, dH(\alpha \mid w)$. And for the equilibrium bidding functions to guarantee the efficient allocation, it would have to be the case that for every α, $b_a(\bar{z}(\alpha), w_a) \geq b_s(\bar{w}(\alpha))$. Together these conditions require that for every α it must be the case that

$$\frac{X_a^*(\bar{z}(\alpha), w_a)}{Q_a^*(\bar{z}(\alpha))} \geq \frac{X_s^*(\bar{w}(\alpha))}{Q_s^*(\bar{w}(\alpha))}.$$

This cannot always hold: for example, for $\alpha = \alpha_{min}$ and setting $w_a < w_{min}(\alpha_{min})$ and $z_{min} = 0$ we have

$$\frac{X_a^*(\bar{z}(\alpha), w_a)}{Q_a^*(\bar{z}(\alpha))} = y + w_a \leq y + w_{min}(\alpha_{min}) < \frac{X_s^*(\bar{w}(\alpha))}{Q_s^*(\bar{w}(\alpha))}$$

which shows that a standard discriminatory auction is generally not optimal. $\square$

Proof of Corollary 5. Denote the active investor's bid for the controlling block by $b_a(z, w_a)$ and a small investor's bid for a share by $b_s = b(w)$. Also, denote by $B = y + \int_{b_0}^{b_{1/2}} 2b \, dG(b)$ the average bid of the marginal small investors competing for the controlling block, i.e., the average of the lower half of the bids, with b_0 as the marginal bid when small investors are allocated all of the shares, $b_0 = b(w_0)$, and $b_{1/2}$ as the marginal bid when small investors are allocated half of the shares,

$b_{1/2} = b(\bar{w}_{1/2})$. Then, the conditions restated are the following:

(i) bids are placed simultaneously;
(ii) allocate one-half unit to the large investor and one-half unit to small investors whenever $\bar{b}_a \geq B$; charge the small investors $\bar{b}_s + b_a$, and charge the large investor $\bar{b}_s + b_a - \pi$, where $\pi = \bar{b}_s - B + b_a - w_a$;
(iii) allocate the full unit to the small investors whenever $b_a < B$ and charge b_0.

To confirm that this method is optimal, note that in equilibrium each investor bids his or her type, $b_a(z, w_a) = z + w_a + y$ and $b_s(w) = w + y$, and that the allocation and pricing rules therefore yield q^* and x^*. In this sale all small investors pay a uniform price equal to the marginal small investor's bid plus a control premium when a block is successfully sold, while the large investor pays a discount, π (always positive), from that same price. Note that the marginal small investor pays a price higher than originally bid, though ex post the higher price is acceptable because it is also the equilibrium price in the secondary market.

$\square$

REFERENCES

Allen, F., Faulhaber, G., 1989. Signaling by underpricing in the IPO market. Journal of Financial Economics 23, 303–323.

Barclay, M., Holderness, C., 1989. Private benefits of control of public corporations. Journal of Financial Economics 25, 371–395.

Barry, C., Muscarella, C., Peavy III, J., Vetsuypens, M., 1990. The role of venture capital in the creation of public companies. Journal of Financial Economics 27, 447–471.

Bebchuk, L., 1994. Efficient and inefficient sales of corporate control. Quarterly Journal of Economics 109, 957–994.

——, Zingales, L., 1995. Private versus social optimality. Discussion paper series, Harvard Law School, Cambridge, MA.

Berle, A., Means, G., 1932. The Modern Corporation and Private Property. World Inc., New York.

Brennan, M., Franks, J., 1995. Underpricing, ownership and control in the initial public offering of equity securities in the U.K., working paper # 12-95, University of California, Los Angeles.

Chemmanur, P., 1993. The pricing of initial public offerings: a dynamic model with information production. Journal of Finance 48, 285–304.

Grinblatt, M., Hwang, C. Y., 1989. Signalling and the underpricing of unseasoned new issues. Journal of Finance 44, 393–420.

Grossman, S., Hart, O., 1980. Takeover bids, the free-rider problem, and the theory of the corporation. Bell Journal of Economics 11, 42–64.

Hanley, K., Wilhelm, W., 1995. Evidence on the strategic allocation of initial public offerings. Journal of Financial Economics 37, 239–257.

Hansen, R., 1985. Auctions with contingent payments. American Economic Review 75 (4), 862–865.

Hirshleifer, D., Titman, S., 1990. Share tendering strategies and the success of hostile takeover bids. Journal of Political Economy 98, 295–324.

Holderness, C., Sheehan, D., 1988. The role of majority shareholders in public held corporations: an exploratory analysis. Journal of Financial Economics 20, 317–347.

Kahan, M., 1993. Sales of corporate control. Journal of Law, Economics and Organization 9, 368–379.

Klein, A., Rosenfeld, J., Beranek, W., 1991. The two stages of an equity carve-out and the price response of parent and subsidiary stock. Managerial and Decision Economics 12, 449–460.

Leland, H., Pyle, D., 1977. Informational asymmetries, financial structure and financial intermediations. Journal of Finance 32, 317–387.

Mikkelson, W., Partch, M., Shah, K., 1995. Performance of companies around initial public offerings, working paper, University of Oregon, Eugene.

——, Ruback, R., 1985. An empirical analysis of the interfirm equity investment process. Journal of Financial Economics 14, 523–553.

Milgrom, P., Stokey, N., 1982. Information, trade and common knowledge. Journal of Economic Theory 26, 177–227.

——, Weber, R., 1982. A theory of auctions and competitive bidding. Econometrica 50 (Sept.), 1089–1122.

Myerson, R., 1981. Optimal auction design. Mathematics of Operations Research 6, 58–63.

Pagano, M., Panetta, F., Zingales, L., 1996. Why do companies go public? An empirical analysis, NBER working Paper 5367, Cambridge, MA.

Riley, J., 1988. Ex-post information in auctions. Review of Economic Studies 55 (3), 409–429.

Rock, K., 1986. Why are new issues underpriced? Journal of Financial Economics 15, 187–212.

Rydqvist, K., Högholm, K., 1994. Going public in the 1980s: evidence from Sweden. European Financial Management 1, 287–316.

Schipper, K., Smith, A., 1986. A comparison of equity carve-outs and seasoned equity offerings. Journal of Financial Economics 15, 153–186.

Shleifer, A., Vishny, R., 1986. Large shareholders and corporate control. Journal of Political Economy 94 (3), 461–488.

Stoughton, N., Zechner, J., 1998. IPO-Mechanisms, monitoring and ownership structure. Journal of Financial Economics 49, 79–109.

Welch, I., 1989. Seasoned offerings, imitation costs, and the underpricing of initial public offerings. The Journal of Finance 44 (2), 421–449.

Weston, F., Chung, K., Hoag, S., 1990. Mergers, Restructuring, and Corporate Control. Prentice Hall, Englewood Cliffs, NJ.

Wruck, K., 1989. Equity ownership concentration and firm value. Journal of Financial Economics 23, 3–28.

Zingales, L., 1995. Insider ownership and the decision to go public. Review of Economic Studies 62, 425–448.

4

Toeholds and Takeovers

JEREMY BULOW, MING HUANG, AND PAUL KLEMPERER

I. INTRODUCTION

Buying a stake or 'toehold' in a takeover target is a common and profitable strategy.[1] The potential acquirer can gain either as a buyer that needs to pay a premium for fewer shares or as a losing bidder that sells out at a profit. A bidder that owns a toehold has an incentive to bid aggressively since every price it quotes represents not just a bid for the remaining shares but also an ask for its own holdings.

But this is the beginning of the story, not the end. There is a crucial difference between auctions among 'strategic' private-value buyers, each of which has a different use in mind for the target assets, and auctions among 'financial' common-value bidders, which primarily differ in their estimates of the returns from largely similar strategies.[2] This paper focuses on the common-values case,[3] where the implications of toeholds are dramatic.[4]

We are very grateful to the referee and editor, as well as to our colleagues and seminar audiences, for helpful comments and suggestions. The views expressed in this paper do not necessarily reflect those of the Federal Trade Commission.

[1] Well-known empirical studies that discuss toeholds include Bradley, Desai, and Kim (1988), Franks and Harris (1989), Jarrell and Poulsen (1989), Stulz, Walkling and Song (1990), Jennings and Mazzeo (1993), Betton and Eckbo (1997), Franks, Mayer, and Renneboog (1997), and Jenkinson and Ljungqvist (1997). These studies indicate that a large percentage of bidders own toeholds, often of 10–20 percent or more, at the time they make offers. (Betton and Eckbo's highly comprehensive data set of 1,353 takeover attempts shows that about half of the initial bidders have toeholds.) We know of no data on options granted to friendly bidders such as Kohlberg, Kravis, and Roberts in its offer for Borden and U.S. Steel in its offer for Marathon Oil, or similar devices that can effectively serve as "toehold substitutes." There is also little information on the differences between the types of bidders that acquire toeholds and those that do not.

[2] For noncontrolling shareholders, stocks are almost entirely common-value assets. For competing leveraged buyout firms, which are likely to apply similar managerial and financing techniques to acquired companies, the common-value element probably dominates. When Wall Street analysts quote a company's "breakup value," they are essentially making common-value estimates of the value of a company's business.

[3] To focus clearly on the strategic effects, we assume pure common values. Of course, in reality takeover targets have both private-value and common-value components, so our model yields some results that are quantitatively implausible, even though we believe that they are qualitatively correct. (The equilibrium we find is continuous as small private-value components are added; Bulow, Huang, and Klemperer (1995) study the general partially common-value, partially private-value, case.)

[4] In a related literature, Shleifer and Vishny (1986), Hirshleifer and Titman (1990), and Chowdhry and Jegadeesh (1994) focus on the use of toeholds by a single bidder to combat the free-rider problem

Because a toehold makes a bidder more aggressive, it increases the winner's curse for a nontoeholder and makes it bid more conservatively in an ascending auction.[5] This reduces the toeholder's winner's curse and allows it to be more aggressive still, creating a powerful feedback loop. So owning a toehold can help a bidder win an auction, and win very cheaply.[6]

But if two or more bidders have toeholds, a toeholder hoping to sell will be more aggressive if an opponent has a large toehold and can be expected to bid high. Our model predicts that if all bidders have toeholds of identical size, they will be more aggressive than if none had a toehold, and prices will be higher.

Our model can explain why bidders sometimes seem to overpay for the companies they take over, without appealing to stories of managerial hubris or of management's pursuit of its own interests at the expense of shareholders. Here, bidding 'too high' maximizes a bidder's ex ante expected profits even though it sometimes loses money ex post.[7]

---

described by Grossman and Hart (1980). Owning a toehold gives a bidder a profit from a successful takeover, even if it has to pay the expected full value for any shares bought in a tender offer. However, the free-rider problem is eliminated if a bidder that acquires a supermajority of the stock is able to force out nontendering shareholders. Also, if buyers do not have to buy out small, untendered minority stakes, the loss of liquidity in those shares may reduce their value, giving bidders an extra incentive to tender. We therefore ignore free-rider issues.

[5] By contrast, with private values, a nontoeholder will be unaffected by an opponent's bidding; a toeholder will become more aggressive if it thinks that there is less chance of its opponent dropping out at any given price.

[6] By contrast with our results, in the private-value models of Engelbrecht-Wiggans (1994), Burkart (1995), and Singh (1998), a small toehold has only a small effect, and toeholds always raise prices. In the "free-rider" models of Shleifer and Vishny, Hirshleifer and Titman, and Chowdhry and Jegadeesh, small toeholds likewise imply small profits because, on average, all of a bidder's profits are accounted for by gains on its toehold. A larger toehold reduces the price a bidder will have to pay in the Shleifer and Vishny and Hirshleifer and Titman models, but increases it in the Chowdhry and Jegadeesh model. None of these models can show how a toehold can make a competitor more conservative and so significantly raise a bidder's expected profits while lowering prices. However, Hirshleifer (1995, sec. 4.5) shows that in the special case of full information, a small toehold can have a big effect on an ascending private-value auction. The firm with the lower value will drop out at a price just below the other bidder's valuation if it has a small toehold (and if any bidding costs are small enough), but if it has no toehold it will bid no further than its own valuation (and will withdraw from the bidding if there are any bidding costs).

[7] Burkart (1995) and Singh (1998) have made this point in the context of a private-value auction, but in their models a small toehold has only a small effect. Chowdhry and Nanda (1993) argue that an indebted firm may commit itself to aggressive bidding (and so sometimes deter competition) by committing to financing the acquisition through additional debt of equal or senior priority and that this might sometimes lead to overpayment.

The free-rider models provide a theoretical foundation for the conventional wisdom that acquirers do not make profits on average, judged by their subsequent stock market performance. However, Loughran and Vijh (1996) show that acquirers that pay cash do make profits whereas those that issue stock underperform the market, just as other nonacquiring equity issuers do. So market prices may overstate the consideration paid in stock takeovers, and market returns may understate the real profitability of these transactions. (Similarly, Rau and Vermaelen (1996) show that "value" companies appear to make profits on tender offers, whereas "glamour" companies, those whose shares sell at a high multiple of book value, decline in the extended period following the issuance of new equity in a takeover.) These papers are therefore consistent with the "bidding contest" models of toeholds,

Our results are consistent with empirical findings that toeholds increase bidders' chances of winning takeover battles (Walking 1985; Betton and Eckbo 1997), but it is unclear whether they decrease (Eckbo and Langohr 1989; Jarrell and Poulsen 1989), increase (Franks and Harris 1989), or have no effect on (Stulz, Walking, and Song 1990) target returns.[8]

The model also implies that an ownership stake of significantly less than 50 percent in a company may be sufficient to guarantee effective control; a toehold may make it much less likely that an outside bidder will enter a takeover battle. This result is consistent with the results of Walkling and Long (1984) and Jennings and Mazzeo (1993), who find that toeholds lower the probability of management resistance; of Stulz et al. (1990), who report much larger toeholds in uncontested than in contested takeovers; and of Betton and Eckbo (1997), who find that greater toeholds increase the probability of a successful single-bid contest by lowering both the chance of entry by a rival bidder and target management resistance.[9]

Our analysis also makes predictions that have not yet been tested because empirical work in the field has not distinguished between financial and strategic bidders or between the single- and multiple-toehold cases. Since a toehold has a much smaller effect on a private-value auction than on a common-value auction, the incentive for acquiring a toehold is much lower for a 'strategic' bidder than for a 'financial' bidder. A financial bidder should generally not compete with a strategic bidder unless it has a toehold or other financial inducement. And bidding should be particularly aggressive when multiple bidders have toeholds.

Since a basic message of the analysis is that if just one bidder has a substantial toehold then it may win an auction cheaply, we consider two ways for target management to counteract this effect.

One way is to limit bidders to a single sealed 'best and final offer,'[10] so the toeholder cannot push up the competitor's price by raising its own bid. Eliminating this incentive reduces the winner's curse faced by a nontoeholder and creates a more competitive auction.

---

including ours, in which bidders make profits on average. Of course, there are many nonpublic investors, such as private entrepreneurs and leveraged buyout firms, that make a business of acquiring and reorganizing companies and appear to be very profitable on average.

[8] The existing empirical literature does not distinguish clearly between the single- and multiple-toehold cases. The case of multiple bidders with toeholds seems rare, but there may be more cases in which multiple bidders have toeholds or "toehold substitutes" such as options (see n. 1).

[9] Except that both Jennings and Mazzeo (1993) and Betton and Eckbo (1997) find that very small toeholds lead to *more* target management resistance than zero toeholds. This result would be explained if, as we argue next, financial bidders were more likely to acquire toeholds and, because they have no private-value advantage, were also more likely to be challenged.

[10] While it may be legally difficult for a board to refuse to consider higher subsequent offers, it may be able to de facto create a "first-price" (i.e., "sealed-bid") auction by awarding the highest sealed bidder a "breakup fee," options to buy stock, or options to purchase some of the company's divisions on favorable terms. (A breakup fee is a fee that would be payable to the highest sealed bidder in the event that it did not ultimately win the company.) Thus our analysis can justify the use of "lockup"

A second approach is to 'level the playing field' by giving a second bidder the opportunity to buy a toehold cheaply. The benefits of a more competitive auction can easily swamp the 'giveaway' aspect of such a deal.

While we primarily focus on auctions of companies, our analysis also applies to several related problems. Consider, for example, the sale of 'stranded assets' by state public utilities commissions, which promise to reimburse the current owners for some percentage of the difference between the assets' sale prices and their book values. If the reimbursement is 80 percent, then the current owner effectively has a toehold of 20 percent in the auctioned asset.[11]

As another example, our analysis applies to whether BSkyB, Rupert Murdoch's satellite television company, should be allowed to acquire Manchester United, England's most successful football club. The U.K. government recently blocked the acquisition, in large part because of concerns that by acquiring Manchester United, which receives the biggest share of the Premier League's television revenues (about 7 percent), BSkyB would be able to shut out other television companies when the contract for the league's broadcasting rights next comes up for auction (see *Economist*, March 20, 1999, p. 35; *Financial Times*, April 10, 1999, p.22; Parliament 1999).

Other applications include the sharing of profits in bidding rings (McAfee and McMillan 1992; Engelbrecht-Wiggans 1994), creditors' bidding in bankruptcy auctions (Burkart 1995), and the negotiation of a partnership's dissolution (Cramton, Gibbons, and Klemperer 1987). More generally, the theory lends insight into situations in which the loser cares how much the winner pays, as when a competitor in several auctions faces an aggregate budget constraint.[12]

Section II sets out our basic 'common-values' model of two bidders with toeholds that have independent private information about the value of a target company. Were the bidders to completely share information, they would have the same valuation for the target.

Section III solves for the unique equilibrium of an ascending auction between the bidders.[13] Section IV derives its properties and shows that asymmetric toeholds tend to lower sale prices.

---

provisions to support the credibility of a first-price auction. For previous analyses of the merits of allowing lockups, see Kahan and Klausner (1996) and the references cited therein.

[11] That is, the current owner is 20 cents better off if the asset is sold to someone else for a dollar more and is only 80 cents worse off if it must bid an extra dollar to win the auction. So its position is strategically identical to that of a toeholder with a 20 percent stake.

[12] The theory here is also very closely related to other examples in which one player has a small advantage (e.g., a small private-value advantage or a reputational advantage) in an otherwise pure common-value auction; see Bikhchandani (1988), Bulow and Klemperer (1999), and Klemperer (1998).

[13] Note that with toeholds we obtain a unique equilibrium in the ascending English auction even with pure common values. It is well known that when bidders have no initial stakes in the object they are competing for, there is a multiplicity of (perfect Bayesian) equilibria, but we show that (even arbitrarily small) toeholds resolve this multiplicity.

Sections V and VI show how a target can make bidding more competitive by using a 'sealed-bid' auction (Section V) or by selling a cheap stake to the bidder with the smaller toehold (Section VI). Section VII extends to bidders that are differentially well informed and shows that most of our results are unaffected.

Section VIII presents conclusions.

II. THE MODEL

Two risk-neutral bidders i and j compete to acquire a company. Bidder k $(k = i,j)$ owns a share θ_k of the company, $0 < \theta_k < \frac{1}{2}$, and observes a private signal t_k. Bidders' shares are common knowledge[14] and exogenous.[15] Bidders' signals are independent, so without loss of generality we can normalize so that both the t_k are uniformly distributed on $[0, 1]$. That is, a signal of $t_k = 0.23$ is more optimistic than 23 percent of the signals k might receive and less optimistic than 77 percent. Conditional on both signals, the expected value of the company to either bidder is $v(t_i,t_j)$. We assume that $v(\cdot, \cdot)$ has strictly positive derivatives $\partial v / \partial t_k$ everywhere.

The company is sold using a conventional ascending-bid (i.e., English) auction. That is, the price starts at zero and rises continuously.

When one bidder drops out, the other bidder buys the fraction of the company that it does not already own at the current price per unit.[16] (If bidders quit simultaneously, we assume that the company is allocated randomly at the current

Our model does not allow for the possibility of firms "jump-bidding," i.e., discontinuously raising the bidding level to intimidate opponents into quitting the auction, as is often observed in practice. Jump-bidding is less likely when there are toeholds since it is harder to discourage an opponent with a toehold from bidding, but it would still arise if there were substantial bidding costs (including costs of entering the auction), especially with smaller toeholds and private-value components. Although we do not expect jump-bidding to affect our basic results and intuitions, it would probably attenuate their quantitative significance by making behavior closer to that in a first-price auction. See Sec. V for our analysis of a first-price auction with toeholds, and see Avery (1998) and Daniel and Hirshleifer (1995) for pure common-value and pure private-value models, respectively, of jump-bidding in the absence of toeholds.

[14] This assumption is consistent with takeover regulations that require bidders to disclose their stakes.

[15] Among the many factors that could affect the size of a bidder's toehold are the liquidity of the company's shares; institutional constraints such as the Williams Act and Securities and Exchange Commission rule 16(b), which may affect some bidders' ability to retain profits if a toehold of 10 percent or more is sold; the effect of accumulating shares on the likelihood of arranging a friendly deal (as in Freeman (1991); the probability that management will find out that a toehold is being accumulated and the range of management response; the risk that information leakage about a potential offer will cause a prebid run-up in the stock price (Schwert (1996) shows that a prebid run-up forces a bidder to pay more to buy a company); and the amount of shares held by the bidder prior to any decision to make an offer for the company (many toeholders own large stakes accumulated years before a buyout offer).

[16] Thus all shareholders (including the two bidders) are assumed to be willing to sell out to the highest bidder, so we are ignoring any free-rider problems of the kind discussed by Grossman and Hart (1980). Also, all offers are assumed to be binding (which is supported by the legal environments of the European Community and the United States). Offers are made for all the outstanding shares. (Partial offers are legal under dominant U.S. law but only if they are nondiscriminating, and we would obtain similar results in this case.) See McAfee et al. (1993, p. 461) and Burkart (1995) for more legal details.

price, though this assumption is unimportant.) Thus a (pure) strategy for bidder k is a price $b_k(t_k)$ at which it will quit if the other bidder has not yet done so. We solve for the Nash equilibrium.[17]

We assume that $v(\cdot,\cdot)$ is symmetric in t_i and t_j. We define i's 'marginal revenue' as

$$ MR_i(t_i, t_j) \equiv v(t_i, t_j) - (1 - t_i)\frac{\partial v}{\partial t_i}(t_i,t_j) $$

and assume that the bidder with the higher signal has the higher marginal revenue, that is, $t_i > t_j \Rightarrow MR_i(t_i, t_j) > MR_j(t_i, t_j)$.[18] This is a standard assumption in auction theory and monopoly theory; it corresponds to assuming that bidders' marginal revenues are downward sloping in symmetric private-value auction problems and the corresponding monopoly problems. The assumption is a much stronger one for common-value auctions than for private-value auctions,[19] but we note that the assumptions of this paragraph are required only for propositions 2 and 6.

We denote the price that the bidding has currently reached by b. We write bidder k's equilibrium profits, conditional on its signal, as $\pi_k(t_k)$ and its unconditional profits (averages across its possible signals) as Π_k. We write the expected profits accruing to all the shareholders except the two bidders as Π_0.

III. SOLVING THE MODEL

In this section, we first establish the necessary and sufficient conditions for the equilibrium strategies of our model (lemmas 1 and 2), next solve for the equilibrium (proposition 1), and then calculate the expected revenue of the bidders and the nonbidding shareholders.

By standard arguments, we obtain the following lemma. (All proofs are in the Appendix.)

---

[17] We shall see that the Nash equilibrium outcome is unique and is also the unique perfect Bayesian equilibrium.

[18] In analyzing our auction using marginal revenues, we are following Bulow and Roberts (1989), who first showed how to interpret private-value auctions in terms of marginal revenues, and Bulow and Klemperer (1996), who extended their interpretation to common-values settings such as this one. Since the marginal revenue of a bidder is exactly the marginal revenue of the customer that is the same fraction of the way down the distribution of potential buyers in the monopoly model, this interpretation allows the direct translation of results from monopoly theory into auction theory and so facilitates the analysis of auctions and the development of intuition about them.

[19] See Bulow and Klemperer (1999) for a discussion of when this assumption holds in the common-value case. See n. 30 for an example for which the assumption fails. See also Myerson (1981), who calls this the "regular" case in his largely private-value analysis; Bulow and Roberts (1989), who refer to this as downward-sloping marginal revenue in their private-value analysis; and Bulow and Klemperer (1996), who also (more loosely) refer to this as downward-sloping marginal revenue in the general case.

Lemma 1. *Bidders' equilibrium strategies must be pure strategies $b_i(t_i)$ and $b_j(t_j)$ that are continuous and strictly increasing functions of their types, with $b_i(0) = b_j(0) > v(0,0)$ and $b_i(1) = b_j(1) = v(1,1)$.*

We can therefore define 'equilibrium correspondence' functions $\phi_i(\cdot)$ and $\phi_j(\cdot)$ by $b_i(\phi_i(t_j)) = b_j(t_j)$ and $b_j(\phi_j(t_i)) = b_i(t_i)$. That is, in equilibrium, type t_i of i and type $\phi_j(t_i)$ of j drop out at the same price, and type t_j of j and type $\phi_i(t_j)$ of i drop out at the same price. So bidder i will defeat an opponent of type t_j if and only if $t_j \le \phi_j(t_i)$, and $\phi_j(t_i)$ is type t_i's probability of winning the company.

Given i's bidding function $b_i(\cdot)$, for any type t_j of j, we can find t_j's equilibrium choice of where to quit or, equivalently, t_j's choice of which t_i to drop out at the same time as, by maximizing t_j's expected revenues

$$\max_{t_i} \left\{ \int_{t=0}^{t_i} [v(t, t_j) - (1 - \theta_j)b_i(t)]dt + \theta_j(1 - t_i)b_i(t_i) \right\}. \tag{1}$$

The term in the integral is j's revenue from buying, and the second term is j's revenue from selling. Setting the derivative of (1) equal to zero[20] and using the fact that $t_j = \phi_j(t_i)$ in equilibrium yields

$$b_i'(t_i) = \frac{1}{\theta_j} \frac{1}{1 - t_i} [b_i(t_i) - v(t_i, \phi_j(t_i))]. \tag{2}$$

The logic is straightforward: given that the price has already reached $b_i(t_i)$, the benefit to j of dropping out against type $t_i + dt_i$ instead of type t_i is $\theta_j b_i'(t_i)dt_i$: j's toehold times the increase in price per share earned by the later exit. The cost is that, with probability $dt_i/(1 - t_i)$, j will 'win' an auction it would otherwise have lost, suffering a loss equal to the amount bid less the value of the asset conditional on both bidders' being marginal.

---

[20] Making this argument assumes that $b_i(t_i)$ is differentiable. Strictly, we should proceed by noting that type $t_j = \phi_j(t_i)$ prefers quitting at $b_i(t_i)$ to $b_i(t_i + \Delta t_i)$. Therefore,

$$\theta_j[b_i(t_i + \Delta t_i) - b_i(t_i)]\left(1 - \frac{\Delta t_i}{1 - t_i}\right) \le \left(\frac{\Delta t_i}{1 - t_i}\right)[b_i(t_i) - v(t_i, \phi_j(t_i))] + o(\Delta b) + o(\Delta v),$$

where $o(\Delta b)$ and $o(\Delta v)$ are terms of smaller orders than, respectively, $\Delta b \equiv b_i(t_i + \Delta t_i) - b_i(t_i)$ and $\Delta v \equiv \Delta t_i \cdot (\partial v/\partial t_i)$. So

$$\limsup_{\Delta t_i \to 0} \frac{b_i(t_i + \Delta t_i) - b_i(t_i)}{\Delta t_i} \le \frac{1}{\theta_j}\left(\frac{1}{1 - t_i}\right)[b_i(t_i) - v(t_i, \phi_j(t_i))].$$

Using the fact that j's type $\phi_j(t_i + \Delta t_i)$ prefers quitting at $b_i(t_i + \Delta t_i)$ to $b_i(t_i)$ yields the same equation except with the inequality reversed and lim inf instead of lim sup, so the right derivative of $b_i(\cdot)$ exists and is given by (2). Examining the incentives for j's type $\phi_j(t_i)$ to quit at $b_i(t_i - \Delta t_i)$ and for j's type of $\phi_j(t_i - \Delta t_i)$ to quit at $b_i(t_i)$ for a small positive Δt_i, completes the argument by showing that the left derivative exists and is also given by (2).

It is easy to check that (2) and the corresponding condition for $b'_j(t_j)$ are sufficient for equilibrium, that is, satisfy global second-order conditions.[21] So we have the following lemma.[22]

Lemma 2. *Necessary and sufficient conditions for the bidding strategies $b_i(t_i)$ and $b_j(t_j)$ to form a Nash equilibrium are that $b_i(\cdot)$ and $b_j(\cdot)$ are increasing functions that satisfy*

$$b'_i(t_i) = \frac{1}{\theta_j}\frac{1}{1-t_i}[b_i(t_i) - v(t_i, \phi_j(t_i))] \tag{3}$$

and

$$b'_j(t_j) = \frac{1}{\theta_i}\frac{1}{1-t_j}[b_j(t_j) - v(\phi_i(t_j), t_j)], \tag{4}$$

where $\phi_i(\cdot) = b_i^{-1}(b_j(\cdot))$ and $\phi_j(\cdot) = b_j^{-1}(b_i(\cdot))$, with boundary conditions given by

$$b_i(0) = b_j(0) > v(0,0) \tag{5}$$

and

$$b_i(1) = b_j(1) > v(1,1). \tag{6}$$

Equation (3) can be integrated to yield

$$b_i(t_i) = \frac{1}{\theta_j}(1-t_i)^{-1/\theta_j}\left[K - \int_0^{t_i} v(t, \phi_j(t))(1-t)^{(1/\theta_j)^{-1}}dt\right],$$

where K is a constant of integration. According to boundary condition (6), it is given by

$$K = \int_0^1 v(t, \phi_j(t))(1-t)^{(1/\theta_j)^{-1}}dt.$$

---

[21] Assume, for contraction, that at some bidding level, type t_i's optimal strategy is to deviate to mimic type $t'_i > t_i$. Observe that at any point a higher type has a greater incentive than a lower type to remain in the bidding (the potential gains from selling out at a higher price are the same and the potential losses from being sold to are less). But the derivation of the first-order condition demonstrates that a type slightly below t'_i does not wish to stay in the bidding to mimic t'_i (see n. 20). So t_i prefers to mimic this type than to mimic t'_i, which is a contradiction.

[22] Bulow et al. (1995) extend this lemma to a more general setting in which the bidders' valuations of the target company have both private- and common-value components, and they prove existence and uniqueness of equilibrium for the general case.

So we have

$$b_i(t_i) = \frac{\int_{t_i}^1 v(t, \phi_j(t))(1-t)^{(1/\theta_j)^{-1}} dt}{\int_{t_i}^1 (1-t)^{(1/\theta_j)^{-1}} dt}. \tag{7}$$

Define $H_k(t_k)$ to be bidder k's hazard rate, that is, the instantaneous rate at which bidder k quits as the price rises, divided by the probability that k is still present. So $H_k(t_k) = [1/b'_k(t_k)]/(1 - t_k)$ since types are distributed uniformly. Since $b_i(t_i) = b_j(\phi_j(t_i))$, dividing equation (3) by equation (4) yields

$$\frac{H_i(t_i)}{H_j(\phi_j(t_i))} = \frac{\theta_j}{\theta_i}. \tag{8}$$

Since boundary conditions (5) and (6) imply that $\phi_j(0) = 0$ and $\phi_j(1) = 1$, the unique solution to (8) is

$$(1 - t_j)^{\theta_j} = (1 - t_i)^{\theta_i}, \tag{9}$$

that is,

$$\phi_j(t_i) = 1 - (1 - t_i)^{\theta_i/\theta_j}. \tag{10}$$

Substituting into (7), we get the following proposition.

Proposition 1. *There exists a unique Nash equilibrium. In it bidder i remains in the bidding until the price reaches*

$$b_i(t_i) = \frac{\int_{t_i}^1 v(t, 1 - (1-t)^{\theta_i/\theta_j})(1-t)^{(1-\theta_j)/\theta_j} dt}{\int_{t_i}^1 (1-t)^{(1-\theta_j)/\theta_j} dt}, \tag{11}$$

and bidder j's strategy can be expressed symmetrically.

Note that our equilibrium is unique, in stark contrast to the case without toeholds in which *every* different weakly increasing function $\phi_j(t_i)$ yields a distinct equilibrium $b_i(t_i) = v(t_i, \phi_j(t_i)) = b_j(\phi_j(t_i))$ (see Milgrom 1981).[23] The reason is that the toeholds determine a precise relationship for each bidder between its opponent's hazard rate and the 'markup' it will bid over what the company would be worth conditional on its opponent's being of the lowest

---

[23] These Nash equilibria are all perfect Bayesian.

remaining type. Without toeholds, these markups are zero, and there is no restriction on the ratio of the hazard rates at any price.[24]

The easiest way to calculate bidder i's profits is to note, by the envelope theorem, that type $t_i + dt_i$'s profits can be computed to first order as though it followed type t_i's strategy, in which case it would earn t_i's profits, except that the company is worth $[\partial v(t_i, t_j)/\partial t_i]dt_i$ more when it wins against a bidder with signal t_j, so

$$\frac{d\pi_i(t_i)}{dt_i} = \int_{t_j=0}^{\phi_j(t_i)} \frac{\partial v}{\partial t_i}(t_i, t_j)\, dt_j,$$

which implies

$$
\begin{aligned}
\pi_i(t_i) &= \pi_i(0) + \int_{t=0}^{t_i} \int_{t_j=0}^{\phi_j(t)} \frac{\partial v}{\partial t}(t, t_j)\, dt_j\, dt \\
&= \theta_i b_i(0) + \int_{t=0}^{t_i} \int_{t_j=0}^{\phi_j(t)} \frac{\partial v}{\partial t}(t, t_j)\, dt_j\, dt,
\end{aligned}
\tag{12}
$$

since a bidder with $t_i = 0$ always sells at $b_i(0)$.

Bidder i's expected profits (after we average across all possible values of its information and simplify) are

$$\Pi_i = \int_{t_i=0}^{1} \pi_i(t_i)dt_i = \theta_i b_i(0) + \int_{t_i=0}^{1} \int_{t_j=0}^{\phi_j(t_i)} (1 - t_i)\frac{\partial v}{\partial t_i}(t_i, t_j)\, dt_j\, dt_i. \tag{13}$$

The expected surplus accruing to all shareholders except the bidders is

$$\Pi_0 = \int_{t_i=0}^{1} \int_{t_j=0}^{1} v(t_i, t_j)\, dt_j\, dt_i - \Pi_i - \Pi_j, \tag{14}$$

and the average sale price is $\Pi_0/(1 - \theta_i - \theta_j)$.

It is also useful to note that (13) can be written as

$$\Pi_i = \theta_i b_i(0) + \int_{t_i=0}^{1} \int_{t_j=0}^{1} p_i(t_i, t_j)(1 - t_i)\frac{\partial v}{\partial t_i}(t_i, t_j)\, dt_j\, dt_i, \tag{15}$$

in which $p_i(t_i, t_j)$ is the probability with which i wins the company if the bidders' signals are t_i and t_j. So substituting $[p_i(t_i, t_j) + p_j(t_i, t_j)]v(t_i, t_j)$ for $v(t_i, t_j)$ we can

---

[24] More precisely, without toeholds, the two bidders' optimization conditions are degenerate and so cannot uniquely determine the two equilibrium strategies. Introducing toeholds breaks this degeneracy, giving two distinct optimization conditions that uniquely determine the equilibrium strategies. Introducing private-value components into valuations would also break the degeneracy.

collect terms to rewrite (14) as

$$\Pi_0 = \int_{t_i=0}^{1} \int_{t_j=0}^{1} \left\{ \left[v(t_i, t_j) - (1 - t_i) \frac{\partial v}{\partial t_i}(t_i, t_j) \right] p_i(t_i, t_j) \right.$$
$$\left. + \left[v(t_i, t_j) - (1 - t_j) \frac{\partial v}{\partial t_j}(t_i, t_j) \right] p_j(t_i, t_j) \right\} dt_j \, dt_i$$
$$- \theta_i b_i(0) - \theta_j b_j(0),$$

or

$$\Pi_0 = E_{t_i, t_j}(MR_{\text{winning bidder}}) - \theta_i b_i(0) - \theta_j b_j(0), \tag{16}$$

in which MR_i is i's 'marginal revenue' as defined in Section II.

Linear Example

As an example, we explicitly compute the case in which the company's value is just the sum of the bidders' signals, $v = t_i + t_j$. Performing the integration in (11), we have

$$b_i(t_i) = 2 - \frac{1}{1 + \theta_j}(1 - t_i) - \frac{1}{1 + \theta_i}(1 - t_i)^{\theta_i/\theta_j}. \tag{17}$$

Hence,

$$\pi_i(t_i) = \theta_i \left(\frac{\theta_i}{\theta_i + 1} + \frac{\theta_j}{\theta_j + 1} \right) + t_i - \left(\frac{\theta_j}{\theta_i + \theta_j} \right) [1 - (1 - t_i)^{(\theta_i + \theta_j)/\theta_j}]. \tag{18}$$

So also

$$\Pi_i = \theta_i \left(\frac{\theta_i}{\theta_i + 1} + \frac{\theta_j}{\theta_j + 1} + \frac{1}{2\theta_i + 4\theta_j} \right), \tag{19}$$

$$\Pi_0 = 1 - (\theta_i + \theta_j) \left(\frac{\theta_i}{\theta_i + 1} + \frac{\theta_j}{\theta_j + 1} \right) - \frac{\theta_i}{2\theta_i + 4\theta_j} - \frac{\theta_j}{4\theta_i + 2\theta_j}, \tag{20}$$

and the average sale price is

$$\frac{\theta_j(2\theta_j + \theta_i + 1)}{(\theta_j + 1)(2\theta_j + \theta_i)} + \frac{\theta_i(2\theta_i + \theta_j + 1)}{(\theta_i + 1)(2\theta_i + \theta_j)}.$$

The bidding functions for this example are illustrated in figure 1 for the case in which the toeholds are $\theta_1 = 0.05$ and $\theta_2 = 0.01$. Observe that the bidder with the larger toehold always bids more than in the symmetric equilibrium without

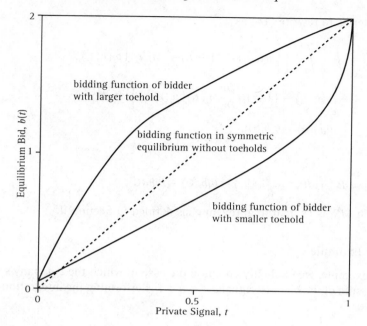

Figure 1. *Equilibrium bidding function with and without toeholds for linear example $v = t_1 + t$*

Note: Dashed line: bidding functions in symmetric equilibrium without toeholds; solid lines: bidding functions with toeholds of 5 percent and 1 percent.

toeholds, whereas the bidder with the smaller toehold bids less than if neither bidder had a toehold except for very low values of its signal. Figure 2 also shows the bidding functions when the toeholds are $\theta_1 = 0.10$ and $\theta_2 = 0.01$; increasing bidder 1's toehold makes that bidder bid more aggressively (and increases its expected profits) for all values of its signal.

The next section describes properties of the equilibrium, including those illustrated in the figures, that apply in the general case.

IV. PROPERTIES OF THE EQUILIBRIUM

If there were no toeholds, type t_i would bid up to the price $v(t_i, \phi_j(t_i))$ at which it would just be indifferent about winning the auction; but it is immediate from equation (7) that every bidder except the highest possible type, $t_i = 1$ bids beyond this price.[25] So except for types $t_i = 1$ and $t_j = 1$, *any bidder that narrowly 'wins' the auction loses money.*

[25] Of course, this does not mean that bidders necessarily bid more than if there were no toeholds, since the functions $\phi_k(\cdot)$ are different.

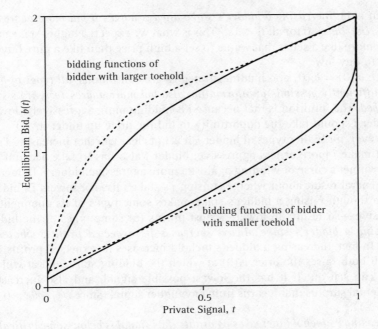

Figure 2. *Equilibrium bidding functions with different size toeholds for linear example $v = t_1 + t_2$*

Note: Dashed lines: bidding functions with toeholds of 10 percent and 1 percent; solid lines: bidding functions with toeholds of 5 percent and 1 percent.

From equation (8), bidder i always quits at a rate θ_j/θ_i times as fast as bidder j, so it follows immediately that i 'wins' the auction, that is, buys the company, with probability $\theta_i/(\theta_i + \theta_j)$. Thus *probabilities of winning the auction are highly sensitive to the relative sizes of bidders' stakes*, and a bidder's probability of winning is increasing in its stake.

It also follows that *increasing a bidder's stake increases its probability of winning, conditional on whatever information it has* (i.e., $\theta_j(t_j)$ is strictly increasing in θ_i for all $0 < t_i < 1$) and that if i's stake is smaller than j's, then bidder i will lose to any bidder j with equally optimistic, or not too much less optimistic, information than it has (i.e., $\theta_i < \theta_j \Rightarrow t_i > \phi_j(t_i)$ for all $0 < t_i < 1$).

Note, in particular, that *a bidder with a zero stake has zero probability of winning*. To see why, observe that it at any point the lowest possible remaining types of i and j were known to be t_i and t_j, then i, with a zero stake, will bid up to $v(t_i, t_j)$ and j, with a positive stake, will bid strictly more. So whatever the current lowest types are, there are always more of i's types that must quit before any of j's types leave.[26]

---

[26] However, the result that a player with *any* positive stake always beats a bidder with no toehold (and, more generally, that bidders' probabilities of winning are in proportion to their toeholds even

From (11), *increasing a bidder's stake always makes it bid more aggressively.* That is, $\partial b_i / \partial \theta_i > 0$ for all $t_i < 1$.[27] This is what we expect: a higher stake makes a bidder more like a seller that wants to set a high price than like a pure buyer that wants to buy low.

Since $b_i(0) = b_j(0)$ and bidding strategies are continuous, *all types of bidder j with sufficiently pessimistic information also bid more aggressively if i's stake is increased.* The intuition is that because i is bidding more aggressively, low types of bidder j should take the opportunity to bid the price up under it.

However, for higher types of bidder j, it is not clear whether increasing i's stake should make j more or less aggressive: bidder j also has to take account of the larger winner's curse of winning against a more aggressive bidder i. In fact, there is no general result about whether raising i's stake raises or lowers j's bid.[28]

Even though raising a bidder's stake makes some types of its opponent more aggressive—so results in lower ex post profits for some types of the bidder— *increasing a bidder's stake always increases its expected profits, whatever its signal.* In fact, increasing a bidder's toehold increases its expected profits in two ways: it both raises the price $b_i(0)$ at which the bidding starts and at which the bidder can sell out if it has the lowest possible signal, and also increases the incremental surplus that it earns from any higher signal (since $\partial \phi_j / \partial \theta_i > 0$ for all $0 < t_i < 1$).

Increasing i's toehold increases j's profits if j's signal is below some critical level, since when j has a low signal it is likely to sell and if j sells it sells for a higher price. (In particular, $\Pi_j(0) = b_j(0)\theta_j = b_i(0)\theta_j$ is larger.) Conversely, however, *it reduces j's profits if its signal is above a certain level,* since when j buys it must pay more. (To check this, recall that $\partial \phi_i / \partial \theta_i < 0$, and it is easy to see that $\partial \pi_j / \partial \theta_i < 0$ at $t_j = 1$ since type $t_j = 1$ always buys and always pays more if θ_i is larger.) *Overall, increasing i's toehold reduces the profits of j averaged over all j's types* (i.e., $\partial \Pi_j / \partial \theta_i < 0$).

The expected price conditional on winning is the same for both bidders (and equals the average sale price) because the relative rates at which the two bidders quit is the same at every price.

---

when the toeholds are arbitrarily small) depends critically on the pure common-values assumption. With any private-value components to valuations, sufficiently small toeholds would have only a small effect on outcomes.

[27] Throughout this section we perform comparative statics thinking of firms' bidding and profit functions as functions of θ_i and θ_j as well as of t_i or t_j.

[28] It is easy to check for the linear case that

$$\frac{\partial b_j}{\partial \theta_i} = \frac{1 - t_j}{(1 + \theta_i)^2} \left[1 + \frac{(1 + \theta_i)^2}{1 + \theta_j} \frac{\theta_j}{\theta_i^2} (1 - t_j)^{(\theta_j - \theta_i)/\theta_i} \log(1 - t_j) \right].$$

So as a result of an increase in the share of the bidder with the larger toehold, the opponent bids more/ less aggressively according to whether its type is below/above some cutoff level. As a result of an increase in the share of the bidder with the smaller toehold, both the weak and strong types of the opponent always bid more aggressively whereas intermediate types bid less aggressively.

Observe that when toeholds are small, $b_i(0) = b_j(0)$ is of first order in $\theta_i + \theta_j$,[29] so $\theta_i b_i(0) + \theta_j b_j(0)$ is of second order in $\theta_i + \theta_j$. From (16), we therefore have $\Pi_0 \approx E_{t_i, t_j}(MR_{\text{winning bidder}})$. Furthermore, by our assumption that the bidder with the higher signal has the higher marginal revenue, the expected marginal revenue of the winner is maximized over all possible mechanisms if and only if the bidder with the higher signals always wins the auction, that is, only when toeholds are symmetric. So with sufficiently small toeholds, the non-bidding shareholders' expected wealth is highest with equal toeholds; the more unequal the toeholds, the more likely it is that the bidder with the lower signal (hence the lower marginal revenue) will win the auction, so the lower the expected wealth of the nonbidding shareholders.[30] The following proposition makes this more precise.

Proposition 2. *The expected sale price is higher from an (ascending) auction when bidders' toeholds are in a less equal ratio, if the toeholds are sufficiently small. (That is, for any given $0 \leq \lambda_1 < \lambda_2 < 1$, there is a $\bar{\theta}$ such that the expected sale price with any $\theta_i < \bar{\theta}$ and $\theta_j = \lambda_2 \theta_i$ exceeds the expected sale price with θ_i and $\theta_j = \lambda_1 \theta_i$.)*

With larger toeholds the terms $\theta_i b_i(0)$ and $\theta_j b_j(0)$ are nontrivial, so Π_0 is not just a function of the expected marginal revenue of the winner. However, it remains true that, for any given $\theta_i + \theta_j$, symmetric toeholds are most desirable from the viewpoint of the nonbidding shareholders provided that the lowest possible bid, $b_i(0) = b_j(0)$, is not too much higher for asymmetric than for symmetric toeholds.

Thus it seems likely that the expected sale price will typically be increasing as the relative sizes of the bidders' toeholds are made more equal, whatever their absolute sizes, and this is confirmed in the linear example from Section III.

Linear example (cont.). In the linear example, $v = t_i + t_j$, the expected price increases as the sizes of the toeholds are made more equal, for any fixed sum of the sizes.[31]

---

[29] For small θ_i and θ_j, we have

$$b_i(0) = b_j(0) \approx \frac{\partial v}{\partial t_j}(0,0)\theta_i + \frac{\partial v}{\partial t_i}(0,0)\theta_j.$$

[30] More asymmetric toeholds may increase the expected wealth of the nonbidding shareholders if the bidder with the higher signal does not necessarily have the higher marginal revenue An example is $v = t_i^3 + t_j^3$. The reason is that even a bidder with an arbitrarily tiny toehold has no reason to quit below the value the company would have if its opponent had the lowest possible signal. Getting this value from the bidder with the smaller toehold—which is equally likely to be the bidder with the better or the worse information—yields a higher price for this valuation function than a more symmetric contest in which the price is more likely to be determined by the bidder with the worse information. For further discussion of the assumption that the bidder with the higher signal has the higher marginal revenue, see Bulow and Klemperer (1999).

[31] Let $\theta_i = \psi x$ and $\theta_j = (1 - \psi)x$. Then

$$\Pi_0 = \frac{1 + 2z}{2 + z} - \left(\frac{1 + 2zx}{1 + x + zx^2}\right)x^2,$$

Note that if $\theta_i + \theta_j$ is small, Π_0 depends, except for high-order terms, only on the ratio $\theta_i : \theta_j$. (This ratio determines the correspondence functions $\phi_k(\cdot)$ and hence determines which bidder wins the company.) It follows that, while toeholds remain small, giving both bidders free shares that proportionally increase their stakes by diluting the remaining shareholders' holdings has no first-order effect on anyone's expected wealth (before they know their types); each bidder's gain from its additional stake is just canceled by its loss from its opponent's more aggressive behavior. For example, in the linear example, giving away 5 percent of a company in equal shares to two bidders that previously had arbitrarily tiny equal toeholds costs the remaining shareholders less than 0.5 percent of their expected wealth.[32]

It also follows that *diluting the stock by giving free shares to the bidder with the smaller toehold can increase the expected sale price per share, that is, increase the nonbidding shareholders' wealth.*

In summary, even small toeholds can have a large effect on the competition between the bidders. A bidder with a large toehold bids more aggressively and wins the auction with a higher probability. If the bidders' toeholds are sufficiently asymmetric, the bidder with a smaller toehold can be forced to quit at a very low price and the auction can generate a much lower expected revenue for the non-bidding shareholders.

V. SEALED-BID AUCTIONS

Since the 'winner's curse' effects we have described mean that the bidder with the larger toehold wins with a high probability and at a low price, it is natural to ask whether the alternative common auction format—the first-price, sealed-bid auction—performs any better from the viewpoint of the nonbidding shareholders.[33] (Of course, without toeholds, first-price and ascending auctions yield the same expected revenue when symmetric buyers are in symmetric equilibrium.)[34]

In a first-price (i.e., sealed-bid) auction, each bidder $k = i, j$ independently makes a single 'best and final offer,' per unit, and the highest bidder buys the fraction of the company, $1 - \theta_k$, that it does not already own at the share price bid. In the equilibrium of this case, type t_i of j will choose to beat all of the

---

where $z \equiv \psi(1 - \psi)$. So Π_0 is increasing in z, and z is increasing in ψ for $0 \leq \psi < \frac{1}{2}$ and decreasing in ψ for $\frac{1}{2} < \psi \leq 1$. So, for fixed $\theta_i + \theta_j$, Π_0 always increases as toeholds become more symmetric. In particular, if $\psi = \frac{1}{2}$ (symmetric toeholds), $\Pi_0 \approx \frac{2}{3} - x^2$ whereas if $\psi = 0$ or $\psi = 1$ (only one bidder has a toehold), $\Pi_0 \approx \frac{1}{2} - x^2$.

[32] Of course, this result relies on $v(0,0) = 0$. More generally, giving away options with an exercise price equal to the lowest possible value of the company, i.e., $v(0, 0)$, has the effects described.

[33] See n. 10 for a discussion of the practical feasibility of the first-price auction.

[34] By the revenue equivalence theorem due to Myerson (1981) and Riley and Samuelson (1981). (See Klemperer (1999a) for a simple exposition and further discussion.) For other considerations that might affect the shareholders' choice between different auction types, see the articles in Klemperer (1999b).

opponent's types below t_i (by bidding $\tilde{b}_i(t_i)$), where t_i is chosen to maximize j's expected revenues

$$\max_{t_i}\left\{\int_{t=0}^{t_i}[v(t,t_j) - (1 - \theta_j)\tilde{b}_i(t_i)]dt + \theta_j\int_{t=t_i}^{1}\tilde{b}_i(t)\,dt\right\}.\tag{21}$$

Setting the derivative equal to zero and substituting $t_j = \tilde{\phi}_j(t_i)$ (i.e., letting $\tilde{\phi}_j(\cdot)$ and $\tilde{\phi}_i(\cdot)$ be the equilibrium correspondence functions) yields

$$\tilde{b}_i'(t_i) = \frac{1}{1 - \theta_j}\cdot\frac{1}{t_i}[v(t_i,\tilde{\phi}_j(t_i)) - \tilde{b}_i(t_i)].\tag{22}$$

The intuition is that, given that j decides not to beat types of i above t_i, bidding even lower to win against dt_i fewer types saves an additional $(1 - \theta_j)\tilde{b}_i'(t_i)dt_i$ in payments when j wins, but the cost is that, with probability dt_i/t_i, j loses an auction it would otherwise have won and so forgoes $v(t_i,t_j) - \tilde{b}_i(t_i)$.

Notice that this intuition, and so also the derivative (22), corresponds exactly to our original problem, with the change of variable θ_k to $1 - \theta_k$ and t_k to $1 - t_k$ except in $v(\cdot,\cdot)$ for $k = i, j$. It follows that the arguments of Section III extend immediately to imply the following lemma.

Lemma 3. *Necessary and sufficient conditions for the bidding strategies $\tilde{b}_i(t_i)$ and $\tilde{b}_j(t_i)$ to form a Nash equilibrium for the first-price auction are that $\tilde{b}_i(\cdot)$ and $\tilde{b}_j(\cdot)$ are increasing functions with*

$$\tilde{b}_i'(t_i) = \frac{1}{1 - \theta_j}\cdot\frac{1}{t_i}[v(t_i,\tilde{\phi}_j(t_i)) - \tilde{b}_i(t_i)]\tag{23}$$

and

$$\tilde{b}_j'(t_j) = \frac{1}{1 - \theta_i}\cdot\frac{1}{t_j}[v(\tilde{\phi}_i(t_j),t_j) - \tilde{b}_j(t_j)],\tag{24}$$

where $\tilde{\phi}_i(\cdot) = \tilde{b}_i^{-1}(\tilde{b}_j(\cdot))$ and $\tilde{\phi}_j(\cdot) = \tilde{b}_j^{-1}(\tilde{b}_i(\cdot))$, with the boundary conditions given by

$$\tilde{b}_i(0) = \tilde{b}_j(0) = v(0,0),$$
$$\tilde{b}_i(1) = \tilde{b}_j(1) < v(1,1).\tag{25}$$

Likewise, we have

$$\tilde{\phi}_j(t_i) = t_i^{(1-\theta_i)/(1-\theta_j)}\tag{26}$$

and the following proposition.

Proposition 3. *There exists a unique Nash equilibrium of the first-price auction. In it i bids*

$$\tilde{b}_i(t_i) = \frac{\int_0^{t_i} v(t, t^{(1-\theta_i)/(1-\theta_j)}) t^{\theta_j/(1-\theta_j)} \, dt}{\int_0^{t_i} t^{\theta_j/(1-\theta_j)} \, dt} \tag{27}$$

and bidder j's bid can be expressed symmetrically.

Now (26) implies that i 'wins' with probability $(1 - \theta_j)/[(1 - \theta_j) + (1 - \theta_i)]$. If $\theta_i > \theta_j$, this is smaller than the probability $\theta_i/(\theta_i + \theta_j)$ with which i would win the ascending auction, so proposition 4 follows.

Proposition 4. *The probability that the bidder with the higher signal wins the auction is greater in the first-price auction than in the ascending auction.*

Thus the outcomes of first-price auctions are less sensitive to toeholds than the outcomes of ascending auctions, although it remains true that the bidder with the larger toehold has a higher probability of winning.

The intuition is that a bidder with a toehold still has an incentive to bid higher than otherwise: bidding more aggressively is less costly when winning the auction means buying only fraction $1 - \theta$ rather than all of the company. However, this effect is generally small unless θ is close to one (in which case the bidder has control anyway; our model therefore assumes $\theta < \frac{1}{2}$). Furthermore, and more important, the indirect or 'strategic' effect due to the winner's curse on the opponent is much smaller in first-price than in ascending auctions.[35] So the extreme outcome of the ascending auction, that a bidder with a relatively small toehold is almost completely driven out of the bidding, does not arise in the first-price auction.

Because toeholds provide greater incentives for bidding aggressively in ascending auctions than in first-price auctions, ascending auctions yield higher prices on average when toeholds are symmetric.

Proposition 5. *With symmetric toeholds, the expected sale price is higher in an ascending auction than in a first-price auction.*[36]

---

[35] In an ascending auction, when bidder i bids more aggressively, bidder j must bid less because, conditional on winning at any price, its revenue is lower. (That is, bidding strategies are "strategic substitutes" in the terminology introduced by Bulow, Geanakoplos, and Klemperer (1985).) In a first-price auction, by contrast, bidder j's response to bidder i's bidding more is ambiguous: when i bids more, j wants to bid *less* on the grounds that its marginal profit when it wins is lower but *more* on the grounds that its probability of winning is lower, so increasing its bid is less costly. So the ascending-auction logic—that when i bids a little more j bids a similar amount less, so i bids a similar amount more, so j bids a similar amount less, etc.—does not apply in first-price auctions.

[36] This result does not depend on the assumption of pure common values. Singh (1998) obtains this result for the pure private-values case.

However, when toeholds are very asymmetric, the winner's curse effect that the bidder with the smaller toehold is forced to quit at a very low value in an ascending auction implies the first-price auctions are likely to perform better.

Proposition 6. *With asymmetric toeholds, the expected sale price is higher in a first-price auction than in an ascending auction if the toeholds are sufficiently small. (That is, for any $\lambda \neq 1$, the first-price auction yields a higher expected price for all θ_i, θ_j such that $\theta_j = \lambda\theta_i \leq \bar{\theta}$, for some $\bar{\theta}$.)*

A more formal way to understand propositions 5 and 6 is to recall that the expected sale price equals $\Pi_0/(1 - \theta_i - \theta_j)$, and Π_0 can be written as in (16) for the ascending auction. By an exactly similar logic, Π_0 for the first-price auction can also be written as in (16) except that the term $b_i(0)$ is replaced by the expected price received by bidder i in a first-price auction if i has the lowest possible signal, that is $\int_{t_j=0}^{1} \tilde{b}_j(t_j)dt_j$, and the term $b_j(0)$ is replaced similarly. There are therefore two differences between a first-price auction and an ascending auction.

First, the price received by bidder i with signal zero in a first-price auction $(\int_{t_j=0}^{1} \tilde{b}_j(t_j)dt_j)$ is the average bid of a bidder j that does not know i's signal, whereas in an ascending auction bidder i must drop out immediately at $b_i(0)$. When toeholds are symmetric, this is the only distinction between the expression for Π_0 for the two types of auction, so the ascending auction yields higher prices for symmetric toeholds (proposition 5).

Second, as proposition 4 demonstrates, the first-price auction is won by the bidder with the higher signal in more cases than in the ascending auction, so the first-price auction is more often won by the bidder with the higher marginal revenue and so is likely to have the higher expected marginal revenue of the winning bidder.[37] In the limit, as toeholds become arbitrarily tiny, this is the only distinction between the expressions for Π_0 for the two types of auction, so we expect the first-price auction to yield higher prices for asymmetric toeholds if the toeholds are not too large (proposition 6).[38]

If bidders' toeholds are neither small nor symmetric, the sale price comparison between the two auction forms is ambiguous, but our leading example suggests that first-price auctions are likely to be better in practice if there is much asymmetry in the relative sizes of the toeholds.

Linear example (cont.). In the linear example $v = t_i + t_j$, a sufficient condition for the expected price to be higher in a first-price auction than in an ascending auction is $\theta_i < \frac{1}{8}\theta_j$ or $\theta_i > 8\theta_j$. If $\theta_k < 0.1$, $k = i,j$, a sufficient condition is $\theta_i < \frac{1}{4}\theta_j$ or $\theta_i > 4\theta_j$.

---

[37] However, this need not be the case, even under our assumption that the bidder with the higher signal has the higher marginal revenue, because it is *not* true that the higher signal wins in the first-price auction in every case in which it wins in the ascending auction.

[38] An example that shows that if the bidder with the higher signal does not always have the higher marginal revenue then an ascending auction may always yield a higher expected price than a first-price auction is $v = t_i^3 + t_j^3$ (see Bulow and Klemperer 1999).

VI. SELLING A SECOND TOEHOLD

An alternative approach to compensating for the advantage that a bidder with a toehold has is to 'level the playing field' by selling shares (or, equivalently, options) to the second bidder so that it has an equal stake.[39] Even if these shares are sold very cheaply (so that all types of the second bidder will wish to buy them), the likely higher price from a fairer contest may more than outweigh the cost to the remaining shareholders of diluting their stake. With sufficiently small toeholds, it always pays to subsidize the smaller toeholder in this way.

For example, with the linear value function $v = t_i + t_j$, if just one of the two bidders has a toehold, say θ, the expected profits of the nonbidding shareholders are $\frac{1}{2} - [\theta^2/(1 + \theta)]$ (from (20)). The bidder without the toehold makes zero expected profit (whatever its signal), so even if it had the lowest possible signal, it would be prepared to pay $2\theta^2/(1 + \theta)$, that is, $\theta b(0)$ when both bidders have a stake of θ, for a stake of equal size. The expected profits of the nonbidding shareholders would then be $2\theta^2/(1 + \theta)$ plus the expected profits from the bidding, $\frac{2}{3} - [4\theta^2/(1 + \theta)]$, which equals $\frac{2}{3} - [2\theta^2/(1 + \theta)]$ in all. This exceeds the expected profits if there were no such sale, $\frac{1}{2} - [\theta^2/(1 + \theta)]$, for all $\theta \leq \frac{1}{2}$.

In fact, even if the stake could only be given away free,[40] giving away the stake would dominate not doing so for all $\theta \leq \frac{1}{4}$.[41]

VII. ASYMMETRIC VALUE FUNCTIONS

Our analysis thus far has assumed that the value function is symmetric in bidders' signals, that is, that bidders have equally valuable private information about the value of the company. In fact, none of our analysis depends on this assumption. However, if the value function is not symmetric, it is implausible that the bidder with the higher signal will always have the higher marginal revenue, and dropping this assumption requires dropping propositions 2 and 6. (Propositions 1, 3, 4, and 5 are unaffected; they depend neither on the symmetry of the value function nor on any assumption about marginal revenues.)

If the bidders' information is not equally valuable, then the bidder to whose information the value is less sensitive—the bidder, k, with the lower $\partial v(\cdot,\cdot)/\partial t_k$— will typically have a higher marginal revenue when $t_i = t_j$, that is, when each bidder receives a signal that is the same fraction of the way down the distribution

---

[39] Selling shares at price p is equivalent in this context to giving options for the same number of shares at exercise price p.

[40] Note that we have set the base price of the stock to be zero if both bidders observe the lowest possible signal. So "given away free" here means selling them at the base price of the stock.

[41] Thus selling shares, or giving options, at a price close to the lowest possible value of the company may be acceptable management behavior in a context in which the value function is hard to assess. In fact, selling, or giving, a second toehold is even more desirable than this if it is done through, e.g., issuing new shares that dilute the size of the first bidder's stake, rather than by just selling a fraction of the nonbidding shareholder's shares. Dilution is probably more realistic, but it is not needed for our result.

of signals that it could have received. Therefore, by contrast with proposition 2, an auction in which the low-information bidder has the larger toehold and so sometimes wins when it has the lower signal may yield higher expected revenue than an auction with symmetric toeholds.[42] Similarly, by contrast with proposition 6, if the low-information bidder has the larger toehold, an ascending auction may be preferred to a first-price auction, since the ascending auction gives a greater bias in favor of the larger toeholder's probability of winning. Of course, if the low-information bidder also has the smaller toehold, then an ascending auction will be particularly disastrous.

VIII. CONCLUSION

Toeholds can dramatically influence takeover battles. A bidder with a large toehold will have an incentive to bid aggressively, essentially because every price it quotes is both a bid for the rest of the company and an ask for its own shares. This increased aggressiveness will cause a competitor to alter its strategy as well. A competitor with a smaller toehold that is relatively pessimistic about the value of the company will become more aggressive, counting on the large toeholder to buy it out at a higher price. If the competitor has an optimistic assessment of the company's prospects, though, the large toeholder's aggressive strategy will cause the competitor to become more conservative because of an exacerbated winner's curse.

Because toeholds make a bidder more aggressive, which can make a competitor more conservative, which can make the bidder still more aggressive, and so on, even small toeholds can have large effects. A toehold can sharply improve a bidder's chance of winning an auction and raise the bidder's expected profits at the expense of both other bidders and stockholders.

The strategic consequences that so benefit the toeholder create a problem for a board of directors interested in attaining the highest possible sale price for its investors. The board of a target company may therefore wish to 'level the playing field' by selling a toehold to a new bidder, or by changing the rules of the auction.

Appendix. Proofs

Proof of Lemma 1. Let $\bar{B}$ be the lowest price level at or below which, with probability one, at least one bidder has dropped out. It is easy to see that if a low type gets the same expected surplus from two different quitting prices and the lower price is below $\bar{B}$, then a higher type always strictly prefers the higher quitting price. So at least up to $\bar{B}$, higher types quit (weakly) after lower types.

---

[42] For example, if the value function is linear but twice as sensitive to i's signal as to j's signal (i.e., $v = 2t_i + t_j$), then in the limit, as all the toeholds become tiny, the expected sale price is maximized when j's toehold is approximately three times as large as i's toehold.

Define the common bidding range as price levels below $\bar{B}$.

Now if i has an 'atom' (i.e., an interval of its types drops out at a single price) within the common range, then j cannot have an atom at the same price, since an interval of j's types cannot all prefer to quit simultaneously with i's atom rather than leave either just before or just after.

We next argue that the equilibrium bidding functions $b_i(t_i)$ and $b_j(t_j)$ are single-valued and continuous on the common range; that is, there are no 'gaps' (no intervals of prices within the common range within which a bidder drops out with probability zero). The reasons is that if i has a gap, then j would do better to raise the price to the top of the gap (thus raising the price j receives for its share) than to drop out during the gap. So j must have a gap that starts no higher than the start of i's gap. Furthermore, unless i has an atom at the start of the gap, j would do better to raise the price to the top of the gap than to drop out just below the start of i's gap; that is, j's gap starts lower than i's. So, since we have already show that i and j cannot both have atoms at the same price, we obtain a contradiction.[43]

Similarly, it follows that $b_i(0) = b_j(0)$, since if $b_i(0) > b_j(0)$, then type 0 of bidder j would do strictly better to increase its bid a little.

Now, observe that if i has an atom in the common range, there cannot be a t_j that is willing to drop out just after the atom quits; t_j would either prefer to quit just before the atom (if t_j's value conditional on i being among the types within the atom is less than the current price) or prefer to quit a finite distance later (since t_j's lowest possible value conditional on i being above the atom must otherwise strictly exceed the current price). So since we have already shown that there are no gaps, any atom must be at the top of the common bidding range.

It now follows that $b_i(0) = b_j(0) > v(0,0)$ since, if not, then type 0 of bidder j would do better to raise its bid slightly; raising its bid by ϵ gains $\epsilon\theta_j$ when it still sells (with probability close to one) and loses less than $\epsilon(1 - \theta_j)$ when it ends up buying (which happens with a probability that can be made arbitrarily small by reducing ϵ).

At the top of the common range, assume, without loss of generality, that j is the player that quits with probability one by or at price $\bar{B}$. Then, for some $\hat{t}_i$, the types (and only the types) $t_i \geq \hat{t}_i$ of i quit at or above $\bar{B}$ (by the argument in the first paragraph of this proof). Then $\bar{B} \geq v(\hat{t}_i, 1)$, so that it is always rational for j to sell at $\bar{B}$. But also $\bar{B} \leq v(\hat{t}_i, 1)$ (because either type $t_i = \hat{t}_i$ is willing to buy at $\bar{B}$ with probability one; or if type $\hat{t}_i$ is not buying with probability one, then j must have an atom at $\bar{B}$ and $\hat{t}_i$ is bidding $\bar{B}$, so $\bar{B} \leq v(\hat{t}_i, 1)$ otherwise $\hat{t}_i$ will quit just before j's atom). So $\bar{B} = v(\hat{t}_i, 1)$. Now we cannot have $\hat{t}_i < 1$ or j's types just below one would prefer quitting just after $\bar{B}$ to just before $\bar{B}$; either i has an atom at $\bar{B}$, so buying just above $\bar{B} = v(\hat{t}_i, 1)$ is profitable or i does not have an atom, so raising t_j's bid by ϵ gains $\epsilon\theta_j$ when it still sells (with probability close to one, conditional

---

[43] Note that without toeholds, gaps would be feasible, since a bidder that knows it will be the next to drop out is indifferent about the price at which it does so.

on having reached price $\bar{B} = v(\hat{t}_i, 1)$) and loses less than $\epsilon(1 - \theta_j)$ when it ends up buying (which happens with a probability that can be made arbitrarily small by reducing ϵ). So $\bar{B} = v(1, 1)$, and it is straightforward that neither player can have an atom at this price (no type below one would wish to win with probability one at this price).[44]

Finally, since we showed that there can be no interval within the bidding range within which a bidder quits with probability zero, note that bidders cannot choose mixed strategies. □

Proof of Proposition 2. Since the correspondence function $\phi_j(t_i)$ is independent of θ_i for any given ratio $\theta_i : \theta_j$, $E_{t_i, t_j}(MR_{\text{winning bidder}})$ is also independent of θ_i for any given ratio and is strictly lower for the ratio λ_1 than the ratio λ_2 by our assumption that $t_i > t_j \Rightarrow MR_i > MR_j$. But for any λ_1 or λ_2, $\lim_{\theta_k \to 0} \pi_k(0) = 0$, $k = i, j$, so the result follows straightforwardly from (16). □

Proof of Proposition 5. From the argument leading up to (14), the expected sale price in the second-price auction is

$$\frac{1}{1 - \theta_i - \theta_j} \left\{ \int_{t_i=0}^{1} \int_{t_j=0}^{1} v(t_i, t_j) \, dt_j dt_i - \left[\pi_i(0) + \int_{t_i=0}^{1} \int_{t_j=0}^{\phi_j(t_i)} (1 - t_i) \frac{dv}{dt_i}(t_i, t_j) \, dt_j dt_i \right] \right.$$
$$\left. - \left[\pi_j(0) + \int_{t_j=0}^{1} \int_{t_i=0}^{\phi_i(t_j)} (1 - t_j) \frac{dv}{dt_j}(t_i, t_j) \, dt_i \, dt_j \right] \right\}.$$

By the same logic, the expected sale price in the first-price auction is the same expression, but $\tilde{\phi}_k(\cdot)$ is substituted for $\phi_k(\cdot)$ and $\tilde{\pi}_k(0)$ for $\pi_k(0)$, $k = i, j$, in which $\tilde{\pi}_k(0)$ is bidder k's surplus when k has its lowest possible signal. If $\theta_i = \theta_j = \theta$, then $\phi_j(t_i) = \tilde{\phi}_j(t_i) = t_i$, so the difference between these expressions is

$$\frac{1}{1 - 2\theta} [\tilde{\pi}_i(0) + \tilde{\pi}_j(0) - \pi_i(0) - \pi_j(0)].$$

Substituting $\pi_i(0) = \theta_i b_i(0)$ and $\tilde{\pi}_i(0) = \theta_i \int_{t_j=0}^{1} \tilde{b}_j(t_j) \, dt_j$ (since a bidder with signal zero always sells) yields (after evaluating $\int_{t_j=0}^{1} \tilde{b}_j(t_j) dt_j$ by parts) that this difference is

$$\frac{1}{1 - 2\theta} \int_{t=0}^{1} 2v(t, t) \{ [(1 - t) - (1 - t)^{(1-\theta)/\theta}] - [t^{\theta/(1-\theta)} - t] \} \, dt.$$

This is positive since $v(t, t)$ is monotonic increasing in t and the expression in braces has expected value zero and is negative for all $t \in (0, \hat{t})$ and positive for all $t \in (\hat{t}, 1)$, for some $\hat{t}$. □

---

[44] Note that we have shown only that players quit by $\bar{B}$ with probability one. Strictly speaking, in a Nash equilibrium, the (zero-probability) types $t_i = 1$ and $t_j = 1$ can quit above $\bar{B}$ since it is a zero-probability event that the price will reach $\bar{B}$. (In a perfect Bayesian equilibrium, however, all types including $t_i = 1$ and $t_j = 1$ must quit by $\bar{B}$.)

Proof of Proposition 6. For a given λ, write $E(\lambda)$ and $\tilde{E}(\lambda)$ for the values of $E_{t_i,t_j}(MR_{\text{winning bidder}})$ for the ascending auction and first-price auction, respectively. The term $E(\lambda)$ is independent of θ_i (since $\phi_i(\cdot)$ is independent of θ_i), and $\tilde{E}(\lambda)$ is monotonic continuous decreasing in θ_i with $\lim_{\theta_i \to 0} \tilde{E}(\lambda) = E(1)$, since $\tilde{\phi}_j(t_i) = t_i^{(1-\theta_i)/(1-\lambda\theta_i)}$ is monotonic and continuous in θ_i for every t_i and $\lim_{\theta_i \to 0} \tilde{\phi}_j(t_i) = t_i$ for every t_i. Furthermore, by our assumption that $t_i > t_j \Rightarrow MR_i > MR_j$, $E(1) > E(\lambda)$ for all $\lambda \neq 1$. Finally, it is straightforward that $\lim_{\theta_k \to 0} \pi_k(0) = \lim_{\theta_k \to 0} \tilde{\pi}_k(0) = 0$, $k = i,j$, for all λ, so the result follows easily from (16).   □

REFERENCES

Avery, Christopher. 'Strategic Jump Bidding in English Auctions.' *Rev. Econ. Studies* 65 (April 1998): 185–210.

Betton, Sandra, and Eckbo, B. Espen. 'State-Contingent Payoffs in Take-overs: New Structural Estimates.' Manuscript. Quebec: Concordia Univ.; Stockholm: Stockholm School Econ., 1997.

Bikhchandani, Sushil. 'Reputation in Repeated Second-Price Auctions.' *J. Econ. Theory* 46 (October 1988): 97–119.

Bradley, Michael; Desai, Anand; and Kim, E. Han. 'Synergistic Gains from Corporate Acquisitions and Their Division between the Stockholders of Target and Acquiring Firms.' *J. Financial Econ.* 21 (May 1988): 3–40.

Bulow, Jeremy, Geanakoplos, John, and Klemperer, Paul. 'Multimarket Oligopoly: Strategic Substitutes and Complements.' *J.P.E.* 93 (June 1985): 488–511.

——, Huang, Ming, and Klemperer, Paul. 'Toeholds and Takeovers: General Characterization, Existence, and Uniqueness of Equilibrium.' Manuscript. Stanford, Calif.: Standford Univ.; Oxford: Nuffield Coll., 1995.

——, and Klemperer, Paul. 'Auctions versus Negotiations.' *A.E.R* 86 (March 1996): 180–94.

——. 'Prices and the Winner's Curse.' Discussion paper. Oxford: Nuffield Coll., 1999.

Bulow, Jeremy, and Roberts, John. 'The Simple Economics of Optimal Auctions.' *J.P.E.* 97 (October 1989): 1060–90.

Burkart, Mike. 'Initial Shareholdings and Overbidding in Takeover Contests.' *J. Finance* 50 (December 1995): 1491–1515.

Chowdhry, Bhagwan, and Jegadeesh, Narasimhan. 'Pre-Tender Offer Share Acquisition Strategy in Takeovers.' *J. Financial and Quantitative Analysis* 29 (March 1994): 117–29.

——, and Nanda, Vikram. 'The Strategic Role of Debt in Takeover Contests.' *J. Finance* 48 (June 1993): 731–45.

Cramton, Peter; Gibbons, Robert; and Klemperer, Paul. 'Dissolving a Partnership Efficiently.' *Econometrica* 55 (May 1987): 615–32.

Daniel, Kent, and Hirshleifer, David. 'A Theory of Costly Sequential Bidding.' Manuscript. Chicago: Univ. Chicago; Ann Arbor: Univ. Michigan, December 1995.

Eckbo, B. Espen, and Langohr, Herwig. 'Information Disclosure, Method of Payment, and Takeover Premiums: Public and Private Tender Offers in France.' *J. Financial Econ.* 24 (October 1989): 363–403.

Engelbrecht-Wiggans, Richard. 'Auctions with Price-Proportional Benefits to Bidders.' *Games and Econ. Behavior* 6 (May 1994): 339–46.

Franks, Julian R., and Harris, Robert S. 'Shareholder Wealth Effects of Corporate Take-overs: The U.K. Experience 1955–1985.' *J. Financial Econ.* 23 (August 1989): 225–49.

——, Mayer, Colin P., and Renneboog, Luc. 'Capital Structure, Ownership and Board Restructuring in Poorly Performing Companies.' Working paper. Oxford: Oxford Univ., 1997.

Freeman, Barry T. 'Friendly vs. Hostile: The Foothold Stake as a Signal of the Bidder's Intentions.' Working paper. Washington: Fed. Trade Comm., 1991.

Grossman, Sanford J., and Hart, Oliver D. 'Takeover Bids, the Free-Rider Problem, and the Theory of the Corporation.' *Bell J. Econ.* 11 (Spring 1980): 42–64.

Hirshleifer, David. 'Mergers and Acquisitions: Strategic and Informational Issues.' In *Finance*, edited by Robert A. Jarrow, Vojislav Maksimovic, and W. T. Ziemba. 3d ed. Handbooks in Operations Research and Management Science, vol. 9. Amsterdam: North-Holland, 1995.

——, and Titman, Sheridan. 'Share Tendering Strategies and the Success of Hostile Take-over Bids.' *J.P.E.* 98 (April 1990): 295–324.

Jarrell, Gregg A., and Poulsen, Annette B. 'Stock Trading before the Announcement of Tender Offers: Insider Trading or Market Anticipation?' *J. Law, Econ., and Organization* 5 (Fall 1989): 225–48.

Jenkinson, Tim, and Ljungqvist, Alexander. 'Hostile Stakes and the Role of Banks in German Corporate Governance.' Working paper. Oxford: Oxford Univ., 1997.

Jennings, Robert H., and Mazzeo, Michael A. 'Competing Bids, Target Management Resistance, and the Structure of Takeover Bids.' *Rev. Financial Studies* 6 (Winter 1993): 883–909.

Kahan, Marcel, and Klausner, Michael. 'Lockups and the Market for Corporate Control.' *Stanford Law Rev.* 48 (July 1996): 1539–71.

Klemperer, Paul. 'Auctions with Almost Common Values: The 'Wallet Game' and Its Applications.' *European Econ. Rev.* 42 (May 1998): 757–69.

——. 'Auction Theory: A Guide to the Literature.' *J. Econ. Surveys* 13 (June 1999). (*a*)

——. *The Economic Theory of Auctions.* Cheltenham, U.K.: Elgar, 1999. (*b*)

Loughran, Tim, and Vijh, Anand M. 'The Form of Payment and Post-acquisition Returns of Mergers and Tender Offers.' Manuscript. Iowa City: Univ. Iowa, 1996.

McAfee, R. Preston, and McMillan, John. 'Bidding Rings.' *A.E.R.* 82 (June 1992): 579–99.

——, Vincent, Daniel, Williams, Michael A., and Havens, Melanie Williams. 'Collusive Bidding in Hostile Takeovers.' *J. Econ. and Management Strategy* 2 (Winter 1993): 449–82.

Milgrom, Paul R. 'Rational Expectations, Information Acquisition, and Competitive Bidding.' *Econometrica* 49 (July 1981): 921–43.

Myerson, Roger B. 'Optimal Auction Design.' *Math. Operations Res.* 6 (February 1981): 58–73.

Rau, Raghavendra P., and Vermaelen, Theo. 'Glamour, Value and the Post-acquisition Performance of Acquiring Firms.' Working paper. Paris: INSEAD, 1996.

Riley, John G., and Samuelson, William F. 'Optimal Auctions.' *A.E.R.* 71 (June 1981): 381–92.

Schwert, G. William. 'Markup Pricing in Mergers and Acquisitions.' *J. Financial Econ.* 41 (June 1996): 153–92.

Shleifer, Andrei, and Vishny, Robert W. 'Large Shareholders and Corporate Control.' *J.P.E.* 94, no. 3, pt. 1 (June 1986): 461–88.

Singh, Rajdeep. 'Takeover Bidding with Toeholds: The Case of the Owner's Curse.' *Rev. Financial Studies* 11 (Winter 1998): 679–704.

Stulz, René M.; Walkling, Ralph A.; and Song, Moon H. 'The Distribution of Target Ownership and the Division of Gains in Successful Takeovers.' *J. Finance* 45 (July 1990): 817–33.

U.K. Parliament. Monopolies and Mergers Commission. *British Sky Broadcasting Group plc and Manchester United PLC: A Revort on the Proposed Merger.* Cm. 4305. April 1999.

Walkling, Ralph A. 'Predicting Tender Offer Success: A Logistic Analysis.' *J. Financial and Quantitative Analysis* 20 (December 1985): 461–78.

——, and Long, Michael S. 'Agency Theory, Managerial Welfare, and Takeover Bid Resistance.' *Rand J. Econ.* 15 (Spring 1984): 54–68.

5

Underpricing and Entrepreneurial Wealth Losses in IPOs: Theory and Evidence

MICHEL A. HABIB AND ALEXANDER P. LJUNGQVIST

Why are some initial public offerings (IPOs) more underpriced than others? For instance, why do IPOs by companies with dot-com in their names suffer average underpricing that is nearly eight times the U.S. average of 13%? Why are Chinese IPOs underpriced by 42%, whereas Malaysian IPOs are underpriced by 6%? And why has average underpricing in Germany quadrupled since the introduction of the *Neuer Markt* in March 1997?[1]

The theoretical literature on IPO underpricing suggests a number of possible answers: Some IPOs are more underpriced than others because there is greater asymmetry of information, more valuation uncertainty, greater risk of lawsuits, and so on.[2]

Although we do not deny that any or all these factors may be at work, we suggest a more fundamental, non-mutually exclusive reason: some IPOs are more underpriced than others because their owners have less reason to care about underpricing. We argue that the extent to which owners care about underpricing depends on how much they sell at the IPO.[3] Owners who sell very few shares suffer only marginally from underpricing. Conversely, the more shares they sell, the greater their incentive to decrease underpricing. As a consequence, we expect that the degree of equilibrium underpricing depends on the extent of insider selling. To return to our examples, the owners of a typical U.S. IPO sell nearly five times more equity than the average dot-com IPO; Malaysian owners sell fifty-eight times more equity in IPOs than do their Chinese counterparts; and the

---

[1] Averages quoted are based on Jenkinson, et al. (1999) and Securities Data Corporation data.

[2] For a survey of these and other reasons for underpricing, see Jenkinson and Ljungqvist (1996). Of course, internet IPOs could be more underpriced due to hype, Chinese IPOs due to political risk, and German IPOs due to a change in the type of business taken public.

[3] How much owners care about underpricing also depends on how many new shares they issue at the IPO, because new shares sold at a discount dilute the owners' stake. For ease of exposition, we mainly discuss the sale of old shares in this introduction. Our formal analysis considers both new and old shares.

companies going public on Germany's *Neuer Markt* sell only half as much equity as do companies on Germany's more established marketplaces.

Controlling for the owners' incentives to decrease underpricing in turn helps us understand the choices they make when going public. To illustrate, in the U.S. and Canada, issuers can choose between a best-efforts offering (which is cheap in terms of cash expenses, but typically leads to high underpricing) and a firm-commitment book-building (which is expensive in terms of fees but leads to lower underpricing). Similarly, a German high-tech company can choose to go public domestically, or obtain a listing on NASDAQ, which will cost more but may result in lower underpricing if U.S. banks and investors are better able to value high-tech companies. Issuers can choose to hire a top-flight investment bank, at a higher fee, and benefit from the quality certification such a bank may provide, or they can hire the cheapest bank available.[4] They can similarly choose different auditors or lawyers based on reputation and certification considerations and different levels of voluntary disclosure based on competitive considerations.[5]

These examples highlight the fact that issuers can, to some extent, make costly choices that lead to lower expected underpricing. In other words, there may be trade-offs between what we label the promotion costs of going public and underpricing. Combining this view with our claim that issuers care about underpricing primarily to the extent that they participate in the offering, we predict that the more issuers plan to sell at the IPO the more they rationally decide to spend when going public. Thus, firm-commitment offerings should, on average, be most attractive for larger issues; a NASDAQ listing will appeal to German high-tech entrepreneurs who plan to cash out; hiring a top-flight investment bank or auditor will be worthwhile for larger issues; and greater voluntary disclosure will be desirable if the benefit from lower underpricing outweighs the competitive disadvantage.

In this chapter, we formalize, develop, and test the ideas that underlie the preceding discussion. There are two main premises to our analysis. The first is that owners care about underpricing to the extent that they stand to lose from it, and that any such losses are proportional to the number of primary (new) and secondary (old) shares being sold. The second is that issuers can affect the level of underpricing by promoting their issues. We assume that issuers choose between different promotion strategies as illustrated in our previous examples. It is clearly impracticable to attempt to capture all the various possible combinations of promotion strategies, such as underwriter, auditor, and lawyer reputations; target investment audience; extent of road shows; multiple listings possibly in different countries; and so on. Instead, we measure the total cost of each issuer's chosen

---

[4] Dunbar (2000) shows that U.S. banks that cut their fees gain market share, indicating that issuers are at least partly influenced in their underwriter choice by the fees they are quoted. Interestingly, he also finds that top-flight banks can gain market share despite charging abnormally high fees, indicating that issuers expect some offsetting benefit from hiring such banks.

[5] Palmiter (1999) notes in his abstract, "There is strong evidence that ... issuers ... disclose at levels beyond that mandated [by the Securities Act of 1933]—as a private, contractual matter."

promotion strategy and compare this cost across issuers. Total promotion costs include the fees paid to underwriters, auditors and lawyers; the cost of road shows; listing fees, and so on, but exclude management time, which cannot easily be measured.[6]

For promotion costs to affect underpricing presumes that promoting an issue can be an alternative to underpricing the issue. This was recognized more than a decade ago by Allen and Faulhaber (1989), Booth and Smith (1986), Carter and Manaster (1990), and Welch (1989). Although their focus was on signaling issue quality through underpricing, Allen and Faulhaber (1989, p. 305) and Welch (1989, pp. 438–439) noted in passing that signaling could also be accomplished through the choice of underwriter and auditor and through advertising, respectively. Carter and Manaster (1990) derived and tested an inverse relation between underpricing and underwriter reputation,[7] which combined Beatty and Ritter's (1986) inverse relation between underpricing and issue quality with Titman and Trueman's (1986) positive relation between issue quality and underwriter reputation. Finally, Booth and Smith (1986, p. 267) specifically discussed the trade-off between the cost of certifying an issue's quality and underpricing: "The more costly is external certification relative to the benefit, the more likely the stock or risky debt to be issued at a discount. The underwriter will incur direct costs of certification only to the point where marginal cost of certification equals marginal benefit so that net issue proceeds are maximized."

Generalizing Booth and Smith's point, we can view promotional activities and underpricing as substitutes. Issuers are then faced with a multidimensional problem when taking a firm public. In addition to the level of underpricing, issuers must choose an optimal promotion strategy, which involves deciding which underwriter and auditor to choose and how much to spend on advertising, as well as all the other promotional activities that may help reduce underpricing.[8] We examine the optimal mix of these activities and show how the choice between underpricing and promotion varies with the number of primary and secondary shares sold at the offering.

We use a simple model based on Benveniste and Wilhelm's (1990) adaptation of the Rock (1986) model to analyze the problem.[9] Our purpose in using a formal model is twofold. First, we use the model to verify our main intuition, specifically that issuers will incur greater promotion costs when selling more shares. An issuer

---

[6] Promotion costs exclude the cost of the underwriting cover, which is a compensation for risk. We return to this distinction in Section 2.

[7] This inverse relation has recently been questioned by Beatty and Welch (1996), who found a positive relation between underpricing and underwriter reputation in the 1990s. We reexamine this issue in Section 3.3.

[8] Of course, the choice of underwriter is not entirely at the discretion of the issuer, for the underwriter may refuse to take part in the offering. But the fact remains that the issuer has some choice in choosing an underwriter. For evidence of such choice, see Dunbar (2000) and note 4.

[9] We note that our use of the Rock (1986) adverse selection rationale for underpricing is without loss of generality. All that is needed for our argument to hold is (i) a reason for underpricing and (ii) one or more alternatives to underpricing.

selling more shares clearly stands to lose more than an issuer selling fewer shares for a given level of underpricing. The former therefore has a greater incentive to incur the promotion costs that we argue decrease underpricing. In the Rock (1986) model, underpricing is necessary to induce uninformed investors to take part in the offering despite the adverse selection problem introduced by the presence of informed investors. Promoting the issue serves to increase the fraction of uninformed investors taking part in the offering (Carter and Manaster, 1990). Promoting the issue, therefore decreases the extent of the adverse selection problem, thereby decreasing the necessary amount of underpricing.[10]

Second, we use the model to derive a number of testable implications and optimality restrictions. Some testable implications are very intuitive. For example, as noted above, promotion costs should increase in the number of shares sold. Incurring these promotion costs is worthwhile only if they decrease underpricing. Underpricing should therefore decrease in promotion costs. Other testable implications are less intuitive. Consider how underpricing varies with the number of shares sold. Our earlier discussion suggests that the incentive to reduce underpricing should be greater for issuers selling more shares. Therefore, the optimal combination of underpricing and promotion should involve higher promotion costs and lower underpricing for large issues than for small issues. This intuition implies that underpricing should decrease in the number of shares sold. However, there are possibly offsetting effects, depending on the origin of the shares sold. Where the IPO consists of primary shares, the costs of promotion are borne by the company in the first instance, thereby reducing both the aftermarket share price and the offer price by the same amount. But because most IPOs are underpriced, the offer price is reduced by more in percentage terms than is the aftermarket share price, resulting in greater underpricing. This second effect works in the opposite direction to the first effect whose intuition we described earlier. Where the IPO consists of secondary shares, there is no second effect because the costs are borne by the selling shareholders. Mixed offerings are more complicated. Tracing these effects cannot easily be achieved in the absence of a formal model.

The optimization problem faced by the issuer imposes testable restrictions on the regression equations we derive. We claim that the issuer acts to minimize wealth losses from going public. These equal the sum of the promotion costs incurred and the losses from underpricing and dilution and should be minimized through the choice of promotion costs.[11] An increase in promotion costs has two effects on wealth losses: (i) a direct effect, which increases wealth losses as promotion costs are part of wealth losses; and (ii) an indirect effect, which decreases wealth losses by decreasing underpricing. Optimality requires these two

---

[10] We formalize this argument in Section 1.

[11] For a discussion of the difference between underpricing and wealth losses, see Barry (1989) and Brennan and Franks (1997).

opposing effects to be equal at the margin. It therefore restricts the coefficient of a regression of wealth losses on promotion costs to be zero.

Our empirical findings support the predictions of our model. Using a large sample of U.S. IPOs from 1991 to 1995, we find that underpricing decreases in promotion costs, and promotion costs increase in the number of shares sold. Furthermore, underpricing decreases in insider selling, as suggested by our earlier discussion of dot-com IPOs. We also find that issuers in our sample are optimizing: at the margin, each dollar spent on promotion reduces wealth losses by 98 cents, indicating that the marginal cost of promotion equals the marginal benefit of reduced wealth losses. Finally, we show that a particular dimension of issuers' promotion strategy, the choice of underwriter, is related to how many shares are sold. Not controlling for this endogeneity of underwriter choice seriously biases the estimated effect of underwriter reputation on underpricing, which seems to account for the counterintuitive positive relation between underpricing and underwriter reputation recently documented by Beatty and Welch (1996) and others. We conduct numerous robustness checks, which leave our basic results unchanged.

In light of our results, we argue that recognizing issuers' ability, and incentives, to make choices when going public matters. Consider an empirical test of Booth and Smith's (1986) certification hypothesis, which predicts that reputable intermediaries, such as investment bankers, auditors, or venture capitalists, can certify to investors that a given IPO is not overpriced. If empirical evidence shows that venture-backed IPOs are less underpriced than nonventure-backed IPOs (Megginson and Weiss 1991), can we infer that investors do in fact credit venture capitalists with certification power? Not necessarily, for it is possible that venture-backed IPOs happen to have a greater incentive to reduce underpricing, by means of their promotion choices, because their owners sold more equity.[12] As a consequence, we argue that empirical tests of IPO underpricing theories should be conditioned on the owners' incentives to take costly actions that reduce underpricing. Ignoring these incentives can lead to omitted variable bias, resulting in incorrect inferences being drawn from empirical work.

1. MODEL AND TESTABLE IMPLICATIONS

1.1 Outline of the Model

We briefly outline the main features of our model before proceeding to its detailed analysis. Our model shares Rock's (1986) adverse selection rationale for underpricing. There are two types of investors. Informed investors know the quality of an issue and naturally subscribe only to "good" issues. Uninformed investors cannot distinguish between "good" and "bad" issues, and so suffer from the winner's curse: They are likely to be allocated a disproportionate share of "bad"

---

[12] Indeed, Table 3 in Megginson and Weiss (1991) suggests that venture-backed firms in the 1980s issued 36% more shares on average than did nonventure-backed firms.

issues, to which informed investors do not subscribe. To induce uninformed investors to take part in the offering, it is therefore necessary to sell the issue at a price below that warranted by its intrinsic quality. As the winner's curse increases in proportion to the fraction of informed investors with whom good issues are shared, so does the necessary amount of underpricing.

The fractions of informed and uninformed investors are exogenously fixed in Rock (1986), but in our model they can be endogenously determined by the issuer. Specifically, we assume that the issuer can increase the fraction of uninformed investors participating in the offering by incurring greater promotion costs. For example, the issuer can, at a cost, hire a more reputable underwriter, whose greater reputational capital will encourage more uninformed investors to take part in the offering.[13] Underpricing decreases as a result.

Though undoubtedly beneficial to the issuer, the decrease in underpricing requires the issuer to incur higher promotion costs. These may offset the benefit of lower underpricing. How the issuer chooses between underpricing and promotion costs naturally depends on how a given combination of promotion costs and the associated underpricing affects wealth losses from going public. This, in turn, depends on the issuer's participation in, and the dilution resulting from the offering.

1.2 The Model

Consider an entrepreneur who wishes to sell part of a firm and/or to raise new capital through an IPO. The entrepreneur owns all N_o original shares of the firm. She sells $N_{o,s} \geq 0$ original (secondary) shares and retains $N_{o,r} = N_o - N_{o,s}$ shares. She issues and sells $N_n \geq 0$ new (primary) shares.

Let a share have value P_G and P_B with equal probability, with $P_G > P_B$. Prior to the IPO, expected share value is $\overline{P} = (P_G + P_B)/2$ with variance $\sigma^2 = \frac{1}{4}\Delta^2$, where $\Delta \equiv P_G - P_B$. Informed investors, who constitute a fraction β_I of the total population of investors, know the true value. Uninformed investors, who constitute a fraction $\beta_U = 1 - \beta_I$, and the entrepreneur do not.

As discussed in Section 1.1, the fractions β_I and β_U depend on the promotion costs incurred by the entrepreneur. Specifically, $\beta_U \equiv \beta_U(\exp)$, where exp denotes the promotion cost per original share. We assume $\beta_U'(\exp) > 0$ and $\beta_U''(\exp) < 0$: higher promotion costs induce more uninformed investors to take part in the offering but at a decreasing rate.

As is the case in practice, we assume that a fraction α of total promotion costs $\mathrm{EXP} \equiv N_o \exp$ is paid by the firm and the remainder $1 - \alpha$ directly by the entrepreneur.[14] $\alpha = N_n/(N_n + N_{o,s}) = n_n/(n_n + n_{o,s})$, as the fraction of the costs paid by the firm is proportional to the firm's fraction of the proceeds from the

---

[13] See Booth and Smith (1986), Carter and Manaster (1990), and Titman and Trueman (1986). For contrary evidence, see Beatty and Welch (1996). We return to this issue in Section 3.3.

[14] Throughout, we will use lowercase letters to denote variables normalized by the number of original shares N_o and capitals to denote untransformed variables.

IPO.[15] $n_{o,s} \equiv N_{o,s}/N_o$ is the number of secondary shares sold normalized by the total number of original shares, and $n_n \equiv N_n/N_o$ is the normalized number of primary shares. We refer to $n_{o,s}$ as the issuer's participation ratio and to n_n as the dilution factor. We use normalized variables because the absolute number of shares is arbitrary: there is evidence that issuers split their shares before an IPO to generate offer prices within certain ranges.[16]

The $N_{o,s}$ secondary shares and the N_n primary shares are sold at a price P_0. Following the IPO, the value of a share of the firm is $P_{1,G} = (N_o P_G + N_n P_0 - \alpha N_o \exp)/(N_o + N_n)$ or $P_{1,B} = (N_o P_B + N_n P_0 - \alpha N_o \exp)/(N_o + N_n)$ with equal probability. Post-IPO, a share therefore has price $\overline{P}_1 = 1/(1 + n_n)\overline{P} + n_n/(1 + n_n)P_0 - (\alpha \cdot \exp)/(1 + n_n)$ and variance $\sigma_1^2 = 1/(1 + n_n)^2 \sigma^2$.

The price P_0 at which shares are sold to investors must be such that uninformed investors expect to break even on average, for they otherwise would not subscribe to the IPO. P_0 is therefore such that $(1/2)\beta_U(P_{1,G} - P_0) + (1/2)(P_{1,B} - P_0) = 0 \iff P_0 = (\beta_U P_G + P_B)/(1 + \beta_U) - \alpha \cdot \exp < \overline{P}$, where the ultimate equality is true by substituting the values of $P_{1,G}$ and $P_{1,B}$ and the inequality is true by noting that $\beta_U < 1$. As noted by Rock (1986), shares must be sold at a discount to their expected pre-IPO value to compensate uninformed investors for the adverse selection introduced by the presence of informed investors.[17]

Shares are also sold at a discount to their expected post-IPO value, $\overline{P}_1$. This can be seen by substituting the expression for P_0 into that for $\overline{P}_1$ to obtain

$$\overline{P} = \frac{1}{1 + n_n}\overline{P} + \frac{n_n}{1 + n_n}\frac{\beta_U P_G + P_B}{1 + \beta_U} - \alpha \cdot \exp$$
$$> \frac{\beta_U P_G + P_B}{1 + \beta_U} - \alpha \cdot \exp = P_0. \tag{1}$$

In common with the IPO literature, underpricing is defined as $UP \equiv (\overline{P}_1 - P_0)/P_0$. The normalized wealth loss suffered by the issuer due to such underpricing, the resulting dilution in the stake (because $\overline{P}_1 < \overline{P}$ as $P_0 < \overline{P}$) and the share of the promotion costs is

$$\text{wl} \equiv \frac{1}{N_o}(N_{o,r}(\overline{P} - \overline{P}_1) + N_{o,s}(\overline{P} - P_0) + (1 - \alpha)N_o \exp)$$
$$= \left(\frac{n_{o,s} + n_n}{1 + n_n}\right)\left(\overline{P} - \frac{\beta_U P_G + P_B}{1 + \beta_U}\right) + \exp. \tag{2}$$

Note that the issuer bears the entirety of the promotion cost exp.

[15] Of course, the entrepreneur, as the firm's original owner, ultimately bears the entirety of the promotion costs EXP. But the distinction between the fraction of promotion costs that is paid directly by the entrepreneur and that paid indirectly through the entrepreneur's ownership of the firm has important implications for our comparative statics results, as Proposition 2 will show.

[16] The median offer price in the U.S. has been virtually unchanged at around $11 since the 1970s even though median gross proceeds have more than tripled, from $8 million in the 1970s to $28 million in the early 1990s.

[17] Note the presence of the $\alpha \cdot \exp$ term: the issue price is further decreased by the fraction of promotion costs that are paid by the firm.

1.3 Results and Discussion

The purpose of our analysis is to examine the variation in the underpricing return UP and the wealth loss wl as a function of the participation ratio $n_{o,s}$, the dilution factor n_n, the uncertainty parameter Δ, and the promotion cost exp. The issuer minimizes wealth losses from going public. She, therefore, solves the optimization problem

$$\underset{\exp}{\text{Min}} \; \text{wl} \iff \underset{\exp}{\text{Max}} \left(\frac{n_{o,s} + n_n}{1 + n_n} \right) \left(\frac{\beta_U P_G + P_B}{1 + \beta_U} \right) - \exp,$$

which has first-order condition

$$\left(\frac{n_{o,s} + n_n}{1 + n_n} \right) \frac{\Delta}{(1 + \beta_U)^2} \beta'_U(\exp) - 1 = 0. \tag{3}$$

The issuer's choice of exp clearly depends on $n_{o,s}$, n_n, and Δ. Indeed, we have:

Proposition 1. *The promotion cost of the IPO, exp, increases in the participation ratio $n_{o,s}$, the dilution factor n_n, and the uncertainty parameter Δ.*

Proof. Immediate from equation (3). □

The results for the participation ratio and the dilution factor confirm our informal discussion in the introduction and in Section 1.1: an issuer who sells a greater fraction of a firm or issues more new shares has a greater incentive to control wealth losses from underpricing. She does so by increasing promotion costs. She also increases promotion costs in response to greater uncertainty because, as we show in Proposition 2, underpricing and hence wealth losses increase in uncertainty.

We can now establish our main result.

Proposition 2. *The wealth loss wl increases in the participation ratio $n_{o,s}$, the dilution factor n_n, and the uncertainty parameter Δ. It is invariant to the promotion cost exp in equilibrium. The underpricing return UP decreases in the promotion cost exp and in the participation ratio $n_{o,s}$. Its variation in the dilution factor n_n is indeterminate. It increases in the uncertainty parameter Δ when controlling for the promotion cost exp, but its variation in Δ is otherwise indeterminate.*

Proof. See Appendix. □

The results for the variation of the wealth loss in the participation ratio, the dilution factor, and the uncertainty parameter are similar to and share the same intuition as those for the promotion cost in Proposition 1. The invariance of the wealth loss to the promotion cost in equilibrium is nothing but the reflection of the zero first-order condition at the optimum. Recall that the first premise of our analysis implies that the issuer chooses promotion costs to minimize wealth loss from going public.

That underpricing decreases in the promotion cost confirms the second premise. The issuer can affect underpricing through the choice of promotion cost. The decrease of underpricing in the participation ratio combines this inverse relation between underpricing and promotion costs with the proportional relation between the promotion cost of the IPO and the participation ratio established in Proposition 1.

That underpricing does not necessarily decrease in the dilution factor, despite the similarity between the dilution factor and the participation ratio, is a consequence of the offsetting effect of the dilution factor on underpricing through the fraction α of the promotion cost that is paid by the issuer. As can be seen from inequality (1), both the issue price and the post-IPO price decrease in α, by the same amount $\alpha \cdot$ exp. This identical absolute effect translates into a greater relative effect on the issue price, which is smaller than the post-IPO price. This increases underpricing.

The proportional relation between underpricing and uncertainty is a well-known result. As in Beatty and Ritter (1986), uncertainty increases the extent of the adverse selection problem faced by uninformed investors. They consequently require a greater discount to be induced to take part in the offering. However, this argument assumes promotion costs are fixed. It does not recognize the issuer's incentive to increase these costs for the purpose of countering the increase in the discount granted uninformed investors. Extending the argument to incorporate the issuer's incentive to increase promotion costs reveals two distinct effects of uncertainty on underpricing: a direct effect, which increases underpricing, and an indirect effect through promotion costs. The variation of underpricing in the combination of these two effects is indeterminate, for the direct effect increases underpricing whereas the indirect effect decreases it.

1.4 Empirical Implications

From the results of Section 1.3, we can write our empirical implications as follows:

1. Wealth losses increase in the participation ratio, the dilution factor, and uncertainty. They are invariant to promotion costs in equilibrium.
2. Promotion costs increase in the participation ratio, the dilution factor, and uncertainty.
3. Underpricing decreases in promotion costs and in the participation ratio. It is indeterminate in the dilution factor. It increases in uncertainty when controlling for promotion costs, but is indeterminate otherwise.

The intuition behind these empirical implications is as in Section 1.3. For a given level of underpricing, wealth losses increase in the number of primary and secondary shares sold. Wealth losses increase in uncertainty because the direct effect of uncertainty is to increase underpricing, which increases wealth losses. Promotion costs are chosen to minimize wealth losses. In equilibrium, wealth losses are therefore invariant to promotion costs.

Promotion costs increase in the participation ratio, the dilution factor, and uncertainty because wealth losses increase in these three variables. The issuer counters the increased wealth losses by increasing promotion costs.

Underpricing decreases in promotion costs because promotion costs increase the fraction of uninformed investors participating in the offering. Underpricing decreases in the participation ratio because underpricing decreases in promotion costs and promotion costs increase in the participation ratio. A similar effect for the dilution factor is countered by the increase in the fraction of promotion costs paid by the firm. For a given level of promotion costs, underpricing increases in uncertainty, but the increase in promotion costs brought about by increased uncertainty counters that first effect.

Recalling that exp, UP, wl, $n_{o,s}$, n_n, and Δ denote promotion costs, underpricing, wealth losses, the participation ratio, the dilution factor, and uncertainty, respectively, we can write the regression equations corresponding to the preceding empirical implications as

$$\exp = \gamma_0 + \gamma_1^+ n_{o,s} + \gamma_2^+ n_n + \gamma_3^+ \Delta + \epsilon \tag{exp1}$$

$$
\begin{aligned}
UP &= \delta_0 + \delta_1^- n_{o,s} + \delta_2^? n_n + \delta_3^+ \Delta + \delta_4^- \exp + \zeta \\
&= (\delta_0 + \delta_4 \cdot \gamma_0) + (\delta_1^- + \delta_4^- \cdot \gamma_1^+) n_{o,s} + (\delta_2^? + \delta_4^- \cdot \gamma_2^+) n_n \\
&\quad + (\delta_3^+ + \delta_4^- \cdot \gamma_3^+)\Delta + \delta_4 \epsilon + \zeta
\end{aligned}
\tag{UP1}
$$

$$\equiv \pi_0 + \pi_1^- n_{o,s} + \pi_2^? n_n + \pi_3^? \Delta + \nu, \tag{UP2}$$

and

$$\mathrm{wl} = \varphi_0 + \varphi_1^+ n_{o,s} + \varphi_2^+ n_n + \varphi_3^+ \Delta + \varphi_4^0 \exp + \eta, \tag{wl1}$$

where ε, ζ, ν, and η are error terms. The signs of the coefficients are as predicted in Propositions 1 and 2 and points 1 to 3 above. Note that the slope coefficient φ_4, which measures the marginal effect of promotion costs on wealth losses, is zero by virtue of the first-order condition for optimality.

There are two nested underpricing equations. Regression (UP2) is obtained from regression (UP1) by substituting regression (exp1) for exp. The two regressions differ in that the slope coefficients of (UP1) constitute partial derivatives, whereas those of (UP2) are total derivatives, which incorporate both the direct effect of the participation ratio, the dilution factor, and uncertainty on underpricing, and their indirect effect through the promotion cost exp. This combination of direct and indirect effects gives rise to the following cross-equation restrictions:

$$H_{0,R1a} : \pi_1 \equiv \delta_1^- + \delta_4^- \gamma_1^+ \implies \pi_1 < \delta_1;$$
$$H_{0,R1b} : \pi_2 \equiv \delta_2^? + \delta_4^- \gamma_2^+ \implies \pi_2 < \delta_2; \qquad \text{(R1)}$$
$$H_{0,R1c} : \pi_3 \equiv \delta_3^+ + \delta_4^- \gamma_3^+ \implies \pi_3 < \delta_3.$$

The intuition is clear. The indirect effect through exp unambiguously decreases underpricing. The slope coefficients that combine both effects should therefore be algebrically smaller than the slope coefficients that include the direct effect alone.

Before we can estimate our regressions, we need to be careful about which variables we treat as exogenous. Clearly, UP and wl each depend on exp, and all three variables depend on $n_{o,s}$, n_n, and Δ. In our empirical work, we will therefore treat exp, UP, and wl as endogenous and $n_{o,s}$, n_n, and Δ as exogenous. We first outline how we deal with endogeneity and then discuss how we test our exogeneity assumption. The usual way to deal with the joint endogeneity of exp, UP, and wl is to use two-stage least squares (2SLS) or generalized method of moments (GMM). However, the two systems of equations (exp1) and (UP1), and (exp1) and (wl1), each form what is called a fully recursive triangular system. Such systems can be written as

$$y_1 = x'\lambda_1 + \epsilon_1$$
$$y_2 = x'\lambda_2 + \mu_{12}y_1 + \epsilon_2$$

In our model, y_1 equals exp; the vector x consists of $n_{o,s}$, n_n, and Δ; and y_2 equals UP when considering regression (UP1) and wl when considering regression (wl1). Regression (UP2) can be viewed as the reduced form of regression (UP1).

By repeated substitution, it can easily be shown that triangular systems can be consistently estimated using equation-by-equation ordinary least squares (OLS), as long as the errors are uncorrelated across regressions (see Greene, 1997, p. 736f; the proof is in Hausman (1978)). We test and fail to reject this restriction in Section 3.1. This confirms the validity of the triangular form assumed, suggests there are no omitted variables common to the regressions, and justifies our use of equation-by-equation OLS. In a previous version of the article, we also reported 2SLS and GMM estimates that were statistically identical to the OLS estimates reported below.

Our model does not endogenize the decision of how many shares to float, so we treat $n_{o,s}$ and n_n as exogenous. This is not to claim that issuers do not choose the offer size, merely that the determinants of offer size are uncorrelated with our variables of interest. If true, it allows us to look at the choice of promotion strategies and wealth loss minimization *conditional on the issuer's choice of offer size*. If not true, our empirical model will be misspecified and our coefficient estimates biased. There are plausible reasons to suppose that offer size may be correlated with our variables of interest. For instance, issuers might use offer size alongside underpricing to signal inside information, as in the signaling models of Allen and Faulhaber (1989), Grinblatt and Hwang (1989), and Welch (1989). Alternatively, issuers might adjust offer size in the light of information gathered during book-building.[18] We show in Section 3.2 that our decision to treat the size of the offer as exogenous can be justified by means of a Hausman (1978) specification test.

2. THE DATA

2.1 Data Sources

Our empirical work uses a sample of U.S. IPOs floated on NASDAQ between 1991 and 1995.[19] Securities Data Company's (SDC) New Issues database lists 1409 NASDAQ IPOs during that period, excluding companies issuing American depository receipts or noncommon shares, real-estate and other investment trusts, and unit offerings. We lost thirty companies for which data on $N_{o,s}$, N_o, N_n, or promotion costs exp was unavailable and excluded three companies that increased their capital at the IPO more than 100-fold.[20] The final sample consists of 1376 companies.

Most cross-sectional data is taken from SDC's database. First-day trading prices come from the Center for Research in Security Prices (CRSP) tapes. Information on overallotment option exercise was gathered from Standard & Poor's *Register of Corporations*, news sources, and subsequent 10-Qs and 10-Ks because we find, as do Ellis et al. (2000), that SDC's exercise information is reported with error. Information about company age at flotation comes from S&P's *Register*. To measure underwriter quality, we use the "tombstone" underwriter reputation rank variable developed by Carter and Manaster (1990), as updated for the 1990s by Carter et al. (1998).

2.2 Variable Definitions and Model Specifications

The three dependent variables in our model are the underpricing return, estimated from the IPO price to the first-day closing price; wl = wealth losses per old share, as calculated in Equation (2); and exp = normalized promotion costs, taken from the SDC's New Issues database. exp includes auditing, legal, road show, exchange, printing, and other expenses of the offering as well as accountable and non-accountable underwriter expenses, but not the underwriter spread, which we view as a payment for underwriting risk and thus not a choice variable.

---

[18] We thank Sheridan Titman for suggesting this alternative explanation.

[19] In a previous draft, we also used Ritter's (1991) sample covering IPOs from 1975 to 1984. Both samples yield similar results.

[20] Their dilution factors ranged from a 575-fold to a 4025-fold increase in shares outstanding. Ratios that high are invariably due to very low reported preflotation N_o and could conceivably be due to data errors. We tried—unsuccessfully—to verify this by means of a Nexis news search. The exclusion is clearly ad hoc, but we note that it in fact *weakens* our empirical results.

The specification of most of our regressors, such as the participation ratio and the dilution factor, is determined by our theoretical model. To control for ex ante uncertainty Δ, we use two alternative types of proxies. The first type is firm characteristics, specifically company age at flotation, the natural log of sales as a measure of firm size, and preflotation leverage ($= debt/[debt + equity]$) as reported by SDC. Prior studies suggest that younger and smaller companies are riskier and thus more underpriced (Ritter, 1984, 1991; Megginson and Weiss 1991), whereas the presence of credit relationships reduces uncertainty and required underpricing (James and Wier, 1990).[21]

The second type of proxy is derived from the put option nature of the underwriting contract. James (1992, p. 1876) argues, "The greater the uncertainty concerning firm value, the greater the risk borne by underwriters in a firm commitment offer. Therefore, a positive relation is expected between [gross] spreads and measures of uncertainty." There is ample empirical support for James's hypothesis that spreads and uncertainty are positively related; see James (1992) on IPOs, Stoll (1976), Booth and Smith (1986), and Gande et al. (1999) on seasoned equity offerings; Dyl and Joehnk (1976) on underwritten corporate bond issues; and Sorensen (1980) on municipal bonds. It seems likely that underwriters are better placed to estimate ex ante uncertainty than an investor who merely observes company age, size, and the existence of credit relationships. We thus expect spreads to be incrementally informative about valuation uncertainty.

Information about gross spreads is readily available in SDC's database. However, instead of the gross spread, we use only one of its components, the so-called underwriting fee. There are two reasons for this. First, the gross spread compensates the investment bank for more than its underwriting services. A narrower proxy, the underwriting fee charged for the underwriting cover, should hence be more informative about valuation uncertainty. Second, Chen and Ritter (2000) document a tendency for gross spreads to be exactly 7% for over 90% of medium-sized IPOs in the mid-to-late 1990s. Though this tendency is less pronounced in our (earlier) sample period, it still affects 60% of sample firms. Underwriting fees, on the other hand, are much less prone to clustering.[22]

We also control for the partial-adjustment phenomenon first documented by Hanley (1993), consistent with Benveniste and Spindt's (1989) prediction that expected underpricing, in a world of asymmetric information, is minimized when discounts are concentrated in states where investors provide strong indications of interest during the bank's promotion effort. Following Hanley, we control for investor interest by including a variable *partadj*, which equals the percentage adjustment between the midpoint of the indicative price range and the offer price. Finally, we control for the possibility of "hot" or "cold" IPO markets (Ritter 1984; Ibbotson et al. 1994) by including time dummies.

---

[21] Another popular proxy is offer size. We refrain from using it because Habib and Ljungqvist (1998) show that as a matter of identities, underpricing is strictly decreasing in offer size *even when holding risk constant*.

[22] Specifically, in our sample they are four times more variable than gross spreads.

2.3 Descriptive Statistics

Table 1 reports descriptive statistics on company (panel A) and offering (panel B) characteristics and the associated costs and wealth losses (panel C).

As in prior studies, the median issuer in panel A is a young company (8 years) with modest sales ($34.1 million) and little debt (5.7% leverage). The averages in each case are higher, indicating positive skewness. The median (average) amount raised in Panel B is $28.5 million ($36.8 million). Much of this represents a capital increase: on average, the original owners sell only 7% of their shares ($n_{o,s}$) while increasing shares outstanding by 50% (n_n). Purely secondary offerings are extremely rare, accounting for only eleven of the 1376 IPOs. Purely primary offerings, around half the sample, are much more common. The remainder combine primary and secondary offerings. The average gross spread (not shown) is 7.149% of the offer price, with a median of 7%. The component of the gross spread that we are interested in, the underwriting fee, averages 1.7%. The quality ranking of lead underwriters is extremely high, averaging 7.26 on Carter and Manaster's 0-9 scale.[23] The median of 8.75 is even higher. For comparison, the average and median rank in Ritter's (1991) sample of 1526 IPOs floated in 1975–1984 is only six. Both the median and the average company go public at a price equal to the midpoint of the filing range, which might thus be interpreted as an unbiased estimate of the offer price. Nonetheless, there is considerable learning: 25% of sample firms are priced below the low filing price, and 23% are priced above the high filing price. Underpricing averages 13.8% in our sample, in line with previous studies. Of the sample firms, 9.5% close strictly below the offer price, and 16.4% close exactly at the offer price. The remaining 74.1% are underpriced.

Wealth losses for the median issuer in panel C are $2.4 million, which include promotion costs of $650,000. Average wealth losses are higher, at $6.5 million, due to the presence of some highly underpriced offerings. On a per-share basis, the average (median) wealth loss is 107 ¢(54 ¢), 17 ¢(13 ¢) of which represents promotion expenses. The remainder is due to the effects of selling underpriced shares and suffering dilution on retained shares.

3. EMPIRICAL RESULTS

3.1 Regression Results

Table 2 presents the equation-by-equation least-squares results for the four regressions (exp1), (UP1), (UP2), and (wl1), adjusted for heteroscedasticity using White's (1980) heteroscedasticity-consistent covariance matrix. The first column estimates the determinants of promotion costs exp. The exp regression exhibits

---

[23] Of our sample firms, 182 use underwriters that are not ranked in Carter and Manaster (1990) or Carter et al. (1998). We inspect the banks they use, only one of which (J. P. Morgan) strikes us as obviously prestigious. We arbitrarily assign it a rank of 8. The remaining banks are assigned a rank of 0. Our results are robust to different treatments.

Table 1. *Descriptive sample statistics*

Variable description	Mean	Standard deviation	Median
Panel A: Company characteristics			
Age at IPO	14.2	19.7	8.0
Sales, in millions of $	79.9	190.3	34.1
Leverage, in %	17.4	23.6	5.7
Panel B: Offering characteristics			
Nominal gross proceeds, in millions of $	36.8	37.9	28.5
Preflotation number of shares	6,636,717	6,825,628	4,986,314
Number of secondary shares sold	424,407	908,219	0
Number of primary shares sold	2,505,365	1,966,985	2,150,000
Participation ratio, in %	7.0	11.9	0.0
Dilution factor, in %	50.1	46.7	42.4
Underwriting fee, in % of offer price	1.69	0.61	1.57
Carter–Manaster underwriter reputation rank	7.26	2.57	8.75
Partial adjustment, in %	0.19	20.08	0.00
Underpricing return, in %	13.8	20.3	7.1
Panel C: Promotion costs and wealth losses			
Wealth losses, in $	6,541,695	12,629,193	2,400,483
of which: promotion costs, in $	*739,000*	*486,872*	*650,000*
Wealth loss per old share, in cents	106.7	154.8	54.2
of which: promotion costs per old share, in cents	*16.6*	*15.6*	*13.0*

Note: The sample covers the 1376 firms floated on NASDAQ between 1991 and 1995. All $ amounts are in nominal terms. Panel A tabulates three company characteristics. Age is IPO year less founding year, taken from S&P's *Corporate Register* and is available for 1357 of the 1376 firms. Sales is annual net sales in the fiscal year prior to the IPO. Leverage is debt over debt plus equity. Panel B tabulates various offering characteristics. Nominal gross proceeds is $P_0(N_n + N_{o,s})$, where P_0 is the offer price and $(N_n + N_{o,s})$ is the sum of primary (new) and secondary (old) shares offered. The participation ratio $n_{o,s}$ is $N_{o,s}/N_o$, that is, the fraction of preflotation shares N_o sold in the IPO. The dilution factor is $n_n = N_n/N_o$, We excluded three firms from the data set for having dilution factors in excess of 10,000%; their inclusion would have strengthened our results. The underwriting fee is that component of the gross spread which represents compensation to the syndicate for providing underwriting cover. The Carter–Manaster (1990) ranks measure underwriter reputation on a scale from 0 (lowest) to 9 (highest). We use the updated ranks provided by Carter *et al.* (1998). Partial adjustment equals the percentage adjustment between the midpoint of the indicative price range and the offer price. Underpricing is $\overline{P}_1/P_0 - 1$, where $\overline{P}_1$ is the closing share price on the first day of trading, extracted from the daily CRSP tapes. Panel C computes marketing costs and wealth losses. The wealth loss per old share is wl in Equation (2), that is, the sum of wealth losses due to dilution, underpricing, and marketing costs per old share exp. Wealth losses are reported both in absolute terms and normalized by N_o. Promotion costs exp are taken from the SDC's New Issue database and include auditing, legal, road show, exchange, printing, and other expenses of the offering as well as accountable and nonaccountable underwriter expenses, but not the underwriter spread.

Table 2. *Ordinary least-squares regressions of promotion costs, underpricing, and wealth losses*

		Promotion costs exp (exp1)		Underpricing (UP1)		(UP2)		Wealth losses wl (wl1)
Constant		0.042**		0.187***		0.186***		0.877***
		0.016		*0.025*		*0.025*		*0.255*
$n_{o,s}$	γ_1	0.153***	δ_1	−0.055*	π_1	−0.071*	φ_1	1.367**
		0.020		*0.028*		*0.028*		*0.444*
n_n	γ_2	0.252***	δ_2	0.007	π_2	−0.023*	φ_2	0.847†
		0.020		*0.011*		*0.009*		*0.446*
exp			δ_4	−0.125***			φ_4	0.023
				0.033				*0.451*
gross proceeds		−0.001***						
		0.000						
partadj				0.509***		0.511***		3.501***
				0.040		*0.040*		*0.285*
Risk proxies	γ_3		δ_3		π_3		φ_3	
underwriting fee		0.009†		0.031**		0.029*		0.115
		0.005		*0.011*		*0.011*		*0.095*
age		−0.0001		−0.0004*		−0.0004*		−0.004**
		0.0001		*0.0002*		*0.0002*		*0.002*
ln(*sales*)		0.005*		−0.007*		−0.007*		−0.042
		0.002		*0.004*		*0.004*		*0.026*
leverage		0.0004		−0.068**		−0.068**		−0.421*
		0.013		*0.021*		*0.021*		*0.169*
Diagnostics								
Adjusted R^2		57.9%		33.2%		32.8%		31.4%
F-statistic		26.61***		25.69***		27.91***		23.95***
Wald test of restrictions				$F = 0.01$ ($p = 99.8\%$)				
Correlation of residuals				−0.006				0.024
Hausman specification test		$\chi^2 = 23.76$ ($p = 9.5\%$)						
Observations		1357		1357		1357		1357

Note: We estimate the following four regressions via equation-by-equation ordinary least-squares:

$$\exp_i = \gamma_0 + \gamma_1 n_{o,si} + \gamma_2 n_{ni} + \gamma_3 \Delta_i + \gamma_4 \, gross \, proceeds_i + \epsilon_i \qquad \text{(exp1)}$$

$$UP_i = \delta_0 + \delta_1 n_{o,si} + \delta_2 n_{ni} + \delta_3 \Delta_i + \delta_4 \exp_i + \delta_5 partadj_i + \zeta_i \qquad \text{(UP1)}$$

$$UP_i = \pi_0 + \pi_1 n_{o,si} + \pi_2 n_{ni} + \pi_3 \Delta_i + \pi_5 \, partadj_i + \nu_i \qquad \text{(UP2)}$$

$$wl_i = \varphi_0 + \varphi_1 n_{o,si} + \varphi_2 n_{ni} + \varphi_3 \Delta_i + \varphi_4 \exp_i + \varphi_5 \, partadj_i + \eta_i \qquad \text{(wl1)}$$

Variables are as defined in Table 1. Underpricing is $\bar{P}/P_0 - 1$. *Gross proceeds* is in \$m. *partadj* is the adjustment between the midpoint of the indicative price range and the offer price. As proxies for ex ante uncertainty about firm value, Δ, we use the underwriting fee, company age at flotation, log sales, and leverage. The γ_i, δ_i, π_i, and φ_i refer to the regression parameters identified in Section 2. Note that H_0: $\varphi_4 = 0$ tests for optimality. Standard errors, given in italics under the coefficient estimates, are adjusted for heteroscedasticity using White's (1980) heteroscedasticity-consistent covariance matrix. One, two, and three asterisk indicate significance at the 5%, 1%, and 0.1% level or better, respectively, and †indicates significance at 10%. The F-test tests the hypothesis that all parameter estimates are jointly zero. The Wald test of restrictions refers to the cross-equation restrictions linking γ_i, δ_i, and π_i. "Correlation of residuals" correlates the residuals of (exp1) and (UP1) and of (exp1) and (wl1). Equation-by-equation least squares is only consistent if these correlations are zero. The Hausman specification test tests of the exogeneity of offer size with respect to underpricing. All regressions include year dummies (coefficients not shown). Results are robust to outliers when estimating the four regressions across quartiles of $n_{o,s}$ and n_n. The sample size is reduced to 1357 due to missing information on company age.

considerable explanatory power with an adjusted R^2 of 58%. The coefficients estimated for $n_{o,s}$ and n_n are positive and statistically significant at the 0.1% level and confirm our prediction that issuers spend more on promotion, the greater their participation ratio and dilution factor. We also include gross proceeds to control for economies of scale in promotion costs (see Ritter, 1987) and find significant support for the expected negative relationship between gross proceeds and promotion costs per share. *Underwriting fees* correlate positively with promotion costs, consistent with the hypothesis that greater valuation uncertainty increases *fees*, though the coefficient is significant only at the 7% level. The other risk proxies, *age*, *log sales*, and *leverage*, perform less well. To assess the economic significance, we consider the effect of two-quartile changes in the independent variables (from the first to the third quartile) on the left-hand-side variable. The regressor with the greatest economic effect is n_n. A two-quartile change in n_n increases promotion costs exp from 11.6 ¢ to 19 ¢ a share, and a two-quartile change in $n_{o,s}$ increases exp from 15.5 ¢ to 17.2 ¢ and a similar change in gross proceeds cuts exp from 18.4 ¢ to 16 ¢, all else equal.

The second column reports the coefficients estimated for regression (UP1). By the standards of the IPO literature, the regression has very high explanatory power, with an adjusted R^2 of 33%. The estimated coefficients strongly support our predictions: Underpricing is lower the larger the participation ratio $n_{o,s}$ ($p = 4.5\%$) and the more issuers spend on promotion ($p < 0.01\%$). A two-quartile increase in promotion costs exp lowers underpricing by 142 basis points to 13.4%. A similar increase in $n_{o,s}$ lowers underpricing by 60 basis points to 13.6%. These effects obtain after controlling for Hanley's (1993) partial adjustment effect, whose existence we confirm in our data set: Underpricing is significantly greater the more the offer price exceeds the midpoint of the filing range. The findings are also robust to controlling for valuation uncertainty using either set of proxies: younger and smaller issuers and issuers with higher put option premia (*underwriting fee*) are significantly more underpriced, and the presence and extent of prior credit relationships (*leverage*) significantly reduce underpricing as in James and Wier (1990).

Regression (UP2) in the third column drops exp from the underpricing equation, forcing the effect of promotional activities on underpricing into the coefficients for $n_{o,s}$, n_n and valuation uncertainty. Adjusted R^2 drops slightly, to 32.8%, and the remaining coefficients appear negatively biased compared to regression (UP1). Our cross-equation restrictions (R1) predict that the size of the bias is exactly $-\delta_4\gamma_i$, using the notation of Section 1.4. Wald tests on the coefficients reported for regressions (UP1) and (UP2) in Table 2 fail to reject these restrictions at any level of significance. Proposition 2 predicts that underpricing decreases in $n_{o,s}$—which the negative and statistically significant coefficient confirms—but leaves the remaining effects unsigned. Still, the coefficients estimated for the remaining effects are intuitive: higher dilution n_n leads to lower underpricing ($p = 1.2\%$) and greater valuation uncertainty leads to higher underpricing ($p = 4.8\%$ or better, depending on the proxy).

The final column of Table 2 investigates the determinants of wealth losses. As predicted in Proposition 2, wealth losses increase significantly in $n_{o,s}$ ($p = 0.2\%$) and n_n ($p = 5.7\%$) as well as valuation uncertainty, all of which confirms the comparative statics of our model—comfortably so in view of the high adjusted R^2 of 31.4%. Furthermore, issuers seem to be choosing their promotion spending *optimally*: The coefficient of 0.023 estimated for exp is virtually zero, as predicted in Proposition 2. Note that the dependent variable here is total wealth losses, including promotion costs. If we regress wealth losses *excluding* promotion costs on the same set of variables, we find that every dollar of promotion spending reduces wealth losses by 98 ¢, which clearly indicates that the marginal cost of promotion equals the marginal benefit, the reduction in wealth losses.[24]

As argued previously, OLS estimates will be consistent and efficient as long as the errors of the exp regression are uncorrelated with the errors of the under-pricing and wealth loss regressions, respectively. Are they? Using the regression residuals, we cannot reject that the errors are indeed uncorrelated across equations, at any significance level, so the equation-by-equation least-squares results presented in Table 2 should be both consistent and efficient.

In summary, the signs and significance levels of the coefficients we estimate as well as the test of the cross-equation restrictions support each of our predictions, including the optimality condition.[25]

3.2 Exogeneity and Feedback

Our empirical modeling has treated the number of shares sold as exogenous with respect to underpricing, ruling out a signaling role for underpricing or a feedback effect of underpricing on the choice of number of shares sold. To see whether the number of shares sold is indeed exogenous, we perform two tests. The first specifically addresses the possibility of feedback. Assume that during the course of book-building, the issuer learns that underpricing is likely to be high, perhaps because the expected winner's curse is high. A rational response for an issuer that does not face capital constraints is to reduce the size of the offering. Our empirical finding that smaller offerings are more underpriced could thus be due to feedback and learning during book-building, rather than promotion and incentives. To see if this is the case, we reestimate our four regressions (exp1), (UP1), (UP2), and (wl1) with the *intended* rather than actual number of shares sold.[26] Our results remain unchanged: issuers spend more on promotion, the more shares they *intend*

---

[24] This follows immediately by subtracting exp from both sides of regression (wl1) in Table 2, giving a coefficient of $(0.023 - 1) = -.977$ for exp.

[25] We have repeated our tests using the absolute number of shares $N_{o,s}$ and N_n as well as the corresponding dollar amounts $N_{o,s} P_0$ and $N_n P_0$ in place of the normalized number of shares $n_{o,s}$ and n_n. The results, in either case, are qualitatively unchanged.

[26] SDC's New Issues database reports the intended number of shares as filed with the Securities and Exchange Commission. Unfortunately, it does not distinguish between primary and secondary shares, so we use $(N_{o,s} + N_n)_{\text{intended}}$, normalized by N_o.

to sell, the more underpricing decreases in promotion costs and the intended number of shares to be sold, and expected wealth losses are invariant to promotion costs at the margin.

The second test is a Hausman (1978) specification test (see Greene, 1997, p. 763). Assume that the number of shares sold is chosen simultaneously with underpricing (as in IPO signaling models) or that expected underpricing affects the number of shares sold (as in the feedback argument). In that case, the least-squares estimates of the effect of the number of shares sold on underpricing reported in Table 2 will be biased and inconsistent, and two- or three-stage least-squares estimates will be consistent. If, on the other hand, the number of shares sold is exogenous with respect to underpricing (as our model assumes), all three estimation techniques will be consistent but only OLS will be efficient (because OLS is the best linear unbiased estimator, or BLUE). Hausman's test statistic measures the bias in the vector of coefficients under these alternative estimation techniques. In our case, we cannot reject the hypothesis that the bias is zero at the 10% level or better. This indicates that allowing the number of shares sold to be affected by underpricing does not significantly alter the least-squares coefficient estimates in Table 2.

3.3 Choice of Underwriters

One of the promotion choices issuers can make is to hire prestigious underwriters who according to Titman and Trueman's (1986) model and Carter and Manaster's (1990) empirical evidence use their reputation capital to reduce underpricing. In the context of our model, we would expect (i) issuers' choice of underwriter prestige to depend on $n_{o,s}$ and n_n assuming that (ii) underpricing is indeed negatively related to underwriter reputation, such that (iii) issuers optimize at the margin, their wealth losses being invariant to changes in choice of underwriter. To test these predictions, we use the Carter–Manaster tombstone reputation variable, *rank*.

The results are in Table 3. The first two columns add *rank* to the underpricing and wealth loss regressions, (UP1) and (w11), from Table 2. The OLS coefficients estimated for *rank* are positive and significant at $p < 1\%$, which leads to the surprising conclusion that more prestigious underwriters are associated with higher underpricing (and wealth losses). To illustrate, the estimated coefficient suggests that every unit increase in underwriter reputation *rank* (say from Volpe & Covington's 5 to First Albany's 6) increases underpricing by half a percentage point (say from 12.7% to 13.2%). In dollars, this would raise wealth losses by 5 ¢ a share, or $365,000 in total. The positive effect of bank reputation on underpricing is clearly at odds with evidence from the 1970s and 1980s, but mirrors the results of Beatty and Welch (1996) and several recent articles that use 1990s data. However, these coefficient estimates tell only half the story. The regressions ignore that the choice of underwriter may be endogenous, which would result in biased OLS coefficients: according to our model, it should be the issuers with the most to gain from lower underpricing who choose the most prestigious underwriters.

Table 3. *Choice of underwriter*

Estimation method	OLS		Probit		2SLS	
Dep. Var	UP	wl	$rank \geq 7$	$rank$	UP	wl
Constant	0.144	0.440	$-0.319^\dagger$	5.857***	0.268***	0.965
	0.028	*0.300*	*0.166*	*0.237*	*0.084*	*0.700*
$n_{o,s}$	-0.058**	1.340**	0.328*	1.959**	$-0.050^\dagger$	1.372***
	0.028	*0.446*	*0.167*	*0.552*	*0.029*	*0.445*
n_n	0.004	$0.815^\dagger$	$0.083^\dagger$	0.555**	0.013	$0.854^\dagger$
	0.011	*0.446*	*0.047*	*0.203*	*0.013*	*0.450*
exp	-0.106***	0.218	-0.547***	-4.001***	-0.162***	-0.017
	0.033	*0.440*	*0.153*	*0.607*	*0.047*	*0.546*
underwriter rank	0.005**	0.049***			-0.009	-0.010
	0.002	*0.012*			*0.009*	*0.075*
partadj	0.506***	3.472***			0.515***	3.507***
	0.040	*0.283*			*0.040*	*0.281*
Risk proxies						
underwriting fee	0.038***	$0.182^\dagger$			0.019	0.101
	0.012	*0.099*			*0.016*	*0.134*
age	-0.0004*	-0.004**			-0.0004*	-0.004**
	0.0002	*0.002*			*0.0002*	*0.002*
$\ln(sales)$	-0.009*	-0.059*			-0.004	-0.038
	0.004	*0.027*			*0.005*	*0.040*
leverage	-0.064**	-0.388*			-0.074***	-0.428*
	0.021	*0.168*			*0.023*	*0.187*
$\ln(assets)$			0.110***	0.549***		
			0.012	*0.054*		
EPS_{-12}			-0.050*	-0.175***		
			0.023	*0.053*		
Diagnostics						
Adjusted R^2 (pseudo for Probit)	33.4%	31.9%	12.2%	12.7%	31.7%	31.8%
F-statistic (χ^2 for Probit)	24.30***	32.51***	114.46***	24.43***	51.15***	48.47***
Observations	1357	1357	1357	1357	1357	1357

Note: We investigate the effect of underwriter reputation on underpricing and wealth losses under two alternative assumptions: that underwriter choice is exogenous (first two columns) and that it is endogenous to firm and offering characteristics (the remaining four columns). Underwriter reputation *rank* is measured using the lead manager's Carter–Manaster ranking. The first two columns and *rank* to regressions (UP1) and (w11) from Table 2. The third column reports the results of a Probit where the dependent variable is a dummy equal to 1 if $rank \geq 7$, and 0 otherwise. The fourth column repeats this using as dependent variable *rank* itself. To allow identification in the 2SLS regressions in the final three columns, we include in the *rank* regressions two new independent variables, $\ln(assets)$, the log of assets, and EPS_{-12}, the earnings per share in the 12 months before the IPO. The final two regressions reestimate (UP1) and (w11) allowing *rank* to be endogenously chosen in the first-stage *rank* regression. Standard errors, given in italics under the coefficient estimates, are adjusted for heteroscedasticity using White's (1980) heteroscedasticity-consistent covariance matrix. One, two, and three asterisks indicate significance at the 5%, 1%, and 0.1% level or better, respectively, and † indicates significance at 10%. The F-test tests the hypothesis that all parameter estimates are jointly zero.

Do they? The third column reports the results of estimating a probit regression of underwriter choice on $n_{o,s}$ and n_n, as well as promotion costs exp to control for substitution effects between underwriter prestige and other promotional activities, In (*assets*) to control for Beatty and Welch's (1996) finding that larger firms use higher-quality underwriters, and the earnings per share for the last 12 months preflotation as reported in the prospectus.[27] The dependent variable is a dummy equaling 1 if the Carter–Manaster *rank* ≥ 7 (Carter et al.'s 1998 definition of prestigious banks) and 0 otherwise. The table reports the marginal effects of the independent variables on the probability of hiring a prestigious lead manager, evaluated at the means of the independent variables. Standard errors are heteroscedasticity-consistent.

The results clearly support the prediction that underwriter choice depends on firm and offering characteristics. The marginal effects estimated for $n_{o,s}$ and n_n are positive and significant and indicate that for every 10% increase in the participation ratio or dilution factor, the probability of hiring a prestigious lead manager increases by 3.3% and 0.8%, respectively.[28] Given the strongly negative marginal effect estimated for exp, prestigious underwriters and other promotional activities appear to be substitutes. The positive marginal effect of ln(*assets*) confirms Beatty and Welch's (1996) earlier observation. Finally, there is a significantly negative association between profitability and under-writer prestige, indicating that top banks are *more* likely to lead-manage speculative IPOs. This is consistent with the spirit of our model, because companies whose values are harder to determine have more to gain from hiring experienced investment banks.

The probit results make it likely that the OLS coefficients indeed suffer from endogeneity bias. The final three columns of Table 3 report consistent 2SLS estimates allowing for the simultaneity of underwriter choice. The first stage estimates a least-squares version of our earlier probit regression, replacing the dummy dependent variable with *rank* itself.[29] The results, reported in the fourth column, confirm the probit estimates. In the second stage, we use the predicted *rank* from the first-stage regression as an instrument in the underpricing (fifth column) and wealth loss regressions (final column). This totally changes the relationship between *rank* and underpricing and wealth losses, compared to OLS: The coefficients estimated for *rank* are no longer significant and in fact become negative. This is more in line with the 1970s and 1980s evidence on the under-pricing-reducing effects of underwriter prestige. It strongly suggests that the

[27] We include *EPS*, a variable we have not hitherto used, to allow instrumentation in what follows.

[28] The results are somewhat sensitive to what cut-off point we choose and cease to be significant (but remain positive) if high reputation is defined as a rank of 8 or higher instead. Therefore, we also estimated an ordered multinomial logit with three categories (below 7, 7 to 8, above 8), which confirmed our results: Higher $n_{o,s}$ or n_n incrementally increase the likelihood of choosing an underwriter in the next highest category.

[29] Because $0 \leq rank \leq 9$, we also tried a Tobit specification with two-sided censoring and found our results qualitatively unchanged.

1990s evidence of the underpricing-*increasing* effects of underwriter prestige is based on the false premise that underwriter choice is exogenous.

The coefficient of *rank* in the wealth loss regression is insignificant, just as we would expect. Changing to a higher-ranked underwriter should not reduce wealth losses at the margin if issuers behave optimally. In the underpricing regression, the coefficient of *rank* is negative, as predicted by certification arguments, but not significant ($t = -1$). Further investigation reveals this to be a problem of extraneous variables affecting the efficiency of our estimate. If we drop either of the insignificant risk proxies, the *underwriting fee* and ln(*sales*), or both, the (still negative) coefficient of *rank* becomes significant at $p = 9\%$, 4%, and 0.3%, respectively.

Finally, we note that our findings concerning the endogeneity of under writer choice are robust to measuring underwriter prestige using market shares, as in Beatty and Welch (1996) and Megginson and Weiss (1991), rather than tomb-stone ranks.[30]

4. CONCLUSION

We began this chapter by asking why some IPOs are more underpriced than others. Notwithstanding the important contributions of the theoretical under pricing literature, we have suggested an alternative, non-mutually exclusive explanation: some owners have less reason to care about the degree of underpricing and therefore, will optimally expend fewer resources to minimize it. This explanation builds on two premises: (i) owners care about underpricing only to the extent that they stand to lose from it, with any such losses being proportional to the number of shares sold; and (ii) owners can affect the level of underpricing through the costs they incur in promoting the issue. Our model derives the empirical implications of these two premises for the relations among issuer wealth losses, underpricing, the costs of promoting the issue, the number of primary and secondary shares sold at the offering, and uncertainty. Our empirical tests on a sample of US IPOs over the period 1991–1995 confirm our empirical predictions. We find that the more shares that are being offered, the more issuers spend to promote their IPOs, and that these promotional activities reduce underpricing. We investigate one particular promotional choice, the choice of lead manager, and find that issuers choose their lead managers optimally once we adjust for the endogeneity of their choice.

We believe two results stand out from our analysis. The first result is that issuers optimize at the margin: each additional dollar spent on promoting an issue reduces wealth losses by 98 cents, so marginal cost equals marginal benefit.[31]

---

[30] We compute underwriters' market shares during the five years ending the quarter before each sample firm goes public. Specifically, we allocate the gross proceeds of each IPO during a five-year window equally to all banks involved as lead, co- or principal underwriters in that IPO (as listed in the top two segments in tombstone advertisements). To obtain each bank's market share, we then cumulate these allocated gross proceeds for each bank and divide by the total gross proceeds raised in all IPOs in the five-year window.

[31] The two-cent difference can presumaby be ascribed to statistical noise.

Such optimizing behavior is hard to reconcile with Loughran and Ritter's (1999) conjecture that "issuers treat the opportunity cost of leaving money on the table as less important than the direct fees." The second result is that accounting for the issuer's endogenous choice of underwriter may help reverse the counterintuitive positive relation between underpricing and the reputation of the lead manager reported for the 1990s by Beatty and Welch (1996) and others.[32] The key to this result is that issuers choose the quality of certification endogenously; it is precisely those issuers who would otherwise be most underpriced who stand to gain the most from choosing a prestigious underwriter to reduce underpricing. Consistent with this, we find that the most speculative companies choose the most prestigious underwriters. They may still be more underpriced than issuers who chose less prestigious underwriters, but less underpriced than they would have been had they chosen less prestigious underwriters themselves.

In conclusion, we caution against making inferences based on a comparison of underpricing alone. Consider, for example, Muscarella and Vetsuypens's (1989) empirical refutation of Baron's (1982) underpricing model. Baron views underpricing as compensation to the investment bank for revealing its superior information about market demand and as payment for marketing effort. Muscarella and Vetsuypens test this by looking at the underpricing experienced by a small sample of banks that underwrite their own flotations, which they find to be just as underpriced as IPOs in general. However, concluding from this that Baron's model does not hold is premature: Though the banks certainly internalize the information rent, there is still the matter of the costs incurred in promoting the issues. Thus, it is at least conceivable that Muscarella and Vetsuypens's banks sell far fewer primary or secondary shares than do issuers in general, thereby leading to lower incentives to promote the issue and decrease underpricing.

Generalizing from this example, we argue that empirical tests should control for issuers' incentives by including the number of shares sold in an offering, and compute wealth losses rather than underpricing returns.

Appendix

Proof of Proposition 2. From the definition of wl, we have

$$\frac{dwl}{dn_{o,s}} = \left(\frac{1}{1 + n_n}\right)\left(\overline{P} - \frac{\beta_U P_G + P_B}{1 + \beta_U}\right) > 0$$

$$\frac{dwl}{dn_n} = \frac{n_{o,r}}{(1 + n_n)^2}\left(\overline{P} - \frac{\beta_U P_G + P_B}{1 + \beta_U}\right) > 0$$

---

[32] For an alternative explanation, see Cooney et al. (1999).

and, noting that $P_G = \overline{P} + \Delta/2$ and $P_B = \overline{P} - \Delta/2$,

$$\frac{dwl}{d\Delta} = -\left(\frac{n_{o,s} + n_n}{1 + n_n}\right)\frac{1}{2}\left(\frac{\beta_U - 1}{\beta_U + 1}\right) > 0$$

Note that we have used the Envelope theorem to neglect changes in exp and β_U. From the definition of UP, we have

$$\frac{\partial UP}{\partial n_{o,s}} = \frac{1}{P_0^2}\left(\frac{\partial \overline{P}_1}{\partial n_{o,s}}P_0 - \overline{P}_1 \frac{\partial P_0}{\partial n_{o,s}}\right)$$

$$= \frac{\exp}{P_0^2}\frac{\partial \alpha}{\partial n_{o,s}}(\overline{P}_1 - P_0) < 0$$

where we have used the relations $\partial \alpha/\partial n_{o,s} = -n_n/(n_{o,s} + n_n)^2 < 0$ and $\overline{P}_1 > P_0$. We also have

$$\frac{\partial UP}{\partial n_n} = \frac{1}{P_0^2}\left(\begin{array}{c}\left(-\frac{1}{(1+n_n)^2}\overline{P} + \frac{1}{(1+n_n)^2}\frac{\beta_U P_G + P_B}{1+\beta_U} - \frac{\partial \alpha}{\partial n_n}\exp\right)\left(\frac{\beta_U P_G + P_B}{1+\beta_U} - \alpha \cdot \exp\right) \\ +\left(\frac{1}{1+n_n}\overline{P} + \frac{n_n}{1+n_n}\frac{\beta_U P_G + P_B}{1+\beta_U} - \alpha \cdot \exp\right)\frac{\partial \alpha}{\partial n_n}\exp\end{array}\right)$$

which cannot be signed, and

$$\frac{\partial UP}{\partial \Delta} = -\frac{1}{P_0^2}\frac{\partial P_0}{\partial \Delta}\frac{1}{1 + n_n}(\overline{P} - \alpha \cdot \exp) > 0$$

where we have used the relations $\partial P_0/\partial \Delta = \frac{1}{2}(\beta_U - 1)/(\beta_U + 1) < 0$ and $\overline{P} - \alpha \cdot \exp > (\beta_U P_G + P_B)/(1 + \beta_U) - \alpha \cdot \exp = P_0 > 0$.

Now turning to the total derivatives, we have

$$\frac{dUP}{dx} = \frac{\partial UP}{\partial x} + \frac{\partial UP}{\partial \exp}\frac{\partial \exp}{\partial x}$$

$x \in \{n_{o,s}, n_n, \Delta\}$ where

$$\frac{\partial UP}{\partial \exp} = -\frac{1}{P_0^2}\frac{1}{1 + n_n}\left(\alpha P_0 + (\overline{P} - \alpha \cdot \exp)\frac{\partial P_0}{\partial \exp}\right) < 0.$$

The preceding inequality is true as

$$\frac{\partial P_0}{\partial \exp} = \frac{\Delta}{(1 + \beta_U)^2}\beta_U'(\exp) - \alpha$$

$$> \left(\frac{n_{o,s} + n_n}{1 + n_n}\right)\frac{\Delta}{(1 + \beta_U)^2}\beta_U'(\exp) - 1 = 0$$

where the inequality is true by recalling that $n_{o,s} < 1$ and $\alpha < 1$ and the equality is true by Equation (3).

Combining the preceding results with those of Proposition 1, we have $dUP/dn_{o,s} < 0$, whereas the signs of dUP/dn_n and $dUP/d\Delta$ are indeterminate. □

REFERENCES

Allen, F., and G. R. Faulhaber, 1989, "Signaling by Underpricing in the IPO Market," *Journal of Financial Economics*, 23, 303–323.

Baron, D. P., 1982, "A Model of the Demand for Investment Banking Advising and Distribution Services for New Issues," *Journal of Finance*, 37, 955–976.

Barry, C. B., 1989, "Initial Public Offering Underpricing: The Issuer's View—A Comment," *Journal of Finance*, 44, 1099–1103.

Beatty, R. P., and J. R. Ritter, 1986, "Investment Banking, Reputation, and the Underpricing of Initial Public Offerings," *Journal of Financial Economics*, 15, 213–232.

Beatty, R. P., and I. Welch, 1996, "Issuer Expenses and Legal Liability in Initial Public Offerings," *Journal of Law and Economics*, 39, 545–602.

Benveniste, L. M., and P. A. Spindt, 1989, "How Investment Bankers Determine the Offer Price and Allocation of New Issues," *Journal of Financial Economics*, 24, 343–361.

Benveniste, L. M., and W. J. Wilhelm, 1990, "A Comparative Analysis of IPO Proceeds under Alternative Regulatory Environments," *Journal of Financial Economics*, 28, 173–207.

Booth, J. R., and R. L. Smith, 1986, "Capital Raising, Underwriting and the Certification Hypothesis," *Journal of Financial Economics*, 15, 261–281.

Brennan, M. J., and J. Franks, 1997, "Underpricing, Ownership, and Control in Initial Public Offerings of Equity Securities in the U.K.," *Journal of Financial Economics*, 45, 391–413.

Carter, R. B., and S. Manaster, 1990, "Initial Public Offerings and Underwriter Reputation," *Journal of Finance*, 45, 1045–1067.

Carter, R. B., F. H. Dark, and A. K. Singh, 1998, "Underwriter Reputation, Initial Returns and the Long-Run Performance of IPO Stocks," *Journal of Finance*, 53, 285–311.

Chen, H. -C., and J. R. Ritter, 2000, "The Seven Percent Solution," *Journal of Finance*, 55, 1105–1131.

Cooney, J. W., A. K. Singh, R. B. Carter, and F. H. Dark, 1999, "The IPO Partial-Adjustment Phenomenon and Underwriter Reputation," working paper, Kansas State University.

Dunbar, C., 2000, "Factors Affecting Investment Bank Initial Public Offering Market Share," *Journal of Financial Economics*, 55, 3–42.

Dyl, E. A., and M. D. Joehnk, 1976, "Competitive versus Negotiated Underwriting of Public Utility Debt," *Bell Journal of Economics*, 7, 680–689.

Ellis, K., R. Michaely, and M. O'Hara, 2000, "When the Underwriter is the Market Maker: An Examination of Trading in the IPO Aftermarket," *Journal of Finance*, 55, 1039–1074.

Gande, A., M. Puri, and A. Saunders, 1999, "Bank Entry, Competition, and the Market for Corporate Securities Underwriting," *Journal of Financial Economics*, 54, 165–196.

Greene, W. H., 1997, *Econometric Analysis* (3rd ed.), Prentice-Hall, Englewood Cliffs, N.J.

Grinblatt, M., and C. Y. Hwang, 1989, "Signaling and the Pricing of New Issues," *Journal of Finance*, 44, 393–420.

Habib, M. A., and A. P. Ljungqvist, 1998, "Underpricing and IPO Proceeds: A Note," *Economics Letters*, 61, 381–383.

Hanley, K. W., 1993, "The Underpricing of Initial Public Offerings and the Partial Adjustment Phenomenon," *Journal of Financial Economics*, 34, 231–250.

Hausman, J. A., 1978, "Specification Tests in Econometrics," *Econometrica*, 46, 1251–1271.

Ibbotson, R. G., J. L. Sindelar, and J. R. Ritter, 1994, "The Market's Problem with the Pricing of Initial Public Offerings," *Journal of Applied Corporate Finance*, 7, 66–74.

James, C., 1992, "Relationship-Specific Assets and the Pricing of Underwriting Services," *Journal of Finance*, 47, 1865–1885.

James E., and P. Wier, 1990, "Borrowing Relationships, Intermediation and the Cost of Issuing Public Securities," *Journal of Financial Economics*, 28, 149–171.

Jenkinson, T. J., and A. P. Ljungqvist, 1996, *Going Public: The Theory and Evidence on How Companies Raise Equity Finance*, Oxford University Press, New York.

Jenkinson, T. J., A. P. Ljungqvist, and W. J. Wilhelm Jr., 1999, "Bookbuilding around the World," working paper, Oxford University.

Loughran, T., and J. R. Ritter, 1999, "Why Issuers Don't Get Upset about Leaving Money on the Table in IPOs?" working paper, University of Notre Dame and University of Florida.

Megginson, W. L., and K. A. Weiss, 1991, "Venture Capitalist Certification in Initial Public Offerings," *Journal of Finance*, 46, 879–903.

Muscarella, C. J., and M. R. Vetsuypens, 1989, "A Simple Test of Baron's Model of IPO Underpricing," *Journal of Financial Economics*, 24, 125–135.

Palmiter, A. R., 1999, "Toward Disclosure Choice in Securities Offerings," *Columbia Business Law Review*, 1999, 1–135.

Ritter, J. R., 1984, "The Hot Issue Market of 1980," *Journal of Business*, 57, 215–240.

Ritter, J. R., 1987, "The Costs of Going Public," *Journal of Financial Economics*, 19, 269–282.

Ritter, J. R., 1991, "The Long-Run Performance of Initial Public Offerings," *Journal of Finance*, 46, 3–27.

Rock, K., 1986, "Why New Issues Are Underpriced," *Journal of Financial Economics*, 15, 187–212.

Sorensen, E. H., 1980, "An Analysis of the Relationship between Underwriter Spread and the Pricing of Municipal Bonds," *Journal of Financial and Quantitative Analysis*, 15, 435–447.

Stoll, H. R., 1976, "The Pricing of Underwritten Offerings of Listed Common Stocks and the Compensation to Underwriters," *Journal of Economics and Business*, 28, 96–103.

Titman, S., and B. Trueman, 1986, "Information Quality and the Valuation of New Issues," *Journal of Accounting and Economics*, 8, 159–172.

Welch, I., 1989, "Seasoned Offerings, Imitation Costs, and the Underpricing of Initial Public Offerings," *Journal of Finance*, 44, 421–449.

White, H., 1980, "A Heteroskedasticity-Consistent Covariance Matrix Estimator and a Direct Test for Heteroskedasticity," *Econometrica*, 48, 817–838.

PART II

FINANCIAL SYSTEM ARCHITECTURE

6

Financial System Architecture

ARNOUD W. A. BOOT AND ANJAN V. THAKOR

A primary function of the financial system is to facilitate the transfer of resources from savers ('surplus units') to those who need funds ('deficit units'). In a well-designed financial system, resources are efficiently allocated. The question we address is, what is the configuration of such a financial system? In particular, we examine why bank lending and capital market financing coexist and the factors—such as regulation and the stage of economic development—that determine which dominates.

These issues are important for many of the current policy debates regarding the structuring of financial systems. How do banks and capital markets emerge and evolve? What services should be provided by banks and what services by the capital market? How is the resolution of informational problems related to how the financial system is configured?

These questions are particularly interesting in the context of Eastern European countries. The financial systems currently in place there are interim arrangements to facilitate transition to systems with lesser emphasis on the central planning of capital allocation [Checchi (1993)]. Although reform discussions have focused largely on the creation of financial markets [Mendelson and Peake (1993)], the more spectacular initial developments are likely to be in banking. For example, privately owned commercial banks were uncommon in Communist Europe until recently. Since then, however, banks have evolved rapidly [Perotti (1993) and

A. V. Thakor would like to thank the Edward J. Frey Chair in Banking and Finance for financial support. A. W. A. Boot thanks the Olin program in Law and Economics at Cornell University for its hospitality during part of the research on this article. The authors would also like to thank Todd Milbourn, Kathleen Petrie, and Anjolein Schmeits for excellent research assistance, and seminar participants at the University of Michigan, Indiana University, University of Amsterdam, Erasmus University, Rotterdam (the Netherlands), University of Minnesota, the JFI Symposium on Market Microstructure and the Design of Financial Systems at Northwestern University (May 1995), the Nordic Finance Symposium at Vendsnu, Norway (February 1995), Queen's University, Cornell University, the London School of Economics, the Stockholm School of Economics, the University of Goteborg (Sweden), McGill University (Canada), and participants at the CEPR meetings in St. Sebastian, Spain (April 1994), and Gerzensee, Switzerland (July 1994), and the American Finance Association meeting, San Francisco (January 1996) for helpful comments. The authors are particularly indebted to Ed Kane, Sudipto Bhattacharya, Paolo Fulghieri, Neil Wallace, Mike Stutzer, Franklin Allen (the editor), and an anonymous referee for helpful suggestions. Address correspondence to A. V. Thakor, University of Michigan Business School, 710 Tappan St., Ann Arbor, MI 48109-1234.

Van Wijnbergen (1994)]. These developments point to a key aspect of financial system architecture: the determination of the roles of the banking system and the financial market.

Despite its importance, the research on this topic is still only emerging. Allen (1993) provides a qualitative assessment and sketches a preliminary framework for analysis. That article links financial system design to the complexity of decision making within firms seeking capital and provides a perspective on the disparate evolutions of financial markets in Europe and the United States. Bhattacharya and Chiesa (1995), Dewatripont and Maskin (1995), von Thadden (1995), and Yosha (1995) examine the comparative allocational efficiencies of 'centralized' (bank-oriented) credit markets versus 'decentralized' (market-oriented) credit markets. Somewhat different approaches are taken by Allen and Gale (1995, forthcoming) who suggest that bank-oriented systems provide better intertemporal risk sharing, whereas market-oriented systems provide better cross-sectional risk sharing, and Sabani (1992) who argues that market-dominated economies will restructure financially distressed borrowers less than bank-dominated economies.

These contributions notwithstanding, there are unanswered questions. For example, how is the informativeness of market prices affected by financial system design? If unfettered by regulation, what determines the design of the financial system? And how does this design affect the borrower's choice of financing source? Does financial system design have real effects?

This article is a modest first attempt to address these issues. We explain how financial institutions and markets form and evolve when economic agents are free to choose the way they organize themselves. Rather than taking the roles of institutions and markets as given and then asking how borrowers make their choice of financing source [e.g., Berlin and Mester (1992), Besanko and Kanatas (1993), Diamond (1991), and Chemmanur and Fulghieri (1994)], we start with assumptions about primitives—endowments and informational frictions—and endogenize the roles of banks and financial markets. The distinction we make between a bank and a market is that agents within a bank can cooperate and coordinate their actions, whereas agents in a market compete;[1] we assume nothing more about what banks and markets do.

We begin by positing three types of informational problems: (i) incomplete information about future projects that is of relevance for firm valuation and real investment decisions within firms, (ii) postlending (asset substitution) moral hazard that can affect payoffs to creditors, and (iii) uncertainty about whether postlending moral hazard will be encountered. Part of the primitives are economic agents who specialize in resolving these informational problems, with each individual agent being atomistic in impact. Our first major result is that problem

---

[1] Perhaps an even more basic distinction is that agents can be anonymous in a market but not in institutions. This may be a way to rationalize the possibility of coordination within a bank and the lack of it in an anonymous, competitive market setting.

(i) is most efficiently resolved in an 'uncoordinated' market setting where individual agents compete with each other, and problems (ii) and (iii) are most efficiently resolved through coordinated action by agents coalescing to form a bank. The scope of banking vis-à-vis the financial market is thereby determined endogenously in an unregulated economy in which the financial market is characterized by many agents and a rational expectations equilibrium price formation process that noisily aggregates information contained in the order flows for securities. A key attribute of the financial market, and one that delineates its role from that of a bank, is that there is valuable information feedback from the equilibrium market prices of securities to the real decisions of firms that impact those market prices.[2] This information loop provides a propagation mechanism by which the effects of financial market trading are felt in the real sector. Bank financing does not have such an information loop. Hence, real decisions are not impacted by the information contained in bank credit contracts. However, banks are shown to be superior in resolving asset substitution moral hazard. Thus, in choosing between banks and financial markets, one trades off the improvement in real decisions due to feedback from market prices against a more efficient attenuation of moral hazard.

The relative levels of credit allocated by banks and the financial market depend on the efficacy of the bank's monitoring and the 'development' (i.e., sophistication or level of financial innovation) of the financial market. We let the latter be reflected in the information acquisition cost for those who wish to become informed. We show that the cost of information acquisition affects the informativeness of equilibrium security prices, and therefore the relative scopes of banks and the financial market in credit allocation. In describing these scopes, our article explains:

- why banks emerge even when every agent in a bank could trade on his own in the market;
- why financial markets develop even when there are no restrictions on banks' activities;
- why a financial market equilibrium in which prices convey information can exist only if prices do not have too much or too little informativeness;[3]
- why borrowers prefer either the financial market or banks based on differences in observable borrower attributes;[4]

---

[2] Allen (1993) suggests that an important role of the stock market is to provide decision-makers in firms with information they would not otherwise have possessed. Holmström and Tirole (1993) examine the role of the stock market as a monitor of managerial performance. They show that a firm's stock price incorporates performance information that cannot be gleaned from the firm's current or future profit data and that this information is useful in structuring managerial incentives.

[3] This is in contrast to the existing literature in which the value of information acquisition is nondecreasing the noisiness of the process by which information is aggregated [e.g., Grossman and Stiglitz (1980)].

[4] Since banks resolve moral hazard in our model, the bank's decision to grant a loan does not trigger an abnormally positive reaction in the borrower's stock price as found empirically by James

- how financial market trading affects firms' real decisions;
- how the state of development of the financial market can impact the borrower's choice of financing source.

The rest of the article is organized as follows. Section 1 contains a description of the basic model. Section 2 analyzes the formation of banks and the financial market. Further analysis is contained in Sections 3 and 4. Section 5 examines model robustness issues. Section 6 explores the implications of the analysis for financial system design. Section 7 concludes. All proofs are in the Appendix.

1 THE BASIC MODEL

1.1. Production Possibilities for Firms

1.1.1. *Preferences and Types of Projects*

There is universal risk neutrality, and the riskless interest rate is zero. The economy consists of firms each with a project that needs a \$1 investment. As shown in Figure 1, each firm has a stochastic investment opportunity set that contains two projects: good and bad. The contractible end-of-period return for the good project has a probability distribution with a two-point support: with probability η the end-of-point return will be $Y > 0$, and with probability $1 - \eta$ it will be 0. The contractible end-of-point return for a bad project will be 0 with probability 1, but this project offers the borrowing firm's manager a noncontractible private rent, N, from investing in the project [see, e.g., O'Hara (1993)]. Let $\eta Y > N$, so that the borrower prefers the good project with self-financing.

1.1.2. *Project Availability and Payoff Enhancement Possibility*

Project availability is stochastic. With probability $\theta \in (\underline{\theta}, \bar{\theta}) \subset (0, 1)$, the firm finds itself in the 'low flexibility' (LF) state in which it has only the good project available. With probability $1 - \theta$, the firm finds itself in the 'high flexibility' (HF) state and has both the good and the bad project available.

We assume that the firm can possibly enhance the return of the good project at a private cost of $K = \bar{K} > 0$, where $K \in \{0, \bar{K}\}$. This investment is unobservable to outsiders, and it enhances the project return by $\alpha \in (0, 1)$, conditional on a favorable realization of an 'environmental' or 'market' random variable $v \in \{0, 1\}$,[5] with $\Pr(v = 1) = \gamma \in (0, 1)$ as the probability that the a priori uninformed assign to the event that $v = 1$. Let $\alpha > \bar{K}$. Note that v is specific to each firm rather than being an economywide variable. Thus, if $v = 1$ and the firm invests $K = \bar{K}$,

---

(1987), Lummer and McConnell (1989), and Shockley and Thakor (1996, forthcoming). Of course, if our model were to be altered to introduce uncertainty about whether the borrower would have a project available, then the bank's decision to grant a loan would signal good news. See Boot and Thakor (1996, forthcoming) for such an approach.

[5] It does not matter much if we assume that K is observable to outsiders. With K unobservable, the firm underinvests relative to first best, whereas with K observable, there is no underinvestment.

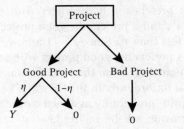

Figure 1. *A schematic of the types of projects (without payoff enhancement) and contractible returns*

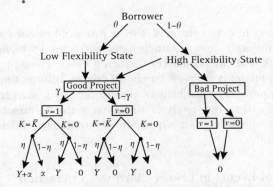

Figure 2. *A schematic of the types of projects (with payoff enhancement) and contractible returns*

then the good project pays off $Y + \alpha$ with probability η and α with probability $1 - \eta$. If a borrower invests $K = 0$, then the good project's return is Y with probability η and 0 with probability $1 - \eta$, regardless of v. If a borrower invests either $K = \bar{K}$ or $K = 0$ in a bad project, the contractible project return is 0 with probability 1, regardless of v. Thus, the improvement in the project return depends on borrower-specific investments as well as the realization of exogenous uncertainties like market demand (see Figure 2).

We assume that the realization of v can only be observed by those who become informed at a cost; we will say more about this later. For now, it suffices that the borrower cannot observe v, but believes that $\Pr(v = 1) = \gamma$. This belief is common knowledge. If the borrower is uninformed about v, an investment $K = \bar{K} > 0$ is suboptimal. That is, we assume $\gamma\alpha - \bar{K} < 0$, where $\gamma\alpha$ is the expected project enhancement if the borrower is uninformed about v. We assume $\eta > \gamma$ and that

$$\gamma\alpha < \bar{K} < \eta\alpha. \tag{1}$$

Further, we assume that exogenous parameter values are such that there exists an interest factor (one plus the interest rate) $r^0 < 1$ satisfying $\eta[Y + \alpha - r^0] - \bar{K} = N$.

Given this, the firm prefers the bad project with external financing if the interest factor exceeds r^0, and it prefers the good project with external financing if the interest factor is less than r^0. Since $r^0 < 1$ and we had earlier assumed that $\eta Y > N$, the firm always prefers the good project with self-financing and the bad project with external financing. From the lender's standpoint, therefore, there is asset-substitution moral hazard only in the HF state. We view the parameter θ as the commonly known prior probability assigned by the market to the event that a randomly selected borrower will be in the LF state and hence pose no moral hazard. Each potential borrower is characterized by its observable $\theta \in (\underline{\theta}, \bar{\theta})$. Let H be the cumulative distribution function over the cross-section of θs.

1.2. Types of Securities

We limit financiers to debt contracts. This is primarily because bank lending is typically done through debt contracts, and we want to have comparability between the bank and capital market financing cases. Thus, the capital market financing in our model is through bonds. Of course, information acquisition in bond markets is probably smaller than that in the stock market. It is therefore important to note that our analysis understates the information acquisition benefits of financial markets, but is qualitatively unaffected if debt is replaced by equity (see Section 5).

1.3. Sequence of Events in Lender–Borrower Interaction

The firm first makes an irreversible decision about whether to borrow from a bank or the financial market. At this stage the only information that it has is about its θ, and this information is common knowledge.[6] Subsequently, the firm learns whether it is in the LF or the HF state, and after this v is realized and learned by those who choose to become informed about it. The lender (either the bank or the financial market) offers a price of credit that the firm can either accept or respond to with a take-it-or-leave-it counteroffer. Moreover, based on the lender's actions (the offered credit price or the market demand for the firm's security in the financial market), the firm makes its inference about the realization of v. Next, the firm makes its initial choice of project if it is in the HF state; in the LF state, this choice is trivially the good project. If the lender can observe this initial choice and monitor, it can force a change to the good project in the event that the firm had initially chosen the bad project. This leads to the firm's final project choice decision and its investment of \$1 in the project. Moreover, at this time the firm

---

[6] We assume that the firm commits to a financing choice at the outset to avoid the situation in which financial market investors produce information about a firm that ends up borrowing from a bank. Although in equilibrium each firm's choice of financing source is unambiguously linked to its θ, and this θ is commonly known at the outset. What we wish to avoid is the firm learning about v from its market price (which is based on investors erroneously believing that the firm will borrow in the financial market) and then borrowing from a bank.

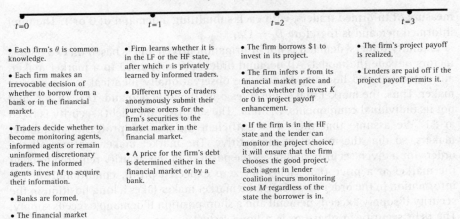

Figure 3. *A description of the sequence of events in the economy*

also makes its decision regarding investing $K \in \{0, \bar{K}\}$ for project payoff enhancement (see Figure 3).

1.4. Types of Agents in the Economy

The structure for the financial market is as follows.[7] There are two types of investors/traders in the market: liquidity traders and discretionary agents. The aggregate asset demand, ℓ, of the liquidity traders is random and exogenously specified by the continuously differentiable probability density function $f(\ell) = A - A^2\ell/2$, where A is a positive constant. Thus, the support of $f(\ell)$ is $[0, 2/A]$. A discretionary agent can become an 'informed' or a 'monitoring' agent at a finite cost $M > 0$. This investment M either generates a signal that perfectly reveals the ν for the firm in question or enables the agent to monitor the firm's investment choice between the good and the bad project. The discretionary agent must decide before investing M whether she wishes to be an informed agent and receive the signal or become a monitoring agent. If the discretionary agent does not invest M, she can be an uninformed discretionary trader who can either invest in the capital market or in bank deposits.

We will first focus on agents who become informed about ν. Each submits a demand order d_I. Let us conjecture that the equilibrium strategy of an informed trader is to set $d_I = 1$ if the signal says $\nu = 1$ and $d_I = 0$ if the signal says $\nu = 0$; we will validate this conjecture later. Each trader is very small but of $\epsilon > 0$ Lebesgue measure on the real line. We will focus on the limiting case in which $\epsilon \to 0$ so that each trader is atomistic, and all traders lie in a continuum. Let Ω be the (Lebesgue)

---

[7] This structure is similar to that in Boot and Thakor (1993a), but richer in that agents can also choose to monitor and there is information feedback from the financial market to the firm.

measure of informed traders, with each submitting a demand of 0 or 1. The total informed demand is therefore $D_I = \Omega d_I$.

Liquidity traders' demand is not information driven and is based on exogenous factors outside the model. All demand orders are submitted to a market maker, and informed and liquidity traders are observationally identical to the market maker. Thus, the market maker observes only the total demand, $D = D_I + \ell$, and not its individual components, D_I and ℓ. The supply of the (debt) security is fixed at \$1. We assume that there is a sufficient number of 'professional' market makers, so that the market is competitive. The market maker receives all the orders for a given security and takes the position in the security required to clear the market at a price that yields her zero expected profit, conditional on the information in the order flow. Thus, the market maker takes a long position in the security if supply exceeds demand and a short position if demand exceeds supply. The debt security in question is a bond issued at par, and the price set by the market maker is the bond's coupon rate (or interest rate).

If the discretionary agent becomes a monitoring agent, she has the ability to monitor the borrower and detect its choice of the bad project; allowing this detection to be noisy is inconsequential. However, since each agent is atomistic, the borrower cannot be prevented from choosing the bad project unless a sufficiently large measure of monitoring agents is involved.[8] We assume that the minimum measure of monitoring agents needed to deter the borrower is $\Lambda^* < 1$. Moreover, while the discretionary agent decides at the outset whether to be an informed trader or a monitoring agent, the actual expense, M, of a monitoring agent, is not incurred until after a loan has been extended to the borrower, whereas the outlay of $M > 0$ by an informed trader occurs prior to her placing her order for the security. This distinguishes information acquisition from post-lending monitoring. For later use, we assume

$$\bar{\theta}[1 + \Lambda^* M] - 1 < 0. \tag{2}$$

This ensures that lending without monitoring and information acquisition is unprofitable, even if the promised interest rate is grossed up to compensate for anticipated monitoring expenses. To understand equation (2) intuitively, note that the following two conditions are sufficient (but not necessary) to obtain equation (2): (i) $\bar{\theta}\eta Y < 1$, which implies that an unmonitored project has a negative net present value (NPV), and (ii) $\eta Y > 1 + \Lambda^* M$, which implies that a monitored project has a positive NPV.

---

[8] The idea is that an individual bondholder who has purchased a \$100 bond as part of a \$50 million IBM bond issue can do little to influence the firm's project choice. However, collectively—as with bank lending—the bondholders who purchased all of IBM's bonds could dictate a lot. Even when a borrower is solvent, 'large block' creditors (either coalitions of bondholders who own significant portions of the firm's public bonds or institutional lenders like banks) can influence specific aspects of a firm's investment policy for reasons related to the borrower's desire to maintain a good relationship with the lender and retain operating flexibility when temporary negative shocks to cash flows elevate the risk of covenant violations.

2. THE EMERGENCE OF BANKS AND THE CAPITAL MARKET

2.1. Definitions of Markets, Institutions, and the Overall Equilibrium

A *financial market* is a collection of traders who all compete to buy debt securities offered by borrowing firms, and where the equilibrium security price is determined through a Walrasian market clearing condition enforced by a market maker. A *bank* is a collection of traders who coalesce to form an institution, provide deposit funding, and coordinate their actions with respect to the borrower. In an interior equilibrium, discretionary agents must be indifferent between becoming informed traders, monitoring agents, or uninformed discretionary traders/depositors.[9] Since the expected equilibrium profit from being an uninformed discretionary trader/depositor is zero, informed traders and monitoring agents must also earn zero expected profit in equilibrium.

2.2. Discretionary Agents' Choices

Consider discretionary agents who have chosen to become informed traders. Each now stands ready to receive a signal about ν. They must decide whether to compete with others in the market in bidding for a debt security or coalesce into a bank and coordinate their actions.

Lemma 1. *Those who invest M to become informed traders will prefer to compete with each other as financial market traders rather than become bankers.*

The monitoring agents must make a similar choice.

Lemma 2. *Those who invest M to become monitoring agents will prefer to coalesce to form a bank and coordinate their actions in monitoring the borrower. Moreover, the measure of monitoring agents in the bank will be exactly Λ^*, the minimum needed to deter the firm from choosing the bad project.*

Given Lemma 1, we see that the financial market will consist of informed traders and liquidity traders. While the informed traders' demand is endogenously determined and the liquidity traders' demand is exogenous, it is possible that their total demand is not equal to 1, the available supply of the security. We assume that some of the uninformed discretionary traders in the market form coalitions called 'market makers,' each of whom is forced by competition to earn zero expected profit and 'correct' the demand-supply imbalance by taking an appropriate position in the security. Moreover, given Lemma 2, the equilibrium measure of monitoring agents equals $\Lambda^* < 1$. Thus, some uninformed discretionary traders join the

---

[9] We will assume throughout that the costs of becoming informed and monitoring agents are such that an interior equilibrium obtains. It is possible, however, that if these costs are sufficiently high, all traders may strictly prefer to remain uninformed and the measures of informed and monitoring agents are zero.

bank as nonmonitoring depositors and provide the remaining funding, $1 - \Lambda^*$. Combining Lemmas 1 and 2 yields the next observation.

Proposition 1. *In equilibrium, the financial market consists of informed traders, uninformed discretionary traders, and liquidity traders. The informed traders are the only ones who learn ν, and their trades have the potential to convey this information. The financial market is ineffective, however, in deterring borrowers from investing in the bad project when they have the choice. In equilibrium, banks consist of monitoring agents and uninformed discretionary agents who act as nonmonitoring depositors. The bank specializes in deterring borrowers from investing in bad projects, but it learns nothing about ν.*

The intuition is as follows. If the informed agents were to form a bank, they could try to communicate information about ν to the borrower. This information communication may be either truthful or not. With truthful communication, the borrower invests $\bar{K}$ whenever optimal. However, once the borrower learns ν, it has no incentive to compensate the bank for its information acquisition cost. It can make a 'take it or leave it' offer to the bank that merely yields the bank a zero expected profit on the loan itself. Since M is a sunk cost, the bank will find it in its own interest to accept the offer, thereby violating the ex ante participation constraints of informed agents. If communication is not truthful, then this problem is exacerbated, as the borrower remains uninformed about ν and thus chooses $K = 0$.[10] On the other hand, if the informed agents compete as traders in the financial market, each can recover his information acquisition cost because the presence of liquidity traders makes prices noisy and sustains the ex post trading profits of those with privileged information.

But if the monitoring agents decide to trade in the financial market as well, they face a coordination failure. Since a certain mass of them must choose to monitor in order to be effective, each monitoring agent must rely on sufficiently many others to monitor as well. But since each agent is arbitrarily small, this arrangement is beset with a free-rider problem in that there is at least one Nash equilibrium in which no agent monitors in the financial market. An effective way to resolve this problem is to form a coalition of monitoring agents whose measure is precisely Λ^*. These monitoring agents can observe each other's actions costlessly and thus implement a coordinated monitoring strategy. This endogenously gives rise to a financial intermediary, as in Ramakrishnan and Thakor (1984). Each monitoring agent contributes his \$1 endowment for lending and an additional \$M for monitoring, so that these agents supply \$$\Lambda^*$ of loanable funds and \$$\Lambda^*M$ of monitoring resources; the remaining \$$1 - \Lambda^*$ of loanable funds is collected from nonmonitoring discretionary depositors.[11] The endogenously

---

[10] We find the case involving no truthful revelation of information to be the most realistic. It also rules out trivial alternative resolutions, for example, a borrower hiring an agent to produce information about ν.

[11] Our modeling of the impact of agents in the information production and monitoring cases is symmetric in the sense that, in both cases, individual agents are viewed as (almost) atomistic in their

emerging role of banks as monitors is reminiscent of the role of banks in Diamond (1984). However, whereas the banks in Diamond's model monitor ex post cash flows, the banks here monitor ex ante project choices.

The role of banks that we have characterized is consistent with the key qualitative asset transformation functions served by real-world depository institutions [see Bhattacharya and Thakor (1993)]. For example, depository institutions that make loans and monitor borrowers to influence credit risk look very much like the banks in our model. Specifically, our banks are mutuals owned by their depositors. The nonmonitoring depositors are 'pure' financiers, whereas the monitoring depositors are both depositors and loan officers since they monitor borrowers. This is akin to real-world mutual depository institutions in which there are depositors who are not involved in the management of the mutual and managers who hold ownership stakes by virtue of their deposits.

3. THE ANALYSIS AND EQUILIBRIUM DEFINITION

3.1. Determination of Interest Rates

3.1.1. *Bank Lending*

The bank monitors the borrower's choice of project but does not learn ν. Thus, there is no information feedback about ν from the bank to the borrower, and by equation (1) the borrower cannot be included to invest $K = \bar{K}$. The competitive bank's loan interest rate is set to yield an expected profit of zero. Thus, the loan interest factor (one plus the interest rate) r_B solves $\eta r_B = 1 + \Lambda^* M$, or

$$r_B = \frac{1 + \Lambda^* M}{\eta}. \tag{3}$$

Note that in deriving equation (3) we have allowed the bank to recoup its monitoring cost. The reason is as follows. The bank's monitoring cost (M times the measure of monitoring agents) is incurred in the postlending stage, and at this stage it is in the bank's best interest to monitor. This is because the lack of bank monitoring means that the borrower will invest in the good project only with probability θ; recall that the realization of whether the borrower has access to a bad project is privately observed by the borrower that precludes realization-contingent monitoring. The bank's expected profit on the loan (if it does not monitor) is

$$\theta \eta \frac{[1 + \Lambda^* M]}{\eta} - 1 = \theta[1 + \Lambda^* M] - 1 < 0$$

by equation (2). Thus, when the competitive bank quotes a price prior to making the loan, its quoted price must include the monitoring cost $\Lambda^* M$ in order to satisfy the bank's participation constraint.

impact. In the financial market equilibrium, it will turn out that there must be sufficiently many informed traders for the security price to be influenced by their trades. And in the banking equilibrium, there must be sufficiently many monitoring agents to deter asset-substitution moral hazard.

3.1.2. Financial Market Funding

As will become apparent later, informed traders submit orders for the security only when their signal reveals that $\nu = 1$. The market maker observes the total order flow and has to decide whether total demand is such that the borrower will be induced to invest $\bar{K}$ in improving the project. From equation (1), we know that this investment is socially efficient (first best) only when the probability that $\nu = 1$ is sufficiently high, that is, when $\Pr(\nu = 1 \mid D)\alpha > \bar{K}$, where $\Pr(\nu = 1 \mid D)$ is the posterior probability that the borrower (or the market maker) assigns to the event $\nu = 1$.[12] Of course, a borrower will be induced to invest only if

$$\Pr(\nu = 1 \mid D)\eta\alpha > \bar{K}. \tag{4}$$

Note that equation (4) is more stringent than the social efficiency condition, because a borrower with a good project benefits from investing $\bar{K}$ only if the project succeeds, even though the improvement, α, occurs in both the successful and unsuccessful states if $\nu = 1$ is realized. The reason is that $\alpha < 1$, so that all of it accrues to the lender (investors in the bond) if the unsuccessful state is realized. This distorts the borrower's decision further away from the first best (attainable with self-financing). This is the usual underinvestment moral hazard or debt overhang problem.

We now define $D_{\min}$ as the minimum total demand to induce the borrower to invest $\bar{K}$ in improving the project. That is (see equation (4)),

$$\Pr(\nu = 1 D_{\min})\eta\alpha = \bar{K}. \tag{5}$$

Since $\Pr(\nu = 1 \mid D)$ is monotonically increasing in D (we will verify this), we have

$$\Pr(\nu = 1 \mid D)\eta\alpha > \bar{K} \quad \text{for} \quad D_{\min}.$$

Therefore, for $D > D_{\min}$, the borrower invests in project improvement. The best decision rule, given the observability problem about ν (second best), would be to choose the cutoff D^* such that $\Pr(\nu = 1 \mid D^*)\alpha = \bar{K}$. The decision rule of investing only when $D > D_{\min}$ is therefore more distortionary. We will later verify that the $D_{\min}$ defined in equation (5) exists.

In Figure 4 we describe the inference process underlying the information feedback that occurs in the financial market. With the help of this figure, we can derive the interest rates that are set in the financial market. Henceforth, we consider the limiting case in which an individual trader's measure $\in = 0$, that is, each trader is atomistic. Where appropriate, we will point out what happens if ϵ is small but positive. Let $r(D)$ be the equilibrium interest factor as a function of the realized demand D. First, for $D \in [0, D_{\min}]$, we have $K = 0$. Thus, $r(D) = r_{\max}$, where $\theta\eta r_{\max} + [1 - \theta] \times 0 = 1$. Thus,

$$r_{\max} = \frac{1}{\theta\eta}. \tag{6}$$

---

[12] Total demand will convey no information about ν if $\Omega = 0$ in equilibrium.

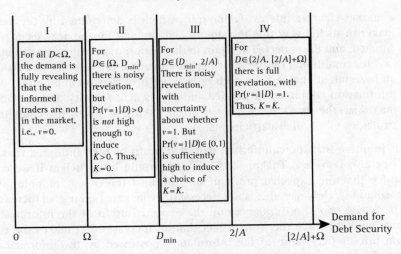

The following table represents the content of the figure:

I	II	III	IV
For all $D < \Omega$, the demand is fully revealing that the informed traders are not in the market, i.e., $v=0$.	For $D \in (\Omega, D_{min})$ there is noisy revelation, but $\Pr(v=1\mid D) > 0$ is *not* high enough to induce $K>0$. Thus, $K=0$.	For $D \in (D_{min}, 2/A)$ There is noisy revelation, with uncertainty about whether $v=1$. But $\Pr(v=1\mid D) \in (0,1)$ is sufficiently high to induce a choice of $K=\bar{K}$.	For $D \in (2/A, [2/A]+\Omega)$ there is full revelation, with $\Pr(v=1\mid D) =1$. Thus, $K=\bar{K}$.

Demand for Debt Security

0   Ω D_{min} $2/A$ $[2/A]+\Omega$

Figure 4. *A schematic of financial market realizations of security demand and inferences*

Note that in deriving equation (6), we have used the result that the financial market does not monitor borrowers. Next, for $D \in (D_{min}, 2/A)$, we have $K = \bar{K}$ and $\Pr(\nu = 1 \mid D) > \bar{K}/\eta\alpha$. Thus (see equation (4)), $r(D) = \hat{r}(D)$, where $\theta\{\Pr(\nu = 1 \mid D)[\eta\hat{r}(D) + [1 - \eta]\alpha] + [1 - \Pr(\nu = 1 \mid D)][\eta\hat{r}(D)]\} = 1$, or

$$\hat{r}(D) = \frac{1 - \theta \Pr(\nu = 1 \mid D)[1 - \eta]\alpha}{\theta\eta}. \tag{7}$$

Finally, for $D \in [\frac{2}{A}, \frac{2}{A} + \Omega]$, we have $K = \hat{K}$ and $\Pr(\nu = 1 \mid D) = 1$. Thus, $r(D) = r_{min}$, where

$$\theta\{\eta r_{min} + [1 - \eta]\alpha\} = 1, \text{ or}$$

$$r_{min} = \frac{1 - \theta[1 - \eta]\alpha}{\theta\eta}. \tag{8}$$

3.2. Definition of Equilibrium in the Financial Market

A noisy rational expectations Nash Equilibrium is:

(i) a measure of informed traders, Ω^*, such that the expected profit of each informed trader is zero (and the first derivative of this expected profit with respect to Ω is negative at Ω^*) when each informed trader takes as given the equilibrium strategies of the other potentially informed traders and the liquidity traders, and all other participants, including banks and borrowing firms, but assumes that the impact of his own trade on the price is negligible;

(ii) an aggregate security demand from informed and uninformed liquidity traders equal to

$$D^*(v, \ell) = \Omega^* d_I(v) + \ell;$$

(iii) a market-clearing interest factor $r(D)$, which is determined by the market maker in such a way that the supply and demand for the debt security are equated, and the expected net gain to the a priori uninformed market maker is zero, conditional on the information contained in the order flow; and

(iv) an investment choice K by each borrowing firm that is conditional on the information contained in the demand for its debt security and is made to maximize the firm's net expected profit, taking as given the equilibrium strategies of all other participants.

It is intuitive that the equilibrium expected profit of each informed trader is zero [see also Boot and Thakor (1993a)]. This would be sufficient if we could guarantee that the expected profit of an informed trader was monotonically decreasing in Ω. However, this is not necessarily true here because an increase in Ω experts two opposing influences on the expected profit of the informed. On the one hand, we have the usual effect that an increase in Ω makes the equilibrium price reflect more of the information possessed by the informed and hence reduces their expected profit. But on the other hand, the increased price informativeness also makes it more likely that the borrower will choose $K = \bar{K}$ when the informed are in the market. This increases the expected profit of the informed as Ω increases. Hence, for an Ω to qualify as the equilibrium measure of informed, it must also be true that, taking both these effects into account, a small increase in Ω reduces the expected profit of an informed trader below zero.

Note that our modeling of markets and institutions is symmetric from the standpoint of competitive structure. Each bank's expected profit is zero in equilibrium, and each informed trader earns a zero expected profit in equilibrium, net of the information acquisition cost.

4. FURTHER ANALYSIS

4.1. Derivation of D_{min}

We wish to ensure that D_{min} is in the interior of its feasible range. By Bayes's rule we know that

$$
\begin{aligned}
\Pr(\nu = 1 \mid D) &= \frac{f(D - \Omega)\gamma}{f(D - \Omega)\gamma + f(D)[1 - \gamma]} \\
&= \frac{\gamma[A - B\{D - \Omega\}]}{\gamma[A - B\{D - \Omega\}] + [1 - \gamma][A - BD]},
\end{aligned}
\tag{9}
$$

where $B \equiv A^2/2$. Note that $\partial \Pr(\nu = 1 \mid D)/\partial D > 0$. We now substitute the above expression in equation (4). Writing $S \equiv \bar{K}/\eta\alpha$ yields (note that $S > \gamma$)

$$
D_{min}^* \equiv D_{min}^*(\Omega) = \frac{A}{B} - \frac{[1 - S]\gamma\Omega}{[S - \gamma]}.
\tag{10}
$$

The solution for $D^*_{\min}$ stated in equation (10) exists if and only if $D_{\min} \geq \Omega$. Otherwise $D_{\min} = \Omega$, and interval II in Figure 4 vanishes. Thus, the desired cutoff demand level, $D_{\min}$, is

$$D_{\min} = \Omega \vee D^*_{\min}, \tag{11}$$

where $\vee$ is the max operator. Thus, the minimum total demand for the security that will induce the borrower to invest is $D^*_{\min}$ (the value of demand such that the expected payoff enhancement to the borrower exactly equals $\bar{K}$, the investment in payoff enhancement) unless $D^*_{\min}$ is less than Ω, the measure of informed agents. In this case, the minimum total demand to induce an investment of $\bar{K}$ must be Ω, since any $D < \Omega$ leads to $\Pr(v = 1 \mid D) = 0$.

4.2. Determination of Equilibrium Measure of Informed Traders

If we assume that $D_{\min} = D^*_{\min}$ (see equation (11)), then the expected profits of the informed, for a given Ω can be expressed as:

$$V = -M + \theta \eta \gamma \int_{D_{\min} - \Omega}^{[2/A] - \Omega} \{\hat{r}(\Omega + \ell) - r_{\min}\} f(\ell) d\ell, \tag{12}$$

where we have $D = \Omega + \ell$ in the range over which the integration in equation (12) is performed. The limits of the integration arise from the fact that it is only when D goes from $D_{\min}$ to $2/A$ that the borrower chooses the value-enhancing investment $\bar{K}$ and revelation is noisy (so that the informed can profit). In this range, the informed are in the market (i.e., they know that $\nu = 1$) and the total demand D is sufficiently revealing so that $r_{\min}$ is the break-even interest factor on the firm's bond. What the firm is being charged is $\hat{r}(\Omega + \ell)$, which is the equilibrium interest factor determined in the financial market. The informed profit because $\hat{r}(\Omega + \ell) > r_{\min}$. We now have the following result.

Proposition 2. *The lowest value of Ω such that the expected profit of each informed trader is zero is given by*

$$\Omega_1 = \sqrt{M/X}, \tag{13}$$

where $X \equiv \theta \gamma \alpha [1 - \eta][1 - \gamma]\{A^2 \gamma \Gamma_1 [1 - \gamma + \gamma \Gamma_1] + \frac{A^2 \gamma (1 - \gamma)}{2} \ln(\Gamma_2)\}$

$$\Gamma_1 \equiv \frac{[1 - \{\bar{K}/\eta \alpha\}]}{[\{\bar{K}/\eta \alpha\} - \gamma]}$$

$$\Gamma_2 \equiv \frac{[\{K/\eta \alpha\} - \gamma]}{[1 - \gamma]}.$$

Moreover, $\partial V / \partial \Omega > 0$ *at* $\Omega = \Omega_1$.

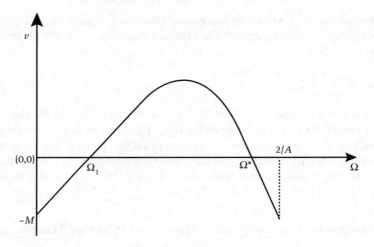

Figure 5. *A graph of the expected profit of an informed trader as a
function of the measure of informed traders*

According to the definition of the equilibrium, Ω^* has to be such that each
informed trader earns an expected profit of zero. Ω_1 satisfies this requirement.
However, because $\partial V / \partial \Omega_1 > 0$, it must be the case that Ω_1 is not the equilibrium
measure of informed traders. At $\Omega = \Omega_1$, the increased informativeness of prices
due to the presence of more informed traders increases the expected profit of each
informed trader. For an equilibrium to exist, the function V must slope down at
some point and become zero again, as shown in Figure 5. That is, we have
multiple solutions in Ω to the equation $V(\Omega) = 0$, and Ω^* is the larger of the two
Ωs satisfying this equation. This situation arises here because, unlike the usual
setting, informed traders here both compete with and complement each other.

If $\epsilon > 0$, then it is transparent that the larger of the two Ωs satisfying $V(\Omega) = 0$
is the unique equilibrium, assuming that $\Omega > 0$.[13] This is because at $\Omega = \Omega_1$, an
additional individual trader can make a positive expected profit from becoming
informed since $\partial V(\Omega) / \partial \Omega \mid_{\Omega = \Omega_l} > 0$, that is, $V(\Omega_1 + \epsilon) > 0$ for $\epsilon > 0$. Thus, Ω_1
cannot be an equilibrium with traders of arbitrarily small but positive measure. It
is only at the limit itself, when $\epsilon = 0$, that we have multiple equilibria—both
values of Ω for which $V(\Omega) = 0$ are possible equilibria under a somewhat less
restrictive definition of equilibrium.[14] The reason why Ω_1 is an equilibrium in this
case is that no additional trader would individually decide to enter the market

---

[13] If the equilibrium $\Omega > 0$, then it must be at least as great as Ω_1 because $V(\Omega) < 0 \; \forall \; \Omega < \Omega_1$. Note
that $\Omega = 0$ is always a candidate for equilibrium; it does not pay any agent of small measure ($\epsilon < \Omega_1$)
to become informed if $\Omega = 0$.

[14] Strictly speaking, according to our definition of equilibrium, Ω_1, is not an equilibrium. But our
discussion here serves to clarify the reason why in our equilibrium definition we imposed the
restriction $\partial V / \partial \Omega < 0$ on the equilibrium Ω. We thank Neil Wallace for discussing this with us.

when $\Omega = \Omega_1$ since his zero measure fails to increase Ω and this keeps V at zero. Because we view this economy as only the limiting case of an economy with small but positive measure agents, we will henceforth focus only on the larger of the two Ωs for which $V(\Omega) = 0$.

We have assumed thus far that $D_{min} = D_{min}^*$, and with this we obtain a solution Ω_1 to $V(\Omega) = 0$ such that $\partial V / \partial \Omega > 0$ at $\Omega = \Omega_1$. As will be shown, increasing Ω above Ω_1 to Ω^* will switch D_{min} in equation (11) to $D_{min} = \Omega^*$. Like equation (12), the expected profit to the informed can now be written as[15]

$$V = -M + \theta\eta\gamma \int_0^{[2/A]-\Omega} \{\hat{r}(\Omega + \ell) - r_{min}\} f(\ell) d\ell. \tag{14}$$

We now have our next result.

Proposition 3. *There is a set of exogenous parameter values for which the equilibrium measure of informed traders, Ω^*, is the solution to*

$$V(\Omega^*) = -M + \theta\gamma\alpha[1 - \eta][1 - \gamma]\{1 - A\gamma\Omega^* + [\Omega^* + (\Omega^*)^2 J(\Omega^*)]\}$$
$$= 0, \tag{15}$$

where

$$J(\Omega^*) \equiv \frac{A^2\gamma}{2} - \frac{A^2}{4} + \frac{A^2\gamma[1 - \gamma]}{2} \left\{ \ell n\left(\frac{A\Omega^*\gamma/2}{1 - [A\Omega^*\{1 - \gamma\}/2]}\right) \right\}.$$

Moreover, $D_{min}^*(\Omega) < \Omega^*$ at $\Omega = \Omega^*$, so that $D_{min} = \Omega^*$ (see equation (11)).

We can now examine some interesting properties of the financial market equilibrium.

Proposition 4. *The equilibrium measure of informed traders is positive only if, for a given M, θ is sufficiently high, or, for a given θ, M is sufficiently low.*

This proposition is intuitive. When the moral hazard problem is severe (the observable θ is low), a potentially informed trader anticipates that even her superior information about ν does not reduce the high probability that she will invest in a firm that chooses a bad project and imposes a loss on her. This reduces

---

[15] In Figure 5, Equation (12) and Equation (14) we have implicitly assumed that $\Omega < 2/A$. It is easy to see why this holds. Note that if $\Omega \geq 2/A$, where $2/A$ is the maximum realization of liquidity demand, then there are only two possibilities: (i) $D < 2/A$, in which case the market maker infers that the probability is 1 that the informed traders are not in the market, and (ii) $D \geq 2/A$, in which case the market maker infers that the probability is 1 that the informed traders are in the market. In both cases, prices are fully revealing and the informed can earn no profit on their information. Hence, $\Omega \geq 2/A$ cannot be the equilibrium measure of informed traders.

her incentive to become informed at a cost. If θ is sufficiently low, no potentially informed trader may choose to acquire costly information. Similarly, for a given θ, an increase in M reduces the expected profit of an informed trader, and a sufficiently high M will cause a breakdown of the market for information. This also highlights another interesting result, which is stated below.

Proposition 5. *The expected profit of an informed trader is always maximized at some $\Omega > 0$.*

In Boot and Thakor (1993a), for example, the expected profit of an informed trader is always maximized at $\Omega = 0$, that is, when there are no other informed traders in the market. This is never true here since a borrower with a good project always eschews its investment in project improvement if it knows there is nothing to be learned from market prices. Given this, it does not pay for any investor to become informed. Thus, as Figure 5 shows, an informed trader earns a higher expected profit when there is a positive measure of informed traders in the market and the borrower views the market price as an information communicator. This means that if the V function were to have a maximum value that was negative,[16] then no one will choose to become informed in equilibrium (i.e., the equilibrium $\Omega = 0$). Another way of saying this is than an investor will become informed only if she believes there will be a sufficiently large number of others who will also choose to become informed.

4.3. The Borrower's Choice of Financing Source

The borrower's expected utility is the expected return net of its borrowing cost. If a borrower chooses the financial market, its borrowing cost depends on the anticipated informativeness of the market price of its debt. We have shown that the equilibrium measure of informed traders is Ω^* and that $D_{min} = \Omega^*$ is the appropriate aggregate demand cutoff [see equation (11) and Proposition 3]. Therefore, whenever the informed discover $v = 1$ and are in the market, the borrower will find that $D \geq D_{min}$, and hence will choose $K = \bar{K}$. But it is possible that the borrower will choose $\bar{K}$ even when the informed have discovered $v = 0$ and do not bid for the firm's debt since $\ell \geq D_{min}$ is possible.

The expected return of the borrower from financial market borrowing is given by

$$E(R^F) = \theta\{\gamma E(R^F \mid v = 1) + [1 - \gamma]E(R^F \mid v = 0)\} + [1 - \theta]N, \qquad (16)$$

where $E(R^F)$ is the unconditional expected return and $E(R^F \mid v)$ is the expected return conditional on the realization of v. To understand equation (16), recall that the borrower invests in the good project with financial market funding only if it is

---

[16] At $\Omega = 0$, it is always the case that $V < 0$.

locked into that project (this happens with probability θ), and invests in the bad project whenever it has a choice (this happens with probability $1 - \theta$). Note that

$$
E(R^F \mid \nu = 1) = \int_0^{[2/A]-\Omega^*} \{\eta[Y + \alpha - \hat{r}^*(D = \ell + \Omega^*)] - \bar{K}\}f(\ell)d\ell
$$
$$
+ \int_{[2/A]-\Omega^*}^{2/A} \{\eta[Y + \alpha - r_{\min}] - \bar{K}\}f(\ell)d\ell \tag{17}
$$

and

$$
E(R^F \mid \nu = 0) = \int_0^{\Omega^*} \{\eta[Y - r_{\max}]f(\ell)d\ell
$$
$$
+ \int_{\Omega^*}^{2/A} \{\eta[Y - \hat{r}^*(D = \ell)] - \bar{K}\}f(\ell)d\ell, \tag{18}
$$

where

$$
\hat{r}^*(\ell) = \frac{1 - \theta \Pr(\nu = 1 \mid D)[1 - \eta]\alpha}{\theta\eta} \tag{19}
$$

and

$$
\Pr(\nu = 1 \mid D) = \frac{\gamma\{A - B[D - \Omega^*]\}}{\gamma\{A - B[D - \Omega^*]\} + [1 - \gamma]\{A - BD\}}. \tag{20}
$$

Next, we turn to bank financing. The cost of bank borrowing is given by equation (3). Thus, the expected return for the borrower is given by

$$
E(R^B) = \eta Y - E(r_B) = \eta Y - 1 - \Lambda^* M, \tag{21}
$$

since interbank competition ensures that $E(r_B) = 1 + \Lambda^* M$. The borrower's choice of financing source is determined by comparing $E(R^F)$ and $E(R^B)$. This gives us the following result.

Proposition 6. *There exists a cutoff value of θ, say $\hat{\theta}$ (assumed to be in the interior of $[\underline{\theta}, \bar{\theta}]$), such that there is a Nash equilibrium in which borrowers with observable $\theta \leq \hat{\theta}$ choose bank financing and borrowers with observable $\theta > \hat{\theta}$ choose financial market financing. Moreover, $\hat{\theta}$ is increasing in M.*

Figure 6 shows how the net return for a borrower changes as a function of its observable quality θ. It is intuitive that borrowers with lower observable quality prefer bank financing. Banks specialize in attenuating asset-substitution moral hazard, so the borrower does not suffer a loss in utility with bank financing as this problem worsens. That is, the borrower's expected return with bank financing is

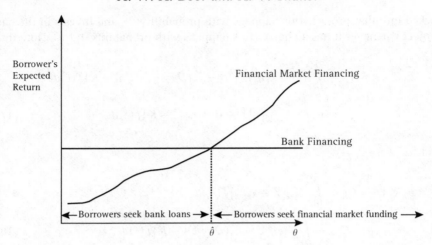

Figure 6. *A graph of the expected returns of a borrower as a
function of the borrower's observable quality*

Note: Borrowers with observable qualities below threshold $\hat{\theta}$ choose bank financing and those
with observable qualities above threshold $\hat{\theta}$ choose financial market financing.

invariant to θ. On the other hand, the benefit of financial market financing to the
borrower is increasing in θ. The reasons are twofold. First, the expected profit of
an informed trader is increasing in θ [see equation (14)], so that the higher the θ,
the larger is the equilibrium measure of the set of informed traders for the debt
security sold by the borrower. This means that the equilibrium interest factor
reflects more of the information possessed by the informed traders and is consequently lower on average. Second, the 'moral hazard premium' paid by borrowers in the financial market is decreasing in θ.

Numerical simulations of the model (details available upon request) illustrate
that $\hat{\theta}$ increases as M increases. The intuition is clear. An increase in M reduces the
expected profit of an informed trader ceteris paribus. This causes a reduction
in Ω^{*} leading to a decline in the value of financial market financing for the
borrower. If the increase in M refers only to an increase in the information
acquisition cost, but not in the monitoring cost, then it is transparent that bank
financing will become more attractive, leading to a larger set of observable
quality levels choosing bank financing. What our numerical analysis shows is that
bank financing becomes more attractive with an increase in M even when this
increase applies equally to the costs of information acquisition and monitoring.

We next consider the implication of permitting only noisy monitoring by the
bank. Suppose that, conditional on being in the state in which the borrower has a
choice of project, the bank can enforce the choice of the good project only with
probability $\xi \in (0, 1)$. We then have the following result.

Proposition 7. *If the bank can prevent the choice of the bad project only with probability* $\xi \in (0, 1)$, *there exists a* θ^0 *(assumed to be in the interior of* $[\theta, \hat{\theta}]$*) such that there is a Nash equilibrium in which borrowers with observable* $\theta \leq \theta^0$ *prefer bank financing and borrowers with observable* $\theta > \theta^0$ *prefer financial market financing. Moreover, the value of bank financing to the borrower is increasing in* θ, *and* $\theta^0 < \hat{\theta}$.

Thus, we see that while noise in the monitoring technology reduces the value of bank financing to the borrower ceteris paribus ($\theta^0 < \hat{\theta}$), we still encounter the earliest result that borrowers with relatively high θs access the financial market and borrowers with relatively low θs approach banks.[17] One noteworthy difference that noisy monitoring makes is that it causes the borrower's net expected payoff with bank financing to be increasing in θ, rather than being invariant to θ. The intuition is that the higher the θ, the lower is the probability that the noise in its monitoring technology will obstruct the bank's ability to deter selection of the bad project, and hence the lower is the bank's loan interest factor. There is a fairly large literature on the borrower's choice of financing source that we do not discuss here. [For example, Diamond (1991), Berlin and Mester (1992), Hirshleifer and Suh (1992), Rajan (1992), Wilson (1994), and Thakor and Wilson (1995). See Bhattacharya and Thakor (1993) for a review.] Unlike that literature, we endogenize banks and the financial market. Moreover, our result here is novel in that it links the borrower's choice to its observable quality in a moral hazard setting and predicates this link on the cost of information acquisition in the financial market.

5. MODEL ROBUSTNESS AND EXTENSIONS

In this section we indicate how our model could be generalized along some important dimensions: the possibility of eliminating noise traders, the use of equity rather than debt in the financial market, information aggregation involving traders with information, the simultaneous use of bank and financial market funding, and the impact of institutional sellers. Our conclusion is that the analysis can be extended in all of these directions without qualitatively altering its results.

5.1. Elimination of Noise Traders and Introduction of Equity

The liquidity traders in our model are 'noise' traders in the sense that they make expected losses from trading. Indeed, their losses enable the informed traders to earn the profits that justify their investment in information. While this is a standard assumption in market microstructure models, one may find the presence of noise traders in our analysis somewhat awkward. In particular, why wouldn't these traders invest exclusively in securities that are immune to adverse selection concerns? Why don't they deal with banks rather than the financial market?

---

[17] Of course, the limit of $\xi \to 0$ involves the financial market dominating banks for all θ.

Clearly, in any model in which agents potentially acquire private information at a cost, there must be sufficient noise in equilibrium prices to make it privately optimal for agents to become informed. However, it is unnecessary for the agents who provide the noise to sustain trading losses. We could assume instead that it is the issuing firm that loses through the systematic underpricing of its security. The liquidity traders could then break even. This would be in the spirit of Rock's (1986) IPO underpricing model. We will show shortly that this approach is consistent with our model.

Consider now the use of debt contracts in our analysis. From an information acquisition standpoint, equity is clearly better than debt to examine in a financial market context. We will also show that using equity instead of debt does not change our conclusions. To deal with this and the liquidity traders issue, we consider a simplified version of our model, an example.

Example 1. *Data*: Suppose $\theta = 1$, $\gamma = 0.4$, and $\eta = 1$. Let S represent the equity ownership share the firm must surrender to outside shareholders to raise the \$1 investment it needs. There are uninformed discretionary traders who can choose to become informed about v at a cost of $M = 0.24\alpha[Y + 0.5\alpha]^{-1}$, and there are liquidity traders whose demand equals $\ell \in \{0, 1/2\}$, with $\Pr(\ell = 0) = 0.6$, and $\Pr(\ell = 1/2) = 0.4$. The prior probability distribution of v is $\Pr(v = 1) = 0.4$, and $\Pr(v = 0) = 0.6$. Assume that $\alpha > 2\bar{K}$ and $\gamma\alpha < \bar{K}$, and that $\bar{K}$ is an unobserved private investment by the firm.

Analysis: We conjecture that $\Omega = 1/2$. Informed traders will submit a purchase order only when $v = 1$. Note that $\alpha > 2\bar{K}$ ensure that the firm invests $\bar{K}$ whenever $D \geq 1/2$. Since the available supply of equity for outsiders to buy is \$1, there are only three relevant states:

(i) $v = 1$ and $\ell = 1/2$, so that the total demand from the liquidity traders and informed traders is \$1. In this case $\Pr(v = 1 \mid D = 1) = 1$, and the uninformed discretionary traders buy 0.

(ii) $v = 1$ and $\ell = 0$ or $v = 0$ and $\ell = 1/2$, so that the total demand D from liquidity traders and informed traders is \$1/2. The UDTs buy \$1/2 worth of equity. Using Bayes's rule, the posterior probability assessment that the firm has that the informed traders have observed $v = 1$ can be determined as

$$
\begin{aligned}
&\Pr(v = 1 \mid D = 1/2) \\
&= \frac{\Pr(D = 1/2 \mid v = 1)\Pr(v = 1)}{\Pr(D = 1/2 \mid v = 1)\Pr(v = 1) + \Pr(D = 1/2 \mid v = 0)\Pr(v = 0)} \\
&= \frac{0.24}{0.48} = \frac{1}{2}.
\end{aligned} \tag{22}
$$

(iii) $v = 0$ and $\ell = 0$, so that the total demand D from liquidity traders and informed traders equals \$0, and $\mathrm{PR}(v = 1 \mid D = 0) = 0$. The uninformed discretionary traders buy \$1 of equity.

Table 1. *Outside investors' ownership fractions for different loan demand realizations*

Description	Realized total demand		
	$D = \$1$	$D = \$1/2$	$D = \$0$
Inference of market maker	$v = 1$ and $\ell = 1/2$	$v = 0$ and $\ell = 1/2$ or $v = 1$ and $\ell = 0$	$v = 0$ and $\ell = 0$
$S_{\text{Fairly Priced}}(D)$ $S_{\text{Underpricing}}(D)$	$[Y + \alpha]^{-1}$ $[Y + 1.25\alpha]\{[Y + 0.5\alpha][Y + \alpha]\}^{-1} >$ $[Y + \alpha]^{-1}$	$[Y + 0.5\alpha]^{-1}$ $[Y + 0.5\alpha]^{-1}$	Y^{-1} Y^{-1}

Table 1 summarizes the ownership fractions outsiders obtain in the three different states. It can be verified that these ownership fractions are such that

(i) The uninformed discretionary traders earn zero expected profit;
(ii) The liquidity traders earn zero expected profit;
(iii) The informed traders earn positive expected profits on their trades, but zero expected profits when their information production costs M are taken into accounts;
(iv) The firm prefers to underprice $D = 1$.
(v) $\Omega = 1/2$ in equilibrium.

A proof of this is available upon request. Thus, our analysis is robust with respect to using equity instead of debt and ensuring that liquidity traders break even on average.

5.2. Information Aggregation

Although we have assumed in our analysis that all informed traders obtain the same information, it is clear that information aggregation is an important element of the intuition behind our story. Without aggregation of heterogeneous signals in the financial market, we must rely solely on the inability of banks to internalize any benefits from information acquisition in order to obtain the sharp dichotomy of functions across banks and the financial market that is described in Proposition 1. Moreover, one might wonder why entrepreneurs can't directly acquire information about v, a single piece of information. That is, in order to simplify, our analysis ignores an important advantage of financial markets, namely to aggregate payoff-relevant information when it is widely dispersed in the economy and difficult to purchase directly.

In what follows, we provide a simple extension of our model that illustrates how financial markets may aggregate diverse information and how the desirability for such aggregation can further diminish the role of banks as pure information sellers.

Example 2: Data: Suppose $\theta = 1$, $\gamma = 0.25$, and $\eta = 1$. There are two distinct signals, $x \in \{0, 1\}$ and $y \in \{0, 1\}$, that are conditionally uncorrelated, that provide information about v. In particular,

$$\Pr(x = 0) = \Pr(y = 0) = 0.5;$$
$$\Pr(v = 1) = 0.25, \Pr(v = 1 \mid x = 1) = \Pr(v = 1 \mid y = 1) = 0.5;$$
$$\Pr(v = 1 \mid x = 1, y = 1) = 1; \text{ and}$$
$$\Pr(v = 1 \mid x = 1, y = 0) = \Pr(v = 1 \mid x = 0, y = 1)$$
$$= \Pr(v = 1 \mid x = 0, y = 0\} = 0.$$

There are liquidity traders whose demand $\ell \in \{0, 1/2\}$, with $\Pr(\ell = 0) = \Pr(\ell = 1/2) = 0.5$. Let S represent the equity ownership share the firm must surrender to outside shareholders to raise the $1 investment it needs. There are uninformed discretionary traders who can choose to become informed about either x or y, but not both, at a cost $M = 0.0625\alpha[Y + 0.5\alpha]^{-1}$.

Analysis: For simplicity, we will assume that the firm's equity is fairly priced and therefore the liquidity traders make losses on average. Let the measure of those who invest to learn x be Ω_x and the measure of those who invest to learn y be Ω_y. We conjecture that $\Omega_x = \Omega_y = \frac{1}{4}$, and that each group of informed traders will submit a purchase order only when the signal for that group takes a value of 1.

There are now five relevant states, each distinguished by a different realization of total demand from the liquidity traders, those who are informed about x and those who are informed about y. Let D represent the total demand from these three groups. As usual, the market maker cannot distinguish the individual components of total demand, the price of the equity is set at its expected value conditional on the information contained in D, and the uninformed discretionary traders purchase equity in the amount needed to clear the market. Thus, $D \in \{0, \frac{1}{4}, \frac{1}{2}, \frac{3}{4}, 1\}$. These five states arise as follows.

(i) $D = 0$: This arises only when $x = 0$, $y = 0$, and $\ell = 0$. The market maker unambiguously infers $v = 0$. The probability of this state is 0.125.

(ii) $D = 1/4$: This arises if $\ell = 0$, $x = 0$, $y = 1$ or $\ell = 0$, $x = 1$, $y = 0$. The marker maker unambiguously infers $v = 0$. The probability of this state is 0.25.

(iii) $D = 1/2$: This arises if $x = 1$, $y = 1$, $\ell = 0$ or $x = 0$, $y = 0$, $\ell = 1/2$. In this state, v could be either 0 or 1. The probability of this state is 0.25.

(iv) $D = 3/4$: This arises if $x = 1$, $y = 0$, $\ell = 1/2$ or $x = 0$, $y = 1$, $\ell = 1/2$. The market maker unambiguously infers $v = 0$. The probability of this state is 0.25.

(v) $D = 1$: This arises only if $x = 1$, $y = 1$, $\ell = 1/2$. The market maker unambiguously infers $v = 1$. The probability of this state is 0.125.

In states (i), (ii), and (iv), $S(D) = 1/Y$. In state (iii), $S(D) = [Y + 0.5\alpha]^{-1}$. In state (v), $S(D) = [Y + \alpha]^{-1}$. It is now straightforward to verify that the expected profit of each group of informed traders, per unit measure of informed traders, is exactly equal to $0.0625\alpha[Y + 0.5\alpha]^{-1}$, which is M. This verifies our conjecture that $\Omega_r = \Omega_y = \frac{1}{4}$.

5.3. Direct Information Elicitation Mechanisms

A natural question that arises in the context of our analysis is why it is not possible to directly elicit the private information possessed by informed traders rather than have it indirectly revealed (noisily) through the equilibrium market price. In particular, one could think of informed traders coalescing to form a bank and selling information directly to the firm.

While this seems reasonable, it is plagued by the potential lack of credibility of the information that is communicated. The problem exists at two levels: within the bank, and between the bank and the firm. Consider the more important intrabank problem first. When there are multiple agents engaged in information production, a free-rider problem arises with unobservable individual inputs in information production since each agent bears the fall cost of his input and only shares in the collective output. Ramakrishnan and Thakor (1984) show that this problem can completely vitiate any risk-sharing gains from coalescing; they therefore examine the benefit of intermediation (coalition formation) when individual agents can costlessly monitor each other's inputs.

Their model has n agents in the intermediary, each producing information about a distinct firm, so that the free-rider problem arises not from information aggregation but from each agent's payoff being a prorata share of the pooled payoff that represents the intermediary's compensation. Without costless internal monitoring, the agents within the intermediary cannot overcome their own free-riding incentives.

Information aggregation exacerbates this problem. This can be seen most readily within the context of Example 2, as well as more generally. In the context of the example, suppose that the bank consists of two groups of informed agents, one group specializing in x and the other in y. Each group provides \$0.5 to the bank to enable it to lend \$1 to the firm. For simplicity, assume that there are no intragroup incentive problems and that members of each group can function as a single entity; we make this assumption to focus on intergroup incentive problems. The bank is competitive and is paid a fee that compensates it for the information acquisition costs of the two groups. Let the measure of each group be 1, so that each group is paid M for its information acquisition.

Consider now the marginal benefit of becoming informed for each group within the bank, assuming that the bank always truthfully reports the information it receives from the two groups to the firm and that it gives each group M plus its prorata share of the output accruing to the bank under its equity contract with the firm. Now, if a particular group produces information, its expected profit (assuming that the other group will also produce information) is zero, since the bank is competitively compensated, and in turn it seeks to just satisfy each group's reservation constraint.

On the other hand, if a particular group decides to always report 0 without producing information, then its expected profit (regardless of what the other group does) is M, since the firm does not make the value-enhancing decision. Similarly, if the group (say the x group) unconditionally reports a signal value of 1, its expected profit (assuming that the other group produces information and truthfully reports) can be shown to be less than M, since now this group bears some of the cost associated with the firm making a value-enhancing decision when it should not.

Thus, each group's dominant strategy is to report 0 without producing information. In particular, it is not a Nash equilibrium for each group to invest in information acquisition, given the intrabank contracting technology of giving each group M plus its prorata share of the output accruing to the bank under its equity contract with the firm. Although mechanisms may be found to restore incentive compatibility in information acquisition within the bank, these are unlikely to be costless.

One such costly mechanism would be for the firm to offer the bank a higher expected payoff when the output is $Y+\alpha$ than when it is Y; this would reduce each group's incentive to unconditionally report 0. If the firm's net payoff enhancement is sufficiently large relative to M, then perhaps each group within the bank can be 'bribed' to report truthfully. What is interesting is that the ability of such a mechanism to restore incentive compatibility is weakened as we increase the number of signals that are being aggregated. To see this, suppose there are three signals, x, y, and z in Example 2, with $\Pr(v = 1 | x = 1, y = 1, z = 0$ or $1) = \Pr(v = 1 | x = 0$ or $1, y = 1, z = 1) = \Pr(v = 1 | x = 1, y = 0$ or $1, z = 1) = 1$ and $\Pr(v = 1 | 0$ for any two or more of x, y, and $z) = 0$. Now, incentive compatibility will be more difficult to achieve because the strategy of unconditionally reporting 0 has become less costly to each group, conditional on the other two groups producing information and reporting truthfully. More generally, the intuition is that as we increase the number of signals being aggregated, each group's signal becomes less pivotal in its impact on the group's share of the output. Thus, misreporting incentives are strengthened with greater aggregation.

The second problem we alluded to earlier was between the bank and the firm. Even apart from the groups within the bank free riding on each other's inputs, the bank's incentive to generate costly and reliable information and truthfully report it may be weak. Firms may attempt to deal with this by appealing to the revelation principle and designing incentive contracts that link the bank's fees to performance in a way that achieves incentive compatibility. For example, the firm could sell the bank a call option with its payoff on the exercise date dependent on the realization of v; the exercise of this option would reveal information about v. However, there are three difficulties with such mechanisms. First, the firm would need to ensure that the option is not resold by the bank, or else the vexing problem of dealing with the coalitional incentive compatibility constraints associated with traded contracts arises.[18] Second, if there are multiple signals

---

[18] See Jacklin (1987) for an analysis of this in the context of traded deposit claims.

that the bank reports to the firm for aggregation, then applying the revelation principle becomes particularly complex as multiple nontraded options must be offered. Third, suppose one interprets 'noise' as agents/banks that mistakenly think they can acquire information, that is, these intermediaries mistakenly buy and exercise options that are valuable if and only if information is acquired. In such a world, the market solution—which requires only the knowledge of the probability distribution of noise—is superior to revelation schemes that require knowledge of the agent type, that is, whether the signal sender in the scheme can indeed acquire the relevant signal. This problem too is exacerbated as one increases the number of signals being aggregated.

Thus the very reason that financial markets have a role for aggregating heterogeneous information puts financial intermediaries at a disadvantage in performing the same task.

Is our theory then at odds with the existence of institutions that sell information?[19] While it is true that bond rating agencies and investment advisory firms sell information about corporations, the credibility of such information sellers and consequently the demand for their services depends on their reputation in possessing the requisite information-processing skills and providing reliable information. To the extent that this reputational mechanism is not perfect, institutional information sales will at best substitute only partially for the direct acquisition of information about v by an informed trader. Thus, the presence of institutional information sellers could diminish the marginal profit from becoming informed, but will not eliminate it entirely. In particular, the preceding analysis suggests that institutional information sellers are likely to be viable only when relatively few pieces of information must be aggregated to provide a relevant set of information, whereas market-based information dissemination is likely to predominate when numerous pieces of information must be aggregated.

5.4. Simultaneous Access to Bank Loans and Financial Market Funding

While in our formulation a firm either chooses bank financing or chooses to fund itself in the financial market, we could envision firms lying along a continuum with sole bank or financial market funding as the polar extremes. This generalized version would allow firms to optimally balance the benefits of bank monitoring and financial market information aggregation. Such 'mixed' financing would be useful in a variety of contexts. For example, Diamond (1993) shows that a mix of private and public debt can improve investment efficiency.

If asset-substitution moral hazard is severe (low θ), a firm is likely to choose considerable bank funding to induce sufficient monitoring. The relatively small

---

[19] Ramakrishnan and Thakor (1984), Millon and Thakor (1985), Allen (1990), Kane and Marks (1990), and Fishman and Hagerty (1995) are examples of articles that rationalize institutions that sell financial information.

amount of funding raised in the financial market would provide some information aggregation benefits, although these would not be large because the
measure of informed traders (Ω) would be rather small in response to the low
funding level. A high-θ borrower is likely to borrow considerably more in the
financial market since its low monitoring demand necessitates only a small
amount of bank funding to mitigate asset-substitution moral hazard. Thus, this
firm can better exploit the information aggregation benefits of financial markets.

This formulation generalizes our results but does not alter them qualitatively.

6. IMPLICATIONS FOR FINANCIAL SYSTEM ARCHITECTURE

Our discussion in this section, which focuses on just a subset of the issues in
financial system architecture, is organized in four parts. First, we examine the
likely starting point for a 'free-market' financial system. That is, if an economy is
making a transition from being centrally planned to being in a free-market mode,
what is likely to be the initial configuration of its financial system? Second, we
examine the potential impact of financial innovation on borrowers' financing
source choices and on real investment decisions. Third, we examine the implications of large ('block') financial market traders who are nonatomistic. Finally,
we discuss what the analysis suggests for overall financial system design.

6.1. The Starting Point of a New Financial System

In a new financial system—one previously managed by a central planner—the
historical absence of profit-motivated banks or financial market traders implies
possibly severe information frictions pertaining to potential borrowers. In particular, asset-substitution moral hazard is likely to be rampant. Consequently,
borrowers will have lower observable qualities (θs) on average. This enhances the
value of bank financing for two reasons. First, borrowers face a large 'moral
hazard premium' in the financial market. Second, lower θs reduce the value of the
informed traders' information, thereby weakening information acquisition
incentives. Moreover, the expected lack of sophistication of financial market
traders in such an economy connotes a higher cost to them of acquiring relevant
borrower-specific information (i.e., M is higher). This leads to a lower Ω^* at the
outset than at the later stages of development of a financial market. Both these
effects—lower Ω^* and higher M—generate a relatively high $\hat{\theta}$. Consequently,
bank financing dominates a financial system during its infancy.

As the financial system evolves, successful borrowers will develop credit reputations that will ameliorate moral hazard and improve the average θ of the borrower
pool [Diamond (1991)]. More borrowers will migrate to the financial market and
traders will become more familiar with firms, leading to a lower M and a higher Ω^*.
Thus, even a financial system that begins as a bank-dominated system will evolve
to a system in which banks lose market share to the financial market.

6.2. Financial Market Sophistication

Greater sophistication in a financial market is often manifested in lower friction in informational flows. There are many ways in which such lower friction is achieved. One is through security design innovations that stimulate greater informed trading and improve liquidity [Back (1993) and Boot and Thakor (1993a)].[20] Another is through improved information transmission mechanisms that permit investors to acquire information at a lower cost. An example is the emergence of information-gathering agencies (e.g., Dun and Bradstreet) that provide lower-cost access to information. We shall focus on this latter characterization of financial market sophistication and assume that it lowers the cost of learning about ν. The effect of a lower information acquisition cost is to increase Ω^*, ceteris paribus. And an increase in Ω^* reduces the borrower's expected cost of funding in the capital market. Nothing changes for bank financing as long as the monitoring cost remains unchanged. Hence, $\hat{\theta}$ decreases and increased financial sophistication of this type results in banks losing market share to the capital market. This is consistent with recent financial history—the greatest shift in corporate borrowing from banks to the capital market has occurred in the United States, which has also led the world in financial market sophistication and efficiency. For a formal analysis of these issues, see Boot and Thakor (1996, forthcoming).

6.3. Large Financial Market Traders

We have assumed that each financial market trader is atomistic. But what if individual traders were allowed to amass 'block' holdings of bonds? This would have two potentially important effects. First, if a trader who acquired information about ν were to be endowed with sufficient investible wealth to submit a demand with positive measure, then such a large demand would noiselessly reveal the trader's superior information to the market maker and lead to a perfectly revealing price. To avoid the Grossman and Stiglitz (1980) paradox, we could provide the informed trader an opportunity to break up her trade into many smaller units, each of which would mimic the trade of an atomistic trader. Alternatively, we could permit liquidity traders to also submit block orders. Either case would change the financial market equilibrium, but is unlikely to alter our principal conclusions.

More interesting, however, is the second effect. If monitoring agents were nonatomistic, an individual monitoring agent could be of measure Λ^*, which would trivially resolve the free-rider problem associated with capital market monitoring. Our model predicts that such larger traders would diminish the

---

[20] A somewhat more subtle way in which security design can resolve informational problems in a dynamic setting is through contractual discretion that stimulates reputation development [see Boot et al. (1993)].

importance of banks and decrease $\hat{\theta}$. This is roughly consistent with the stylized facts in the United States in that the emergence of institutional investors (like CALPERS and TIAA-CREF) as active players in monitoring firms has coincided with a decline in banks' lending to corporations.

6.4. Tentative Thoughts on Financial System Design

Our analysis predicts that an optimal financial system will configure itself skewed toward bank financing if borrowers have relatively poor credit reputations (a higher moral hazard propensity) and toward capital market financing if borrowers have relatively good credit reputations, but can improve real decisions based on the information conveyed by market prices. Moreover, capital market financing is more valuable for those borrowers who attach a high value to information regarding ν.

Do these observations have anything to say about how a financial system will evolve if left to its own machinations? Our analysis provides some indications. In particular, our earlier observations on emerging financial systems suggest that the welfare relevance of financial markets should grow through time as the financial system develops. However, financial market growth will come at the expense of commercial banks. This implies that some institutional resistance from existing banks should be expected as financial markets grow in prominence. But unless the actions of banks are coordinated—in contrast to our assumption that competitive banks do not coordinate—it is unlikely that financial market growth can be retarded. Thus, it is possible that a critical factor in the development of the financial market is the fragmentation of the banking industry, which in turn may depend on the number of banks in the industry.

7. CONCLUSION

We have rationalized the coexistence of banks and financial markets based on assumptions about primitives—endowments, types of agents, and informational constraints. Banks arise as coalitions of agents who coordinate their actions to resolve asset-substitution moral hazard. The financial market arises to permit noncolluding agents to compete, and this facilitates the transmission of valuable information about market conditions with a concomitant impact on firms' real decisions. We find that borrowers who pose relatively onerous asset-substitution moral hazards prefer bank financing, and borrowers who pose less serious moral hazards go directly to the capital market. Moreover, increased financial market sophistication diminishes banks' market share.

The predictions of our theory match up with cross-sectional differences across industries. For example, our theory predicts that firms in industries with substantial state verification use financial markets, while firms in industries that require a lot of monitoring use banks. An example of this is the choice of venture capital versus financial market funding. Borrowers who have few tangible assets to offer as collateral pose particularly onerous moral hazards [see, e.g., Boot,

Thakor and Udell (1991)] and require a lot of monitoring. We do find that such borrowers tend to seek financing from venture capitalists who specialize in monitoring. On the other hand, firms that rely on more complex technologies have more to gain from the feedback role of market prices and should prefer financial market funding. The evidence on cross-sectional financing patterns in the United States (e.g., the recent explosion of biotech and computer technology firms' IPOs) seems consistent with this. Allen (1993) comprehensively discusses the consistency of this aspect of our model with the cross-sectional and inter-temporal evidence on global financing patterns. For example, Allen points out that stock market-based financial systems have been associated with 19th-century U.K., which was the first country to go through the Industrial Revolution, when managerial decision making ostensibly increased in complexity. Similarly, Mayer (1988) points out that between 1970 and 1985, companies in France, Germany, Japan, and the U.K. relied primarily on retained earnings and bank loans to finance investment, in contrast to U.S. firms that raised significant amounts in the bond markets. Allen (1993) suggests a possible explanation for this that is consistent with our model. He provides evidence that significantly more firms are covered by financial analysts in the United States than in these other countries, so that stock prices in U.S. financial markets are likely to reflect much more information of relevance to mangers.

Recently, Carey (1995) provided empirical evidence that is supportive of our analysis. He found that informational asymmetries are not an important factor in bank loan contracting with large borrowers, but moral hazard is. He concludes from his evidence that bank loans are special primarily because of their moral hazard attenuation implications.

Our article has scratched only the surface of financial system design. There are other significant unresolved issues. Foremost is understanding how regulatory policies, aimed principally at banking scope, affect the financial system, parti-cularly when one considers not only incentive problems between banks on the one hand and depositors and regulators on the other, but also between regulators and taxpayers [see Boot and Thakor (1993b) and Kane (1989, 1990)]. Such an exercise may point to potentially interesting multiperiod extensions of the analy-sis, creating a role for reputational rents and their interaction with regulation.

Appendix

Proof of Lemma 1. Suppose, counterfactually, that traders whose combined measure integrates to 1, including a strictly positive measure of traders each having invested M to learn about ν, coalesce to form a bank that can lend \$1 to the same borrower. Suppose first that information communication is truthful. Then, once the borrower learns ν, it will find it optimal to offer to pay the bank $\{\theta^{-1} - [1 - \eta]\alpha\}\{\eta\}^{-1} + t$ if $\nu = 1$ and $[1/\eta\theta] + t$ if $\nu = 0$, where t is an arbitrarily small positive scalar approaching zero. This will be a 'take it or leave it' offer. At these interest factors, each bank makes an expected profit of t on the loan itself, thereby incurring a net expected loss because of its inability to recoup its information acquisition cost (M times the measure of informed traders in the bank). Of course, if information communication is not truthful, the borrower does not invest in $\bar{K}$. Thus, informed traders do not form a bank.

If these traders choose to trade independently in the capital market, however, they compete with each other. The presence of liquidity traders means that the equilibrium security price will not always fully reflect all of the informed traders' information. This noise in prices is sufficient to enable each informed trader to recoup M.   □

Proof of Lemma 2. Suppose, counterfactually, that the monitoring agents trade in the capital market. Since actions in the capital market are uncoordinated, we may view the measure of monitoring agents as being greater or less than Λ^*. We show below, however, that agents must believe that it is either 0 or Λ^*. If it is believed to be less than Λ^*, then it must be zero in a Nash equilibrium since each agent recognizes that her investment in monitoring is useless due to the assumption that any measure less than Λ^* leads to ineffective monitoring. If it is conjectured to be greater than Λ^*, then there is a free-rider problem in that any agent can arbitrarily choose to not monitor without affecting the efficacy of monitoring. If the measure is believed to be precisely Λ^*, then the assumption that each agent is atomistic implies that the dominant strategy of each agent is not to monitor. The reason is as follows. If the set of monitoring agents is Z (with measure Λ^*), then if agent $i \in Z$ believes that no other agent $j \in Z$ will monitor, i's best response is to not monitor either. If agent $i \in Z$ believes that all other agents $j \in Z$ will monitor, then once again her best response is not to monitor since agents i's measure is zero, and her lack of monitoring does not affect the measure of those who monitor. (This proof clarifies that if each agent had measure $\epsilon > 0$, we would obtain two Nash equilibria, one in which all agents in Z monitor and one in which none of them do.) Thus, monitoring agents will not trade in the financial market.

Monitoring agents will form a bank, however, since exactly Λ^* monitoring agents can coalesce and invite measure $1 - \Lambda^*$ of discretionary uninformed agents to join as nonmonitoring depositors. Given that monitoring inputs of individual agents are costlessly observed within the bank, the free-rider problem is trivially resolved. When it comes to contracting with the borrower, the bank can charge an interest factor $\{1 + \Lambda^* M\}\eta^{-1}$ and thus recoup the cost of monitoring, $\Lambda^* M$, since lending without monitoring is unprofitable [see equation (2)]. Given the competitive environment, no higher or lower rate is feasible.   □

Proof of Proposition 1. Follows readily from Lemmas 1 and 2.   □

Proof of Proposition 2. Using equations (7) and (8) and simplifying, we can write

$$\hat{r}(\Omega + \ell) - r_{\min} = \frac{\alpha[1 - \eta]}{\eta} \left\{ \frac{[1 - \gamma]\{A - B[\Omega + \ell]\}}{\gamma[A - B\ell] + [1 - \gamma][A - B\{\Omega + \ell\}]} \right\}.$$

Substituting the above in equation (12) and simplifying yields

$$V = -M + \theta\gamma\alpha[1 - \eta][1 - \gamma]$$
$$\times \int_{D_{\min}-\Omega}^{[2/A]-\Omega} \left\{ \frac{B^2\ell^2 + [B^2\Omega - 2AB]\ell + A^2 - AB\Omega}{-B\ell + A - B\Omega[1 - \gamma]} \right\} d\ell. \tag{A1}$$

Tedious algebra enables one to simplify equation (A1) and express it as

$$V = -M + X\Omega^2. \tag{A2}$$

Ω_1 is obtained by setting $V = 0$ in equation (A2) and choosing the positive root. This leads to equation (13). Tedious algebra shows that $\partial V/\partial\Omega > 0$ at $\Omega = \Omega_1$. $\qquad\square$

Proof of Proposition 3. We substitute equations (7) and (8) in equation (14) and simplify. With some tedious algebra, this leads to equation (15). Note that since $\Omega < 2/A$, we have $A\Omega\gamma/2 < 1 - \{A\Omega[1 - \gamma]/2\}$, so that $ln([A\Omega\gamma/2]/(1 - [A\Omega\{1 - \gamma\}/2]))$ is negative. Although signing $\partial V/\partial\Omega$ analytically does not seem possible, we have verified through numerical analysis that there exist sets of exogenous parameter values for which $\partial V/\partial\Omega < 0$ for some $\Omega > \Omega_1$ and that V cuts the x axis only once at Ω^* for all $\Omega > \Omega_1$. The numerical analysis also helps to verify that $D_{\min}^*(\Omega^*)$ defined in equation (10) is less than Ω^*. $\qquad\square$

Proof of Proposition 4. The proof follows immediately from equation (15). For any $M > 0$, V becomes negative at $\theta = 0$ independently of Ω^*. Similarly, for a given θ, V become negative if M is sufficiently high, once again for any $\Omega^* \geq 0$. $\qquad\square$

Proof of Proposition 5. From Proposition 1 we know that $\partial V/\partial\Omega > 0$ at $\Omega = \Omega_1 > 0$. Hence, an increase in Ω beyond Ω_1 can increase an informed trader's expected profit. $\qquad\square$

Proof of Proposition 6. The proof follows immediately from comparing equation (16) and (21). $E(R^B)$ is independent of θ and $E(R^F)$ is increasing in θ. Moreover, $E(R^B) > E(R^F) = 0$ at $\theta = 0$ and $E(R^F) > E(R^B)$ at $\theta = 1$. Thus, given continuity of $E(R^F)$ in θ, $\exists\theta \in [\underline{\theta}, \bar{\theta}] \subset (0, 1) \ni a\hat{\theta} \in (\underline{\theta}, \bar{\theta})$ can be found to satisfy $E(R^F) > E(R^B) \forall \theta > \hat{\theta}$ and $E(R^F) \leq E(R^B) \forall \theta \leq \hat{\theta}$. $\qquad\square$

Proof of Proposition 7. With noisy monitoring, the zero expected profit interest factor charged by the bank, r_B^0, satisfies

$$r_B^0\eta[\theta + \{1 - \theta\}\xi] = 1 + \Lambda^*M,$$

which yields

$$r_B^0 = \frac{1 + \Lambda^* M}{\eta[\theta + \{1 - \theta\}\xi]}.$$

(A3)

The borrower's net payoff from bank financing is

$$E(R_0^B) = [\theta + \{1 - \theta\}\xi]\eta[Y - r_B^0] + [1 - \theta][1 - \xi]N.$$

(A4)

Substituting equation (A3) in equation (A4) and using the fact that $\eta Y > N$, we see that $\partial E(R_0^B)/\partial\theta > 0$. Moreover, comparing equation (21) and equation (A4) also shows that $E(R_0^B) < E(R^B)$ for every $\theta \in [\underline{\theta}, \bar{\theta}]$.

To show that there exists a cutoff θ^0, note that $E(R^F) = 0$ at $\theta = 0$ [see equation (16)], and by Proposition 5 and the fact that $E(R_0^B) < E(R^B)\,\forall\theta$, we know that $E(R^F) > E(R_0^B)$ at $\theta = \bar{\theta}$. Thus, continuity of $E(R^F)$ and $E(R_0^B)$ in θ guarantees that $E(R_0^B) = E(R^F)$ for an interior $\theta > 0$ sufficiently small (assuming that $\underline{\theta}$ is small enough). This then establishes that $\exists\theta^0 \in (\underline{\theta}, \bar{\theta}) \ni E(R^F) > E(R_0^B)\,\forall\theta > \theta^0$ and $E(R^F) \le E(R_0^B)\,\forall\theta \le \theta^0$. The result that $\theta^0 < \bar{\theta}$ follows from the result that $E(R_0^B) < E(R^B)\,\forall\theta \in [\underline{\theta}, \bar{\theta}]$. $\qquad\square$

REFERENCES

Allen, F., 1990, 'The Market for Information and the Origin of Financial Intermediation,' *Journal of Financial Intermediation*, 1, 3–30.

——, 1993, 'Stock Markets and Resource Allocation' in C. Mayer and X. Vives (eds.), *Capital Markets and Financial Intermediation*, Cambridge University Press, Cambridge.

——, and D. Gale, 1995, 'A Welfare Comparison of the German and U.S. Financial Systems,' *European Economic Review*, 39, 179–209.

——, and ——, 'Financial Markets, Intermediaries and Intertemporal Smoothing,' forthcoming in *Journal of Political Economy*.

Back, K., 1993, 'Asymmetric Information and Options,' *Review of Financial Studies*, 6, 435–472.

Berlin, M., and L. Mester, 1992, 'Debt Covenants and Renegotiation,' *Journal of Financial Intermediation*, 2, 95–133.

Besanko, D., and G. Kanatas, 1993, 'Credit Market Equilibrium with Bank Monitoring and Moral Hazard,' *Review of Financial Studies*, 6, 213–232.

Bhattacharya, S., and G. Chiesa, 1995, 'Financial Intermediation with Proprietary Information,' *Journal of Financial Intermediation*, 4, 328–357.

——, and A. V. Thakor, 1993, 'Contemporary Banking Theory,' *Journal of Financial Intermediation*, 3, 2–50.

Boot, A. W., S. I. Greenbaum, and A. V. Thakor, 1993, 'Reputation and Discretion in Financial Contracting,' *American Economic Review*, 83, 1165–1183.

——, and A. V. Thakor, 1993a, 'Security Design,' *Journal of Finance*, 48, 1394–1378.

——, and ——, 1993b, 'Self-interested Bank Regulation,' *American Economic Review*, 83, 206–212.

Boot, A. W., and A. V. Thakor, 1996, 'Banking Scope and Financial Innovation,' working paper, University of Michigan and Tinbergen Institute/University of Amsterdam, presented at the Western Finance Association Meeting, Sunriver, Oregon, June; forth-coming in *Review of Financial Studies*.

——, and G. F. Udell, 1991, 'Secured Lending and Default Risk: Equilibrium Analysis and Monetary Policy Implication,' *Economic Journal*, 101, 458–472.

Carey, M., 1995, 'Some Evidence on the Nature of Information Problems in Debt Contracting and Financial Intermediation,' manuscript, Board of Governors of the Federal Reserve System, December.

Checchi, D., 1993, 'Creation of Financial Markets in (Previously) Centrally Planned Economies,' *Journal of Banking and Finance*, 17, 819–847.

Chemmanur, T. J., and P. Fulghieri, 1994, 'Reputation, Renegotiation, and the Choice Between Bank Loans and Publicly Traded Debt,' *Review of Financial Studies*, 7, 475–506.

Dewatripont, M., and E. Maskin, 1995, 'Credit and Efficiency in Centralized Versus Decentralized Markets,' *Review of Economic Studies*, 62, 541–555.

Diamond, D., 1984, 'Financial Intermediation and Delegated Monitoring,' *Review of Economic Studies*, 51, 393–414.

——, 1991, 'Monitoring and Reputation: The Choice Between Bank Loans and Privately Placed Debt,' *Journal of Political Economy*, 99, 688–721.

Diamond, D. W., 1993, 'Seniority and Maturity of Debt Contracts,' *Journal of Financial Economics*, 33, 341–368.

Fishman, M. J., and K. M. Hagerty, 1995, 'The Incentive to Sell Financial Market Information,' *Journal of Financial Intermediation*, 4, 95–115.

Grossman, S. J., and J. E. Stiglitz, 1980, 'On the Impossibility of Informationally Efficient Markets,' *American Economic Review*, 70, 393–408.

Hirshleifer, D., and Y. Suh, 1992, 'Risk, Managerial Effort and Project Choice,' *Journal of Financial Intermediation*, 2, 308–345.

Holmström, B., and J. Tirole, 1993, 'Market Liquidity and Performance Monitoring,' *Journal of Political Economy*, 101, 678–709.

Jacklin, C., 1987, 'Demand Deposits, Trading Restrictions, and Risk Sharing,' in E. C. Prescott and N. Wallace (eds.), *Contractual Arrangements for Intertemporal Trade*, University of Minnesota Press, Minneapolis, pp. 26–47.

James, C., 1987, 'Some Evidence on the Uniqueness of Bank Loans,' *Journal of Financial Economics*, 19, 217–235.

Kane, A., and S. G. Marks, 1990, 'The Delivery of Market Timing Services: Newsletters versus Market Timing Funds,' *Journal of Financial Intermediation*, 1, 150–166.

Kane, E. J., 1989, 'Changing Incentives Facing Financial-Services Regulators,' *Journal of Financial Services Research*, 2, 263–272.

——, 1990, 'Principal-Agent Problem in S & L Salvage,' *Journal of Finance*, 45, 755–764.

Lummer, S. L., and J. J. McConnell, 1989, 'Further Evidence on the Bank Lending Process and the Capital Market Response to Bank Loan Agreements,' *Journal of Financial Economics*, 25, 99–122.

Mayer, C., 1988, 'New Issues in Corporate Finance,' *European Economic Review*, 32, 1167–1188.

Mendelson, M., and J. W. Peake, 1993, 'Equity Markets in Economies in Transition,' *Journal of Banking and Finance*, 17, 913–929.

Millon, M., and A. V. Thakor, 1985, 'Moral Hazard and Information Sharing: A Model of Financial Information Gathering Agencies,' *Journal of Finance*, 40, 1403–1422.

O'Hara, M., 1993, 'Real Bills Revisited: Market Value Accounting and Loan Maturity,' *Journal of Financial Intermediation*, 3, 51–76.

Perotti, E. C., 1993, 'Bank Lending in Transition Economies,' *Journal of Banking and Finance*, 17, 1021–1032.

Rajan, R., 1992, 'Insiders and Outsiders: The Choice between Informed and Arm's Length Debt,' *Journal of Finance*, 47, 1267–1400.

Ramakrishnan, R. T. S., and A. V. Thakor, 1984, 'Information Reliability and a Theory of Financial Intermediation,' *Review of Economic Studies*, 51, 415–432.

Rock, K., 1986, 'Why New Issues are Underpriced,' *Journal of Financial Economics*, 15, 187–212.

Sabani, L., 1992, 'Market Oriented Versus Bank Oriented Financial Systems: Incomplete Contracts and Long Term Commitments,' unpublished manuscript, Universita' di Roma 'La Sapienza' Dipartimento di Economia Pubblica and Trinity College, Cambridge, September.

Shockley, R., and A. V. Thakor, 1996, 'The Structure of Loan Commitment Contracts: Data, Theory, and Tests,' working paper, Indiana University and University of Michigan, September, forthcoming in *Journal of Money, Credit and Banking*.

Thakor, A.V., and P. Wilson, 1995, 'Capital Requirements, Loan Renegotiation and the Borrower's Choice of Financing Source,' *Journal of Banking and Finance*, 19, 693–712.

Van Wijnbergen, S., 1994, 'The Role of Banks in Corporate Restructuring: The Polish Example,' working paper, CEPR, London, November.

von Thadden, E. L., 1995, 'Long-Term Contracts, Short-Term Investment and Monitoring,' *Review of Economic Studies*, 62, 557–575.

Wilson, P., 1994, 'Public Ownership, Delegated Project Selection and Corporate Financial Policy,' working paper, Indiana University, February.

Yosha, O., 1995, 'Information Disclosure Costs and the Choice of Financing Source,' *Journal of Financial Intermediation*, 4, 3–20.

7

Banking Scope and Financial Innovation

ARNOUD W. A. BOOT AND ANJAN V. THAKOR

> Perhaps it is this specter that most haunts the working men and women: the planned obsolescence of people that is of a piece with the planned obsolescence of the things they make.
>
> Studs Terkel

We study the implications of alternative designs of the financial system with a view to improving our understanding of the pros and cons of functionally separated banking (the U.S. system, for example) vis-à-vis universal banking (the German system, for example). There has been a great deal of practical interest in this subject as exemplified by the following quote from *The Economist* (1994):

What do the Porsche 911 and Deutsche Bank have in common? The answer is that both these German creations are widely considered to be perfect models—and nowhere more so than in Central Europe. While car lovers around the world admire the Porsche's sleek lines, bankers and policy makers in Warsaw, Prague and Budapest are impressed by lines of another kind: those on Deutsche's balance sheet.... This model of "universal" banking has sometimes been seen as a cornerstone of Germany's post-war economic success. Unsurprisingly, neighboring countries that are rebuilding their financial systems from the rubble of communism are tempted to copy it. That would be a mistake.

Academic research has kept abreast of the practical interest in this topic. There are three strands of the literature that are relevant. First is the research on financial innovation and security design [see, e.g., Allen and Gale (1988, 1991, 1994), Bhattacharya and Nanda (1996), Boot and Thakor (1993), Duffie and Rahi

The authors thank Anjolein Schmeits (in particular) and Kathleen Petrie for research assistance. For their many helpful comments, we gratefully acknowledge Franklin Allen (the editor), an anonymous referee, Andy Winton (discussant at the WFA-RFS Symposium), and participants at the NYU/Salomon Brothers Conference on Universal Banking (1996) and the Western Finance Association Meeting in Sunriver (1996), as well as participants of finance workshops at the University of Miami, University of Utah, University of Iowa, Indiana University, London School of Economics, University of Lausanne, Universitat Pompeu Fabra (Barcelona), University of Amsterdam, and Tilburg University for their helpful comments. We alone are responsible for the contents of this article. Address correspondence to Anjan V. Thakor, Edward J. Frey Professor of Banking and Finance, University of Michigan Business School, 701 Tappan Street, Ann Arbor, MI 48109.

(1995), Nanda and Yun (1994), and Riddiough (1997)]. This literature explains what motivates financial innovation and how securities are designed, priced, and marketed. A second literature—that has grown somewhat independently—is concerned with the policy question of banking scope, that is, whether the banking system should contain functionally separated commercial and investment banks or universal banks [see, e.g., Berlin, John, and Saunders (1994), Kanatas and Qi (1994), Puri (1994), Kroszner and Rajan (1994a, 1994b), and Rajan (1993)]. The focus here has largely been on potential conflicts of interest associated with universal banking. Somewhat more recently, attention has focused on the broader issue of *financial system design* [see, e.g., Allen (1992), Allen and Gale (1995), Boot and Thakor (1997), Neave and Johnson (1993), Sabani (1992), and Titman and Subrahmanyam (1996)]. This literature has addressed a comprehensive set of questions concerned with how financial system design affects individual risk-sharing opportunities, the allocation and cost of capital for corporations, corporate governance, and the restructuring of firms in financial distress. Since the design of contracts, institutions, and markets, as well as the determination of banking scope, are all part of the details of how a financial system should be configured, the emerging literature on financial system design promises to provide valuable unifying insights.

This article focuses on the effect of financial system design on financial innovation. In particular, we examine the impact of banking scope—the choice between universal and functionally separated banking—on the endogenously determined incentives of institutions to engage in financial innovation, and thus on each borrower's choice of financing source and its cost of capital. In addition to explaining how financial innovation is influenced by banking scope, the analysis speaks to a host of related system design issues, such as the implications of banking industry fragmentation or consolidation, the potential path dependence in the evolution of the financial system, and the desirable starting point of a new financial system. Thus our research touches all three strands of the literature mentioned earlier—financial innovation and security design, the implications of banking scope, and overall financial system design and evolution.

The model is characterized by four key players: commercial banks, investment banks, borrowing firms, and the financial market. The actions of each are endogenously determined according to an optimization program. Commercial banks specialize in postlending monitoring to deter asset-substitution moral hazard. Investment banks assist borrowers in raising funds in the capital market and design securities (through financial innovation) to lower their borrowers' cost of capital. Borrowers optimize through their choice of financing source, which is predicated on an observable attribute that varies cross-sectionally. The financial market consists of informed and other traders. How many traders become informed (and hence trading volume) depends on the design of securities and the attributes of firms that access the capital market. Thus the actions of investment banks and borrowers impact the "price efficiency" of the capital market. The advantage of capital market financing for the borrower is that informed traders possess payoff-relevant information that the borrower does not have and this information is noisily transmitted to the borrower through the market price of its debt security, thereby leading to improved real decisions and an enhanced payoff.

In this setting, the borrower trades off the advantage of bank financing (which lies in the bank's ability to attenuate asset-substitution moral hazard) against the advantage of capital-market financing (which stems from the feedback role of capital market prices).[1] We assume that the severity of the borrower's moral hazard is captured by a publicly observable quality attribute, with lower values of this attribute representing more severe moral hazard. It can then be shown that there is a "quality cutoff" in the borrower's choice of financing source. Borrowers below this quality cutoff approach banks because the moral hazard problem is the most severe for them, whereas borrowers above this cutoff access the capital market. Since this cutoff is endogenously determined by the tension faced by the borrower between the value of moral hazard amelioration and the value of the information conveyed by the capital market price, financial innovation affects this cutoff as well. If an investment bank can design a *new* security that results in the equilibrium security price reflecting more of the information possessed by the informed agents, then this innovation will cause the quality cutoff to decline as more borrowers gravitate to the capital market.

If the financial system has functional separation between commercial and investment banks, then each investment bank will choose its investment in innovation based on the cost of the innovation relative to the expected increase in its fee revenue that comes from sharing in the borrower's elevated payoff due to the innovation. But the decision rule is different if we have universal banking. Now the investment banking arm of the universal bank internalizes the potentially pernicious effect of financial innovation on the customer base of the commercial banking arm, that is, the commercial bank's borrowers may defect to the efficiency-enhanced financial market. The equilibrium level of financial innovation is lowered as a consequence. This provides one perspective on the higher rate of financial innovation in the U.S. relative to Europe.

The structure of the banking industry, manifested in its fragmentation/competitiveness, affects *interbank* competition and hence the price at which commercial bank credit is available. This leads to a link between banking industry structure, either with functional separation or with universal banking, and the quality cutoff that delineates bank borrowers from capital market borrowers (even ignoring financial innovation incentives). Moreover, the sophistication of the financial market is an important determinant of the impact of a financial innovation. For example, the introduction of an exotic new option is likely to be

---

[1] Thus our analysis sidesteps the issue of the relationship between the borrower's choice of financing source and the extent to which there is leakage of proprietary information (that the borrower does not wish to disclose) to the borrower's competitors due to the process of raising financing. These issues are examined in Bhattacharya and Chiesa (1995) and Yosha (1995).

less successful in an underdeveloped financial market than in a more developed, sophisticated financial market. But the success or failure of the financial innovation in turn affects the *future* evolution of the financial market. Hence the evolution of the financial market is likely to be path-dependent [see also Dinc (1994)].

Our analysis points, therefore, to the many important effects that financial system design is likely to have on credit allocation and economic development. The ramifications of this for the structuring of financial systems in ex-communist economies are transparent and echoed in the following quote from *The Economist* (1994):

Yet the German model may not be suitable for economies that are making the painful transition from central planning to capitalism. One priority should be to create a stable banking system that wins depositors' trust while allocating credit on the basis of market forces. A second should be to encourage a rapid restructuring of the hugely inefficient industries that central planning has created. And a third should be to promote the development of efficient and competitive capital markets. An unthinking dash for a universal-banking system could make it harder to meet any of these priorities.

We have focused in our analysis on the impact of two key aspects of financial system design on financial innovation: the degree to which the banking system is functionally separated (or universal) and the degree of fragmentation in the banking system. Both aspects are important in driving our results. In particular, the deleterious effect of universal banking on financial innovation predicted by our analysis presupposes a high degree of consolidation with universal banks. Without such consolidation, a universal bank would not discern a dampening of the demand for its loans due to its own financial innovation. Thus, in a very fragmented universal banking system—perhaps like that which existed in the United States prior to the Glass–Steagall Act—financial innovation would not be significantly discouraged by the universal nature of banking.

The rest is organized as follows. Section 1 presents the model. Section 2 presents an analysis of the borrower's choice of financing source. Section 3 contains an analysis of the decisions of commercial and investment banks for a financial system with functionally separated commercial and investment banking as well as for a financial system with universal banking. Section 4 discusses key implications. Section 5 concludes. All proofs are in the Appendix at the end of the article.

1. THE MODEL

1.1. Investment Choices of Firms

There is universal risk neutrality, and the riskless rate is zero. Each firm in the economy has the potential to invest in a single-period project that needs a $1 investment. Whether the project will actually become available to a borrower one period hence is uncertain at the outset; this uncertainty will be resolved at $t = 1$.

Moreover, conditional on a project being available, the quality of the project is random. Conditional on an investment opportunity being available, the probability is $\theta \in (0, 1)$ that the firm has only a good project available. This project yields a terminal payoff of $\$Y > 0$ with probability (w.p.) $\eta \in (0, 1)$ and 0 w.p. $1 - \eta$. With probability $1 - \theta$, the firm will have a choice between this good project and a bad project. The latter yields a contractible payoff of 0, but generates a noncontractible private rent $R > 0$ for the firm's manager; this could be viewed as a control rent as in O'Hara (1993). We will later impose parametric restrictions that ensure that the manager will always prefer the bad project with external financing even though he would prefer the good project if he could self-finance (the firm's cash constraints preclude self-financing).

Each potential borrower is characterized by an observable parameter $\theta \in (0, 1)$. Each borrower knows its own θ at the outset, but others observe it only a period later. Let G be the cumulative distribution over the cross-section of θ's, and $g(\theta)$ the associated density function that outsiders associate with θ. This parameter θ is the commonly known prior probability assigned by the market to the event that a borrower with that θ will have access only to the good project, and therefore pose no asset-substitution moral hazard problem.

1.2. Role of Commercial Banks

Commercial banks (CBs) specialize in postlending monitoring that resolves asset-substitution moral hazard. Thus, if a firm borrows from a bank, the choice of the good project can be ensured w.p. 1. The bank incurs a cost $C > 0$ to monitor each borrower, and it must decide at the outset how much monitoring capacity to acquire for the period. Let N_0 denote the monitoring capacity the bank acquires at the beginning of the period, at a total cost of CN_0. With this capacity, the bank can monitor at the most N_0 borrowers. The loan demand the bank faces is random, however. The realized loan demand for a bank depends on numerous factors, including the number of borrowers who will need funds, the realizations of θ, and the decisions of borrowers about whether to go to banks or the capital market. If loan demand exceeds N_0, then the demand in excess of N_0 must either be rationed or extended loans without postlending monitoring. If loan demand falls short of N_0, then the excess of N_0 over the realized loan demand remains unutilized.

We visualize an imperfectly competitive banking industry. As in Besanko and Thakor (1992), we can imagine banks lying along the circumference of a circle, engaging in competition constrained by spatial considerations on the part of borrowers.[2] In particular, we view the lack of perfect competition—and any rents arising therefrom—as related to the bank's monitoring ability. Each bank realizes a particular (random) loan demand in its "area" and "transportation costs," for borrowers permit the bank to earn a rent of $\tau > C$ on each borrower it monitors,

---

[2] The spatial representation is best viewed as an allegory for more general product-differentiation-based imperfections in competition.

that is, the bank earns a rent that is such that the borrower is indifferent between paying that rent and incurring the cost to go to the next most convenient bank.

We can view τ as a rent that compensates the bank for some previously incurred fixed cost of entry into the banking industry and having acquired the expertise to monitor borrowers at a cost. Another interpretation is that these rents arise from ex post informational monopolies stemming from information flows in durable bank-borrower relationships [e.g., Rajan (1992)]. Clearly the assumption that this rent is fixed per borrower is strong. In general, we would expect the rent to arise from an explicit consideration of the borrower's various financing alternatives, in which case it is likely that τ would be decreasing in θ since the bank would have to settle for a lower rent from higher quality borrowers who have a lower "need" for bank monitoring. This will not affect the qualitative nature of our results. In any case, our goal is not to explain the existence of banking rents, but rather the implications of these rents for lending policy and innovation incentives. Nonetheless, a more fully developed model in which these rents arise endogenously would be interesting.

One approach to building such a model is suggested by the work of Kreps and Scheinkman (1983) on the relationship between Bertrand and Cournot competition. They show that to reach the perfectly competitive outcome that is usually associated with Bertrand competition requires *both* the assumption that firms compete on prices and the assumption that production occurs after demand is determined in response to the announced prices. If one assumes a two-stage game in which in the first stage firms determine their production capacities independently and simultaneously, then produce and bring these quantities to the market, and in the second stage engage in Bertrand-like price competition, then it is possible for the Cournot outcome to be the unique equilibrium. This kind of two-stage game fits our commercial banking system nicely since banks are first building up monitoring capacities and then competing (imperfectly) for borrowers. The Kreps and Scheinkman (1983) results indicate that banks can earn rents (like Cournot oligopolists) even when they are engaged in Bertrand competition of this sort.[3]

1.3. The Capital Market

The basic idea we want to model is that the capital market includes traders who acquire costly information relevant to the real decisions of firms that even the managers of these firms may not possess. This perspective differs from traditional

---

[3] Proceeding formally along the lines of Kreps and Scheinkman (1983) in our context is complicated, however, because loan demand is random and exogenously specified for each θ in our model for the set of θ's that approach banks, whereas they consider a deterministic, downward-sloping, price-dependent demand schedule. Endogenizing loan demand would significantly complicate our analysis since then τ would depend on the *number* of competing banks which would then also affect the quality (θ) cutoff determining which borrowers go to banks and which go to the capital market. We do not believe this will change our qualitative results, however.

signaling models in finance where the firm's manager is the one endowed with proprietary information. While we do not dispute the assumption that managers often know more about their firms than anyone else, we also believe that there are situations in which managers could learn something of value from the market. For instance, we could envision traders/analysts who are industry specialists who develop special skills in assessing shifts in customer preferences, changes in the competitive structure of the industry, and so on.

These security analysts may acquire privileged information randomly. For example, a security analyst who specializes in the pharmaceutical industry may learn something that may be of value to Eli Lilly's managers in a particular period. The analyst may or may not be able to credibly communicate to Lilly management that he has proprietary information that they should pay for; Fishman and Hagerty (1995) explain why informed traders may wish to sell their information, and Allen (1990) analyzes the credibility problem in direct information sales. In the next period, there may be a different analyst who acquires proprietary information. In a market with many analysts following the industry, it would be difficult for Lilly to ascertain who knows what and when. This would preclude Lilly from going out and hiring these traders to acquire their information directly.[4] Alternatively, even if no individual analyst/investor is better informed than the managers, it is nevertheless possible for the capital market in the aggregate to be better informed. For example, if individual traders who invest in information were to receive identical, and independently distributed (noisy) signals, the market price could aggregate their information and reveal something that the firm's management was unaware of.[5]

---

[4] An exception to this would be when a significant portion of the firm's stock is owned by institutional investors who are informed. In this case, management could directly ask these investors for input. Pound (1997) describes a meeting convened by NewTech Corporation to which the company's largest institutional investors were invited to provide input that would help the company formulate strategies.

[5] The notion that there may be those in the market who know something of decision relevance that the firm's managers don't is evidenced by the NewTech Corporation case described by Pound (1997). We quote from Pound:

In July of 1995, an unusual meeting took place at the Intercontinental Hotel in New York. It was convened by NewTech Corporation—a growing, successful public company, operating in two broad areas of applied information technology .... The subject of the meeting was of broad and fundamental importance to NewTech. The Company's officers had gathered for an all-day retreat to assess the Corporation's overall corporate structure, strategy, and prospects in the next five years .... The unusual aspect of the NewTech meeting was not the decision to hold such an offsite strategic review. Instead, the remarkable part of the NewTech meeting was the presence around the conference table of ten additional individuals. These individuals were not members of NewTech's management or its board; nor did they represent the usual coterie of paid corporate advisers. Instead, they represented ten of NewTech's largest and best-informed institutional shareholders .... Now, NewTech was faced with developing a defining strategy that would guide corporate policy going forward. This would require not execution, but creative insight—vision .... That, Strideman emphasized was the key reason that NewTech's top institutional investors had been invited to sit around the table .... Who better to judge the Company's initiatives in the context of what its competitors were doing—firms

The key to the information-feedback role of prices is that the informed traders will attempt to profit from their information by taking positions in the securities issued by the firms about which they have superior information. Although the presence of liquidity-motivated trades will mask the trades of the informed traders, the total order flow will at least noisily reveal informed trading. Based on this, the firm may be able to infer some of the information possessed by the informed traders and this may lead it to make a value-enhancing real decision.[6] This is one way to visualize the information aggregation role of the capital market and the feedback role of prices. The informed traders observe a market opportunity that they conjecture the firm will exploit and thus take a position in the firm's securities based on that conjecture, and the firm noisily infers the availability of this opportunity from the order flow for its securities and acts on it, thereby rationalizing the initial conjecture. We will now formalize this intuition about the interaction between the real decisions of firms and capital market price determination.

Suppose there are two types of investors/traders in the capital market: liquidity traders and discretionary agents. The aggregate demand of the liquidity traders for any asset is random and exogenously specified. A discretionary agent can become an "informed" agent at a private cost. This investment generates a privately observed signal, ϕ, that reveals payoff-relevant information about the firm's operating environment. Each informed agent receives exactly the same signal. This information can be "favorable" (f) or "unfavorable" (u). If $\phi = f$, then the firm can make real investment decisions that can enhance its good project's payoff to $Y + \alpha$ w.p. η and α w.p $1 - \eta$, where $\alpha \in (0,1)$; the cost of this payoff-enhancing investment is $K > 0$. If $\phi = u$, then the payoff enhancement opportunity does not exist. This signal ϕ is unavailable to the firm's manager, but if the informed agents demand the security only when $\phi = f$, then the manager can infer valuable information from the aggregate demand for the security or its price. This inference will be noisy, however, because of liquidity trade randomness. For a similar approach to modeling the real impact of the capital market, see Allen (1992), Boot and Thakor (1996), and Holmstrom and Tirole (1993).[7]

---

that the institutional investors in the room also followed and had detailed knowledge of? ... Strideman emphasized that the purpose of the day's proceedings was thus not to give shareholders any new quantitative information about NewTech. Instead, the purpose of the day was for NewTech to get information from *them*.

Clearly, direct communication like this is possible if *all* investors with valuable information can be identified ex ante. If this is not possible, the next best alternative may be to infer what they know from market prices.

[6] Consider the following example of a value-enhancing decision. Suppose we have one company producing VHS VCRs and another producing BETA VCRs, and each must decide how much to invest in expanding productive capacity. Whether this investment is good for the company's shareholders depends on which "standard" will ultimately prevail. Each company's stock price will reveal the aggregated information of the market about whether BETA or VHS will become the standard, and this could in turn guide each company's investment decision.

[7] We are assuming in our formal modeling that the prospects of firms seeking external financing are completely idiosyncratic. In reality, this will not always be true, so that even a firm that opts for a

The larger the fraction of the total trade volume that is potentially accounted for by informed traders, the more revealing is the order flow, and the smaller is the expected gain to each informed trader from his information. Thus the measure of informed traders, Ω, is endogenously determined through an equilibrium condition which states that the equilibrium value of Ω should be such that each discretionary agent is indifferent between becoming informed and staying uninformed, that is, the expected profit of each informed agent, net of the cost of becoming informed, should be zero.

The equilibrium price of the security is set to be equal to its expected value, with the expectation conditioned on the information contained in the aggregate demand, D, for the security; thus the discretionary uninformed traders earn zero expected profit on their trading. One can think of a competitive market maker setting the equilibrium price to clear the market, after observing D but being unable to distinguish the individual components of the demand attributable to the different types of traders. We also assume no short sales by agents other than the market maker and that the market maker absorbs any supply/demand imbalances.

The capital market has no monitoring capability. Thus, if the firm has a project available and further has a choice of project (conditional on a project being available, the probability of this is $1 - \theta$), it is anticipated that the bad project will be chosen by the manager. The market maker takes this into account in setting the security price. Moreover, she also accounts for the fact that there are some (sufficiently high) values of D such that project-payoff enhancement will occur and other (sufficiently low) values of D for which it will not. To ensure comparability with the bank financing case, we assume that capital market funds are raised through debt securities. It should be noted, however, that the type of security used for financing does not affect the analysis. In particular, the asset-substitution moral hazard problem here cannot be resolved by using equity instead of debt. The borrower always prefers the bad project with external financing, and only bank monitoring can ensure selection of the good project.

1.4. The Role of the Investment Bank

The investment bank's (IB's) role is to underwrite the firm's debt offering in the capital market. Moreover, the IB can engage in security design innovation that improves the information sensitivity of the securities offered by the firm, as in the model developed by Boot and Thakor (1993). In the formal Boot–Thakor analysis, financial innovation takes the form of splitting a composite cash-flow security into debt and equity. This splitting creates one security (equity) that is more

---

bank loan will be able to learn something from the prices of other firms' securities issued by investment banks. This will reduce the value of capital market financing relative to bank financing. We thank the referee for this observation.

information-sensitive than the original composite security and one (debt) that is less information sensitive than the composite security. Traders are wealth-constrained and therefore have limited wealth to invest in securities. Financial innovation permits informed traders to devote their entire investment to the most information-sensitive security and thus increases their marginal return on investment in costly information. This induces more traders to become informed, leading to a higher endogenously determined measure of informed traders in equilibrium. As a consequence, order flow becomes more informative for the market maker and the good (undervalued) firm is able to realize a higher expected *total* equilibrium revenue for its debt and equity issues[8] than it could when it issued a single composite security.

In our analysis, we simplify by shying away from the details of financial innovation, viewing it instead as the creation of an unspecified feature in the design of the debt contract—for example, an option or a callability feature—that makes that security more information sensitive, and this induces more informed trading. This benefits the firm in two ways when it invests in the good project. First, it improves the information content of D, and thus leads to a higher probability of realizing the project payoff enhancement. Second, the higher probability of payoff enhancement reduces the expected cost of borrowing in the capital market.[9]

To come up with the financial innovation, the IB must understand the borrower's idiosyncratic project. This means that the IB must invest some resources to study the borrower *before* it knows whether it will get the borrower's business. Thus the manner in which IBs compete is as follows. At $t = 0$, each IB decides which borrower it will study. To ensure a competitive market, we assume that borrowers are scarce relative to IBs, so that each borrower may have multiple IBs studying it. After an IB knows how many other IBs it is competing with, it innovates with an endogenously determined innovation probability. If it innovates, it will make an investment of $\xi > 0$, which covers its cost of studying the firm and innovating. This investment results in a successful innovation with probability one. It does not matter to the analysis if we make the outcome of the innovation initiative random.

We assume that the IB captures the entire gain to the issuing firm from financial innovation through an increase in its fee, as long as it faces no competition from other IBs. This is possible only if the IB is the only institution that comes up with the innovation. If there is another IB that comes up with the same innovation, then none can profit from the innovation because they compete away

---

[8] The security splitting in Boot and Thakor (1993) creates a riskless debt security for which the firm receives a first-best price.

[9] When the informed bid for the security and D is high enough to convince the firm to take advantage of the opportunity to enhance the good project's payoff, the payoff to bondholders increases by α in the state in which it would be 0 without the enhancement initiative. This lowers the interest rate the firm must pay.

their rents through a standard Bertrand undercutting argument. Moreover, none can recoup ξ.

1.5. Sequence of Events

There are three dates: $t = 0, 1, 2$. At $t = 0$, each commercial bank chooses its monitoring capacity N_0, and each investment bank determines the probability with which it will invest in financial innovation. Each borrower knows its own θ, but no one else does. Corresponding to each θ is a continuum of borrowers. After it is known how many investment banks have successfully innovated, each borrower approaches either a commercial bank or the capital market for funds; whether all of these borrowers will actually need loans will be determined stochastically only at $t = 1$ according to the probability of project availability for individual borrowers. The random variable that determines the project availability is identically and independently distributed (i.i.d.) across borrowers and independent of θ.

At $t = 1$, each borrower comes to know whether there is a project available, and each borrower's project availability as well as quality (θ) become common knowledge. Thus total loan demand is realized. That is, corresponding to each θ, there is a distinct total loan demand, and across θs the loan demand realizations are i.i.d. random variables. Based on the earlier financing-source choice decisions of borrowers, we now come to know the realized loan demand for commercial banks and the aggregate volume of debt to be underwritten in the capital market. Those who opted to borrow from commercial banks will be extended monitored loans at an interest factor r_B until the monitoring capacities of the banks they applied to are exhausted; if there is any loan demand left over, it will be satisfied by extending unmonitored loans at an interest factor r_{NB}.[10] We view this descriptively as a process whereby all those seeking loans are viewed as belonging to a homogeneous pool, and the commercial bank selects all at once a random subset of these borrowers to extend monitored loans to at r_B. Thus, prior to the bank's selection of this subset, each borrower views the probability of receiving a monitored loan at r_B as P, with $P \in (0, 1)$ if loan demand exceeds the bank's monitoring capacity, and $P = 1$ otherwise. The interest factors r_B and r_{NB} and the probability P are all derived endogenously in the next section.

Also observed at $t = 1$ is the aggregate order flow D, but not how much of it came from each type of trader. The measure of informed traders, although not directly observable, is inferred. Thus at $t = 1$, each firm chooses its project, the price of each firm's debt is determined, and payoff-enhancing investment decisions by firms are also made (or not). Finally, at $t = 2$ all payoffs are realized and creditors are paid off if possible. Figure 1 summarizes this sequence of events pictorially.

---

[10] In an ex-post sense, these borrowers would have been better off going to the capital market. However, they are locked into their choice of financing source by this stage.

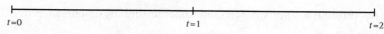

$t=0$	$t=1$	$t=2$

*Each borrower knows its θ (conditional on a project being available) but outsiders can only assess a commonly-known probability density function over θ, $g(\theta)$.

*Each borrower assesses a probability of project availability at $t=1$.

*Each commercial bank chooses its monitoring capacity N_0, and each investment bank determines the probability with which it will invest in financial innovation for a particular borrower.

*The investment bank contacts the borrower and announces whether it has developed a financial innovation for that borrower.

*Each borrower also (irrevocably) decides whether to borrower from a bank or the capital market, depending on its θ.

*Each borrower comes to know whether it has a project to invest in, and if it has a project, then it proceeds to request funds from the financing source chosen at $t=0$.

*Each borrower's θ becomes common knowledge.

*Aggregate loan demand and its division between commercial banks and the capital market become known.

*After the borrower has taken its loan, its manager determines its project choice (good or bad project), depending on whether it has a choice between the good and bad projects and whether there is bank monitoring.

*Based on the realized loan demand, each bank determines which loans to monitor and which not to monitor, i.e., the monitoring probability P is determined.

*Each borrower going to the capital market has its security issued by the chosen investment bank.

*The market maker observes the aggregate order flow, D, for each firm's capital market debt. Based upon this order flow, each firm determines whether or not to undertake project payoff enhancement.

* Project payoffs are realized and creditors are paid off if possible.

Figure 1. *Time line and sequence of events for the model*

2. ANALYSIS OF THE BORROWING FIRM'S CHOICE OF FINANCING SOURCE

2.1. Cost of Borrowing from a Commercial Bank

If the CB plans to monitor the borrower, then it knows that the borrower will choose the good project w.p. 1, and the CB will be repaid w.p. η. The equilibrium repayment obligation, r_B, thus solves:

$$\eta r_B = 1 + \tau,$$

which yields

$$r_B = \frac{1 + \tau}{\eta}. \tag{1}$$

If the CB does not monitor, then it knows that the probability is θ that the borrower will invest in the good project and $1 - \theta$ that it will invest in the bad project. The equilibrium repayment obligation, r_{NB}, thus solves

$$\theta \eta r_{NB} + \{[1 - \theta] \times 0\} = 1,$$

which yields

$$r_{NB} = 1/\eta\theta. \tag{2}$$

The borrower's expected payoff if it is monitored is $\eta[Y - r_B]$. Its expected payoff if it is not monitored is $\theta\eta[Y - r_{NB}] + [1 - \theta]R$. To ensure that the borrower prefers to be monitored, we need

$$\eta[Y - r_B] > \theta\eta[Y - r_{NB}] + [1 - \theta]R. \tag{3}$$

We assume that exogenous parameters are restricted such that

$$\eta Y > R + \tau. \tag{PR-1}$$

Given Equation (PR-1), Equation (3) will hold for all $\theta < 1 - \tau[\eta Y - R]^{-1} \equiv \theta^0$. Note that Equation (PR-1) also guarantees that the borrower would prefer the good project if it could self-finance (which is not possible due to wealth constraints). We also need to ensure that the borrower prefers the bad project with external financing, even when external financing involves the payoff enhancement α. The sufficient condition for this is[11]

$$\eta[Y + \alpha - 1] < R. \tag{PR-2}$$

Next we check to see whether the bank prefers to monitor. If the bank extends a loan at r_B and monitors the borrower, its expected profit will be $1 + \tau$. At this loan price, if the bank does not monitor, its expected profit will be $\theta[1 + \tau]$, which is less than its expected profit from pursuing a monitoring strategy. Similarly, if the bank extends a loan at r_{NB}, then its expected payoff if it monitors will be $\eta r_{NB} = 1/\theta$, and its expected payoff if it does not monitor will be $\theta\eta r_{NB} = 1 < 1/\theta$. Thus, regardless of the price at which the bank extends a loan, it will strictly prefer to monitor.

Recall that P is the probability that a borrower will receive a loan at r_B from the bank and $1 - P$ is the probability that a borrower will receive an unmonitored loan at r_{NB}. Define $\bar{\theta} \equiv [1 + \tau]^{-1}$. Then for a borrower with $\theta < \bar{\theta}$, the expected payoff is

$$\Pi_B(\theta) = P\eta[Y - r_B] + [1 - P][\theta\eta\{Y - r_{NB}\} + \{1 - \theta\}R]$$
$$= P\eta Y - P\tau + [1 - P][\theta\eta Y + \{1 - \theta\}R] - 1. \tag{4}$$

2.2. Cost of Borrowing in the Capital Market

Let $\Pr(\phi) = f | D)$ denote the conditional probability assessed by the uninformed traders that the informed traders have received a favorable signal. This probability

---

[11] Equations (PR-1) and (PR-2) imply the joint restriction $\eta Y \in (R + \tau, R + \eta - \eta\alpha)$, which implies $\tau < \eta[1 - \alpha]$.

is conditioned on the total demand, D, for the security. A higher realization of D implies a higher probability that the informed traders are in the market, and hence a greater willingness on the borrowing firm's part to engage in the value-enhancing decision. We assume that the value-enhancing decision requires an unverifiable (by outsiders) investment of K. Thus there will be a critical D, call it D^*, such that the firm will make the value-enhancing decision for all $D \geq D^*$ and not otherwise. We will address shortly how D^* is determined. Let $\Pr^*(\phi = f \mid D)$ represent the probability that the firm invests in value enhancement and actually realizes this enhancement. Thus

$$\Pr^*(\phi = f \mid D) = \begin{cases} 0 & \text{if } D < D^* \\ \Pr(\phi = f \mid D) & \text{if } D \geq D^*. \end{cases}$$

We can now write the equilibrium repayment obligation, $\bar{r}_F(D)$, of the firm as a function of the realized demand for its security. It is a solution to

$$\theta\{\Pr^*(\phi = f \mid D)[\eta \hat{r}_F(D) + \{1 - \eta\}\alpha] + [1 - \Pr^*(\phi = f \mid (D)][\eta \hat{r}_F(D)]\} = 1.$$
(5)

Note that in writing Equation (5) we recognize that bondholders get repaid only if the firm is locked into the good project since there is no monitoring in the capital market to deter asset substitution by the firm; the probability of the good project being taken is θ. Moreover, wherever project payoff enhancement occurs, bondholders are repaid in full in the successful state (this happens w.p. η) and recover $\alpha < 1 < \hat{r}_F(D)$ in the unsuccessful state (this happens w.p. $1 - \eta$). Solving Equation (5) yields

$$\hat{r}_F(D) = \frac{1 - \theta\Pr^*(\phi = f \mid D)[1 - \eta]\alpha}{\theta\eta}.$$
(6)

Let $\Lambda(D \mid \Omega)$ represent the cumulative distribution function for D, conditional on the measure of informed traders, Ω. Then the firm's expected payoff is

$$\Pi_F(\theta) = \theta\Bigg[\int_\eta [Y + \alpha\Pr^*(\phi = f \mid D) - \hat{r}_F(D)]d\Lambda(D \mid \Omega)$$

$$- K \int_{D \geq D^*} d\Lambda(D \mid \Omega) \Bigg] + [1 - \theta]R.$$
(7)

Define $q \equiv q(\Omega) \equiv \int \Pr^*(\phi = f \mid D)d\Lambda(D \mid \Omega)$, $r_F \equiv r_F(\Omega) \equiv \int \hat{r}_F(D)d\Lambda(D \mid \Omega)$, and $\bar{K} \equiv K \int_{D \geq D^*} d\Lambda(D \mid \Omega)$. Then we can write Equation (7) as

$$\Pi_F(\theta) = \theta\eta[Y + \alpha q - r_F] - \theta\bar{K} + [1 - \theta]R.$$
(8)

We will now determine D^*. Investing K (which happens only when the firm is locked into a good project) when the observed market demand is D produces an expected benefit of $\eta\alpha \Pr(\phi=f|D)$ and has a cost of K. It is transparent that $\Pr(\phi=f|D)$ is increasing in D. Thus there exists a D^* such that

$$\eta\alpha\Pr(\phi = f|D^*) = K, \text{ and}$$
$$\eta\alpha\Pr(\phi = f|D) > K \forall D > D^*, \text{ and}$$
$$\eta\alpha\Pr(\phi = f|D) < K \forall D < D^*.$$

2.3. Firm's Choice of Financing Source

The firm will make its financing source choice by comparing $\Pi_B(\theta)$ in Equation (4) with $\Pi_F(\theta)$ in Equation (8). Making this comparison, we obtain the following result.

Proposition 1. *Define*

$$\hat{\theta} \equiv \frac{P[\eta Y - R - \tau]}{\alpha q + P[\eta Y - R] - \bar{K}} \in (0, 1). \tag{9}$$

Then the firm prefers bank financing if its $\theta \leq \hat{\theta}$ and capital market financing if $\theta > \hat{\theta}$. Moreover, all bank-financed borrowers pay a lower interest rate on monitored loans than on nonmonitored loans.

Thus we see that the borrower's choice depends on the publicly observable quality parameter θ. A higher θ means a lower likelihood that the borrower will substitute projects to the lender's detriment, so that θ can be viewed as a representation of the severity of moral hazard. The more severe the moral hazard, the more valuable is the CB's monitoring service. As θ increases, the monitoring becomes less valuable, and at some point the value lost due to not monitoring is more than offset by the expected project payoff enhancement due to capital market financing. At this point the borrower, who has sufficiently high quality, will switch to capital market financing.

3. ANALYSIS OF THE DECISIONS OF COMMERCIAL AND INVESTMENT BANKS

3.1. The Commercial Bank's Choice of Lending Capacity in a Functionally Separated Banking System

We assume that total loan demand N for each θ is uniformly distributed over $(\underline{N}, \bar{N})$ and that the θ faced by a given CB is uniformly distributed over $(0, 1)$. Thus a CB's *realized* loan demand is N if $\theta < \hat{\theta}$ and 0 if $\theta > \hat{\theta}$.[12] Then the CB's choice of

---

[12] Descriptively, one should view this as a market with a finite number of banks, with each bank being uncertain about both the θ of its borrower pool and the loan demand from this pool at the time it

lending capacity, N_0, is made to maximize

$$W(\hat{\theta}) = \int_0^{\hat{\theta}} \left[\int_{\underline{N}}^{N_0} \frac{N\tau}{[\hat{N} - \underline{N}]} \, dN + \int_{N_0}^{\bar{N}} \frac{N_0\tau}{[\bar{N} - \underline{N}]} \, dN \right] d\theta - CN_0. \tag{10}$$

There are a few points worth noting about Equation (10). First, the CB's lending to the unmonitored borrowers does not appear here because the CB's expected profit on those loans is zero and hence leaves its overall expected profit W unchanged. Second, CB's expected profit depends both on the realized θ and the realized N. If the CB's monitoring capacity $N_0 > N$ and $\theta \le \hat{\theta}$, then lending equals demand and some monitoring capacity is wasted. On the other hand, if $N_0 < N$ and $\theta \le \hat{\theta}$, then lending equals the monitoring capacity and some loans are extended without monitoring. If $\theta > \hat{\theta}$, then lending is zero regardless of N, and all monitoring capacity is wasted. The following proposition follows readily from Equation (10).

Proposition 2. *The CB's optimal monitoring capacity is given by*

$$N_0^* = \bar{N} - C[\bar{N} - \underline{N}][\tau\hat{\theta}]^{-1} < \bar{N}. \tag{11}$$

The probability that a borrower with $\theta \le \hat{\theta}$ will receive a monitored loan with a repayment obligation of r_B is

$$P = 1 + \frac{\bar{N}}{[\bar{N} - \underline{N}]} \ln \left(\frac{\bar{N}\tau\hat{\theta}}{\bar{N}\tau\hat{\theta} - C[\bar{N} - \underline{N}]} \right)$$

$$- \frac{C}{\tau\hat{\theta}} \left[1 + \ln \left(\frac{\bar{N}\tau\hat{\theta}}{\bar{N}\tau\hat{\theta} - C[\bar{N} - \underline{N}]} \right) \right]. \tag{12}$$

Next we present a corollary that provides some useful comparative statics.

Corollary 1. $\partial N_0^*/\partial\tau > 0$ *and* $\partial P/\partial\tau > 0$.

It is intuitive that N_0^* and P are increasing in τ. Since the CB earns a rent τ on its lending only if it extends a monitored loan, the higher this rent the greater is the investment the CB makes in monitoring. And the greater this investment in monitoring capacity, the higher is the probability that a borrower will receive a monitored loan.

---

determines its lending capacity N. Each bank views the θ it will face as being drawn from a uniform distribution over $[0, 1]$ and the N it will face as being drawn from a uniform distribution over $[\underline{N}, \bar{N}]$. Since there is a finite number of banks, there is only a finite number of relevant θ realizations. Clearly the distribution of N depends on the measure of borrowers associated with each θ as well as the probability distribution of the random variable that determines whether a borrower will have a project to invest in. Since the distribution of N is independent of θ, the simplest case in which the measure of borrowers associated with each θ is the same across all θs and the project-availability random variable is i.i.d. across θs.

Holding fixed Ω, the measure of informed traders in the capital market, Equations (9), (11), and (12) completely characterize the commercial banking equilibrium with functionally separated banking. Next we turn to the IB's problem.

3.2. The Investment Bank's Problem in a Functionally Separated Banking System

Inspection of Equation (6) reveals that the reduction in the firm's cost of borrowing due to informed trading is captured in the term $\theta \Pr^*(\phi = f|D) \times [1 - \eta]\alpha/\theta\eta$. The expected value of this is $q(\Omega)[1 - \eta]\alpha/\eta$, where the expectation is taken with respect to D [see the definition following Equation (7)]. This is the cost saving available to the firm with the *existing* security. We assume that the role of financial innovation is to alter security design and *increase* the measure of informed traders from to Ω to $\Omega^* > \Omega$. Boot and Thakor (1993) explain how altered security design can achieve this by making more information-sensitive securities available to wealth-constrained informed traders. Define $\Delta \equiv q(\Omega^*) - q(\Omega)$. Then the cost reduction attributable to the financial innovation is $\Delta[1 - \eta]\alpha/\eta$ and its expected value is $\theta\Delta[1 - \eta]\alpha$ for a type-θ borrower, with this expectation taken with respect to whether the firm will be locked into a good project and whether that project will succeed. In addition to this cost saving, there is an expected enhancement in the firm's project payoff due to the innovation, which is $\theta\eta\Delta\alpha - \theta\bar{K}_0$, where $\bar{K}_0 \equiv \bar{K}(\Omega^*) - \bar{K}(\Omega)$ and $\bar{K}(\Omega^*) \equiv K \times \int_{D \geq D^*} d\Lambda(D|\Omega^*)$, $\bar{K}(\Omega) \equiv K \int_{D \geq D^*} d\Lambda(D|\Omega)$. If the IB responsible for the innovation is the only one to bring it to market, then it captures all of the borrowing firm's cost saving and payoff enhancement due to the innovation. Thus its reward for the innovation is an increase in its fee revenue by an amount $F \equiv \theta\Delta[1 - \eta]\alpha + \theta\eta\Delta\alpha - \theta\bar{K}_0 = \theta[\Delta\alpha - \bar{K}_0] > \xi$, where $\xi > 0$ is what the IB must invest in order to come up with the financial innovation. It is assumed that there are many IBs in the market and any can avail of the financial innovation by investing ξ. For later use, define $S \equiv \Delta\alpha - \bar{K}_0$, so that $F \equiv \theta S$.

Proposition 3. *There does not exist a symmetric pure strategy Nash equilibrium in the game in which multiple IBs compete to innovate. If there are $M > 1$ IBs competing, then the probability, z_s, with which each IB innovates in a mixed-strategy Nash equilibrium with functionally separated banking is*

$$z_s = 1 - \sqrt[M-1]{\frac{2\xi}{F[\underline{N} + \bar{N}][1 - \hat{\theta}]}}. \tag{13}$$

A remark about the interpretation of this equilibrium is in order. Since this is a mixed-strategy equilibrium, each IB is indifferent (in equilibrium) between innovating and not innovating. However, this indifference is based on the IB's assumption that every other IB will innovate with probability z_s. Since the particular IB will then be indifferent, we are free to choose any probability of innovation for it, and the only one that is consistent with the Nash equilibrium assumptions of the other IBs is z_s. We therefore interpret z_s as the probability with which each IB will invest in innovation. For simplicity, we will assume henceforth that $M = 2$.

3.3. The Universal Bank's Problem

With universal banking, the CB and the IB are part of the same bank. Assume that there are two universal banks. Thus the universal bank maximizes the sum of its expected profits from commercial and investment banking [see Equation (10) and Equation (A-2) in the Appendix]. Conditional on the universal bank investing in financial innovation, the total expected profit maximized by the universal bank is

$$zW(\hat{\theta}_2) + [1 - z]W(\hat{\theta}) + \frac{F[\underline{N} + \bar{N}][1 - \hat{\theta}][1 - z]}{2} - \xi \tag{14}$$

where z is the probability with which each universal bank innovates, and $W(\cdot)$, the profit from the commercial bank's lending, was defined in Equation (10). Note that there are two quality cutoffs, $\hat{\theta}$ and $\hat{\theta}_2$. The cutoff $\hat{\theta}$ is that which obtains when only one universal bank innovates, and this is the same as the cutoff without innovation. The reason is that when only one bank innovates, all the benefits of innovation accrue to the bank and the borrower is indifferent between purchasing that innovation and not purchasing it. If both universal banks innovate, then the borrower extracts the entire innovation gain F, and a new cutoff $\hat{\theta}_2$ emerges.

The borrower's expected utility from financial market financing with only one universal bank innovating is $\Pi_F^1(\theta) \equiv \Pi_F(\theta)$, where $\Pi_F(\theta)$ is given by Equation (8), so that the quality cutoff remains $\hat{\theta}$.

The borrower's expected utility from financial market financing with two universal banks present is

$$\Pi_F^2(\theta) = \Pi_F^1(\theta) + z^2\theta S. \tag{15}$$

In writing Equation (15) we recognize that the borrower benefits from the financial innovation only when *both* universal banks innovate (the probability of which is z^2). Now, $\hat{\theta}_2$ is obtained by equating Equations (4) and (15). This yields

$$\hat{\theta}_2 = \frac{P[\eta Y - R - \tau]}{\alpha q + P[\eta Y - R] - \bar{K} + z^2 S}. \tag{16}$$

Observe that $\hat{\theta}_2 < \hat{\theta}$. We now have our main result.

Proposition 4. *The equilibrium probability of financial innovation in a universal banking system, z_u, is lower than the equilibrium probability of financial innovation in a functionally separated banking system, z_s.*

The intuition is as follows. When a functionally separated IB determines whether to innovate, it is unconcerned about the impact the innovation will have on the loan demand faced by a CB. However, when it is the universal bank that determines whether to innovate, it internalizes the depressing effect that the innovation will have on the loan demand faced by its CB unit; this result is independent of the organizational details of the universal bank—whether the IB and the CB are divisions or subsidiaries—and depends only on the fact that the universal bank maximizes the sum of the expected profits of its IB and CB. Consequently the universal bank needs a higher expected profit from the innovation than does a functionally separated IB. Since a positive profit from innovation is available only if the universal bank in question is the only bank that innovates, the only way to increase the expected profit from innovation is to lower the probability with which each competing bank innovates in a mixed-strategy Nash equilibrium. Note also that it follows from Proposition 4 that the depressing effect of universal banking on financial innovation is dependent on industry structure. With greater concentration in universal banking, z_u is lower since each universal bank internalizes to a greater degree the impact of its own innovation on its commercial banking profits.

Proposition 4 is obtained in a static setting. As we discuss in Section 4A, the propensity of a universal banking system to innovate less is likely to be exacerbated in a dynamic setting.

4. IMPLICATIONS OF ANALYSIS

In this section we discuss the implications of our analysis for various aspects of financial system design.

4.1. Intertemporal Considerations

An important consideration precluded by our static analysis is reusability of information by CBs. A CB's investment in monitoring is likely to be intertemporally reusable [see Bhattacharya and Thakor (1993) and Boot, Greenbaum and Thakor (1993)]. This means that the cost of monitoring a borrower at date $t + 1$ is likely to be lower than the cost of having monitored the same borrower at date t. The customers of a CB will therefore be more profitable to the CB over time.[13] By contrast, financial innovation yields only a single-shot gain due to imitation by rivals.

When this consideration is introduced in our analysis, we see that a universal bank innovates with an even lower probability since it now imputes a greater cost

---

[13] See Greenbaum and Thakor (1995) for empirical evidence. Sharpe (1990) and Rajan (1992) develop models in which the accumulation of proprietary borrower-specific information during the course of a lending relationship creates an informational monopoly for the bank and produces ex post rents.

to the loss in loan demand suffered by its CB due to the financial innovation. Thus intertemporal considerations are likely to strengthen the result that there will be less financial innovation in economies with universal banks.

4.2. Banking Scope and Capital Market Development

Perhaps the clearest implication of our analysis is that banking scope—a regulatory choice variable—affects the development of the capital market. In our model this effect arises from the lower incentives for financial innovation with universal banking than with functionally separated banking. This stochastic lowering of financial innovation with universal banking means a higher $\hat{\theta}$ and hence fewer borrowers accessing the capital market. With lower aggregate trading volume as well as less financial innovation, we should expect capital markets in economies with universal banking to be less developed than those in economies with functionally separated banking. Moreover, since capital market funding becomes more attractive for borrowers over time due to financial innovation, CBs are likely to lose *more* market share to the capital markets over time in functionally separated financial systems than in universal banking economies. These observations are consistent with the higher incidence of financial innovation and the greater intertemporal loss of market share by CBs in the United States relative to the continental European universal banking economies of Germany, Switzerland, and The Netherlands, for example.

Consistent with the predictions of our model, the corporate bond markets in many of these universal banking economies are not well developed.[14] However, we have assumed in our formal model that universal banks operate in fairly liquid bond markets, which implies that our analysis overstates the importance of bond markets in universal banking economies. Note also that the applicability of our analysis is unaffected by whether the financial contract used is debt or equity. Thus we could readily view our analysis as focusing on the borrower's choice between public equity underwritten by the investment banking arm of a universal bank and private equity offered by the commercial banking arm of a universal bank.

We doubt that the architects of the Glass–Steagall Act foresaw the enormously positive impact the act would have on the development of U.S. capital markets or on the incentives for financial innovation. The act had its roots in the desire to limit the power of banks, reduce conflicts of interest, and limit the scope of the deposit insurance safety net. Nonetheless, our analysis provides a framework within which to understand the unintended consequences of banking scope legislation like the Glass–Steagall Act.

---

[14] The Netherlands is particularly illustrative. The government bond market there is very liquid, suggesting that an adequate infrastructure for bond trading exists. However, the corporate bond market is not as well developed, suggesting that the incentives for (private) universal banks to innovate and facilitate development of the corporate bond market may be particularly weak.

4.3. Path Dependence in the Evolution of Financial Systems

Financial innovation is likely to be path dependent. Although we have assumed that an investment in financial innovation will succeed with probability one, it would be straightforward to let the success probability be less than one. While this by itself will not alter our analysis, we could incorporate the insight offered by Gale (1992) and argue that the success probability will be a function of the sophistication of financial market participants. The ability of market participants to appreciate the payoff implications of a new security will likely depend on their experience with existing securities, the attributes of which may depend on the development of the capital market. Thus the probability of financial innovation will be higher in a better-developed capital market. Over time this will lead to differences in the rate at which financial innovation proceeds in different markets. This difference in the pace of financial innovation further widens the development gap between better-developed capital markets and their less-developed counterparts.

This implies that even if the regulation of banks and capital markets were to be perfectly harmonized internationally, different financial systems are likely to display disparate levels of financial innovation and differing fractions of total credit allocation accounted for by CBs simply due to disparities in the sophistication of their capital markets. Moreover, how sophisticated a capital market is at date t is likely to depend on the history of financial innovation until date t. A financial system that has historically been dominated by universal banks is likely to have a poorer history of financial innovation, according to our earlier arguments. This appears consistent with the different patterns of capital market development in continental Europe and the United States.

4.4. Commercial Banking Fragmentation Implications

Greater fragmentation of commercial banking is typically taken to mean greater competition among CBs. In our model this implies a lower τ for each CB. From Equation (9) we know that $\partial \hat{\theta} / \partial \tau < 0$. Thus increased fragmentation in commercial banking will lead to an increase in $\hat{\theta}$ and hence more business for CBs.[15] This elevates borrower welfare as well as the average quality of bank loans (since $\hat{\theta}$ increases, the average quality of bank loans increases with it).[16] Nevertheless, Corollary 1 also tells us that the probability, P, of extending a monitored loan declines as τ decreases. Moreover, the effect of increased competition on the bank's investement in monitoring capacity is ambiguous since a higher $\hat{\theta}$ implies

---

[15] The observation that more competitive commercial banking results in more use of banks may seem counter to actual experience, not only in universal-banking Germany but also in functionally separated Japan. This is probably because increased bank competition may be accompanied (and perhaps caused) by improved information technology, which also increases the efficiency of public markets.

[16] One may wonder why CBs do not reduce τ for borrowers with θ just above $\hat{\theta}$. The reason they don't do this is that borrowers precommit to a choice of financing source prior to knowing whether they will receive a monitored loan.

a higher N_0^* ceteris paribus but a lower τ (which leads to a higher $\hat{\theta}$) diminishes N_0^* for a fixed $\hat{\theta}$.

4.5. Implications of Increased Competition in Investment Banking

Fragmentation and the resulting increased competition in investment banking will diminish the inclination of any IB to introduce a financial innovation. Recall that the probability of each IB innovating is chosen such that the net present value of the innovation to the IB is zero. From Equation (13) we see that $\partial z_s / \partial M < 0$. More importantly, however, the probability that there will be any innovation at all—the probability that at least one out of M IBs will innovate—declines as M increases.[17] Hence, increased competition among IBs leads to stochastically lower innovation.

4.6. Overall Financial System Design

Our analysis shows that financial systems with universal banking can be expected to innovate less and have capital markets that display lower development than financial systems with functionally separated banking. Since an important role of the financial market in our model is to provide informational feedback to managers of firms that facilitate improved real decisions, borrowers make better real decisions on average in functionally separated financial systems.

On the other hand, there is on average better attenuation of asset-substitution moral hazard in a financial system with universal banking because a larger measure of borrowers use CBs. The welfare implications of financial system design are therefore ambiguous. Of course, because our capital market model has exogenously specified security demand from liquidity traders, it is not amenable to welfare analysis. However, one could adapt the model in such a way that it is the firm rather than the liquidity traders who provide compensation to the informed traders: welfare analysis would then be possible.

Stepping outside our model, a factor that might favor universal banking is related to scope economies based on information sharing made possible by the marriage of commercial and investment banking. However, potential gains from scope economies could be vitiated by conflicts of interest in a universal bank [see Kroszner and Rajan (1994b) and Rajan (1993)].

4.7. Mixed Financial Systems

We have considered functionally separated banking and universal banking as two extremes. What about "mixed" financial systems in which stand-alone IBs and CBs compete with universal banks?

---

[17] To see this, note from Equation (13) that Pr (at least one bank innovates) $= 1 - [1 - z_s]^M$, where z_s is defined in Equation (13) and $0 < (2\xi/F[\bar{N} + \underline{N}][1 - \hat{\theta}]) < 1$. It can now be shown that ∂Pr (at least one bank innovates)$/\partial M < 0$. In a takeover bidding context, Spatt (1989) proves a similar claim. See also Thakor (1996) for a proof in a credit rationing context.

We believe that stand-alone banks would be competitively disadvantaged in a universal banking system for two reasons. First, scope economies would give universal banks a competitive edge over their stand-alone counterparts. In the context of our model, one way to introduce scope economies would be to assume that if there is any redundant monitoring capacity in the CB unit of the universal bank, it could be used to support the underwriting activities of the IB. This would lower expected underwriting costs, and some of the savings could be passed along to the universal bank's customers.

Second, although we don't have a good theory that provides testable links between organization size and its influence-peddling ability, casual observation suggests that a larger universal bank typically deals with larger, more politically visible clients, has "deeper pockets" and enjoys greater implicit "too big to fail" (TBTF) protection than its smaller (particularly stand-alone) competitors [see Kane (1996)]. Thus it seems reasonable to posit that large universal banks have greater influence over regulators than (smaller) stand-alone IBs or CBs, which means that regulatory policy could also be slanted in favor of universal banks.[18] For example, financial innovations where scope economies could be exploited more fully may be favored over others when it comes to regulatory approval. A good example is commercial paper with backup loan commitments. The universal bank can underwrite the commercial paper issue and also sell the backup loan commitment.

Both of these considerations imply that stand-alone banks, even though viable, are unlikely to be major players in universal banking economies, an observation that appears consistent with what we observe. Hence it seems improbable that overall financial innovation in a universal banking system with some stand-alone CBs and IBs could match the financial innovation in a functionally separated financial system.

4.8. Global Competition Among Institutions from Different Systems

At a more general level, the issue of stand-alone investment banks competing with universal banks raises the important issue of competitiveness of different financial systems in an increasingly integrated global economy. While cross-border competition is limited at present, it does exist nonetheless. How would a bank-dominated (universal banking) system compete with a market-dominated (functionally separated) system? This is an interesting question for future research.

---

[18] Of course, if there are numerous small banks that collectively represent a large fraction of banking industry assets, these banks could coordinate to collectively lobby regulators and politicians. This has been the case in the United States. However, unlike the United States, in economies traditionally dominated by large universal banks, small stand-alone banks are unlikely to represent a sufficiently large fraction of industry assets to have significant political clout. And they would be further hampered by the fact that the interests of stand-alone CBs would differ from those of stand-alone IBs, leading to collective lobbying being frustrated by the usual coordination problems.

Our analysis does suggest, however, that IBs from functionally separated financial systems would have an innovation-based advantage in competing with universal banks from universal banking systems. Thus if these IBs were allowed to operate in universal banking economies, they would wrest some market share away from local universal banks, particularly when it came to large corporate borrowers seeking capital market funding. Interestingly this is precisely what has happened with U.S. banks entering Germany. We quote from the *Wall Street Journal* (October 1995):

Bavaria's $4 billion sale of its electric utility was the largest deal in Germany last year. But the Bavarian state government didn't choose Deutsche Bank AG or another big German bank to lead the auction. Instead, it turned to Lehman Brothers, Inc.

The choice of a American adviser for such a significant deal shows the growing influence of U.S. investment banks in Germany.

The breakthrough came with German reunification in 1990, when the nation's financing needs soared. U.S. banks stood ready to fill that need. And since then, whether it has been privatizations, mergers or stock offerings, they have won one assignment after another. They have come to dominate futures and options trading on the Frankfurt Stock Exchange. And they have scored points for introducing aggressive American concepts such as structured notes and leveraged buyouts to the staid German market.

It's that innovative edge, U.S. bankers say, that sets them apart.

5. CONCLUSION

We have focused on the financial innovation implications of financial system design. Our main findings and observations are summarized below.

There is an observable quality cutoff such that borrowers with observable qualities below that are funded by commercial banks and borrowers with observable qualities above that are funded in the capital market. As commercial banking becomes more competitive, this cutoff increases.

There exists a mixed-strategy Nash equilibrium in the financial innovation game such that each competing investment bank invests in financial innovation with some probability less than one. The equilibrium probability of innovation is lower in a financial system with universal banking than in a financial system with functionally separated banking.

The evolution of a financial system is likely to be path-dependent. Well-developed financial systems provide stronger incentives for financial innovation and develop faster.

Banks are likely to lose more market share over time to capital markets in financial systems with functionally separated banking than in a universal banking system.

The choice of financial system design rests on the trade-off between the superior attenuation of asset-substitution moral hazard in a universal banking system versus superior financial innovation and better real decisions in a functionally separated financial system.

Perhaps the most significant point of our article is that there is a vital link between the behavior of commercial banks and developments in capital markets, and that any discussion of financial system design must adopt an essentially integrated approach.[19] Moreover, bank regulation and capital market regulation, which are typically the responsibilities of different regulatory agencies, should be conducted in an integrated manner.

Future research should perhaps attempt to join together the implications of financial system design derived in recent articles. For example, Allen and Gale (1995) conclude that bank-dominated financial systems provide better inter-generational risk sharing and market-dominated systems provide better cross-sectional risk sharing. That is, generally speaking, financial innovation should be thought of more broadly as improving risk sharing and providing tax advantages, in addition to increasing information sensitivity. It would be interesting to incorporate risk-sharing considerations in the approach we have taken. In particular, including liquidity demand considerations [e.g., as in Kahn and Winton (1996)] in a framework like ours could open the door for interesting welfare analyses. Moreover, one could also consider innovations that have *synergies* with bank lending, such as swaps and forward contracts. Our analysis suggest that commercial banks would be aggressive in introducing them, which is what we observe.

Appendix

Proof of Proposition 1. We know that $\hat{\theta}$ solves $\Pi_B(\theta) = \Pi_F(\theta)$, where $\Pi_B(\theta)$ is defined in Equation (4) and $\Pi_F(\theta)$ in Equation (8). Thus the borrower prefers capital market funding to a CB loan if

$$\theta\eta[Y + \alpha q - r_F] - \theta\bar{K} + [1 - \theta]R > P\eta Y - P\tau + [1 - P][\theta\eta Y + \{1 - \theta\}R] - 1.$$

Substituting $r_F = ((1 - \theta q[1 - \eta]\alpha)/\theta\eta)$ in the above inequality and performing a few algebraic manipulations, we obtain the result that the borrower strictly prefers capital-market funding if

$$\theta > \frac{P[\eta Y - R - \tau]}{\alpha q + P[\eta Y - R] - \bar{K}} \equiv \hat{\theta},$$

prefers CB financing if $\theta < \hat{\theta}$, and is indifferent if $\theta = \hat{\theta}$. Moreover, it is straightforward to show that $\hat{\theta} < \theta^0$. Now, define $\bar{\theta} \equiv [1 + \tau]^{-1}$. Then it is transparent that $r_B < r_{NB} \forall \theta < \bar{\theta}$. It is easy to show that $\hat{\theta} < \bar{\theta}$. Thus all those who apply for bank loans find that $r_B < r_{NB}$. This completes the proof. □

---

[19] Benveniste, Singh and Wilhelm (1993) provide interesting empirical support for the notion that commercial banks and capital markets are significantly linked. They document that the failure of Drexel, Burnham and Lambert led to an abnormal increase in the prices of banks whose loans were viewed as close substitutes for the junk bonds underwritten by Drexel.

Proof of Proposition 2. Performing the necessary integration, Equation (10) can be written as

$$W(\hat\theta) = \frac{\hat\theta\tau[N_0^2 - \underline{N}^2]}{2[\bar{N} - \underline{N}]} + \frac{\hat\theta\tau N_0[\bar{N} - N_0]}{[\bar{N} - \underline{N}]} - N_0 C.$$

The first-order condition, $\partial W(\hat\theta)/\partial N_0 = 0$, yields

$$\frac{\hat\theta\tau\bar{N}}{[\bar{N} - \underline{N}]} - \frac{\hat\theta\tau N_0^*}{[\bar{N} - \underline{N}]} - C = 0,$$

which then gives us Equation (11). The second-order condition is

$$\partial^2 W(\hat\theta)/\partial N_0^2 = \frac{-\tau\hat\theta}{[\bar{N} - \underline{N}]} < 0.$$

It is transparent from Equation (11) that $N_0^* < \bar{N}$.

To derive P, note that

$$
\begin{aligned}
P &= \text{Pr (no shortage of monitoring capacity)} \times \text{Pr (each loan will be} \\
&\quad \text{monitored when there is no monitoring capacity shortage)} \\
&\quad + \text{Pr (Shortage of monitoring capacity)} \times \text{Pr (loan will be monitored} \\
&\quad \text{when there is a capacity shortage)} \\
&= \text{Pr (no monitoring capacity shortage)} \times 1 \\
&\quad + \text{Pr (monitoring capacity shortage)} \times \frac{\text{monitoring capacity}}{\text{loan demand}} \\
&= \int_{\underline{N}}^{N_0^*} \frac{1}{[\bar{N} - \underline{N}]} \, dN + \int_{N_0^*}^{\bar{N}} \frac{N_0^*}{N[\bar{N} - \underline{N}]} \, dN \\
&= \frac{[N_0^* - \underline{N}]}{[\bar{N} - \underline{N}]} + \frac{N_0^* \ln(\bar{N}/N_0^*)}{[\bar{N} - \underline{N}]}.
\end{aligned}
\tag{A1}
$$

Substituting for N_0^* from Equation (12) into Equation (A1) yields Equation (12). $\square$

Proof of Corollary 1. Differentiating Equation (12) with respect to τ gives

$$\partial N_0^*/\partial\tau = \frac{C[\bar{N} - \underline{N}]}{\tau^2\hat\theta} > 0.$$

Moreover, differentiating Equation (12) with respect to τ and doing a little algebra shows that

$$\partial P/\partial\tau > 0. \qquad\qquad \square$$

Proof of Proposition 3. To show that there cannot be a symmetric pure strategy Nash equilibrium in the innovation game, suppose that we conjecture that no IB innovates in equilibrium. Then it must pay for one IB to innovate since it will have a monopoly on the innovation and therefore earn positive expected profit. Thus no innovation cannot be an equilibrium. Next, suppose that it is an equilibrium for each IB to innovate w.p. 1. Then no IB can profit from the innovation and hence cannot recover its investment of ξ in innovation. Thus it cannot be an equilibrium for each IB to innovate w.p. 1.

Let $z \in (0, 1)$ be the probability with which each IB innovates in a symmetric mixed strategy Nash equilibrium. Consider a particular IB. Its expected profit from innovation is

$$[1 - \hat{\theta}] \times \frac{[\bar{N} + \underline{N}]}{2} \times [1 - z]^{M-1} \times F - \xi. \tag{A2}$$

Note also that the quality cutoff $\hat{\theta}$ in (A2) is the same as the quality cutoff without financial innovation. The reason is that Equation (A2) is relevant only for the case in which only one IB innovates. As indicated in Section 2.4, in that case, all the benefits of innovation accrue to the investment bank and the quality cutoff $\hat{\theta}$ remains unaffected. In writing Equation (A2), note that the expected credit demand faced by the IB is

$$\int_{\hat{\theta}}^{1} \int_{\underline{N}}^{\bar{N}} \frac{N}{[\bar{N} - \underline{N}]} \, dN \, d\theta = \frac{[1 - \hat{\theta}][\bar{N} + \underline{N}]}{2}.$$

Moreover, the IB in question can profit from its financial innovation only if no other IB innovates. Since the probability that an IB will not innovate is $[1 - z]$ and there are $M - 1$ other IBs, the probability that the remaining $M - 1$ banks will not innovate is $[1 - z]^{M-1}$.

To obtain a symmetric mixed strategy Nash equilibrium, we have to ensure that the IB is indifferent between innovating and not innovating. Since the IB's expected profit from not innovating is zero, this means the required equilibrium condition is

$$\frac{[1 - \hat{\theta}][\bar{N} + \underline{N}][1 - z]^{M-1} \times F}{2} - \xi = 0. \tag{A3}$$

Solving Equation (A3) yields Equation (13). $\qquad\square$

Proof of Proposition 4. With universal banking, the bank's objective is to maximize Equation (14). Let z_u be the probability with which each universal bank innovates in a mixed strategy Nash equilibrium. Note that the rule by which innovation rents are shared between the IB and the borrower is immaterial to the analysis. From our earlier analysis, $\hat{\theta} > \hat{\theta}_2$.

Consider now a particular universal bank and assume that there are two universal banks in the market. If the universal bank in question innovates, its expected profit is

$$z_u[W(\hat{\theta}_2) + 0] + [1 - z_u]\left[W(\hat{\theta}) + \frac{F\{\bar{N} + \underline{N}\}\{1 - \hat{\theta}\}}{2} \right] - \xi. \tag{A4}$$

Note that the probability that the other universal bank will innovate is z_u, and in this case each bank earns zero profits in investment banking and an expected profit of $W(\hat{\theta}_2)$ from commercial banking. The probability that the other universal bank will not innovate is $1 - z_u$, and in this case the universal bank in question earns an expected profit of $(F\{\bar{N} + \underline{N}\}\{1 - \hat{\theta}\})/2$ on its innovation and an expected profit of $W(\hat{\theta}_1)$ on its CB lending. If the universal bank in question does not innovate, then its expected profit is

$$z_u[W(\hat{\theta})] + [1 - z_u][W(\hat{\theta})]. \tag{A5}$$

A key difference between Equation (A4) and Equation (A5) is that now if the other universal bank does not innovate, then no bank innovates and the expected profit on commercial bank lending is $W(\hat{\theta})$ since the quality cutoff is $\hat{\theta}$.

Now, z_u is obtained by setting Equation (A4) equal to Equation (A5). Solving this gives us

$$z_u = \frac{FN_m[1 - \hat{\theta}] - \xi}{FN_m[1 - \hat{\theta}] + 2W(\hat{\theta}) - W(\hat{\theta}) - W(\hat{\theta}_2)} \tag{A6}$$

where $N_m \equiv [\bar{N} + \underline{N}]/2$. Note that $W(\hat{\theta}) < W(\hat{\theta}_2)$ since W is increasing in $\hat{\theta}$. We wish to compare Equation (A6) and Equation (13). Note first that Equation (13) can be stated as

$$z_s = \frac{FN_m[1 - \hat{\theta}] - \xi}{FN_m[1 - \hat{\theta}]}. \tag{A7}$$

Comparing Equation (A6) and Equation (A7) and recalling that $W(\hat{\theta}) > W(\hat{\theta}_2)$, we see that $z_u < z_s$. □

REFERENCES

Allen, F., 1990, "The Market for Information and the Origin of Financial Intermediation," *Journal of Financial Intermediation*, 1, 3–30.

——, 1992, "Stock Market and Resource Allocation" in C. Mayer and X. Vives (eds.), *Capital Markets and Financial Intermediation*, Cambridge University Press, Cambridge.

——, and D. Gale, 1988, "Optimal Security Design," *Review of Financial Studies*, 1, 229–263.

——, and ——, 1991, "Arbitrage, Short Sales, and Financial Innovation," *Econometrica*, 59, 1041–1068.

——, and ——, 1994, *Financial Innovation and Risk Sharing*, MIT Press, Cambridge, Mass.

——, and ——, 1995, "A Welfare Comparison of the German and U.S. Financial Systems," *European Economic Review*, 39, 179–209.

Benveniste, L. M., M. Singh, and W. J. Wilhelm, Jr., 1993, "The Failure of Drexel Burnham Lambert: Evidence on the Implications for Commercial Banks," *Journal of Financial Intermediation*, 3, 104–137.

Berlin, M., K. Johon, and A. Saunders, 1994, "Bank Equity Stakes in Borrowing Firms and Financial Distress," working paper, Indiana University.

Besanko, D., and A. V. Thakor, 1992, "Relationship Banking, Deposit Insurance, and Portfolio Choice," in C. Mayer and X. Vives (eds.), *Capital Markets and Financial Intermediation*, Cambridge University Press, Cambridge.

Bhattacharya, S., and V. Nanda, 1996, "Client Discretion, Switching Costs and the Introduction of New Financial Products," working paper, University of Michigan.

——, and G. Chiesa, 1995, "Proprietary Information, Financial Intermediation, and Research Incentives," *Journal of Financial Intermediation*, 4, 328–357.

——, and A. V. Thakor, 1993, "Contemporary Banking Theory," *Journal of Financial Intermediation*, 3, 2–50.

Boot, A. W., and A. V. Thakor, 1993, "Security Design," *Journal of Finance*, 48, 1349–1378.

——, and ——, 1997, "Financial System Architecture," *Review of Financial Studies*, 10, 693–733.

——, S. I. Greenbaum, and A. V. Thakor, 1993, "Reputation and Discretion in Financial Contracting," *American Economic Review*, 83, 1165–1183.

Dinc, S., 1994, "Integration of Financial System and Institutional Path Dependence," working paper, Stanford University.

Duffie, D., and R. Rahi, 1995, "Financial Market Innovation and Security Design," *Journal of Economic Theory*, 65, 1–42.

The Economist, 1994, "Central Europe's Model Bank," August 27–September 2.

Fishman, M., and K. Hagerty, 1995, "The Incentive to Sell Financial Market Information," *Journal of Financial Intermediation*, 4, 95–115.

Gale, D., 1992, "Information Capacity and Financial Collapse," in C. Mayer and X. Vives (eds.), *Capital Markets and Financial Intermediation*, Cambridge University Press, Cambridge.

Greenbaum, S. I., and A. V. Thakor, 1995, *Contemporary Financial Intermediation*, Dryden Press, Fort Worth, Texas.

Holmstrom, B., and J. Tirole, 1993, "Market Liquidity and Performance Monitoring," *Journal of Political Economy*, 101, 678–709.

Kanatas, G., and J. Qi, 1994, "Should Commercial Banks be Prohibited from Underwriting Corporate Securities?," working paper, University of South Florida.

Kahn, C., and A. Winton, 1996, "Ownership Structure, Liquidity Demand, and Shareholder Monitoring," working paper, University of Illinois and Northwestern University.

Kane, E. J., 1996, "Foundations of Financial Regulation," paper presented at a conference, *Monetary and Financial Integration in an Expanding (N)AFA: Organization and Consequences*, Toronto, Canada.

Kreps, D. M., and J. A. Scheinkman, 1993, "Quantity Precommitment and Bertrand Competition Yield Cournot Outcomes," *Bell Journal of Economics*, 14, 326–337.

Kroszner, R. S., and R. G. Rajan, 1994a, "Is the Glass-Steagall Act Justified? A Study of the U.S. Experience with Universal Banking Before 1933," *American Economic Review*, 84, 810-832.

——, and ——, 1994b, "The Role of Firewalls in Universal Banks," working paper, University of Chicago.

Nanda, V., and Y. Yun, 1994, "Competition and Cooperation Among Investment Banks in the Market for Financial Innovations," working paper, University of Southern California.

Neave, E. H., and L. D., Johnson, 1993, "Governance and Financial System Organization," Working Paper 93-26, School of Business Research Program, Queen's University.

O'Hara, M., 1993, "Real Bills Revisited: Market Value Accounting and Loan Maturity," *Journal of Financial Intermediation*, 3, 51-76.

Pound, J., 1997, "The Resurrection of NewTech," excerpted from *The New Public Corporation*, forthcoming.

Puri, M., 1994, "The Long-Term Default Performance of Bank Underwritten Security Issues," *Journal of Banking and Finance*, 18, 397-418.

Rajan, R. G., 1992, "Insiders and Outsiders: The Choice Between Informed and Arm's-Length Debt," *Journal of Finance*, 47, 1367-1423.

——, 1993, "A Theory of the Costs and Benefits of Universal Banking," working paper, University of Chicago.

Riddiough, T., 1997, "Optimal Design and Governance of Asset-Backed Securities," *Journal of Financial Intermediation*, 6, 121-152.

Sabani, L., 1992, "Market Oriented Versus Bank Oriented Financial Systems: Incomplete Contracts and Long Term Commitments," unpublished manuscript, Universita' di Roma "La Sapienza" Dipartimento di Economia Pubblica and Trinity College, Cambridge.

Sharpe, S. A., 1990, "Asymmetric Information, Bank Lending and Implicit Contracts: A Stylized Model of Customer Relationship," *Journal of Finance*, 55, 1069-1087.

Spatt, C. S., 1989, "Strategies Analyses of Takeover Bids," in S. Bhattacharya and G. Constantinides (eds.), *Financial Markets and Incomplete Information: Frontiers of Modern Financial Theory, Volume 2*, Rowman Littlefield Publishers, Inc., N.J.

Thakor, A. V., 1996, "Capital Requirements, Monetary Policy and Aggregate Bank Lending: Theory and Empirical Evidence," *Journal of Finance*, 51, 279-324.

Titman, S., and A. Subrahmanyam, 1996, "Information, Resource Allocation and the Development of Financial Markets," unpublished manuscript, Boston College and UCLA.

Yosha, O., 1995, "Information Disclosure Costs and the Choice of Financing Source," *Journal of Financial Intermediation*, 4, 3-20.

PART III

DESIGN OF CREDIT CONTRACTS AND INSTITUTIONS

8

Optimal Debt Structure and
the Number of Creditors

PATRICK BOLTON AND DAVID S. SCHARFSTEIN

I. INTRODUCTION

Much of corporate finance theory is devoted to understanding the trade-off between debt and equity financing. Yet it is striking that firms almost always resolve this trade-off by choosing debt over equity. From 1946 to 1987, debt issues accounted for 85 percent of all external financing and equity only 7 percent. Thus if one wants a theory of the composition of external financing, it may be more important to understand the structure of debt financing than the choice between debt and equity.

The goal of this paper is to analyze debt structure using an optimal (but incomplete) contracting framework. We focus on three aspects of debt structure. First, what determines the number of creditors a company should borrow from? Second, how should security interests be allocated among creditors? Third, what sort of voting rules should govern changes in the debt contract?

In our model, an optimal debt structure tries to meet two objectives. First, there should be little loss in value when the firm is liquidated: the costs of financial distress should be low. Second, it should discourage firms from defaulting. As we shall see, these objectives sometimes conflict, and an optimal debt structure must balance the two.

We make this point in a model similar to those of Hart and Moore (1989) and Bolton and Scharfstein (1990). In these models, there are two types of defaults: *liquidity* defaults, in which a firm does not have the cash to make debt payments; and *strategic* defaults, in which a firm defaults because managers want to divert cash to themselves. In the absence of default penalties, firms would always choose to default and creditors would be unwilling to lend. Debt contracts reduce the incentive for strategic defaults by giving creditors the right to liquidate the

We thank Bengt Holmstrom, Julio Rotemberg, an anonymous referee, and seminar participants at Toulouse and the European Science Foundation conference at Gerzensee for helpful comments. We are also grateful for financial support from the National Science Foundation and the International Financial Services Research Center at MIT. Some of this work was done while Scharfstein was on a Sloan Foundation Research fellowship.

company's assets following a default. But the right to liquidate results in inefficiencies following liquidity defaults. An optimal contract balances the benefits of deterring strategic defaults against the costs of realizing a low liquidation value in a liquidity default.

Debt structure affects this trade-off because it affects the price at which creditors can sell the firm's assets following a default. Suppose that the firm's assets are worth more combined than separated: the whole is worth more than the sum of the parts. Then if there are many creditors, each of whom is secured by a different asset, a buyer would have to get a large number of them to agree to a sale to maximize the combined value of the assets. But once the buyer has struck a deal with one creditor, his marginal valuation of the other assets rises. So he will end up paying more for the remaining assets than if those assets were sold on a stand-alone basis.

By influencing the price at which creditors sell the firm's assets, debt structure affects both the manager's incentive to default strategically and the expected liquidation value of the firm. Following a strategic default, the manager will have to pay more to stop the creditors from liquidating the assets when there are many creditors than when there is only one creditor. Therefore, borrowing from many creditors disciplines managers by lowering their payoffs from a strategic default; they have less incentive to divert cash flow to themselves.

However, there is a cost of having multiple creditors. When the firm defaults for liquidity reasons, creditors will try to sell their assets to another firm—the second-best user of the assets. This firm will have to pay more for the assets if there are multiple creditors. But while the high price of the assets benefits creditors if there is a buyer willing to bid, there is a potential downside: the buyer may not have the incentive to sink the costs of becoming informed about the firm's assets. Thus, from an ex ante perspective, the liquidation value can actually be lower when there are multiple creditors. While borrowing from multiple creditors provides managerial discipline, doing so can also reduce efficiency when the firm defaults because of liquidity problems.

If a firm chooses to borrow from more than one creditor, then the allocation of security interests among creditors and the voting rules that govern the sale of assets also affect efficiency. We show that security interests and voting rules can be chosen to balance the benefits of deterring strategic defaults against the cost of liquidity defaults.

In addition, we try to link each of these aspects of debt structure—the number of creditors, the allocation of security interests, and voting covenants—to observable firm characteristics. Our principal finding is that it is optimal for firms with low credit quality to maximize liquidation values: by borrowing from just one creditor, by giving only one creditor a security interest, and by adopting voting rules that make it easier to complete an asset sale or debt restructuring.

By contrast, it is optimal for firms with high credit quality to have debt structures that make strategic default less attractive: by borrowing from multiple creditors, by giving each equal security interests, and by adopting voting rules that allow some creditors to block asset sales.

Finally, we show how optimal debt structure depends on how efficiently assets can be redeployed to other users, the cyclicality of the industry, and the degree to which the assets are worth more together than apart (what we call asset complementarity).

Our results on the number of creditors could be interpreted as suggesting a trade-off between bank debt and public debt since firms often have many public debt holders but few banks. The model would therefore suggest that firms with low credit quality, those in noncyclical industries, and those with highly complementary assets will issue bank debt, whereas firms with the opposite characteristics will issue public debt. However, it would be misleading to put too much weight on this interpretation. Bank debt can be syndicated to many banks, and some public debt instruments are held by only a few investors. Thus we would prefer to interpret the results as suggesting when bank debt is syndicated and when public debt is widely held.

Of course, we are not the first to consider debt structure issues. There are a number of strands of the literature. One strand, which includes Bulow and Shoven (1978), White (1980), and Gertner and Scharfstein (1991), analyzes how debt structure affects liquidation values when firms are in financial distress. But there is no consideration of how this, in turn, affects optimal debt structure. Another strand, including papers by Smith and Warner (1979), Berkovitch and Kim (1990), and Hart and Moore (1990), considers how priority and security can be allocated to mitigate over- and underinvestment problems. Diamond (1991) and Hoshi, Kashyap, and Scharfstein (1992) consider the trade-off between bank debt and public debt. The line of work closest in spirit to ours includes Hart and Moore (1989), Diamond (1992, 1993), Rajan (1992), and Dewatripont and Maskin (1995), who examine how optimal debt structure is determined by ex post bargaining considerations.

This paper is also related to the literature on corporate governance. While that literature explores optimal voting rules for shareholders (e.g., whether one share–one vote is optimal as in Grossman and Hart [1988], Harris and Raviv [1988], and Gromb [1993]) and the optimality of having large shareholders (as in Zingales [1991]), our paper is the first to analyze similar governance issues for debt holders.

The paper is organized as follows: Section II outlines the basic model. Section III presents the trade-off between one and two creditors. Section IV discusses the optimal allocation of security interests, and Section V takes up the issue of voting rules. Concluding comments are in Section VI.

II. THE BASIC MODEL

We study a two-period investment project that requires an outlay of K at an initial date 0 for the purchase of two physical assets, A and B. The project is run by a manager who has no wealth. At date 1, the project produces a random cash flow of x with probability θ or zero with probability $1 - \theta$.

The project also produces cash flow at date 2, which depends on how the assets are deployed at date 1. If the manager continues to manage the assets, the date 2 cash flow is y. This alternative generates the highest possible cash flow. The project can also be liquidated (separated from the manager) in one of two ways. The project's investors can manage the assets, in which case they generate no cash flow at date 2. Or the assets can be managed by another manager, generating a date 2 cash flow of αy, where $\alpha \leq 1$. One might think of this other manager as another firm in the industry. These assumptions reflect the idea that other managers can get more out of the assets than the investors, but perhaps not as much as the original manager. The assumption that investors get zero is just a normalization. Everyone is risk neutral, and the riskless interest rate is zero.

If one were able to write a complete financial contract, it would specify date 1 and date 2 payments from the firm to the investors conditional on the uncertain first-period cash flow. The project would never be liquidated, and investors would receive payments with an expected value of K. There is a continuum of contracts that satisfy these conditions.

We assume, however, that contracts are incomplete in that they cannot be made contingent on cash flow. Although cash flow is assumed to be observable to both the manager and the investors, it is not observable to outside parties. Thus a court could not enforce a contract contingent on realized cash flows. In the language of Grossman and Hart (1986), cash flow is "observable" but not "verifiable."

This assumption is meant to capture the idea that managers have some ability to divert corporate resources to themselves at the expense of outside investors. We do not mean that managers actually "take the money and run," but rather that they may choose to spend it on perquisites or unprofitable new projects that they value more than investors. Such perk consumption and investment may be difficult to distinguish from appropriate business decisions and thus impossible to control through contracts.

While one cannot write contracts contingent on cash flows, we do assume that contracts contingent on the firm's physical assets are feasible. This assumption is based on the idea that it is harder to divert physical assets than to divert cash flow. This distinction between cash flows and assets is emphasized by Hart and Moore (1989).

In our model, the most general type of contract specifies that if the firm makes a payment R^t at date t, creditors have the right to liquidate some fraction of the assets, $z^t(R^t) \leq 1$, with probability $\beta^t(R^t) \leq 1$. A special case of this contract is a standard debt contract with the principal and interest due at date 1. The contract specifies that if the firm repays some amount, say D, at date 1, then it has the right to continue without intervention by creditors. If, however, the firm does not make the payment, the creditor has the right to seize the company's assets. This amounts to setting $z^1 = \beta^1 = 1$ if $R^1 < D$, $z^1 = \beta^1 = 0$ if $R^1 \geq D$, and $z^2 = \beta^2 = 0$.

In our model, however, the standard debt contract is not, in general, optimal. Such a contract is generally too harsh: it leads to too much liquidation if the firm does not make the payment D. It may be better not to liquidate all the firm's assets, and only with probability less than one. (We shall show that partial liquidation is not optimal, though we shall see that probabilistic liquidations are optimal.)

The contract therefore specifies that if the manager makes the payment R_r when cash flow is x, investors have the right to liquidate the assets with probability β_r. If the manager makes the payment R_0 when cash flow is zero, investors have the right to liquidate the assets with probability β_0. Note that investors cannot induce the manager to pay anything at date 2 because there are no assets to liquidate.

Given this contract, the firm's expected payoffs are

$$\theta[x - R_r + (1 - \beta_r)y] + (1 - \theta)[-R_0 + (1 - \beta_0)y]. \tag{1}$$

The investor's expected profits are

$$\theta(R_r + \beta_r L_r) + (1 - \theta)(R_0 + \beta_0 L_0) - K, \tag{2}$$

where L_r and L_0 refer to the liquidation value of the assets in the hands of the creditor when cash flow is x and zero, respectively. Although investors get no direct value from owning the assets, we shall see later that they can sell the assets. For the moment, we write the proceeds of this asset sale as L_r and L_0.

Given that the manager has no wealth of his own, payments cannot exceed the available funds at date 1, that is, $R_0 \leq 0$ and $R_r \leq x$. These payments must also satisfy an incentive constraint that ensures that the manager has an incentive to pay R_r when cash flow is x. One can write this incentive constraint as

$$x - R_r + (1 - \beta_r)y \geq x + \beta_0 S + (1 - \beta_0)y. \tag{3}$$

Two points are worth noting about this constraint. First, S denotes the utility the manager receives from paying out R_0 when cash flow is really x and the creditor is entitled to liquidate the asset. One might be tempted to think that this is zero. However, this assumes that it is optimal to follow through with the liquidation with probability β_0 when the firm pays out zero. We shall see that this is not the case, so for the moment we write the payoff as S.

Second, in principle, there should also be another constraint stating that the manager has an incentive to pay out R_0 when cash flow is zero rather than R_r. However, since R_r will be greater than zero, it is never feasible for the manager to pay out R_r when he has no cash flow. So this constraint is not binding.

The optimal contract maximizes the firm's expected payoffs (1) subject to the incentive constraint (3) and the constraint that the creditor's profits (2) are nonnegative. It is straightforward to establish two preliminary results: (i) $\beta_r = 0$: it is never optimal to liquidate when the firm makes the payment R_r; and (ii) $R_0 = 0$.

Setting $\beta_r = 0$ is optimal because it achieves the two goals of maximizing the surplus from the contract and providing the manager with incentives to pay out cash flow. If β_r were strictly positive, then the creditor could be made no worse off by reducing β_r by some infinitesimal amount ϵ and increasing R_r by ϵL_r. Such a change would increase the manager's expected payoff by $\theta\epsilon(y - L_r)$ and relax the incentive constraint.

Setting $R_0 = 0$ also maximizes the surplus from the contract and provides the manager with incentives. The only alternative is to set $R_0 < 0$ that is, pay the manager something in the bad state. But it would be better to increase R_0 and reduce β_0. As before, given that liquidation is inefficient, this increases the manager's expected payoff while making investors no worse off.

Given these results, the incentive constraint reduces to

$$R_r \leq \beta_0(y - S). \tag{4}$$

This constraint must be binding at an optimum; otherwise it would be optimal to set $\beta_0 = 0$ and the manager would have no incentive to pay out any cash flow. The nonnegative profit constraint must also be binding; otherwise R_r could be reduced while making the manager better off and still satisfying the constraint. Thus substituting the incentive constraint into the nonnegative profit constraint implies that

$$\beta_0[\theta(y - S) + (1 - \theta)L_0] - K = 0. \tag{5}$$

Using (5), we can write the manager's expected payoff as

$$\theta x + y - K - (1 - \theta)\beta_0(y - L_0). \tag{6}$$

The first three terms in (6) sum to the net present value of the project in the first-best case of no liquidation. The last term is the expected efficiency loss from contractual incompleteness; it is the probability of a liquidation, $(1 - \theta)\beta_0$, times the loss in value from a liquidation, $y - L_0$. Given that the manager's expected payoff is decreasing in β_0 and the creditor's profits are increasing in β_0, the optimal solution is to set β_0 equal to its minimum feasible level, that is, the solution to (5). Thus

$$\beta_0 = \frac{K}{\theta(y - S) + (1 - \theta)L_0}. \tag{7}$$

There is a feasible solution provided that the β_0 that solves (7) is no greater than one. That is, there will be a solution if K is less than the maximum feasible gross profit of the creditors, $\pi \equiv \theta(y - S) + (1 - \theta)L_0$.

The main feature of the optimal contract is that there is liquidation when the firm's first-period performance is poor. This is not because poor early performance signals poor future performance, that is, they are uncorrelated. Rather, the threat of liquidation serves as a way of inducing the manager to pay out cash flow instead of diverting it to himself. If he were to keep the first-period cash flow, the creditor would be given the right to liquidate the assets with probability β_0, which generates a second-period payoff of $S < y$. When the first-period cash flow is in fact x, the manager would (weakly) prefer to pay $R_x = \beta_0(y - S)$ than to keep the cash and forfeit $\beta_0(y - S)$. Unfortunately, if first-period cash flow turns out to be zero, the manager has no choice but to have the assets liquidated with probability β_0 since he lacks the cash to prevent such a liquidation.

Recall that we have ruled out contracts in which creditors limit themselves to liquidating only one of the assets. We show in the Appendix that it is never optimal for creditors to limit themselves in this way. There are two reasons why such contracts are not optimal. First, liquidating only part of the asset means that β_0 must be higher than if all of the asset is liquidated. Given asset complementarity, it is better to liquidate all of the asset less often than to liquidate only one of the assets more often. Second, when only one of the assets is liquidated, an outside buyer has less to gain from incurring a fixed transaction cost of becoming informed. Therefore, the asset is sold with lower probability, and the expected liquidation value is lower under partial liquidation.

III. ONE CREDITOR OR TWO?

The model above is incomplete because it is not specific about the liquidation value L_0 and the manager's payoff following default, S. In this section, we fill in these important details and begin to address the question of when it is optimal to borrow from one or two creditors. The trade-offs that emerge in this model capture all the trade-offs that would emerge in a model of more than two creditors. In fact, we have analyzed such a model, and all the basic results carry through.

To emphasize the dependence of the variables on the number of creditors, we write $L_0(n)$, $S(n)$, and $\beta_0(n)$, where n is the number of creditors. We first consider the case of one creditor.

A. One Creditor

We have assumed that creditors get no value from managing the asset. Therefore, they may choose to sell the asset to an outside buyer—another firm in the industry or some other investor who can manage the asset. As noted, the outside buyer's value of the asset is αy, where $0 < \alpha \leq 1$. Suppose that the buyer incurs a cost, c, to bargain for control of the assets. This cost c is unknown at date 0 and is distributed uniformly along the interval $[0, \bar{c}]$. Thus the buyer will bargain provided that c is less than his share of the surplus from bargaining.

Now suppose that cash flow is zero and the firm defaults. Control of the assets passes to the creditor. We assume Nash bargaining so that the buyer and the creditor share the surplus αy equally provided that the buyer incurs the transaction cost. Thus the buyer gets $\frac{1}{2}\alpha y$ and the creditor receives the remaining $\frac{1}{2}\alpha y$.

It pays for the buyer to bargain provided that $c \leq \frac{1}{2}\alpha y$; the assets are therefore sold with probability $(\frac{1}{2}\alpha y)/\bar{c}$ assuming, as we do, that $\frac{1}{2}\alpha y < \bar{c}$. So, at date 0, the expected value of the liquidation payoff when cash flow is zero is given by

$$L_0(1) = \frac{\alpha^2 y^2}{4\bar{c}}. \tag{8}$$

One should keep in mind that we have assumed that the buyer has the up-front cash to pay for the asset at date 1. Given that cash flow is not verifiable, the buyer would not be able to borrow the purchase price, promising to repay the loan out of date 2 cash flows. Thus, as Shleifer and Vishny (1992) have argued, assets may get sold to the most liquid bidder rather than to the highest-value user.

What happens following a strategic default? There are now three potential parties to the negotiations: the outside buyer, the creditor, and the original manager. Since the original manager is the most efficient user of the assets, he will buy them back from the creditor (assuming as we do that x is large enough). To analyze this case, we would need a model of three-person bargaining such as the Shapley value generalization of Nash bargaining. In such a model, even though the outside buyer never ends up buying the assets, the manager would end up paying the outsider something because of his positive Shapley value. (One can show that this is $\frac{1}{6}\alpha y$.)

However, for several reasons, we assume that the outside buyer does not enter the bargaining following a strategic default. First, because the Shapley value model implies that the outsider gets payments without getting control of the assets, 'bogus' buyers could claim to value the assets at αy in order to extract some payment from the manager. So it may be hard to distinguish between genuine outside buyers and bogus ones. Second, in an alternative model in which the manager and the outside buyer bid against each other, the outsider would always lose against the more efficient manager. Therefore, he would have no incentive to incur the transaction cost of becoming informed about the assets. Finally, we have solved the model under the alternative assumption that the outside buyer does bargain. Nothing of substance changes.

Without the outside buyer, there are two parties to the bargain, so the manager and the creditor split the surplus of y equally according to Nash bargaining. Thus

$$S(1) = \frac{y}{2}. \tag{9}$$

Note that the manager does not incur a cost to bargain. The assumption that the cost is zero is just a normalization and reflects the idea that the manager is more informed about the firm and therefore has a lower cost of preparing a bid.

We can now use (8) and (9) to write β_0 in terms of the exogenous parameters, α, y, and $\bar{c}$. Specifically, $\beta_0(1) = K/\pi(1)$, where

$$\pi(1) \equiv \theta \frac{y}{2} + (1 - \theta)\left(\frac{\alpha^2 y^2}{4\bar{c}}\right). \tag{10}$$

It is straightforward to establish that $\beta_0(1)$ is decreasing in θ so that the inefficiency, $(1 - \theta)\beta_0(1)[y - L_0(1)]$, is lower for high-$\theta$ (low-default-risk) firms. Also, $\beta_0(1)$ is decreasing in α and $L_0(1)$ is increasing in α, so the inefficiency is also decreasing in α.

B. Two Creditors

Now suppose that the firm raises capital from two creditors to purchase the two assets, A and B. In order to analyze this case, we have to specify what happens in a default. Suppose, for the moment, that creditor a is "secured" by asset A and gets to liquidate that asset only, and creditor b is secured by asset B and gets to liquidate that asset only. Each creditor makes his own decision about whether to take possession of the asset, renegotiate with the manager, or sell it to an outside buyer. In Section V, we shall consider alternative mechanisms by which creditors decide when to sell the assets.

The critical assumption that drives the analysis is that assets A and B are worth more together than apart. Let y^A be the date 2 cash flow from asset A if it is used without asset B, and let y^B be the date 2 cash flow from asset B if it is used without asset A. Our assumption amounts to the condition that $y - y^A - y^B > 0$. We label this difference Δ.

There are two rationales behind the assumption that Δ is strictly positive. The first is that the two assets are essentially the same and there are increasing returns to scale. For example, asset A may be one plant and asset B another, and there are benefits to having a large market share.

The second rationale—and the one we shall stress—is that there are project-specific complementarities between the assets. For example, a building designed to manufacture aircraft equipment is more valuable when used together with the machines designed to build aircraft. The building could be used to manufacture something else, or even other aircraft, but it is most efficient to use it for its original purpose. Certainly not all assets exhibit this sort of complementarity. Farmland and farm equipment can both be separated from each other without any real diminution in value: a tractor can be used just as efficiently on other farms, and farmland can be used just as efficiently with other tractors.[1]

Following a liquidity default, there are three parties to the bargaining: the outside buyer and the two creditors. As before, the manager is not in a position to buy the assets from the creditors because he has no cash to offer. Since the most efficient use of the assets is to keep the assets together, the outside buyer will buy both of them if it pays for him to incur the transaction cost c.

In this case, we have to calculate the creditors' Shapley values. The basic idea of the Shapley value is that the bargaining power of each agent is related to his marginal value to the various coalitions that could form in the process of

---

[1] It might also be possible for Δ to be negative if there are decreasing returns to scale. We do not consider this possibility because we think that the case of asset complementarity is more relevant.

bargaining. In particular, the Shapley value gives each agent his expected marginal value to a coalition, where the expectation is taken over all coalitions to which the agent might belong.

Creditor a's Shapley value is $\frac{1}{2}\alpha y^A + \frac{1}{3}\alpha\Delta$. This was calculated as follows. With probability $\frac{1}{3}$, creditor a is part of a coalition with creditor b and the buyer. His marginal value to this coalition is $\alpha(y - y^B)$ since the buyer and b can get αy^B without a, but with a they can get αy. With probability $\frac{1}{6}$, creditor a is in a coalition with only the buyer, and his marginal value is αy^A. With probability $\frac{1}{6}$, creditor a is in a coalition only with creditor b, and his marginal value is zero since they need the buyer to get any value from the assets. Finally, with probability $\frac{1}{3}$, creditor a is in a coalition by himself, which has no value. The weighted average of these marginal values is creditor a's Shapley value, $\frac{1}{3}\alpha(y - y^B) + \frac{1}{6}\alpha y^A$. This can be written as $\frac{1}{2}\alpha y^A + \frac{1}{3}\alpha\Delta$.

Analogously, creditor b's Shapley value is $\frac{1}{2}\alpha y^B + \frac{1}{3}\alpha\Delta$. The sum of the two creditors' Shapley values is $\frac{1}{2}\alpha y + \frac{1}{6}\Delta$. Thus the two creditors together get more than a single creditor would if he controlled both assets A and B.

This result clearly depends on the assumption of asset complementarity ($\Delta > 0$). Recall that an agent's Shapley value is higher to the extent that he adds value to each possible coalition of agents. For example, creditor a adds a value of $\alpha(y^A + \Delta)$ to the coalition of creditor b and the outside buyer, but adds a value of αy^A only if creditor b is not in the coalition. So creditor a is able to capture some of the benefits of asset complementarity.

Although the Shapley value is not based on an explicit model of multiperson bargaining, it captures some of the holdup problems arising in multiperson bargaining. These effects are modeled, for example, by Gertner (1990) in an extensive-form bargaining game with three players, asymmetric information, and asset complementarity.

It follows then that the outside buyer's Shapley value is $\frac{1}{2}\alpha y - \frac{1}{6}\alpha\Delta$ in the event he bargains, and therefore he will bargain with probability $(1/\bar{c})(\frac{1}{2}\alpha y - \frac{1}{6}\alpha\Delta)$. So the expected payoff to the two creditors is

$$
\begin{aligned}
L_0(2) &= \frac{1}{\bar{c}}\left(\frac{\alpha y}{2} + \frac{\alpha\Delta}{6}\right)\left(\frac{\alpha y}{2} - \frac{\alpha\Delta}{6}\right) \\
&= \frac{\alpha^2 y^2}{4\bar{c}} - \frac{\alpha^2\Delta^2}{36\bar{c}} \\
&< \frac{\alpha^2 y^2}{4\bar{c}} \\
&= L_0(1).
\end{aligned}
\tag{11}
$$

Thus two creditors receive more than one if the outside buyer enters the bargain, but they receive less from an ex ante perspective since they are less likely to find a buyer of the assets. The reason is that the low payoff of making the bid discourages the outside buyer from incurring the cost c of bidding. That the latter effect is strong enough to outweigh the former follows from our assumption that the transaction costs are uniformly distributed. We discuss the importance of these assumptions later in this section.

The calculation of $S(2)$ follows similarly. Again, there are three parties to the bargain: the outside buyer and the two creditors. Since the manager is the most efficient user of the assets, he will end up buying them back from the creditors. The manager's Shapley value is given by

$$S(2) = \frac{y}{2} - \frac{\Delta}{6}. \tag{12}$$

Given $\Delta > 0$, this value is clearly lower than the original manager's Shapley value when there is only one creditor, $\frac{1}{2}y$. As in the case of a liquidity default, asset complementarity forces the buyer (in this case the manager) to pay more because control of an asset is worth more if the buyer already owns the complementary asset.[2]

Given (7), we know that $\beta_0(2) = K/\pi(2)$, where

$$
\begin{aligned}
\pi(2) &= \theta\left(\frac{y}{2} + \frac{\Delta}{6}\right) + (1 - \theta)\left(\frac{\alpha^2 y^2}{4\bar{c}} - \frac{\alpha^2 \Delta^2}{36\bar{c}}\right) \\
&= \pi(1) + \theta\frac{\Delta}{6} - (1 - \theta)\frac{\alpha^2 \Delta^2}{36\bar{c}}.
\end{aligned}
\tag{13}
$$

Thus the two creditors' maximum gross profit could be greater or less than the single creditor's gross profit.

Borrowing from two creditors is beneficial in that the manager has to pay them more than one creditor following a strategic default (thus disciplining the manager), but it is costly in that two creditors are paid less than one creditor following a liquidity default (thus leading to more costly financial distress). The result that two creditors receive more following a strategic default but less following a liquidity default may seem inconsistent, but there is an important idea underlying it. In a liquidity default, the high price of the assets required when there are two creditors is costly in that it discourages outside buyers from bidding. But when there is a strategic default, the original manager always buys back the assets, so there is no cost of borrowing from two creditors.

C. Which Is Better?

We are now in a position to compare the two alternatives. Recall that the inefficiency is proportional to $\beta_0(n)[y - L_0(n)]$. Thus there are two ways in which the

---

[2] When there are two creditors, there is the possibility that the manager could default on one creditor and not on the other. However, one can show that when $\Delta > 0$, the manager has no incentive to do so. That is, the manager is better off making no payment and renegotiating with both creditors than making the payment to one creditor and renegotiating with the other creditor. In the case in which $\Delta < 0$, the manager *would* have an incentive to default on only one creditor. To avoid such an outcome, the contract could specify a cross-default provision (as is common in practice) giving each creditor the right to seize all the firm's assets in the event of a partial default. There would then be no gain from defaulting on only one of the creditors.

number of creditors affects this measure. First, it affects the liquidation value. From (11), we know that the liquidation value is always higher when there is only one creditor. So, on this score, the manager would always choose to borrow from one creditor.

Second, the number of creditors affects the liquidation probability; low values of β_0 reduce the inefficiency. This liquidation probability, in turn, is low when creditors can require high payments in the good state (because S is low) or when the liquidation value, L_0, is high (see eq. [7]). While S is lower with the two creditors, L_0 is higher with one creditor. So $\beta_0(2)$ could be greater or less than $\beta_0(1)$.

The following three propositions characterize the conditions under which the two-creditor arrangement is more or less efficient than the one-creditor arrangement.

Proposition 1. *The firm borrows from two creditors when default risk is low (θ high) and from one creditor when default risk is high (θ low).*

The rationale is simple. When default risk is high, the best way to reduce β_0 is to have a high liquidation value. This is best achieved with one creditor. By contrast, when default risk is low, the more effective way to reduce β_0 is to limit the manager's renegotiation rents, thereby allowing a larger payment in the good state. This is best achieved with two creditors.

The proposition assumes that it is feasible for the firm to borrow from one or from two creditors. However, for low enough θ, neither may be feasible or only one of the alternatives may be feasible. Indeed, there are parameters for which the optimal number of creditors is nonmonotonic in θ. For high values of θ, the firm borrows from two creditors; for intermediate values of θ, the firm borrows from one creditor; and for low values of θ, the firm borrows from two creditors. This last region is possible because at low θ it may not be feasible to borrow from one creditor, but it may be feasible to borrow from two creditors. In particular, this occurs when

$$\theta\frac{y}{2} + (1-\theta)\left(\frac{\alpha^2 y^2}{4\bar{c}}\right) < K < \theta\frac{y}{2} + (1-\theta)\left(\frac{\alpha^2 y^2}{4\bar{c}}\right) + \theta\frac{\Delta}{6} - (1-\theta)\frac{\alpha^2\Delta^2}{36\bar{c}}.$$

$$(14)$$

Proposition 2. *The firm borrows from two creditors when asset complementarity is low (Δ low) and from one creditor when asset complementarity is high (Δ high).*

On the one hand, a large Δ is beneficial in that it reduces the manager's renegotiation rent; on the other hand, it is detrimental in that it lowers liquidation payoffs. However, as one can see from (11) and (12), Δ has a first-order effect on renegotiation rents but only a second-order effect on liquidation payoffs.

Thus small increases in Δ from zero increase efficiency. Beyond a certain point, the liquidation costs outweigh the renegotiation benefits.

Proposition 3. *The firm borrows from two creditors when outside buyers place low valuations on the assets (α small) and from one creditor when their valuations are high (α high).*

As α increases, liquidation values rise. But, more important, the one-creditor liquidation value rises faster than the two-creditor liquidation value. This effect makes it more attractive for firms to borrow from one creditor when α is high.

One way to interpret the results is to view α as a measure of the ease with which assets can be redeployed. Firms with easily redeployable assets will borrow from one creditor. For example, an office building is likely to be easily redeployable: an outside buyer can get just as much value from the office building as the manager. However, highly redeployable assets probably also do not exhibit much complementarity. Indeed, one of the reasons they can be easily redeployed is that they can be easily combined with other assets. The office building is highly redeployable because it can just as easily be combined with the office equipment of an accounting firm as with the office equipment of a law firm. Thus, while firms with highly redeployable assets might want to borrow from one creditor, those assets may exhibit low asset complementarity, suggesting that the firm should borrow from two creditors. Which effect is more important is an open question.

Another interpretation of α is that it reflects the extent to which outside buyers have liquid resources to purchase the assets. Loosely speaking, when α is low, buyers do not have the resources to pay for the assets up front, even if they have high fundamental valuations of the assets.

To make this idea more precise, we need to introduce some notation. Let p be the probability that the buyer has enough cash to buy the asset; $1 - p$ is the probability that the buyer has no cash at all. If cash flows are correlated in an industry, and we think of the outside buyer as another firm in the industry, then p should be lower in the low-cash flow state than in the high-cash flow state. Let p_0 be the probability that the outside buyer has the cash when the firm's cash flow is low, and let p_r be the corresponding probability when cash flow is high. Low values of p_0 relative to p_r would be characteristic of cyclical industries (such as durables) or those in which firms are subject mainly to common shocks (such as oil).[3] For simplicity, let $p_r = 1$.

In this setup, the expected liquidation values can be written as

$$L_0(1) = p_0 \frac{\alpha^2 y^2}{4\bar{c}} \tag{15}$$

---

[3] This point is made by Shleifer and Vishny (1992), who go on to argue that firms in these industries will choose low leverage as a result. Asquith, Gertner, and Scharfstein (1994) present evidence that financially distressed firms are less likely to sell assets when the other firms in the industry are also distressed.

and

$$L_0(2) = p_0\left(\frac{\alpha^2 y^2}{4\bar{c}} - \frac{\alpha^2 \Delta^2}{36\bar{c}}\right). \tag{16}$$

These are just the standard liquidation values, given in (8) and (11), times the probability that buyers have enough liquidity in the low-cash flow state to buy the assets.

As p_0 falls, expected liquidation values fall and, more important, the difference between the one-creditor and two-creditor expected liquidation values falls. Thus, when p_0 is small, the cost of borrowing from two creditors (a lower liquidation value) is small. The firm, therefore, borrows from two creditors.

Thus one might argue that firms in cyclical industries or in industries exposed to common shocks will choose to borrow from two creditors. These firms are likely to realize low liquidation values for their assets regardless of the number of creditors, so they are better off taking advantage of the discipline provided by two creditors. By contrast, firms in noncyclical industries or those in industries subject to idiosyncratic shocks—industries in which liquidation values can be high—should borrow from one creditor to maximize the liquidation value.

IV. SECURITY ALLOCATION

Our framework also has implications for how security should be allocated between creditors. Should creditor a be secured by asset A and creditor b secured by asset B, as we have assumed? Or should creditor a be secured by both assets while creditor b has no security?

Let R_x^a be the payment to creditor a and R_x^b be the payment to creditor b. If only a is secured, then there is only one creditor with whom to negotiate. The liquidation value is therefore equal to $L_0(1)$ and the renegotiation rent is $S(1)$. Each creditor makes zero profits in equilibrium:

$$\theta R_x^a + (1-\theta)\beta_0 L_0(1) = K^A, \tag{17}$$

$$\theta R_x^b = K^B, \tag{18}$$

where K^A is the capital invested by creditor a to purchase asset A, and K^B is analogous for creditor b.

Equation (18) pins down R_x^b. Combining this with the binding incentive constraint pins down R_x^a:

$$R_x^a + R_x^b = \beta_0[y - S(1)]. \tag{19}$$

Substituting (18) and (19) into (17), we see that β_0 is solved by

$$\beta_0\{\theta[y - S(1)] + (1-\theta)L_0(1)\} = K, \tag{20}$$

which is precisely the condition determining $\beta_0(1)$. Thus giving one creditor all of the security replicates the one-creditor solution. It generates a relatively high liquidation value, but also high renegotiation rents. Giving both creditors security generates a low liquidation value, but also low renegotiation rents.

It follows then that one can use propositions 1, 2, and 3 to characterize when both creditors will be secured and when only one of them will be secured. Firms with high θ, low α, and low Δ will give equal security interests to both creditors, whereas firms with low θ, high α, and high Δ will grant security to only one creditor.

V. VOTING RULES

Although we do not have an explicit model of bargaining, we have implicitly assumed that each creditor negotiates on an individual basis with the manager or the outside buyer. However, indentures in credit agreements typically specify voting rules that determine how creditors make collective decisions regarding debt renegotiation, asset sales, and many other terms of the debt contract. For example, an indenture to a bank loan might specify that the terms of the agreement can be changed only if a majority of the creditors agree to do so.

In this section, we take up the question of the optimal voting rule to govern' renegotiation. To do this in the simplest possible way, we assume that there is only one asset and that it generates a date 2 value of y. We also assume that there are $n > 1$ creditors, each of whom is secured by an equal amount of the asset.

A voting rule specifies that if m creditors agree to sell the asset to the outsider (in the case of a liquidity default) or the manager (in the case of a strategic default), then the asset gets sold and the proceeds are paid out pro rata. A *majority voting* rule occurs when $m/n = \frac{1}{2}$, a *supermajority voting* rule occurs when $m/n > \frac{1}{2}$, and a *submajority voting* rule occurs when $m/n < \frac{1}{2}$.

The goal here is to solve for the optimal voting rule, m/n. To do this, we need to first calculate the creditors' payoffs in a liquidity default and the manager's payoff in a strategic default, which we denote by $L_0(m, n)$ and $S(m, n)$, respectively.

First, consider a strategic default. If the voting rule requires m of the n creditors to agree, then the manager will contribute a positive value of y only to those coalitions that have at least m creditors. Since there are $n + 1$ parties in the bargaining, this occurs with probability $1 - [m/(n + 1)]$. Thus

$$S(m, n) = \left(1 - \frac{m}{n + 1}\right) y. \tag{21}$$

Note that the higher m is—the more stringent the voting rule—the lower the manager's surplus from renegotiation.

Similarly, following a liquidity default, the outside buyer will add value only to coalitions with m creditors. So his Shapley value is $\{1 - [m/(n + 1)]\}\alpha y$ and the probability that he bargains is therefore $\{1 - [m/(n + 1)]\}(\alpha y/\bar{c})$. The creditors get the remaining surplus of $[m/(n + 1)]\alpha y$. Thus

$$L_0(m, n) = \frac{m}{n + 1} \left(1 - \frac{m}{n + 1}\right) \frac{\alpha^2 y}{\bar{c}}. \tag{22}$$

In this case, an increase in m has ambiguous effects on L_0. On the one hand, it increases creditors' payoffs in liquidation because it increases the probability that they will have a positive value to a coalition. On the other hand, it reduces the buyer's Shapley value and discourages him from becoming informed. Differentiating (22) with respect to $m/(n + 1)$, we see that the value of $m/(n + 1)$ that maximizes $L_0(m, n)$ is $\frac{1}{2}$. Thus the maximal value of $L_0(m, n)$ is $\alpha^2 y^2/4\bar{c}$ (which is exactly the payoff in the one-creditor case under the alternative mechanism considered in Sec. III).

A couple of points are worth noting before we continue. First, $m/(n + 1) = \frac{1}{2}$ is not quite majority rule since $m/n = \frac{1}{2}(n + 1)/n > \frac{1}{2}$. However, as $n \to \infty$, $m/n \to \frac{1}{2}$. So we shall consider this majority rule. Second, majority rule maximizes the expected liquidation value because we assumed a uniform distribution of bidding costs. This is by no means a general result.

Given these values of L_0 and S, the expected efficiency loss given m and n, $EL(m, n)$, can be written as

$$EL(m, n) = (1 - \theta)\beta_0(m, n)[y - L_0(m, n)]$$

$$= (1 - \theta)K \frac{1 - v(1 - v)(\alpha^2 y/\bar{c})}{v[\theta + (1 - \theta)v(1 - v)(\alpha^2 y/\bar{c})]}, \tag{23}$$

where $v \equiv m/(n + 1)$.

If integer problems are ignored, the optimal v minimizes (23). Thus differentiating with respect to v gives the following first-order condition:

$$\theta v^2 \frac{\alpha^2 y}{\bar{c}} - \theta - (1 - \theta)(1 - 2v) \frac{\alpha^2 y}{\bar{c}} = 0. \tag{24}$$

The second-order condition is always satisfied.

First, note that the optimal v, v^*, is greater than $\frac{1}{2}$, the voting rule that maximizes the liquidation value. At $v = \frac{1}{2}$, (24) is negative, indicating that the efficiency loss could be reduced by increasing v above $\frac{1}{2}$. The reason is that a small increase in v has a second-order effect in lowering the liquidation value but a first-order effect in lowering the renegotiation rent. This in turn lowers β_0.

Thus, in our model, supermajority voting is always optimal. However, this result is not general; it is driven by the assumption of uniform distribution of c. What is general is the idea that the optimal voting rule is more stringent than the rule that maximizes liquidation values.

Two results follow immediately from (23).

Proposition 4. (i) *The optimal voting rule is more stringent for firms with lower default risk* (v^* *is increasing in* θ). (ii) *The optimal voting rule is more stringent when outside buyers have a low valuation of the firm's assets* (v^* *is decreasing in* α).

The reasoning behind these results is simple. High-θ firms are less likely to default, so the higher liquidation value creditors receive under a lenient voting rule is not particularly valuable. But the lower renegotiation rents made possible by a more stringent rule allow the firm to pay out more cash flow in the good state, which is particularly valuable when θ is high.

More stringent voting rules are also preferred by low-α firms. When α is low, a stringent voting rule has little impact on liquidation values. So the cost of such a rule is small. As a result, low-α firms prefer more stringent voting rules.

Note that this version of the model does not pin down an optimal number of creditors. The trade-offs that emerge in the model of Section III do not arise here because the voting rule can be used to undo the undesirable aspect of having too many or too few creditors.

VI. CONCLUSION

This paper analyzes some aspects of debt structure within an optimal contracting framework. Our basic point is that debt structure affects the negotiations that follow default. These negotiation outcomes can be affected by varying the number of creditors, by distributing security interests more or less widely, or by imposing more or less stringent voting rules. An optimal debt structure balances two concerns: on the one hand, it should deter defaults; on the other hand, it should not make unavoidable defaults too costly. The model predicts that low-default risk firms, those with strong asset complementarities, and those in non-cyclical businesses will tend to borrow from more creditors, spread out security interests, and adopt more stringent voting rules.

One issue that we have not considered is the role of bankruptcy law. We have unrealistically assumed that firms cannot file for bankruptcy and that creditors pursue their liquidation rights as specified in the debt contract. This issue is important in the context of our model because Chapter 8 specifies a detailed set of rules that govern debt renegotiation.

For example, Chapter 8 imposes a particular voting rule on debt renegotiation: one-half of the creditors in number or two-thirds of the creditors in the face value of their claims need to agree. This voting rule could be more or less stringent than the optimal voting rule, v^*. If it is less stringent, creditors might choose other aspects of debt structure that make it harder to renegotiate, for example, by borrowing from more creditors or spreading out security interests. Chapter 8 also includes an automatic stay and an exclusivity period, in which debtors can defer debt payments and remain in Chapter 8 for long periods. This lowers the creditors' liquidation value and increases the payoff from strategic default. In response, the optimal debt contract will specify a higher liquidation probability, β_0, to compensate for the lower payouts to creditors.

Appendix

Proof That Partial Liquidation Is Not Optimal. Let L_0^i be the liquidation value when asset set $i = \{A\}, \{B\}, \{AB\}$ is liquidated following a liquidity default. Let S^i be the manager's payoff following a strategic default when creditors have the right to liquidate asset set i. In the text we consider the case in which $i = \{AB\}$. Here we show that $i = \{AB\}$ is optimal.

The incentive constraint can now be written as

$$R_r \leq \beta_0(y - S^i). \tag{A1}$$

Given the binding incentive constraint, the nonnegative profit constraint is

$$\beta_0[\theta(y - S^i) + (1 - \theta)L_0^i] - K \geq 0, \tag{A2}$$

The manager's expected payoff can be written as

$$\theta x + y - K - \beta_0(1 - \theta)(y - y^{-i} - L_0^i), \tag{A3}$$

where $-i$ is the set of assets not in i.

Given that β_0 solves (A2) with equality, the efficiency loss in the case in which i is liquidated can be written as

$$EL^i = \frac{y - y^{-i} - L_0^i}{\theta(y - S^i) + (1 - \theta)L_0^i}(1 - \theta)K. \tag{A4}$$

Total liquidation is preferred to partial liquidation provided that $EL^{AB} < EL^A$ and $EL^{AB} < EL^B$. We shall compare EL^{AB} to EL^A. The comparison to EL^B is basically the same. The condition is met provided that

$$\frac{y - L_0^{AB}}{\theta(y - S^{AB}) + (1 - \theta)L_0^{AB}} < \frac{y - y^B - L_0^B}{\theta(y - S^A) + (1 - \theta)L_0^A}. \tag{A5}$$

Consider first the case of a single creditor. The values of $S^{AB}(1)$ and $L_0^{AB}(1)$ are given in the text. We need to calculate the payoffs in liquidation and following strategic default when there is partial liquidation. Following a strategic default, the surplus from renegotiating is $y - y^B$ since the manager can get y^B without the involvement of the creditor. Thus

$$S^A(1) = y^B + \tfrac{1}{2}(y - y^B)$$
$$= \frac{y + y^B}{2}. \tag{A6}$$

This is greater than $S^{AB}(1) = y/2$ given in equation (9).

The analysis of $L_0^A(1)$ is a bit more complex. Implicit in (A2) is the assumption that the manager holds on to asset B and the creditor sells asset A. In order for this to be the case, it must be that

$$\alpha y^A + y^B > \alpha y, \tag{A7}$$

which can be written as

$$\alpha < \frac{y^B}{y^B + \Delta}. \tag{A8}$$

Thus if α and Δ are relatively small, this condition will be satisfied.

If this condition is met, the buyer just buys asset A from the creditor. It is straightforward to show that

$$L_0^A(1) = \frac{\alpha^2 (y^A)^2}{4\bar{c}}, \tag{A9}$$

which is clearly less than $L_0^{AB}(1)$.

Thus substituting these values of $S^A(1)$ and $L_0^A(1)$ into inequality (A5) yields

$$\frac{y - (\alpha^2 y^2 / 4\bar{c})}{\theta(y/2) + (1 - \theta)(\alpha^2 y^2 / 4\bar{c})} < \frac{y - y^B - (\alpha^2 (y^A)^2 / 4\bar{c})}{\theta((y - y^B)/2) + (1 - \theta)(\alpha^2 (y^A)^2 / 4\bar{c})}. \tag{A10}$$

Dividing the numerator and denominator of the left-hand side by y and the numerator and the denominator of the right-hand side by $y - y^B$ gives us

$$\frac{1 - (\alpha^2 y / 4\bar{c})}{(\theta/2) + (1 - \theta)(\alpha^2 y / 4\bar{c})} < \frac{1 - (\alpha^2 (y^A)^2 / 4\bar{c}(y - y^B))}{(\theta/2) + (1 - \theta)(\alpha^2 (y^A)^2 / 4\bar{c}(y - y^B))}. \tag{A11}$$

Given that $y^A < y - y^B < y$, this inequality is satisfied.

If condition (A7) is violated, then the outside buyer buys asset A from the creditor and asset B from the manager. The outside buyer's Shapley value is

$$\tfrac{1}{2}\alpha y^A + \tfrac{1}{3}(\alpha y - \alpha y^A - y^B). \tag{A12}$$

Thus the probability that the outside buyer buys the assets is (A12) divided by $\bar{c}$. The creditor's Shapley value is the same as (A12). Given that $\alpha y - \alpha y^A - y^B > 0$ by (A7), this payoff is greater than $\tfrac{1}{2}\alpha y^A$. Let $\tfrac{1}{3}(\alpha y - \alpha y^A - y^B) \equiv z$.

The expression for the efficiency loss is slightly different in this case. It can be written as

$$\frac{y - y^B - (1/\bar{c})(\tfrac{1}{2}\alpha y^A + z)(\tfrac{1}{2}\alpha y^A + 2z)}{\theta((y - y^B)/2) + (1 - \theta)(1/\bar{c})(\tfrac{1}{2}\alpha y^A + z)^2}(1 - \theta)K. \tag{A13}$$

We compare the left-hand side of (A11) with (A13). First, divide the numerator and the denominator of (A13) by $y - y^B$. Expression (A13) will be greater than (A11) if

$$\frac{\alpha^2 y}{4\bar{c}} > \frac{(\frac{1}{2}\alpha y^A + z)(\frac{1}{2}\alpha y^A + 2z)}{\bar{c}(y - y^B)}. \tag{A14}$$

Tedious but straightforward calculations establish that (A14) is indeed satisfied. Thus, in both cases, that is, when (A7) is satisfied and when it is violated, total liquidation is more efficient than partial liquidation.

Finally, it remains to show that total liquidation is preferred to partial liquidation when there are two creditors. Note, however, that partial liquidation with two creditors is the same as partial liquidation with one creditor since only one of the creditors is given the right to liquidate one of the assets. But we have already shown that one-creditor total liquidation is preferable to one-creditor partial liquidation. Therefore, the relevant choice is between total liquidation with two creditors and total liquidation with one creditor. This is the case we consider in the paper.

Proof of Proposition 1. The firm is indifferent between borrowing from one and borrowing from two creditors when the efficiency losses under the two regimes are equal, $EL(1) - EL(2) = 0$, or

$$\frac{y - L_0(1)}{\theta[y - S(1)] + (1 - \theta)L_0(1)} - \frac{y - L_0(2)}{\theta[y - S(2)] + (1 - \theta)L_0(2)} = 0. \tag{A15}$$

This condition can be written as

$$\frac{\Delta y}{6}\left[\theta\left(\frac{\alpha^2\Delta}{12\bar{c}} + 1 - \frac{\alpha^2 y}{4\bar{c}}\right) - \frac{\alpha^2\Delta}{6\bar{c}}\right] = 0. \tag{A16}$$

The condition is met when $\Delta = 0$ or, for $\Delta > 0$, when

$$\theta = \frac{\alpha^2\Delta}{3\alpha^2\Delta + 36\bar{c} - 9\alpha^2 y} \equiv \hat{\theta} < 1. \tag{A17}$$

Since (A16) is increasing in θ, the firm borrows from two creditors for all $\theta > \hat{\theta}$, and the firm borrows from one creditor for all $\theta < \hat{\theta}$.   □

Proof of Proposition 2. From (A16), it is clear that $EL(1) = EL(2)$ at two values of Δ: at $\Delta = 0$ and at some positive Δ. The positive value of Δ, $\hat{\Delta}$, is given by

$$\hat{\Delta} = \frac{\theta(1 - \alpha^2 y/4\bar{c})}{(1 - \theta/2)(\alpha^2/6\bar{c})}. \tag{A18}$$

This $\hat{\Delta}$ exists provided that $\hat{\Delta} < y$. This condition can be written as

$$\frac{\theta}{1 + (\theta/2)} < \frac{\alpha^2 y}{4\bar{c}}, \tag{A19}$$

which is clearly satisfied for large enough α and small enough θ. Differentiating $EL(2)$ with respect to Δ, we get

$$\frac{dEL(2)}{d\Delta} = -\frac{1}{\pi(2)^2}\left\{[y - \theta S(2)]\frac{dL_2}{d\Delta} - [y - L(2)]\theta\frac{dS(2)}{d\Delta}\right\}$$

$$= \frac{1}{\pi(2)^2}\left\{\left[\left(1 - \frac{\theta}{2}\right)y + \theta\frac{\Delta}{6}\right]\frac{\alpha^2\Delta}{18\bar{c}} - \left(y - \frac{\alpha^2 y^2}{4\bar{c}} + \frac{\alpha\Delta^2}{36\bar{c}}\right)\frac{\theta}{6}\right\}. \tag{A20}$$

At $\Delta = 0$, $EL(2)$ is decreasing in Δ, and for large enough Δ, $EL(2)$ is increasing in Δ.

It follows then that at $\hat{\Delta}$ (if it exists), $EL(2)$ is increasing in Δ. Thus, for all $\Delta > \hat{\Delta}$, $EL(2) > EL(1)$, and the firm borrows from one creditor; for all $\Delta < \hat{\Delta}$, $EL(1) > EL(2)$, and the firm borrows from two creditors. $\qquad\square$

Proof of Proposition 3. Equation (A16) implies that the firm is indifferent between borrowing from one creditor and borrowing from two creditors for $\alpha = \hat{\alpha}$, where $\hat{\alpha}$ is defined implicitly by

$$\hat{\alpha}^2 = \frac{12\theta\bar{c}}{\theta(3y - \Delta) + 2\Delta}. \tag{A21}$$

This cutoff level of $\hat{\alpha}$ exists provided that it is less than one, which will be true when θ is small or y and Δ are large.

Given that (A16) is decreasing in α, it follows that the firm borrows from one creditor when $\alpha > \hat{\alpha}$ and borrows from two creditors when $\alpha < \hat{\alpha}$. $\qquad\square$

Proof of Proposition 4.

(i) Totally differentiating (24) with respect to v yields

$$\frac{dv^*}{d\theta} = \frac{1 - (1 - 2v)(\alpha^2 y/\bar{c}) - v^2(\alpha^2 y/\bar{c})}{(\alpha^2 y/\bar{c})[2\theta v + 2(1 - \theta)]}. \tag{A22}$$

Substituting the first-order condition reduces the numerator of (A22) to $-(1 - 2v^*)(\alpha^2 y/\theta\bar{c})$, which is positive given that $v^* > \frac{1}{2}$. Since the denominator is also positive, $dv^*/d\theta > 0$.

(ii) Similarly, totally differentiating (24) with respect to α shows that $dv^*/d\alpha$ has the same sign as

$$\frac{2\alpha y}{\bar{c}}[(1 - \theta)(1 - 2v^*) - \theta v^{*2}]. \tag{A23}$$

Given that $v^* > \frac{1}{2}$, this expression is negative. $\qquad\square$

REFERENCES

Asquith, Paul; Gertner, Robert; and Scharfstein, David S. "Anatomy of Financial Distress: An Examination of Junk-Bond Issuers." *Q.J.E.* 109 (August 1994): 625–58.

Berkovitch, Elazar, and Kim, E. Han. "Financial Contracting and Leverage Induced Over- and Under-investment Incentives." *J. Finance* 45 (July 1900): 765–94.

Bolton, Patrick, and Scharfstein, David S. "A Theory of Predation Based on Agency Problems in Financial Contracting." *A.E.R.* 80 (March 1990): 93–106.

Bulow, Jeremy I., and Shoven, John B. "The Bankruptcy Decision." *Bell J. Econ.* 9 (Autumn 1978): 437–56.

Dewatripont, Mathias, and Maskin, Eric. "Credit and Efficiency in Centralized and Decentralized Economies." *Rev. Econ. Studies* (1995), in press.

Diamond, Douglas W. "Monitoring and Reputation: The Choice between Bank Loans and Directly Placed Debt." *J.P.E.* 99 (August 1991): 689–721.

——. "Bank Loan Maturity and Priority When Borrowers Can Refinance." In *Financial Intermediation in the Construction of Europe*, edited by Colin Mayer and Xavier Vives. Cambridge: Cambridge Univ. Press, 1992.

——. "Seniority and Maturity Structure of Debt Contracts." *J. Financial Econ.* 33 (June 1993): 341–68.

Gertner, Robert. "Inefficiency in Three-Person Bargaining." Manuscript. Chicago: Univ. Chicago, Grad. School Bus., 1990.

Gertner, Robert, and Scharfstein, David S. "A Theory of Workouts and the Effect of Reorganization Law." *J. Finance* 46 (September 1991): 1189–1222.

Gromb, Denis. "Is One Share–One Vote Optimal?" Manuscript. London: London School Econ., 1993.

Grossman, Sanford J., and Hart, Oliver D. "The Costs and Benefits of Ownership: A Theory of Vertical and Lateral Integration." *J.P.E.* 94 (August 1986): 691–719.

——. "One Share–One Vote and the Market for Corporate Control." *J. Financial Econ.* 20 (January/March 1988): 175–202.

Harris, Milton, and Raviv, Artur. "Corporate Governance: Voting Rights and Majority Rules." *J. Financial Econ.* 20 (January/March 1988): 203–35.

Hart, Oliver D., and Moore, John. "Default and Renegotiation: A Dynamic Model of Debt." Manuscript. Cambridge: Massachusetts Inst. Tech., Dept. Econ., 1989.

——. "A Theory of Corporate Financial Structure Based on the Seniority of Claims." Manuscript. Cambridge: Massachusetts Inst. Tech., Dept. Econ., 1990.

Hoshi, Takeo; Kashyap, Anil; and Scharfstein, David S. "The Choice between Public and Private Debt: An Examination of Post-deregulation Corporate Financing in Japan." Manuscript. Cambridge: Massachusetts Inst. Tech., Finance Dept., 1992.

Rajan, Raghuram G. "Insiders and Outsiders: The Choice between Informed and Arm's-Length Debt." *J. Finance* 47 (September 1992): 1367–1400.

Shleifer, Andrei, and Vishny, Robert W. "Liquidation Values and Debt Capacity: A Market Equilibrium Approach." *J. Finance* 47 (September 1992): 1343–66.

Smith, Clifford W., Jr., and Warner, Jerold B. "On Financial Contracting: An Analysis of Bond Covenants." *J. Financial Econ.* 7 (June 1979): 117–61.

White, Michelle J. "Public Policy toward Bankruptcy: Me-First and Other Priority Rules." *Bell J. Econ.* 11 (Autumn 1980): 550–64.

Zingales, Luigi. "Insiders' Ownership and the Decision to Go Public." Manuscript. Cambridge: Massachusetts Inst. Tech., Dept. Econ., 1991.

9

Information Sharing in Credit Markets

MARCO PAGANO AND TULLIO JAPPELLI

A large body of literature on credit markets has shown that asymmetric information may prevent the efficient allocation of lending, leading to credit rationing (e.g., Jaffee and Russell (1976), Stiglitz and Weiss (1981)) or to a wedge between lending and borrowing rates (e.g., King (1986)). In this literature informational asymmetries are taken to be exogenous: lenders fail to observe some relevant characteristic or action of potential borrowers and have no way of learning about it. In some countries, however, lenders can improve their knowledge about new customers by exchanging information with other lenders through information brokers, generally known as 'credit bureaus.' The latter collect, file, and distribute the information voluntarily supplied by their members, and operate on the principle of reciprocity: lenders who do not provide data are denied access to the bureau's files. In other countries, instead, these institutions do not exist. The literature offers no guide to identify the factors that lead to endogenous communication between lenders. This paper is an attempt to fill the gap.

Information sharing is important for a number of reasons: it may increase the degree of competitiveness within credit markets (Vives (1990)), improve efficiency in the allocation of credit, increase volume of lending, and may also have policy implications (e.g., for the issue of debt neutrality, see Yotsuzuka (1987)). Even if we focus on credit markets, the implications of our analysis extend to a variety of situations where an informational asymmetry exists: employers may have an incentive to share records about their former employees, landlords may want to exchange information about tenants, insurance companies about their former customers.

We gratefully acknowledge the helpful comments of an anonymous referee, Richard Arnott, Patrick Bolton, Michael Brennan, Ian Cooper, Julian Franks, Michalis Haliassos, Fumio Hayashi, Julio Rotemberg, Antti Suvanto, and particularly Jorge Padilla and Xavier Vives. We also thank participants in seminars at Barcelona, Bilbao, Boston College, Helsinki, IGIER, LBS, University of Pennsylvania, MIT, and at the 1991 Symposium of the ESF Network of Financial Markets. Bruce Bargon, William Detlefsan, and Stuart Pratt have helped in understanding the operation of credit bureaus. We acknowledge financial support from CEPR under its SPES Programme (no. E89300105/RES) and from the Italian Ministry for Universities and Scientific and Technological Research.

We present a model of the credit market with adverse selection to analyze when information sharing arises endogenously.[1] The model focuses on lending to households, but its insights apply also to lenders' decisions to share information about the creditworthiness of firms. We find that information is more likely to be shared when the mobility of households is high, borrowers are heterogeneous, the underlying credit market is large, and the cost of exchanging information is low. Once some banks agree to share information, there are increasing returns to the scale of information sharing: the credit bureau is a natural monopoly.

We further find that when safe borrowers are priced out of the market because of adverse selection, information sharing leads to an increase in the volume of lending. This creates the potential for two-way causation: an increase in the size of the credit market may generate information sharing, which may in turn lead to more lending activity. Finally we note that membership in a credit bureau entails both benefits and costs: more accurate information about potential borrowers set against the loss of one's informational advantage relative to competitors. Thus, another of the model's predictions is that the incentive to share information is greater when competition is limited by cost or regulatory factors (such as limits to branching).

These predictions are tested on international and historical evidence in the context of the consumer credit market. International comparison shows that the geographical mobility of the population correlates with the amount and quality of information provided by credit bureaus. The amount of information intermediated by credit bureaus is greatest in the United States, Britain, and Japan, which feature relatively high geographical mobility. At the opposite extreme, information sharing is minimal in Belgium, Italy, and Spain, where internal mobility is low. The evidence also reveals a positive correlation between information sharing and the size of the consumer credit market; but this correlation disappears when one controls for geographical mobility. Further, regulatory safeguards for consumer privacy can reduce the amount of information that credit bureaus intermediate, as in France until 1990.

The historical experience of the United States over the last century brings out a similar pattern. Increases in mobility and growth in the market for consumer credit are associated with the rise and spread of credit bureaus. More recently, the activity of credit bureaus has been greatly enhanced by the cost reductions due to the introduction of computerized filing systems. The paper is organized as follows. In Section I we develop the model. Section II presents the international and historical evidence. In Section III we summarize the main results of the paper.

---

[1] It is uncommon to find models that analyze these issues in relation to financial intermediation (exceptions are Jaynes (1978) and Hellwig (1986)). Many studies have analyzed the oligopolists' incentives to share information about their demand or cost functions. Vives (1990) notes that the results of these studies are highly sensitive to their particular assumptions about 'the strategic variables (prices instead of quantities), or the source of uncertainty (demand instead of cost), or the type of uncertainty (common value versus private value)' (p. 413). These results cannot be applied to the analysis of information sharing among lenders, where uncertainty concerns the quality of borrowers rather than the level of demand or costs.

I. THE MODEL

Consider a country with M towns. Each town consists of a continuum of households uniformly distributed on the interval $[0, 1]$ and served by a single bank. Households can borrow to finance their consumption by taking out a loan of size one.[2] They differ in two respects. First, with probability p a household is a 'safe' potential borrower repaying with probability q_s, and with probability $1 - p$ it is 'risky' and repays with probability q_r, where $q_s > q_r$.[3] Second, tastes differ, in that each household i sets a potentially different subjective value v_i on the loan. The loan's value v_i can be thought of as a reflection of household i's discount rate: more impatient people are more eager to borrow. We assume that v_i is uniformly distributed across households, with support $[0, V]$. Letting the index $i \in [0, 1]$ rank households by decreasing values of v_i, we have

$$v_i = V(1 - i), \tag{1}$$

so that i is the fraction of households who value the loan more than v_i (in fact for $v_i = V$, $i = 0$).

Each lender faces some turnover in his customer base. In every period a proportion m of the population moves to other towns, and is replaced by an equal fraction of immigrants (m) from other towns. The bank has acquired information on the households that have previously lived in town (the 'residents'), so it can distinguish their type. Immigrants, by contrast, are a 'black box': the bank knows only that with probability p they are safe and with probability $1 - p$ they are risky.[4] For all classes of households, the reservation values v_i are private information.

The interest factor charged is R_s for safe borrowers, R_r for risky borrowers, and R_m for immigrants. The cost of capital to the bank is R. We assume throughout that $R < V$: together with imperfect competition, this allows banks to earn positive expected profits.

---

[2] If instead individuals could borrow from different lenders, each bank would consider the existing debt exposure of a client as valuable private information about the client's repayment probability. This creates a strategic interaction among lenders, that will in general affect their incentives to exchange information, as in the Jaynes (1978) and Hellwig (1986) models of monopolistically competitive insurance markets. Since we rule out borrowing from different lenders, this interaction is absent from our model. However, this does not prevent other forms of strategic interaction affecting the incentives to share information (see Section I.C below).

[3] This assumption is standard in the literature on asymmetric information. The repayment probabilities may differ because the future incomes of borrowers have different variances (due to endowments or technology). This assumption implies that ex post lenders observe the realization of borrowers' incomes, so that the latter cannot lie about their type.

[4] Although this is a static model, it can be viewed as the steady state of an overlapping generations model where people live for two periods. At the start of each period, they borrow and at the end of the same period they either repay or default. Everyone stays in his home town when young, and moves with probability m to a different town when old. The local bank learns young agents' types, so that it knows the creditworthiness of residents when old (but not of immigrants). The model in this paper describes then lending to people in the old generation.

A. Banks as Local Monopolies

We posit initially that borrowing from another town's bank is prohibitively expensive. This may be because serving the local market is more costly for 'foreign' banks or because of regulatory barriers to intercity branching. Thus, each bank is a local monopolist. In Section I.C below, we relax this assumption and introduce competition.

The monopolistic bank can discriminate among three groups: safe residents, risky residents, and newcomers. Among resident households, the marginal safe borrower i_s and the marginal risky borrower i_r are defined respectively by

$$i_s = 1 - q_s R_s / V, \quad i_r = 1 - q_r R_r / V. \tag{2}$$

For these two households, in fact, the marginal value of the loan equals its interest cost. The expected volume of loans demanded by residents is pi_s for safe borrowers and $(1 - p)i_r$ for risky ones. Immigrants, regardless of type, are charged a common interest factor R_m. Among immigrants, the two marginal borrowers are defined by

$$i_{ms} = 1 - q_s R_m / V, \quad i_{mr} = 1 - q_r R_m / V, \tag{3}$$

where i_{ms} and i_{mr} denote the marginal safe immigrant and the marginal risky immigrant, respectively. The expected volume of loans demanded by immigrants is pi_{ms} and $(1 - p)i_{mr}$, for the safe and risky types respectively. The bank's expected profits are

$$
\begin{aligned}
E(\pi) = {} & (1 - m)[p(q_s R_s - R)i_s + (1 - p)(q_r R_r - R)i_r] \\
& + m[p(q_s R_m - R)i_{ms} + (1 - p)(q_r R_m - R)i_{mr}].
\end{aligned}
\tag{4}
$$

Maximizing this expression with respect to R_s and R_r, one finds the interest rates charged to risky and safe borrowers

$$R_s^* = (V + R)/2q_s, \quad R_r^* = (V + R)/2q_r, \tag{5}$$

where clearly $R_r^* > R_s^*$.

To derive the interest charged to immigrants (R_m), one must take into account the fact that a rise in R_m will shrink the pool of credit applicants. If R_m goes above a certain level, only risky types (among immigrants) will borrow, and the bank will accordingly charge R_r to all newcomers. For some parameter values, the bank has an incentive to do so, because this strategy increases its expected profits by driving safe borrowers out of the market.

We must therefore distinguish between two cases: in Case (a) both types of immigrants borrow, while in Case (b) safe types drop out of the pool of borrowers. We first characterize the two equilibria (Propositions 1 and 2) and then establish the regions of parameter values in which each equilibrium applies (Proposition 3).

As we shall see, the main difference between the two cases is that information sharing has different implications for lending activity and for welfare.

Case (a). When safe types stay in the market, the profit-maximizing interest factor is obtained by taking the first order conditions with respect to R_m in equation (4):

$$R_{m,a}^* = \frac{pq_s + (1-p)q_r}{pq_s^2 + (1-p)q_r^2} \frac{V+R}{2},$$

(6)

where $R_s^* < R_{m,a}^* < R_r^*$. Substituting equations (5) and (6) in equation (4), one obtains the maximum value of expected profits:

$$E(\pi_a^*) = \frac{1}{V}\left[\left(\frac{V-R}{2}\right)^2 - m(1-\lambda)\left(\frac{V+R}{2}\right)^2\right], \quad \text{where}$$

$$\lambda = \frac{[pq_s + (1-p)q_r]^2}{pq_s^2 + (1-p)q_r^2}.$$

(7)

As is shown in the Appendix, $1 - \lambda$ is an index of heterogeneity of the population, since it increases with the distance between the two repayment probabilities $(q_s - q_r)$.

Proposition 1. *When safe types stay in the market, higher mobility (m) and heterogeneity of the population (i.e., a mean-preserving spread in q_s and q_r) lower equilibrium expected profits. If the additional condition $pq_s > (1-p)q_r$ holds, an increase in the proportion of safe borrowers (p) raises expected profits.*

This proposition is proved in the Appendix. Mobility and heterogeneity lower profits because they increase the size and the riskiness of the pool of immigrants. A reduction in the proportion of safe borrowers also lowers profits if it worsens the average quality of applicants: the relevant condition is $pq_s > (1-p)q_r$, i.e., the probability of lending to a safe borrower and being repaid is greater than the probability of lending to a risky borrower and being repaid.

Case (b). If, in equilibrium, safe types drop out of the pool of borrowers, the rate of interest charged to immigrants equals that charged to risky residents:

$$R_{m,b}^* = R_r^* = (V+R)/2q_r.$$

(8)

The maximum value of profits is found by substituting (5) and (8) into (4), positing $i_{ms} = 0$:

$$E(\pi_b^*) = \frac{1-mp}{V}\left(\frac{V-R}{2}\right)^2.$$

(9)

Proposition 2. *If safe types drop out of the pool of borrowers, higher mobility (m) and a higher proportion of safe borrowers (p) lower the equilibrium value of expected profits.*

This result follows from equation (9). Mobility lowers profits as in Case (a). Heterogeneity no longer affects profits because in Case (b) the only immigrants who apply for credit are the bad risks. The proportion of safe borrowers p has the opposite effect from Case (a): since the bank only lends to bad risks among immigrants, and high values of p reduce the proportion of bad risks, a high value of p reduces the number of its customers and expected profits.[5]

Proposition 3. $E(\pi_a^*) < E(\pi_b^*)$ i.f.f. $(1 - \lambda/p) > [(V - r)/(V + R)]^2$.

This proposition is obtained by comparing (7) and (9). It determines the parameter regions where Cases (a) and (b) apply. When the condition holds, we have Case (b): safe borrowers drop out. As shown in the Appendix, this can happen either because the interest factor $R_{m,a}^*$ is too high to attract any safe borrower ($q_s R_{m,a}^* > V$), or because the bank *chooses* to charge the higher interest factor R_r^* even though at $R_{m,a}^*$ safe borrowers are willing to borrow ($q_s R_{m,a}^* < V$).

It can be shown that in Case (b) the volume of lending is lower than in Case (a).[6] This is because in Case (b) the adverse selection problem is more severe. Proposition 3 indicates under which conditions this occurs. Other things equal, safe borrowers are more likely to be priced out of the market if: (1) the pool of immigrants is very heterogeneous ($1 - \lambda$ is high); (2) the fraction of safe borrowers (p) is low; (3) the reservation value is low relative to the cost of capital ($V - R$ is small), so that safe borrowers prefer not to borrow rather than to pay high interest to the bank.

B. Information Sharing

The next step is to allow for the possibility of information sharing. Suppose that all or some of the banks in the country agree to set up a credit bureau. The bureau merges the information provided by all banks into a single database, which the members of the system can access for information about the quality of their credit applicants. Typically, setting up such a system entails a fixed cost (purchase of equipment, filing systems, etc.), which we denote by K.

Assume for simplicity that each member of the bureau contributes equally towards this cost, that all towns are identical, and that all banks agree to participate. Then the cost of the bureau for each participant is K/M. In return all

---

[5] In both Cases (a) and (b), profits are increasing in V, and decreasing in R. An increase in V implies that the average reservation value of loans increases, so that the demand for loans shifts outward. On the other hand, if the cost of capital R rises, the markup falls.

[6] To show this, compare the expressions for i_m^a and i_m^b in the Appendix (Proof of Proposition 4).

lenders operate with full information. Expected profits are then given by

$$E(\pi^*_f) = \frac{1}{V}\left(\frac{V-R}{2}\right)^2 - \frac{K}{M}, \tag{10}$$

where the subscript f stands for 'full information.' The credit bureau will operate if it leads to an increase in expected profits, after netting out the costs of setting up the bureau. The proposition below shows the conditions under which information is shared in Case (a) and Case (b).

Proposition 4. (*i*) *Information sharing increases profits if, respectively*

$$\text{in Case (a):} \quad E(\pi^*_f) - E(\pi^*_a) = \frac{m(1-\lambda)}{V}\left(\frac{V+R}{2}\right)^2 - \frac{K}{M} > 0, \tag{11a}$$

$$\text{in Case (b):} \quad E(\pi^*_f) - E(\pi^*_b) = \frac{mp}{V}\left(\frac{V-R}{2}\right)^2 - \frac{K}{M} > 0. \tag{11b}$$

(*ii*) *Information sharing increases lending volume in Case (a) and reduces it in Case (b).*

The proposition is proved in the Appendix. The first term in (11a) and (11b) represents the profits that banks obtain from the reduction in the risk of lending: when information is shared, default rates fall in both cases.[7] Credit bureaus are more advantageous the greater the demand for loans (captured by V), the higher the geographical mobility (m), the lower the cost of operating the system (K) and the greater the number of participants (M). In Case (a), where both types of immigrants borrow, the heterogeneity of borrowers ($1-\lambda$) raises the net benefit from the creation of a credit bureau: the gain from eliminating the asymmetry of information between borrowers and banks increases with the uncertainty about the quality of applicants.[8]

The main difference between the two cases is the effect of information sharing on the volume of lending, which expands in Case (b) and contracts in Case (a). In Case (b), information sharing makes credit accessible to immigrants that would otherwise have been priced out of the market—with the rates charged to other borrowers remaining unchanged. As we know from Proposition 3, Case (b) arises when the pool of applicants is heterogeneous and of poor quality, and when the desire to borrow is low relative to the cost of credit, i.e., when, in the absence of information sharing, the credit market is thin. In this case, communication

---

[7] Denoting by d_a, d_b, and d_f the default rates of migrants in Case (a), in Case (b), and under full information respectively, it can be shown that

$$d_a - d_f = [(1-\lambda)/(2-\lambda)][pq_s + (1-p)q_r] > 0, \quad \text{and} \quad d_b - d_f = p(q_s - q_r) > 0.$$

[8] The parameter p may have different effects in the two cases. In Case (a), a higher p reduces the gain from sharing if and only if it increases heterogeneity (the relevant condition is $pq_s > (1-p)q_r$, which implies $\partial\lambda/\partial p > 0$). In Case (b), instead, an increase in p will always increase the gain from information sharing, since it implies that the proportion of safe borrowers that can be drawn into the market when the bureau is established is larger.

between lenders is a Pareto improvement: profits increase, safe borrowers benefit, and risky borrowers are indifferent.

In Case (a), on the contrary, information sharing reduces the volume of loans, because it has two effects: it enables the monopolist to practice price discrimination, and it eliminates uncertainty about borrowers' types. With no uncertainty and linear demand, price discrimination does not affect the optimal quantity for a monopolist (Tirole (1988)): the increase in the quantity purchased by one group of customers is matched by the reduction in the demand by other customers. But in our uncertain environment, the introduction of price discrimination coincides with the elimination of uncertainty about types, so that the increase in lending to safe borrowers does not fully compensate for the reduction in lending to the risky, and total lending falls.[9]

So far we have assumed that all M banks cooperate in the institution of the credit bureau. Now consider the case when only M' banks ($M' < M$) agree to pool their information, possibly because they are better managed than the remaining $M - M'$. For ease of handling we take the symmetric case, where all towns are identical and the migrants from each town distribute themselves equally among all the other towns, so that each town receives m/M percent of them.

The gain from this partial information sharing is a fraction M'/M of what it would be if all lenders joined. If costs are equally shared by the M' banks, the cost per participant is K/M'. Thus, in Case (a), the net benefit per participant increases with the number of participants M':

$$\frac{M'}{M}\frac{m(1-\lambda)}{V}\left(\frac{V+R}{2}\right)^2 - \frac{K}{M'}.\tag{12}$$

Setting (12) equal to zero yields the minimum number of banks for the system to be profitable:

$$M^* = \frac{2}{V+R}\sqrt{\frac{KMV}{m(1-\lambda)}}.\tag{13}$$

A similar expression for M^* can be obtained for Case (b).

Equation (13) highlights the possibility that only a subset—conceivably, a small one—of the banks may agree to institute a credit bureau. However, as equation (12) shows, once M^* banks have agreed to participate, there is a tendency for the system to encompass the whole of the market: as $M' > M^*$, nonmembers derive a net benefit from joining and incumbents have an incentive to let outsiders join. Note that this result does not depend on the assumption of fixed costs. The net benefit per member increases with M' even if costs are proportional to the number of members (e.g., $K = kM'$, where k is a constant): the extension of the system's coverage itself enhances its effectiveness. In this sense, the credit bureau is a natural monopoly.

---

[9] In Case (a) the change in welfare, defined as the sum of consumer surplus and profits, is $(1-\lambda)\{R^2 - [(V-R)/2]^2\}/2V$, and is positive if and only if $V < 3R$. In contrast to Case (b), welfare does not always increase, because profits rise but consumer surplus falls.

C. Competition and the Gains from Information Sharing

So far it has been assumed that regulation or prohibitively high costs prevent banks from extending loans to citizens of other towns. This assumption precludes all competition between banks. A more realistic assumption is that credit markets are contestable. When this feature is included in the model, it becomes clear that in deciding whether to join a credit bureau lenders must take an additional effect into account, besides those already examined.

When a bank supplies information about its own customers to a competitor, in effect it is helping the latter to compete more aggressively. Monopoly profits will thus be reduced. This effect reduces the expected gain from information sharing and may deter banks from sharing information. To illustrate the interaction between market contestability and information sharing, we introduce competition via assumptions that require minimal changes in the model's structure.

1. Banks can extend credit to households living in neighboring towns at an additional cost c that reflects their lower efficiency in competing outside their market area or the presence of regulatory barriers.[10] Effectively, the cost of capital for potential entrants is $R + c$. The cost of extending credit to residents of 'distant' towns stays instead prohibitive, as in the monopoly case.

2. Immigrants move to distant towns, so that their former lender is unable to retain them as customers (no bank has national coverage). It follows that immigrants are still a 'black box' for the local bank as well as for any potential entrant.

3. Outside competitors can sort out migrants from residents. Their only informational disadvantage relative to the local bank is that they are unable to sort out safe from risky borrowers *among residents*.

4. The order of moves by the players is the following. First, the local bank announces a menu of interest rates, one for each group of borrowers (R_s, R_r and R_m in Case (a): R_s and R_r in Case (b)). These rates maximize expected profits, taking into account the entrant's best response. Second, the entrant announces the interest rate(s) that maximize his profits, conditional on the rates offered by the local bank in the first stage. Third, each borrower chooses a lender. To break ties between the players, borrowers are assumed to always prefer the local bank when they are offered the same interest rate by the two banks.

5. In the absence of information sharing, an entrant can compete only for risky borrowers, who are willing to pay an interest rate high enough to cover the entrant's addition cost c. Thus the only contestable segment of the market is that formed by borrowers who pay the highest rate: risky residents in Case (a), and both risky residents and risky immigrants in Case (b).[11] In all other market segments the local lender remains a monopolist. For brevity we concentrate on

[10] Alternatively, the parameter c may reflect the cost of switching from the local lender to an outside competitor. Ausubel (1991) reports evidence for the United States pointing to the existence of substantial switching costs in the credit card industry (pp. 68, 69).

[11] Recall that in Case (b) immigrants are charged the same rate as risky residents, while safe types drop out of the pool of immigrant borrowers.

this situation only. Even when outside banks can compete in all market segments, the basic insight of this section is still valid: information sharing calls for more aggressive competition.

C.1. *Case (a)*

As just explained, the entrant's cost disadvantage c is assumed to be low enough that the market for risky borrowers is contestable, but high enough that other segments of the local market are not. Thus c lies within an interval $(\underline{c}, \bar{c})$. The upper bound $\bar{c}$ is found by equating to zero the entrant's profits from lending to risky borrowers at the monopolistic rate R_r^*: if $c < \bar{c}$, these profits are positive, and the entrant has an incentive to undercut the incumbent in this market segment (if $c > \bar{c}$, one reverts to the local monopoly case of I.A). The lower bound $\underline{c}$ is computed by setting to zero the profits that the entrant can obtain by lending to immigrants at the same rate as the monopolistic incumbent ($R_{m,a}^*$). If $c > \underline{c}$, the entrant has no incentive to compete away these customers from the incumbent. The relevant condition is

$$\frac{\left[\dfrac{V-R}{2}\right]^2 - (1-\lambda)\left[\dfrac{V+R}{2}\right]^2}{V - \lambda\left[\dfrac{V+R}{2}\right]} \equiv \underline{c} < c < \bar{c} \equiv \frac{V-R}{2}. \tag{14}$$

The expression for $\underline{c}$ can be shown to be the profit per customer that the local bank obtains by lending to immigrants at the monopolistic rate $R_{m,a}^*$: the left-hand side inequality says that this potential profit is wiped out by the entrant's cost disadvantage per customer, c. Similarly, the expression for $\bar{c}$ is the profit per customer that the incumbent earns by lending to risky residents at the monopolistic rate R_r^*: the right-hand side inequality states that this potential profit exceeds the entrant's cost disadvantage per customer, c. The interval defined by (14) is nonempty.

The game has a unique Nash equilibrium, where the local bank sets $R_s = R_s^*$; $R_m = R_{m,a}^*$; $R_r = (R+c)/q_r$, and entry does not occur (see Pagano and Jappelli (1991), pp. 16 and 17, for a proof).

The value of equilibrium expected profits when information is not shared is then

$$E(\pi_a^*) = \frac{1}{V}\left\{ [(1-m)(1-p)c(V-R-c)] + \left[(1-m)p\left(\frac{V-R}{2}\right)^2\right] \right.$$
$$\left. + m\left[\left(\frac{V-R}{2}\right)^2 - (1-\lambda)\left(\frac{V+R}{2}\right)^2\right] \right\}. \tag{15}$$

The first term in square brackets is the profit on risky loans to residents, and it is lower than under monopoly. The other two terms in square brackets are the profits on safe loans to residents and to (all) immigrants respectively, and are unchanged from the case of monopoly.

If the local bank agrees to share information with all other lenders it learns how to distinguish between risky and safe borrowers among immigrants, but it loses its informational advantage concerning residents, for now outside competitors can sort out safe and risky borrowers just as well as the local bank. So all market segments become contestable. To prevent entry, the local bank will charge the limit prices $(R + c)/q_s$ and $(R + c)/q_r$ on safe and risky borrowers respectively. Again, this is the unique Nash equilibrium for the game. At this equilibrium the local bank can make positive expected profits only because it retains the cost advantage c:

$$E(\pi^*_f) = c(V - R - c)/V - K/M. \tag{16}$$

The change in expected profits associated with information sharing is then

$$E(\pi^*_f) - E(\pi^*_a)$$
$$= \frac{1}{V} \left\{ m(1 - \lambda) \left(\frac{V + R}{2} \right)^2 - [m + p(1 - m)] \left(\frac{V - R}{2} - c \right)^2 \right\} - \frac{K}{M}. \tag{17}$$

The first term in braces is the gain from information sharing that accrues to the bank under monopoly (equation 11a). The second term—absent when the bank acted as a local monopoly—is the loss due to the increased competition associated with information sharing. While this increase in competition reduces profits, it increases the volume of loans if the parameter c is low enough. Under monopoly this effect is absent in Case (a): lending increases only in Case (b).[12]

C.2. *Case (b)*

Here the marginal group includes all risky borrowers—residents and immigrants alike. For brevity, we analyze only the case in which the interest factor $R^*_{m,a}$ is too high to attract any safe borrower, i.e., $q_s R^*_{m,a} > V$. The condition implied by assumption (5) reduces to

$$0 \equiv \underline{c} < c < \bar{c} \equiv \frac{V - R}{2}. \tag{18}$$

The only change relative to condition (14) is that now the lower bound for c is zero: even if outside competitors are not burdened by a cost disadvantage, they are unable to compete safe borrowers away from the local bank. Their informational disadvantage is sufficient to prevent entry in this market segment.[13]

---

[12] See footnote 16 in Pagano and Jappelli (1991).

[13] To attract safe borrowers, the entrant would have to offer a rate below R^*_s. By (5), $R^*_s < V/q_s$, so that the entrant's offer should be lower than V/q_s. But at this rate he would make losses, as shown in Figure A1: to the left of V/q_s, the relevant profit function (the thick line) is below zero.

The unique Nash equilibrium is now $R_s = R_s^*$, $R_m = R_r = (R + c)/q_r$, with no entry. The resulting expression for expected profits in the absence of information sharing is

$$E(\pi^*_b) = \frac{1}{V}\left\{(1 - p)c(V - R - c) + (1 - m)p\left(\frac{V - R}{2}\right)^2\right\}. \tag{19}$$

Subtracting expression (19) from (16), we find that the net gain from information sharing is

$$E(\pi^*_f) - E(\pi^*_b) = \frac{1}{V}\left\{mp\left(\frac{V - R}{2}\right)^2 - p\left(\frac{V - R}{2} - c\right)^2\right\} - \frac{K}{M}. \tag{20}$$

As in Case (a), the expression can be broken down into two parts: the expected gain under monopoly (the first term in braces, identical to (11b)) and the loss that the bank incurs by revealing its privileged information to its competitors (the second term).

From (17) and (20), it appears that in both cases the loss that the bank incurs by disclosing its information decreases with its cost advantage c. When the local bank agrees to share information, a lower c reduces the profits it extracts from all market segments. When it refuses to share information, a lower c reduces only the profits extracted from risky borrowers. So the bank's incentive to share information falls with c.

Considering that the cost differential c is an index of barriers to entry, contestability reduces the gain from information sharing, and may even turn it into a loss.[14] In this case, information sharing will not occur because it triggers unwanted competitive forces. But if lenders choose to share information, the resulting increase in competition is likely to increase lending activity. Recall that under local monopoly information sharing leads to an expansion in lending only in Case (b), due to the elimination of the adverse selection problem. When credit markets are contestable, it may lead to an increase in lending also in Case (a).

II. THE EVIDENCE

The foregoing theoretical framework has a number of empirical implications. First, the extent to which lenders share information on customers' creditworthiness should correlate positively with mobility, whereas its predicted correlation with the size of the consumer credit market is ambiguous. Second,

---

[14] For instance, information sharing will definitely lower profits if $c = 0$: in this case, under full information, competition reduces expected profits to zero on all loans, and in addition each bank would have to pay the fixed cost K/M to share information. In fact, in Case (b), with $c = 0$ information sharing is unprofitable even if it is costless $(K = 0)$: expression (20) is negative with $c = K = 0$. This is to be contrasted with the local monopoly case, where, information sharing is always profitable if it is costless: expression (11b) is positive if $K = 0$.

once some lenders have agreed to pool their information in a credit bureau, there will be a tendency for others to join, leading to comprehensive coverage of the population of would-be borrowers: the credit bureaus are natural monopolies. Third, information sharing may be deterred by fear of competition. Finally, any technical innovation that reduces the costs of filing, organizing, and distributing information should foster information exchange.

In order to compare these theoretical predictions with the evidence, we have collected data on the extent of information sharing in the consumer credit market, the degree of geographical mobility, and the size of the consumer credit market in 14 countries belonging to the Organization for Economic Cooperation and Development (OECD).[15] The evidence on credit bureaus is gathered from direct interviews and questionnaires sent to credit bureaus and their associations. In the second part of this section, the validity of the model's predictions is assessed on the basis of the long historical record of the United States, where credit bureaus appeared as early as the end of the 19th century.

A. International Comparative Evidence

In all countries where lenders (banks, finance companies, or retailers) share information, the operation of credit bureaus has common features, the main ones being the principle of reciprocity and the related sanctions. A lender is entitled to access only the type of information that he is willing to contribute to the bureau. The main distinction here is between 'black' (or negative) information, concerning only defaults, and 'white' (or positive) information, i.e., data about the credit history and the current debt exposure of all customers. In all cases, failure to comply with the rules (for instance, by providing late or inaccurate information) is sanctioned by the denial of further access.

Even if the operation of credit bureaus is basically standard around the world, there are enormous differences in the amount and type of information shared. Table I gives the key indicators of the credit-reporting activity in the consumer credit market of 14 OECD countries. The data exclude all credit reports associated with the purchase of houses. The number of consumer credit reports in millions (column 1) is a gauge of the quantity of information exchanged by lenders. To compare information sharing across countries, we also report the number of reports per capita (column 2) and per 10,000 dollars of consumption expenditure (column 3). Column 4 provides an indicator of the quality of the information pooled by lenders. Information sharing systems also differ in the length of time they have existed (column 5): whereas in the United States and Sweden credit bureaus have operated for almost a century, they were not introduced until 1987 in Belgium, and until 1990 in France, Italy, and Spain.

---

[15] In principle, the appropriate variable is the mobility of customers between lenders, rather than between geographic locations. In the model the two concepts coincide, whereas in reality they may be only imperfectly correlated. Thus geographic mobility should be taken only as a proxy for the customer turnover faced by lenders in different countries.

On the basis of Table I, the countries surveyed divide into two groups. In the first group of countries, information sharing is widespread. In the United States, Japan, and Britain, the number of credit reports per person is highest, lenders exchange black as well as white information, and credit bureaus have been active for at least thirty years. The responses to the questionnaires also indicate that in these countries credit bureaus possess information on the entire population of credit seekers. Credit bureaus operate also in Finland, the Netherlands, Australia, Germany, and Sweden, but on a smaller scale. In Australia and Finland reports are available on any credit seeker, but the bureaus provide black information only.

In a second group of countries, information sharing is not practiced at all or is in its infancy. In Belgium, a 1987 law obliged lenders to provide information on defaults to a public agency managed by the central bank and to request a report on every application for credit. In France a similar scheme has just been set up, implementing a law passed in October 1989. These compulsory schemes contrast with the spontaneous nature of information sharing in all other countries. In Italy and Spain, credit bureaus did not exist until 1990, and are just starting to operate on a very limited scale. In Greece, no such experiment is under way.

Columns 6 and 7 display estimates of *residential* and *long-range mobility*, respectively. The first is a measure of the frequency with which the typical household changes residence in a year, irrespective of the distance travelled. The second is the frequency of moves between communities with average population of 1 million, such as cities or regions. Column 8 displays total *consumer credit* as a percentage of private consumption in 1985 to 1987.

By international standards the group of countries where credit bureaus are most active also exhibits high mobility and deep consumer credit markets. The countries where there is very little information sharing or none at all are characterized by scanty mobility and thin markets. In fact, the correlation between the number of credit reports (scaled by consumer spending) and long-range mobility is 0.77.[16] Its correlation with the size of the consumer credit market is positive but rather small—only 0.11. This is confirmed by the following regression:

$$\text{Number of credit reports} = \underset{(-0.69)}{-0.14} + \underset{(3.19)}{0.06} \text{ residential mobility}$$

$$\underset{(-1.23)}{-0.01} \text{ consumer credit, } \bar{R}^2 = 0.41,$$

where credit reports and consumer credit are both scaled by consumption, and *t*-statistics are reported in parentheses (the data are those of Table I, excluding Greece). This regression is merely intended to summarize the partial correlations

---

[16] One possible objection is that the correlation between mobility and credit reports is spurious, because in some countries when people move and purchase a house, a credit report is often requested by their lender. But this objection does not apply to our data, which refer to the consumer credit market only, and excludes credit reports associated with housing loans.

Table I. Information sharing, mobility, and consumer credit in 14 OECD countries

Country	Number of Credit Reports[a]			Type of Information[b] (4)	Period Started[c] (5)	Mobility Rate[d]		Consumer Credit (Percent of Private Consumption) (8)
	Level (Millions) (1)	Per Capita (2)	Per $10,000 of Consumption (3)			Residential (6)	Long Range (7)	
United States	400	1.62	1.08	black + white	1890s	18.40	5.52	22.8
United Kingdom	60	1.05	1.08	black + white	1960s	11.93	2.91	14.0
Japan	110	0.89	0.67	black + white	1960s	12.78	3.47	16.5
Finland	3.5	0.70	0.52	black	n.a.	11.92	1.31	30.5
Netherlands	7.5	0.50	0.52	black + white	1960s	10.20	1.75	5.1
Australia	5.8	0.34	0.33	black	1930s	15.62	2.65	22.1
West Germany	18	0.29	0.26	black + white	1920s	10.00	n.a.	15.4
Sweden	2.2	0.26	0.20	black + white	1890s	13.30	1.91	36.8
Belgium	1.3	0.13	0.12	black	1987	4.53	0.70	9.7
Norway	0.5	0.12	0.10	black	n.a.	10.67	1.05	42.7
France	0	0	0	black	1990	10.31	2.48	6.0
Italy	0	0	0	—	1990	3.69	0.90	2.7
Spain	0	0	0	—	1990	1.47	0.33	7.6
Greece	0	0	0	—	—	n.a.	n.a.	0.3

n.a., not available

Note: The number of credit reports refers to 1989 for the United States, the United Kingdom, Germany, France, Italy, and Spain, to 1988 for Japan, and to 1990 for all other countries. The term 'black' indicates that only default information is shared; 'white' indicates that lenders also share data on credit history and debt exposure of borrowers. Residential mobility is the household's probability of changing residence in a year. Long-range mobility measures the probability of moving in a year across communities with average population of 1 million inhabitants. The figures for consumer credit are averages of 1985–87 values (1987 for the United Kingdom, 1989 for Australia, 1985–86 for Sweden); see Pagano and Jappelli (1991, Appendix B) for sources and definitions. Private consumption is drawn from the OECD National Accounts.

[a] The United Kingdom figure is a lower bound, based on data supplied by the two largest credit reference agencies.

[b] In Japan, the affiliates of the three major credit bureaus exchange white information; in turn, these three bureaus exchange only black information through a network. In the United Kingdom, finance companies and local banks share black and white information, but exchange only black information with national banks. In Germany 12,000 lenders exchange white information and 2,000 lenders share only black information. In Finland privacy protection laws prevent the collection of white information.

[c] In Belgium and France, since 1987 and 1990 respectively, all the defaulted consumer loans must be reported to a consumer credit register managed by the Central Bank. In Italy and Spain private credit bureaus started operating in 1990. In both countries a public credit reporting system also exists: banks must report to a credit register managed by the Central Bank all defaults above 80 million lire and above 4 million pesetas respectively, but very few personal loans exceed these limits.

[d] Mobility rates computed from census data are not comparable between countries because they count people who move between administrative areas of different sizes. To overcome this problem, following Courgeau (1973), we estimate distance decay functions for mobility rates across areas of different size by fitting the relationship $p_r = a \log(P_0/P_1)$, where p_i is the probability of moving across areas of average population P_i, and P_0 is the total population of the country. In the table we report the fitted values of p_i for $P_i = 4$ and $P_i = 1,000,000$. The data for the United States, the United Kingdom, Japan, Finland, the Netherlands, Sweden, Belgium, and France refer to 1971 and are drawn from Long (1989), Tables 8.1 and 8.5. Residential mobility in Australia is also drawn from Long (1989); other data for Australia are from *Labour Statistics*, Australian Bureau of Statistics, 1986, Tables 1.6 and 1.7, and refer to 1986. The figure for Germany is drawn from J. O'Loughlin and G. Glebe, Intraurban migration in West German cities, *Geographical Review* 74,1984, p. 4 Data for Italy refer to 1984, and are drawn from *Statistiche Demografiche*, 34, Part 2, 1987, Table 1.6, p. 19. Data for Spain refer to 1982, and are from the *Anuario de Estadística*, 1983, Table 3.1, and from S. Bentolila and J Dolado, Mismatch and internal migration in Spain, 1962–1986, Banco de España, Documento de Trabajo no. 9006, 1990.

between information sharing and the other two variables, since according to the model consumer credit is an endogenous variable. The regression explains a large proportion of the international differences in information sharing, and is consistent with the main prediction of the model. The coefficient of mobility is positive and significantly different from zero; the insignificant coefficient of consumer credit does not contradict the model. We obtain a similar pattern of results by replacing residential with long-range mobility (here Germany is also dropped for lack of data on mobility):

$$\text{Number of credit reports} = -0.06 \quad + \quad 0.21 \quad \text{long range mobility}$$
$$(-0.36) \quad (3.58)$$
$$+0.01 \text{ consumer credit}, \quad \bar{R}^2 = 0.50.$$
$$(0.15)$$

The results are qualitatively unaffected if credit reports are scaled by population.

The largest negative residual in the regressions refers to France. In fact, this is a country where mobility is relatively high (in the same range of the Netherlands and the United Kingdom) but there was no information sharing until 1990. The reason is that in France *regulations* protecting consumer privacy thwart private incentives to share information about households. The person investigated must be notified in advance of requests to access a credit file, and no report can be issued without his or her consent. The French provisions are stricter than those of other countries, even though the activity of credit bureaus is regulated almost everywhere so as to prevent excessive infringement of privacy and civil liberties.

In all countries, at most a few large credit bureaus dominate the market: in 1990, three giant bureaus were operating in the United States, three in Japan, and four in the United Kingdom; in Australia, Germany, Sweden, and the Netherlands the market is dominated by a single credit bureau. This high degree of concentration is a relatively new feature of the industry: historically, credit bureaus were born to serve local business communities, and accordingly they tended to be numerous and relatively small (in the 1950s there were 1,700 credit bureaus in the United States and 30 in Australia, and in the 1970s there were at least 30 in Japan). The emergence of a few dominant bureaus with nationwide coverage has stemmed from rapid and extensive mergers and acquisitions of smaller bureaus, especially in the 1970s and 1980s. We interpret this tendency as confirmation that information sharing is indeed, as shown in Section I, a *natural monopoly*.

Another of the model's predictions is that information sharing makes *competition* tougher by depriving lenders of the monopoly power attached to exclusive customer information. Fear of competition may inhibit or limit information sharing.[17] But if lenders are well protected by barriers to entry, they should be

---

[17] This tradeoff was already stressed in a 1940 National Bureau of Economic Research report: '... a complete interchange of information [between lenders] is greatly to be desired. Under such conditions the costs of investigation and the risks of lending would be reduced substantially. The possession of credit information, however, is sometimes viewed by individual lenders and by groups as an important

more willing to share information. Some evidence supports this theoretical prediction. In the United States, branching regulations have traditionally limited competition among banks in different states, an entry barrier that may help explain why credit bureaus arose so early and lenders began sharing both black and white information as far back as the 1920s.[18] In Britain, by contrast, banks are free to compete nationwide, and have refused a 1989 proposal from finance companies to share white information on a reciprocal basis. As a result, finance companies share only black information with banks (though sharing white information as well among themselves). Conceivably, this is because with their nationwide presence British banks feel more exposed to competition than finance companies, whose customer bases are more concentrated geographically. Similarly in Italy, where banks compete nationwide, the initiative to create the first credit bureau in 1990 was taken by local lending institutions, with national banks joining only later.

B. Evidence from the History of the United States

The beginnings of information sharing in the United States are closely connected with the high mobility of households and the development of consumer credit. Before 1870 lending to households was limited, and the role of the family and of small communities in the provision of credit was predominant. An organized consumer credit market appeared following the Civil War and the dramatic socioeconomic changes after 1870. In the words of Nugent (1939),

The Civil War... marked for many communities the beginning of the breakdown in the social cohesiveness that made mutual assistance beneficial... [Immigrants] were transplanted from intimate communities, where they had enjoyed the security of partial self-sufficiency and the protection of family and neighborhood facilities for mutual assistance, to impersonal cities, where... their nearest neighbors were usually anonymous (pp. 65, 66).

Mass urbanization led to informational asymmetries in the relationship between lenders and immigrant loan applicants. As a result, banks changed their lending policies:

Liberal credit policies could readily be maintained in small and stable communities, where the financial worth, earning capacity, family history, and personal qualities of applicants were matters of common knowledge. In metropolitan cities, on the other hand, the difficulty of appraising credit worth on any basis other than the ownership of readily

---

asset, not to be shared with competitors... Consequently, the growth of an adequate interchange of credit information between personal finance companies has been inhibited, though such interchange has been developed to a certain degree' (Young (1940) p. 160).

[18] In principle, limits to interstate branching do not prevent lending to households in other states. Banks can lend out of state provided they do not collect deposits out of their state. Since the cheapest way to acquire information on households' solvency is by monitoring their asset position, in practice this inhibits informed lending to households in other states.

negotiable collateral led to the denial of credit to classes of consumers whose credit needs were supplied by banks in intimate communities (p. 82).

The low quality of public information, coupled with the interest in financing the consumption of immigrants with scanty assets, engendered the need to organize the exchange of information about households. At the end of the century few credit bureaus operated, and those that did collected almost exclusively information on defaults from public records and credit pay habits, specializing in a certain local area (typically, a county) and serving the local community only.[19] But the high geographical mobility of households created the need for organized interbureau reporting. In 1906 six credit bureaus agreed to cooperate in the exchange of information and founded the National Association of Mercantile Agencies (NAMA)—forerunner of the still active Associated Credit Bureau of America, Inc. (ACB), founded in 1937: the aim was to exchange data about consumers moving from one town to another, and to act as a clearing house for the payment of interbureau credit reports (Phelps (1949)).

In the 20th century, there have been three spurts of growth in information sharing: in the 1920s, in the 1950s, and in the 1980s. The 1920s witnessed a credit bureau explosion, the membership of NAMA soaring from 88 in 1916 to 267 in 1924 and 800 in 1927; at the same time the information exchanged was upgraded, with lenders beginning to supply the local bureaus with white as well as black information.

In the 1950s, the number of credit bureaus rose further—ACB membership rose from 1,453 in 1948 to 1,700 in 1955. The number of credit reports reached 60 million in 1960, as coverage of the consumer credit market became virtually total (in 1954 credit bureaus could already report on anyone in the United States, with 70 million consumers on file). The range of the information also widened (including data about the liabilities and employment of household members, law suits, family history, etc.), and interbureau reporting expanded tremendously. The third spurt of growth in information sharing started in the mid 1970s: the number of consumer credit reports grew fourfold, from 100 million in 1970 to 400 million in 1989.

Figure 1 shows that of these three waves (marked by the shaded areas), the first two are associated with an increase in households' mobility and in the volume of consumer credit. As an indicator of household mobility, we plot the percentage of the U.S. population not living in the state of birth in census years (Long, 1989, Table 2.1), which rose from 20.6 percent in 1900 to 23.5 in 1930, and from 25.6 percent in 1950 to 27.3 in 1960. Consumer credit as a percentage of gross national product (GNP) saw buoyant growth in the 1920s and in the 1950s.

---

[19] The first information brokers, associated with the massive European immigration to industrial cities of the Northeast in the late 19th century, were probably the 'customer peddlers.' These were English-speaking members of the immigrant group who established relations with the newly arrived, and acted as intermediaries between the credit stores and the borrowers. 'The intimacy of the relationship between the peddler and his customers . . . generally compelled scrupulous honesty and fair dealing' (Nugent (1939), p. 68).

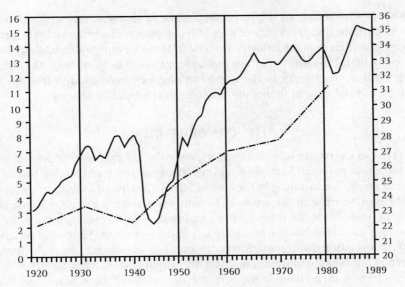

Figure 1. *Information sharing, consumer credit, and household mobility in the United States (1919 to 1989).*

Note: The figure reports consumer credit as a percentage of GNP (*solid line and left-hand scale*) and the percentage of the population not living in the state of birth (an indicator of household mobility) (*broken line and right-hand scale*). The *shaded areas* mark periods of rapid growth in the activity of credit bureaus. For 1919 to 1949, consumer credit data are drawn from the *Survey of Current Business* (1972), Series X, 393–409, and for 1950 to 1989 from the *Economic Report of the President* (1990). For GNP, data up to 1929 are drawn from N. S. Balke and R. J. Gordon, The estimation of prewar gross national product: Methodology and new evidence, *Journal of Political Economy* 97, 1989, pp. 38–92; after 1929, we rely on the *Economic Report of the President* (various years). Data on mobility are drawn from Long (1989), Table 2.1.

The third wave of growth in information sharing is probably related to the dramatic technological changes due to the introduction of computers in the 1970s and 1980s. Not only did computerization lower costs and further stimulate the exchange of information among lenders; the new technology eliminated the spatial segmentation that had previously limited competition among local credit bureaus. Creditors started to centralize their databases and no longer felt obliged to provide their information to the credit bureau in their local trade area. This deprived many local bureaus of the information earlier furnished by the local branches of the creditors' offices, to the advantage of the credit bureaus in the large cities. This advantage was compounded by more aggressive marketing by the larger, computerized bureaus. From a network of local monopolies, credit bureaus began to evolve into a nationwide oligopoly.

Despite a deliberate effort by the ACB to help the smaller credit bureaus survive (by mandating parity of access to creditors' files with the larger, automated bureaus), the powerful tendency to concentration has prevailed. The 1970s and

1980s have witnessed an unprecedented wave of closures, mergers, and acquisitions, with the disappearance of over 900 independent bureaus and the eventual emergence of three giant industry leaders. In terms of our model, while reducing the costs of information sharing, computerization has eliminated the original geographic segmentation in the operation of credit bureaus, and this has fully brought out the natural monopoly inherent in information sharing.

III. CONCLUSIONS

Lenders can overcome informational asymmetries by exchanging private information about potential borrowers. This exchange varies considerably by country and over time. For instance, in the United States, the United Kingdom, and Japan, information sharing in the consumer credit market takes place on a vast scale, while in other countries it is absent or embryonic. In this respect, there are two important questions that the literature has failed to address. First, why do lenders share information in certain instances but not in others? Second, does the agreement to share information foster the expansion of credit markets? This paper offers a theoretical framework for approaching these issues, and some evidence to assess its relevance.

The incentive to create credit bureaus is greatest, it is argued, where each lender is confronted by large numbers of customers on which it has no previous information, e.g., where borrowers are very mobile. The size of the credit market also increases the incentives to share information. On the other hand, the model indicates that sharing information does not always increase lending activity. Credit bureaus increase lending only if, in the absence of information sharing, safe borrowers would be priced out of the market by adverse selection. Finally, the model sheds light on several other features of credit bureaus: information sharing is a natural monopoly, it is discouraged by the fear of competition from potential entrants and fostered by cost-reducing innovations in information processing technology. These predictions are consistent with international and historical evidence in the context of the consumer credit market.

Appendix

Proof of Proposition 1. To show that $\partial E(\pi_a^*)/\partial m < 0$, note that by Jensen's inequality $[pq_s + (1-p)q_r]^2 < pq_s^2 + (1-p)q_r^2$, so that $\lambda < 1$, i.e., $1 - \lambda > 0$. To show that $1 - \lambda$ is an index of heterogeneity, let a mean-preserving spread be an increase in q_s to $q_s' = q_s + \epsilon$ and a reduction in q_r to $q_r' = q_r - \epsilon p/(1-p)$. Then, $[pq_s' + (1-p)q_r']^2 = [pq_s + (1-p)q_r]^2$, but $pq_s'^2 + (1-p)q_r'^2 > pq_s^2 + (1-p)q_r^2$, implying that $\lambda(q_s', q_r') < \lambda(q_s, q_r)$, i.e., $1 - \lambda(q_s', q_r') > 1 - \lambda(q_s, q_r)$. Since $\partial E(\pi_a^*)/\partial(1-\lambda) < 0$, a mean-preserving spread (an increase in heterogeneity) decreases $E(\pi_a^*)$. Finally, differentiation of equation (7) shows that $\partial E(\pi_a^*)/\partial p > 0$, provided $pq_s > (1-p)q_r$.

Discussion of Proposition 3. The expected profit function is linear-quadratic in R_m. If both types borrow, it is

$$E(\pi_a) = \frac{1-m}{V}\left(\frac{V-R}{2}\right)^2 + \frac{m}{V}\{-[pq_s^2 + (1-p)q_r^2]R_m^2$$

$$+ [pq_s + (1-p)q_r](V+R)R_m - RV\}.$$

If instead only risky types borrow, it becomes

$$E(\pi_b) = \frac{1-m}{V}\left(\frac{V-R}{2}\right)^2 + \frac{m}{V}\{(1-p)[-q_r^2 R_m^2 + (V+R)q_r R_m - RV]\}.$$

Each expression is composed of two terms: the first, multiplied by $(1-m)$, is the profit obtained by lending to residents; the second, multiplied by m, is that obtained from loans to immigrants.

Case (a) occurs when the maximum of $E(\pi_a)$ is greater than the maximum of $E(\pi_b)$, and Case (b) occurs when the opposite is true. Here we concentrate on Case (b) and show that it may arise in two different contexts, as illustrated in Figures A1 and A2. In both figures we graph only the expected profits obtained by lending to immigrants, i.e., the second terms in $E(\pi_a)$ (the thick line) and $E(\pi_b)$ (the thin line).

It can be shown that the two functions intersect twice, at $R_m = R/q_r$ and at $R_m = V/q_s$. If $E(\pi_a)$ is increasing at $R_m = V/q_s$ as in Figure A1, then its maximum $E(\pi^*_a)$ lies below $E(\pi_b)$, so that $R^*_{m,a} > V/q_s$. The relevant condition ensuring that $E(\pi_a)$ is increasing at V/q_s,

$$\frac{1-\lambda}{p} > \left(\frac{V-R}{V+R}\right)^2\left(1 + \frac{p}{1-p}(q_s/q_r)^2\right),$$

is more stringent than the condition in Proposition 3—it is sufficient but not necessary for $E(\pi^*_a) < E(\pi^*_b)$. Intuitively, $R^*_{m,a}$ is too high to attract any safe borrower.

If instead $E(\pi_a)$ is decreasing at $R_m = V/q_s$ as in Figure A2, then its maximum $E(\pi^*_a)$ lies above $E(\pi_b)$, so that $R^*_{m,a} < V/q_s$. Here the above condition is not met but Proposition 3 is still satisfied. Intuitively, safe types would be willing to borrow at $R^*_{m,a}$, but the bank chooses to charge $R^*_{m,b} = R^*_r$ and to price out safe borrowers.

Proof of Proposition 4. (*i*) Conditions (11a) and (11b) are obtained respectively by subtracting (7) and (9) from (10). (ii) The expected volume of loans extended to immigrants is $pi_{ms} + (1-p)i_{mr}$. With no information sharing, it takes different values in Cases (a) and (b), denoted by i_m^a and i_m^b respectively. Given information sharing, the volume of loans is i_m^f. To compute i_m^a, one evaluates $pi_{ms} + (1-p)i_{mr}$

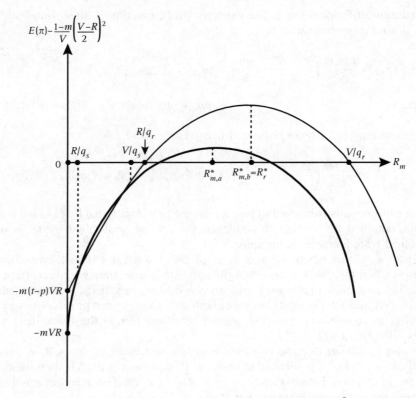

Figure A1. *Expected profits from lending to immigrants when $R^*_{m,a} > V/q_s$.*
The figure graphs the expected profits that banks earn on the pool of immigrants as a function of the interest rate charged to them (R_m). The *thick line* represents profits earned when both safe and risky immigrants obtain credit; the *thin line* graphs profits when only risky immigrants borrow. The parameter V is the maximum value that households place on the loan, R the cost of capital, m the proportion of immigrants, p the proportion of safe borrowers, and q_s and q_r are the repayment probabilities of safe and risky borrowers, respectively. Here the interest rate that maximizes profits when both types of borrowers apply for credit ($R^*_{m,a}$) is too high to attract safe borrowers, because V/q_s is the maximum interest rate that the latter are willing to pay. As a result, the relevant profit function is that drawn under the assumption that only risky borrowers apply for credit (the *thin line*).

by using (3) for i_{ms} and i_{mr}, and substituting $R^*_{m,a}$ from (6):

$$i^a_m = \frac{m}{V}\left[V - \frac{\lambda}{2}(V + R)\right].$$

To compute i^b_m, one evaluates $pi_{ms} + (1-p)i_{mr}$ at $i_{ms}=0$ and i_{mr} at $R^*_{m,b}=R^*_r$ from (5):

$$i^b_m = \frac{m}{V}(1-p)\frac{V-R}{2}.$$

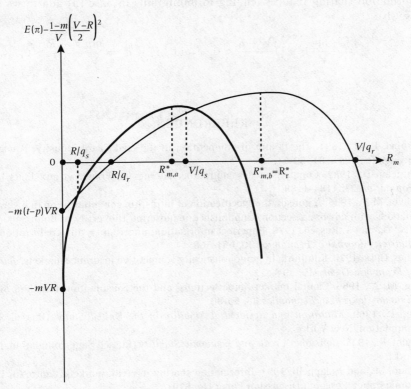

Figure A2. *Expected profits from lending to immigrants when* $R^*_{m,a} < V/q_s$.

The figure graphs the expected profits earned on the pool of immigrants as a function of the interest rate charged to them (R_{in}). The *thick line* represents profits earned when both safe and risky immigrants obtain credit; the *thin line* graphs profits earned when only risky immigrants borrow. The parameter V is the maximum value that households place on the loan, R the cost of capital, m the proportion of migrants, p the proportion of safe borrowers; and q_s and q, are the repayment probabilities of safe and risky borrowers, respectively. In contrast with Figure A1, here safe immigrants are willing to borrow at the interest rate that maximizes profits when both types borrow ($R^*_{m,a}$). However, banks can increase profits by setting the higher rate $R^*_{m,a}$, thus pricing safe borrowers out of the market. As a result, the relevant profit function is that drawn under the assumption that only risky immigrants borrow (the *thin line*), as in Figure A1.

Finally, i^f_m is obtained by evaluating i_{ms} at R^*_s and i_{mr} at R^*_r from (5), and substituting the results in $pi_{ms} + (1-p)i_{mr}$:

$$i^f_m = \frac{m}{V} \frac{V - R}{2}.$$

Information sharing reduces lending to immigrants in Case (a) and raises it in Case (b):

$$i_m^f - i_m^a = -\frac{m}{V}(1 - \lambda)\frac{V + R}{2} < 0, \quad \text{and} \quad i_m^f - i_m^b = \frac{mp}{V}\frac{V - R}{2} > 0.$$

REFERENCES

Ausubel, L. M., 1991, The failure of competition in the credit card industry, *American Economic Review* 81, 50–81.

Courgeau, D., 1982, Comparison des migrations internes en France et aux Etats Unis, *Population* 37, 1184–1188.

Hellwig, M. F., 1986, A note on the specification of intra-firm communication in insurance markets with adverse selection, Unpublished manuscript, University of Bonn.

Jaffee, D., and T. Russell, 1976, Imperfect information, uncertainty, and credit rationing, *Quarterly Journal of Economics* 90, 651–666.

Jaynes, G. D., 1978, Equilibria in monopolistically competitive insurance markets, *Journal of Economic Theory* 19, 394–422.

King, M. A., 1986, Capital market 'imperfections' and the consumption function, *Scandinavian Journal of Economics* 88, 59–80.

Long, L., 1989, *Migration and Residential Mobility in the United States* (Russell Sage Foundation, New York).

Nugent, R., 1939, *Consumer Credit and Economic Stability* (Russell Sage Foundation, New York).

Pagano, M., and T. Jappelli, 1991, Information sharing in credit markets, Centre for Economic Policy Research Discussion Paper No. 579.

Phelps, C. W., 1949, *Retail Credit Management* (McGraw-Hill, New York).

Stiglitz, J., and A. Weiss, 1981, Credit rationing in markets with imperfect information, *American Economic Review* 71, 393–410.

Tirole, J., 1988, *The Theory of Industrial Organization* (The MIT Press, Cambridge, Mass.).

Vives, X., 1990, Trade association disclosure rules, incentives to share information, and welfare, *RAND Journal of Economics* 21, 409–430.

Yotsuzuka, T., 1987, Ricardian equivalence in the presence of capital market imperfections, *Journal of Monetary Economics* 20, 411–486.

Young, R. A., 1940, *Personal Finance Companies and Their Credit Practices*, National Bureau of Economic Research, Studies in Consumer Installment Financing (National Bureau of Economic Research, Cambridge, Mass.).

10

Endogenous Communication among Lenders and Entrepreneurial Incentives

A. JORGE PADILLA AND MARCO PAGANO

One often observes that lenders communicate to each other information about the creditworthiness of their customers. Sometimes this informational exchange is so intense and frequent as to be intermediated by information brokers, such as credit bureaus and credit rating agencies. Typically these information brokers gather information about past defaults or delays in payment ('black information') or about the current debt exposure, performance, and riskiness of the borrower ('white information'). These data are mainly provided by banks, finance companies, and suppliers, and are consolidated in a file for each company or individual. This file is later accessed to provide information upon request via a credit report. In most instances, only lenders and suppliers who provide data are allowed to access this consolidated information, albeit at a small fee. The accuracy of the reported information is routinely verified—for instance, by cross-checking lenders' and borrowers' financial and accounting statements—and misreporting is sanctioned by exclusion from further access to the database.

This information exchange concerns companies as well as households. One of the main U.S. rating agencies, Dun & Bradstreet Information Services, collects and delivers information on 32 million companies worldwide, of which 18 million are in the United States, and much of it comes from banks and suppliers. More than 300 banks regularly contribute data on loan and average account size electronically, and thousands more do it by phone or mail. Over 600,000 companies provide payment references with data about delays and defaults by

This article has benefited from the comments of participants at the CEPR-Fundación BBV 1994 Conference on Industrial Organization and Finance, at the CEEA 1994 Conference on Banking and Finance in a Changing World, at the 1994 European Summer Symposium in Economic Theory, and at the universities of Chicago, Lausanne, and Princeton. In particular, we wish to thank Franklin Allen, Bernard Caillaud, Thomas Gehrig, Denis Gromb, Ian Jewitt, Steve Kaplan, Massimo Marrelli, Ragu Rajan, and an anonymous referee for their insightful remarks. We acknowledge financial support by the Fundación BBV, the Italian National Research Council (CNR), and the Italian Ministry for Universities and Scientific and Technological Research (MURST). The usual caveats apply. Address correspondence to Marco Pagano, Via Catullo 64, 80122 Napoli, Italy.

downstream companies. In 1992, Dun & Bradstreet received 3,700,000 banking reports and 207,400,000 payment reports. Also, in the United Kingdom credit reference agencies collect and disseminate vast amounts of data about businesses, mostly reported by finance companies. Credit bureaus provide a similar service for the consumer credit market. In the United States they currently issue some 400 million reports per year about credit seekers, and coverage of the households that have applied for consumer credit is virtually complete. Credit bureaus are also very active in the United Kingdom, Japan, and several other countries [see Pagano and Jappelli (1993)].

Information sharing among banks produces two types of effects. On the one hand, it tends to diminish informational asymmetries between lenders and borrowers, and thus reduces the impact of adverse selection and moral hazard on lending decisions. On the other hand, it stimulates harsher competition between banks, slashing their informational rents. The net effect on banks' profits is ambiguous: the improved performance of entrepreneurs need not translate into higher profits, since the latter may be dissipated by increased competition. Depending on the balance between these factors, banks may have the incentive to pool their private information with competitors or keep their information private. Focusing on this trade-off, one can identify the circumstances in which lenders will share spontaneously their private information, as well as the type and precision of the information that they will release to competitors.

Even though we develop the analysis with reference to credit markets, we would like to stress that our story can be seen as an instance of a more general principle—that information sharing, by raising ex post competition among principals, can sharpen agents' incentives, which in some cases can benefit the principals themselves. It is easy to think of other examples. By agreeing to provide references about their former employees, firms can induce them to work harder while they are in the job. Similarly, the U.S. graduate schools' standard practice of writing reference letters for their students in the job market improves the average quality of their research. Other examples can also be found in the housing market and in the insurance market.

We develop the analysis in the context of a two-period model with imperfectly competitive banks and heterogeneous entrepreneurs. The performance of each loan depends both on the intrinsic qualities of the entrepreneur and on his effort choice. In the first period, each bank has better information than its competitors about the characteristics of some entrepreneurs, and can thus extract informational rents from them. However, the very presence of such monopoly power thwarts its borrowers' incentives to perform: fearing that the return to their effort will be partly appropriated by their bank via high future interest rates, borrowers will tend to exert a low level of effort and perform badly in the current period.

Banks can correct this incentive problem by committing to share with other lenders their private information about the quality of their customers at the end of the first period. The resulting competitive pressure forces them to forgo opportunistic behavior in the second period. Anticipating this, borrowers step up their initial effort level. This raises banks' profits in the first period, when each bank still retains an informational advantage. But the fiercer competition that intervenes later reduces second-period profits. The ex ante decision to sign an information sharing agreement depends on which effect is expected to prevail. We study how the model parameters impinge on this decision and how its outcome affects the efficiency of the credit market, the volume of lending, and the interest rates charged to entrepreneurs.

To be viable an information sharing agreement must consider that ex post each bank will be tempted to cheat: once a customer has performed well, the inside bank has the incentive to abstain from informing outside competitors (or to misreport its information) and predate on the customer. Thus the agreement must contemplate a system to issue and enforce sanctions against deviant banks. In the context of our model, a simple decentralized reputation system can prevent such deviant behavior under mild conditions about the banks' discount rate, provided information can be transmitted across generations costlessly: if subsequent customers can learn about the deviation, they will 'force' the deviant bank toward the equilibrium with no information sharing.

In practice, one finds that the private enforcement mechanism used in these cases relies on more than a decentralized reputation system: wherever lenders spontaneously agree to share information via credit bureaus, the sanction against opportunistic behavior is subsequent exclusion from the system [Pagano and Jappelli (1993)]. Why in practice do banks need the explicit threat of exclusion from the informational exchange?

In this article, we develop the following explanation. We show that no individual borrower has the incentive to detect past deviations, nor to inform subsequent customers if he has been 'squeezed' by his bank. Borrowers are short-lived agents who care only about payoffs in their own lifetime and are thus unwilling to bear the cost of communicating with future generations, even if this cost is small. No individual bank has such an incentive either. Therefore, a decentralized reputation system cannot sustain the information sharing agreement if the transmission of information across generations is costly.[1]

But the effectiveness of the reputation mechanism can be restored by a multilateral institution, such as a credit bureau. The bureau is formed and financed by long-lived banks and is instructed to detect deviants, exclude them from further access to the bureau, and let any customer freely ascertain if its potential lender is still a valid member of the system. So the credit bureau ensures the transmission of information across generations of would-be customers, and thus the viability of the reputation mechanism. We show that, if the costs incurred by the bureau (most

---

[1] If a decentralized reputation system can sustain an information sharing agreement among lenders, it can also sustain the lenders' commitment to a sequence of low interest rates, which has the same implications on entrepreneurs' incentives and overall market efficiency as information sharing [see Sharpe (1990)]. But the commitment to low interest rates faces the very same problems of sustainability as an information sharing agreement supported by a decentralized reputation system. (See Section 1.3.)

importantly, the costs of verifying the information provided by members) are not too large, lenders are willing to finance the bureau in order to be able to lend profitably in the future. The same argument has been proposed to explain other private enforcement mechanisms, such as the system of private judges that sanctioned dishonest merchants in medieval Champagne fairs: 'in a large community, [...] it would be too costly to keep everyone informed about what transpires in all trading relationships, as a simple reputation system might require' [Milgrom, North, and Weingast (1990, p. 3); see also Greif, Milgrom, and Weingast (1994)].

This is not the first article to focus on the incentive problems that arise from the exclusive relationship with a bank: Rajan (1992) shows that a company can limit the ex post monopoly power of the inside bank by borrowing from uninformed outside lenders and assigning different priorities to its creditors; in a similar spirit, von Thadden (1992) argues that duplicated monitoring can dominate exclusive monitoring in banking. Also in our model, outside lenders compete with the inside bank, but the effect of competition on entrepreneurial incentives depends on the information that the inside bank optimally precommits to release. As noticed by von Thadden (1992) and Dewatripont and Tirole (1994), the argument that competition can offer protection against the predatory behavior of the inside bank is reminiscent of the 'dual sourcing theory' in industrial organization, as developed by Farrell and Gallini (1988) and Shepard (1988). These last two articles analyzed models in which a buyer invests in a specific asset (e.g., a mainframe computer) and a seller chooses, ex post, some variable that affects the value of the asset and is not contractible ex ante (e.g., the quality of service and maintenance). Ex post the seller has an incentive to choose a low quality and, therefore, ex ante the buyer invests little in the asset. Dual sourcing consists of having two or more suppliers, who compete ex post, increasing the equilibrium level of quality and thus raising ex ante efficiency.

The role of information sharing in inducing good behavior by entrepreneurs has also been analyzed in Padilla and Pagano (1996b). The main insight added in that paper is that the incentive effects of information sharing may be greater when banks disclose to each other only data about defaults, rather than more complete information about the credit worthiness of their customers. Another feature of the model in Padilla and Pagano (1996b) is that, due to unrestrained *ex ante* competition, banks always make zero expected profits and the net benefit from information sharing accrues entirely to their customers. Here, instead, we assume imperfect competition, so that banks retain their initial informational rents and internalize part of the incentive effects of information sharing.[2]

---

[2] Also Pagano and Jappelli (1993) focus on spontaneous information sharing by banks, but in the context of a pure adverse selection model. They show that, by agreeing to share information, each bank earns more profits from customers who happen to 'migrate' into its market area, but loses part of its informational rents on its local customer base due to more aggressive outside competition. Also in that model, banks must have some monopoly power (irrespective of their decision to share information) for them to ever want to share information. [See also Van Cayseele, Bouckaert, and Degryse (1994).]

The article proceeds as follows. In Section 1 we present the basic model, where two types of entrepreneurs—high- and low-ability—can borrow to finance a project of a fixed size: we show that, if low-ability entrepreneurs invariably choose negative-NPV projects, information sharing is required for the credit market to operate at all. We also analyze the conditions to prevent cheating by the banks who participate in the information sharing agreement, and compare the sustainability (and thus the actual efficiency properties) of information sharing agreements vis-à-vis that of commitments to low interest rates. In Section 2 we generalize the model in various directions. Relaxing some of the assumptions of the basic model, we find—more realistically—that banks can operate also if they fail to share information, and study in which circumstances one would expect them to communicate and how this affects the size of the credit market and the rates charged to borrowers. Section 3 concludes the article.

1. THE BASIC MODEL

1.1. Description

We consider a two-period model of the credit market with risk-neutral borrowers and banks, where only one-period loan contracts are available.[3] Our economy is composed of many (strictly speaking, $N \geq 3$) 'towns,' each of which hosts a single bank and a continuum $[0, 1]$ of entrepreneurs. The local bank has superior information on local entrepreneurs, while it must incur a cost to learn about borrowers located in other towns.[4] Apart from this, competition among banks is unrestrained. Competition ensures that no bank will acquire costly information about lenders located in other towns: all the resulting rents would be dissipated to the benefit of entrepreneurs.

Entrepreneurs differ as to their ability to identify profitable projects. They fall in two classes: high- (H) and low-ability (L) types, whose respective proportions in the population are γ and $1 - \gamma$ for $\gamma \in (0, 1)$. High-ability entrepreneurs choose projects which, if successful, yield R^* units of output per period and, if unsuccessful, yield nothing. The probability of success, $p \in [0, \hat{p}]$, depends on their level of effort, which is nonobservable noncontractible, by assumption. (We define $\hat{p}$ as the first-best full information effort level, that is, the level of effort that would be chosen by high-ability entrepreneurs when banks charge actuarially fair interest

---

[3] In this model, by the time the loan contract is signed, the effort choice is sunk (see below), so that in the absence of repeated interaction long-term contracts cannot be used by the bank to precommit to anything other than the time-consistent policy. So the assumption of one-period contracts is not restrictive: the sequence of one-period contracts derived below coincides with the optimal *time-consistent* two-period contract. Otherwise, if the bank could precommit, it could always do better by offering *nonlinear* long-term contracts. (We thank Ian Jewitt for pointing this out to us.)

[4] Hannan (1991) presents evidence that U.S. firms mainly borrow from local lenders because of prohibitive informational and transactional costs. Petersen and Rajan (1995) also report that in their sample 'over half the firms are within 2 miles of their primary institution. 90% of the firms are within 15 miles of their primary institution.'

rates.) Effort is chosen once and for all prior to any borrowing.[5] Since the probability of success p is monotonic in effort, we shall consider it as the borrowers' choice variable. Low-ability entrepreneurs, instead, are not creditworthy: whatever the rate at which they get credit, they choose projects with no return and are insolvent.

Each investment project requires one unit of capital, that entrepreneurs must always borrow entirely from one of the competing banks (entrepreneurs have zero initial wealth available for investment, and the project's output cannot be stored, so it does not generate additional collateral for subsequent operations). We assume that each individual investment project is run as a private limited liability company[6] and that the entrepreneur cannot be disqualified after default, so that (1) once the project matures the company is liquidated, (2) if the project fails to produce positive returns, the entrepreneur cannot be held liable for the losses incurred, so that his future investment projects are free from any floating charge, and (3) the failure of the current project has no bearing on the entrepreneur's legal capacity to promote new investment projects.[7] Furthermore, we assume that the profitability of any investment project is observable and contractible by the current lender, but not observable by any other outside lender. This last assumption implies that if the project succeeds the entrepreneur must repay the loan, and that if the entrepreneur defaults the event is only observed by his current lender.

If the high-ability entrepreneur i gets no credit, his expected utility is zero. If, instead, he gets credit and chooses a success probability $p(i)$, his total discounted utility is equal to

$$U_H(p(i)) = p(i)[(R^* - R_{h1}) + \beta(R^* - E(R_{h2}))] - V(p(i)), \qquad (1)$$

where R_{h1} is the period 1 gross interest rate charged by bank h; $E(R_{h2})$ is the expected period 2 gross interest rate charged by bank h; $\beta \in (0, 1)$ is the discount factor; and finally, $V(p(i))$ is the total disutility of effort exerted to achieve $p(i)$. $V(\cdot)$ is increasing and convex ($\infty > V' \geq 0$ and $V'' > 0$), and $V(0) = V'(0) = 0$.

---

[5] Relevant examples may be the effort spent on hiring a good manager or on laying out a good business plan. These choices must be made *prior* to raising any external finance. But our main results would extend to a more general model, where some effort is also exerted after the loan contract is signed. In this case the bank and the customer would want to sign a two-period contract to correct the incentives of the borrower. This contract would solve the incentive problem for the portion of the effort to be exerted after the contract is signed, but our model would still apply for the portion of the effort that is sunk when the contract is signed.

[6] This is a simplifying assumption that makes our algebra simpler. We relax this assumption at the end of Section 1.2 to consider the case of entrepreneurs' unlimited liability, showing that our main results are robust to alternative bankruptcy rules.

[7] In most countries company managers are disqualified only if the company becomes insolvent because of fraud, negligence, or in general, if the conduct of the entrepreneur as a manager of the company makes him unfit to be concerned in the management of a company (see, for instance, the U.K. Company Directors Disqualification Act 1986). None of these reasons applies to our high-ability but unlucky entrepreneurs.

Entrepreneurs rationally anticipate future interest rates, but assume that they cannot affect them, that is, behave as price takers. Notice that no high-quality entrepreneur will demand credit at rates strictly exceeding R^* (but since his effort is sunk, he is willing to borrow and run his project even if the bank charges him the rate R^*). Low-ability entrepreneurs derive no monetary payoff from borrowing, because their projects yield no return with certainty, and for the same reason they spend no effort on their project. But since they are assumed to derive positive, although arbitrarily small, utility from 'being in business,' they still participate in the credit market.[8]

In each period, lenders raise capital at a cost $\bar{R}$ and compete in interest rates given their respective information sets. At the beginning of the first period, each bank can costlessly distinguish between high- and low-ability entrepreneurs located in its town. It also knows the average ex ante probability of success, p, of the local high-ability entrepreneurs. Thus it has an informational advantage over its rivals with respect to these entrepreneurs. More precisely, we assume that

$$\gamma \hat{p} R^* < \bar{R} < \hat{p} R^*, \tag{2}$$

which implies that in the absence of information sharing the local bank enjoys monopoly power in its own town in both periods, and that there are effort levels for which such a power is indeed profitable.[9] Define $\underline{p} > 0$ such that $\underline{p} R^* \equiv \bar{R}$, that is, as the minimum effort level by high-ability types that allows the bank to break even. Then equation (2) ensures that, for all $p \in [\underline{p}, \hat{p}]$, lending to high-ability entrepreneurs is a profitable activity.

Since effort is assumed to be noncontractible, then interest rates cannot be conditioned on the individual borrower's probability of repayment $p(i)$, albeit they will obviously depend on the ex ante average probability of repayment, p. In period 2, bank h sets R_{h2} so as to maximize its current profits, Π_{h2}. In period 1, it chooses R_{h1} to maximize its total discounted expected profits, $\Pi_h = \Pi_{h1} + \beta \Pi_{h2}$, where Π_{h2} is evaluated at the equilibrium period 2 rates. This reflects the inability of banks to precommit to a given path of interest rates. The rates posted by each bank are public knowledge, but the rival bank cannot observe to whom they are offered. The sequence of events described above is summarized by the time line in Figure 1.

In Section 1.2 we analyze the model under two different scenarios. First, we assume that banks do not communicate any information about their borrowers. Second, we analyze the case in which they share information about the entrepreneurs' ability *and* can commit to report it honestly. (The case in which they cannot commit to honest reporting is analyzed in Section 1.3.)

---

[8] Notice that, with some slight changes, the model can be reinterpreted as referring to consumer credit rather than to business lending. More precisely, it can apply to the credit extended by a retailer for the purchase of a consumer durable, which is repossessed by the retailer in case of default. R^* can be thought of as the flow utility from the services of the durable and p as the effort that the consumer must undertake to avoid default, for instance by working overtime.

[9] We shall discuss the implications of relaxing this assumption in Sections 2.1 and 2.2.

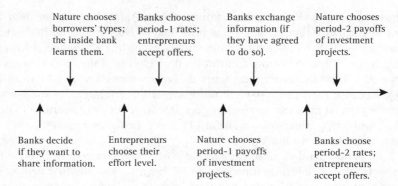

Figure 1. *Timing of actions in the model*

In each case, we look for the subgame perfect equilibria (SPE) of the model, that is, a vector $\{p, (R_{h1}, R_{h2}), \forall\, h\}$, such that

1. Each high-ability entrepreneur i chooses $p(i)$ to maximize his expected utility, correctly anticipating the interest rates R_{ht} for $t = 1, 2$ and all h, and taking as given the effort choices of the other entrepreneurs in his town. Since high-ability entrepreneurs are all identical, we have that, in equilibrium, $p(i) = p$ for all i.
2. Banks maximize their profits given the average ex ante probability of success p, so that the interest rates $(R_{h1}, R_{h2}), \forall\, h$, constitute a subgame perfect equilibrium for the banking competition subgame.

1.2. The Main Result

Suppose for the moment that the entrepreneurs' average effort level, p, is exogenously given. In the absence of communication among banks, our previous assumptions imply that each bank can extract all surplus from the entrepreneurs at its location. Therefore, if $p \geq \underline{p}$, high-ability entrepreneurs are charged the reservation rate R^*, whereas low-ability entrepreneurs are denied access to credit. Otherwise, if $p < \underline{p}$, both classes of entrepreneurs are left without credit. The total discounted profits of each bank in the absence of communication are thus equal to

$$\Pi^{ns}(p) = \begin{cases} (1 + \beta)\gamma(pR^* - \bar{R}) & \text{if } p \geq \underline{p}, \\ 0 & \text{otherwise.} \end{cases} \tag{3}$$

By sharing information on the types of local entrepreneurs in period 2, banks give away their informational rents and so forgo all monopoly profits in this period. In fact, rate-setting competition among fully informed banks in period 2 leads to actuarially fair interest rates for high-quality entrepreneurs, that is,

$R_2^{is} = \bar{R}/p$, and no credit to low-ability entrepreneurs if $p \geq \underline{p}$. As before, credit is refused to everybody if $p < \underline{p}$. Therefore, period 2 profits are equal to zero for all banks. But in period 1 banks retain their informational advantage in their respective towns, so that they can extract all the surplus from high-ability entrepreneurs by lending to them at a rate R^*, and simultaneously refuse credit to low-ability entrepreneurs if $p \geq \underline{p}$. The total discounted profits of each bank under information sharing are equal to

$$\Pi^{is}(p) = \begin{cases} \gamma(pR^* - \bar{R}) & \text{if } p \geq \underline{p}, \\ 0 & \text{otherwise}, \end{cases} \tag{4}$$

so that

$$\Pi^{is}(p) \leq \Pi^{ns}(p) \text{ for all } p. \tag{5}$$

Therefore, if effort levels were exogenous banks would have no incentive to communicate their borrowers' types, as this would only have the effect of fostering competition in period 2. But of course effort levels are endogenously chosen. When banks do not communicate, high-quality entrepreneurs know that, if they are given credit, their bank will appropriate the entire surplus of the project ex post. So they choose to exert zero effort ex ante: in equilibrium, $p^{ns} = 0$. This implies that in the absence of communication among banks the credit market *collapses*, since banks have to close down or else incur losses. This need not happen under information sharing. In this case, there may be multiple SPE for our model: there is always an equilibrium involving zero effort and market collapse, but there may be other equilibria involving positive effort levels that strictly Pareto dominate the zero effort equilibrium. The intuition behind this multiplicity is clear: if the average borrower chooses a low p^{is}, the interest rate will be high, so that each individual borrower is induced to choose a low effort level, and p^{is} will be low in a symmetric equilibrium (and vice versa if the average borrower chooses a high p^{is}). Hence, in those cases where multiple equilibria do exist, the credit market will be active under information sharing provided entrepreneurs can coordinate on an equilibrium with positive effort. This indicates that information sharing is a necessary but not sufficient condition for an active credit market: in a depressed economy where entrepreneurs are expected to slack, setting up an information sharing system among banks will not per se induce lending. These results are formally stated in the following lemma and proposition (proofs are in Appendix A).

Lemma 1. *Under information sharing, the repayment probability optimally chosen by a high-quality entrepreneur is no lower than under no information sharing, that is, $p^{is} \geq p^{ns} = 0$. Furthermore, there are functional forms for the total disutility of effort $V(\cdot)$, such that there is at least an SPE (which is not Pareto dominated) with $p^{is} > \underline{p} > p^{ns} = 0$.*

From Lemma 1 and Equations (3), (4), and (5), we can directly establish our main result:

Proposition 1. *Under information sharing, equilibrium profits are no lower than under no information sharing, that is, $\Pi^{is}(p^{is}) \geq \Pi^{ns}(p^{ns}) = 0$. Furthermore, there are functional forms for the total disutility of effort $V(\cdot)$, such that there is at least an SPE (which is not Pareto dominated) with $\Pi^{is}(p^{is}) > 0 = \Pi^{ns}(p^{ns})$.*

In conclusion, in this simple model communication among lenders is a necessary condition for the existence of an active credit market. In the absence of communication, lending is always unprofitable; in its presence, lending can become profitable. If it does, the welfare level of borrowers rises so that information sharing brings about a strict Pareto improvement. This result is independent of the precise bankruptcy rules described in Section 1.1, which put a limit on the entrepreneurs' liability in case of default. Consider what happens if entrepreneurs have *unlimited liability* (though, as before, are not disqualified from business in case of failure). This means that, if the period 1 project fails, the unpaid debt and interest is carried over to period 2, and this liability is senior relative to period 2 interest. Under a condition analogous to Equation (2), which ensures that without information sharing the inside bank enjoys local monopoly power in both periods, we can show that (1) in the absence of communication the credit market collapses, since in equilibrium high-ability entrepreneurs optimally choose to exert no effort; (2) under information sharing, lending can be profitable: high-ability entrepreneurs exert positive effort in any non-Pareto dominated SPE, irrespectively of whether they can avoid past liabilities by switching banks or not. These results are shown in Appendix B.

1.3. Sustainability of the Information Sharing Agreement

While in this basic model information sharing is needed for the viability of the credit market, the information sharing agreement itself will not be viable if it does not contemplate sanctions against deviant banks. In fact, once its customers have performed well, each bank has the incentive to renege on its commitment to honestly reveal its private information to outside competitors so that it can predate on its customers. Obviously, if customers anticipate this behavior, they do not exert any effort in the first place. Thus one must make sure that the punishment for deviant banks exceeds the temptation to deviate. This requires that the game described in the previous section be repeated over time. We assume that infinite-lived banks face overlapping generations of two-period-lived customers (where each generation is identical to the single generation in the original model): at each date, in the equilibrium with information sharing, they lend monopolistically to young customers in their market area and compete with other banks for old customers. Banks' payoffs are now determined as the discounted sum of their periodic profits. The timing of events is as described in Figure 1 with the additional assumption that the effort choices of any newborn generation are sunk by the time banks post their rates for young and old customers, respectively.

1.3.1. *Game 1. Informationally Isolated Generations*

Our first model represents the situation of entrepreneurs who only know the lending rates offered to them: in particular, when young, they cannot observe the interest rates charged on old customers nor communicate with previous and/or future generations of entrepreneurs any information regarding the behavior of their banks. In this game, it is immediate that

Proposition 2. *No Nash equilibrium of game 1 can support the information sharing outcome* $\{p^{is}, (R^*, \bar{R}/p^{is}), \forall\ h\}$.

In other words, no reputation mechanism based only on sanctions from those who are cheated can sustain the most efficient information sharing equilibrium. As emphasized by Greif, Milgrom, and Weingast (1994), Nash equilibrium is the relevant concept to use here, since we just want to show that even with the most inclusive of noncooperative equilibrium concepts, there is no way to sustain the information sharing agreement.

1.3.2. *Game 2. Informationally Linked Generations: a Decentralized Communication Mechanism*

Suppose now that entrepreneurs learn about the interest rates charged to previous generations, because, in any period, old customers can credibly and costlessly communicate their experiences and those of their predecessors to young customers in the same market area. That is, we assume that young entrepreneurs always know whether a bank behaved dishonestly with any preceding generation.

Proposition 3. *There is an SPE for game 2 in which information sharing is sustainable over time if and only if* $\beta > 0.62$.

Thus, under mild restrictions on the discount factor, a simple reputational mechanism ensures that banks do not cheat. But this requires that the old customers 'squeezed' by the local bank can credibly and costlessly communicate their experiences to younger customers in the same market area. Moreover, it requires that the would-be customers of the local bank in each generation inform those in the subsequent generation that the bank misbehaved in the past, so that the latter's bad reputation lingers on. But none of these agents has any incentive to pass on this information: entrepreneurs who were 'squeezed' have nothing to gain from doing so, and they strictly lose if documenting the fact involves a cost. The same holds for subsequent generations of would-be customers. Nor does any individual bank have such an incentive since (1) detecting a deviation at a location different from its own amounts to learning the true types of the entrepreneurs at that location, which involves a cost, and (2) there is no direct gain to benefit from, since competition with the local bank will dissipate all rents to the benefit of the local entrepreneurs.

In summary, if communication across generations involves any cost, entrepreneurs—being short-lived and self-interested—will not inform future generations of their experiences and the decentralized reputation system will collapse. The problem is similar to that analyzed in Allen (1984), Klein and Leffler (1981), and Shapiro (1983). These authors show that, in markets for experience goods, firms cannot credibly commit to offer high quality unless they can earn nonnegligible rents from honest behavior and there is perfect communication among buyers so that cheating firms lose all their future sales. It is this last requirement that, according to our previous reasoning, is unlikely to hold in practice.

1.3.3. *Game 3. Informationally Linked Generations: Credit Bureaus*

The problems just discussed explain why in practice information sharing agreements among lenders require an institution like a credit bureau to be viable. The credit bureau must be designed to enforce compliance by individual banks: it must detect and credibly sanction any deviation by excluding the deviant bank from further access to the bureau, and it must inform current and future generations of entrepreneurs about any such deviation.

Suppose that at t_0, N banks choose to form a credit bureau. The credit bureau is an independent legal entity, which acts as a principal with respect to the member banks at $i \geq t_0$ and whose statutes are designed at t_0. We assume that creating and organizing a credit bureau involves a fixed start-up cost $K > 0$, which is equally shared among the bureau's members at t_0. Its statutes instruct the personnel of the credit bureau to collect information about entrepreneurs' types from their local banks, verify it, and make it available to all the members of the bureau, and only to them. We assume that the credit bureau can perfectly monitor, albeit at a cost, all reports provided by its members.[10] Once failure to report or misreporting is detected, these statutes mandate the bureau exclude the deviant bank from the common database. The statutes of the bureau also include a clause forbidding the readmission in the bureau of past deviators.[11] At any point in time, the bureau publicizes the list of its current members as well as the list of previous members who deviated in the past. So entrepreneurs at any location can always freely ascertain whether their potential lenders are still valid members of the bureau or if they misbehaved in the past.

On top of its fraction of the start-up fixed cost K, each member of the credit bureau must pay a membership fee $c \geq 0$ in each period $t \geq t_0$ to cover the costs

---

[10] There are many ways in which banks can verify the information provided by their members. Misleading information may eventually emerge if the borrower goes bankrupt or may be simply revealed by word of mouth. In practice, credit bureaus cross-check the information they obtain from lenders with that provided by suppliers, by the debtors themselves, as well as from public sources, such as courts, public registers, accounting statements, etc. Our results are qualitatively unaffected if misreporting is not detected with probability one. Basically this would reduce the parameter region in which the credit bureau is sustainable, just like an increase in the cost of verifying the truthfulness of the members' reports.

[11] In the absence of such a clause, the deviator could bribe the remaining members of the bureau to admit it back into the bureau and delete its name from the bureau's black list. Hence, the exclusion threat would not be renegotiation-proof, which would destroy the credibility of the credit bureau.

incurred by the bureau to handle the files of the member bank's customers and to verify the information contained in them. A bank qualifies for membership only if it pays the fee c in each period.

Proposition 4. *For any $c \in [0, c^*]$, where $0 < c^* < \infty$, there exists a real number $\underline{\beta}(c) \in [0, 1]$, strictly increasing in c, such that there is an SPE for game 3 for which information sharing is sustainable over time if and only if $\beta > \underline{\beta}(c) \geq 0.62$.*

Intuitively, for the credit bureau to be viable its costs of verifying reported information must not be too large, that is, its fees c must be below the critical level c^*. Within that range its viability will depend on the discount factor of banks. An expensive credit bureau (a high c) is viable only if banks are sufficiently farsighted (a high β).

Two important remarks are in order. First, if (β, c) satisfy Proposition 4, there is a range of values of K, $0 < K < N(\gamma(p^{is}R^* - \bar{R}) - c)/(1 - \beta))$, for which every bank will pay its share of the fixed costs, K/N, at t_0 and remain a faithful member of the bureau at $t \geq t_0$. That is, the credit bureau is viable: at t_0 every bank finds it privately optimal to join the credit bureau. Second, the multilateral arrangement analyzed here is less efficient than the decentralized reputation system in game 2 whenever the latter is also viable: if information can be costlessly transmitted across generations, for all $c > 0$ and discount factors $\beta \in (0.62, \underline{\beta}(c))$ the information exchange is viable in game 2 and not in game 3. But if borrowers of different generations are informationally isolated, the information exchange cannot be sustained without a mechanism such as a credit bureau.

The creation of such a multilateral institution entails a commitment at the *collective* level. In a situation where banks and borrowers at different locations, as well as borrowers of different generations, are informationally isolated, misbehavior can still be detected, publicized, and punished by a collective institution that acts as a third party vis-à-vis any of its members and their customers. The same argument has been offered by Greif, Milgrom, and Weingast (1994) and Milgrom, North, and Weingast (1990) to explain the successful performance of other private collective enforcement mechanisms, such as the private judicial system of medieval trade fairs or the merchant guilds that 'emerged during the late medieval period to allow rulers of trade centers to commit to the security of alien merchants.' Milgrom and Roberts (1992, pp. 266–269) provide a number of examples that support the theory, which lies at the heart of this subsection, that private multilateral institutions, such as credit bureaus, can help enhance the efficiency of a reputation system.

1.4. Information Sharing Versus Alternative Precommitment Devices

One may wonder if to solve our incentive problem banks really need to sign an information sharing agreement. Why cannot banks precommit at the individual level to a sequence of interest rates via a *decentralized reputational mechanism,* solving the incentive problem even in the absence of information sharing? Under the informational assumptions of game 2 in the previous section, banks could indeed credibly precommit to a sequence of rates $(R^*, \bar{R}/p^{is})$ offered to high-ability entrepreneurs only, which would induce the latter to exert a positive effort level p^{is}, leading to the very same equilibrium outcome that prevails under information sharing. This outcome could be achieved in a simpler bilateral setting, in which each local bank only deals with the current and future generations of entrepreneurs at its location (without interacting with rival banks based at other locations). But the sustainability of commitments to a sequence of interest rates via a decentralized reputation mechanism is exposed to the same objections raised in the discussion of game 2. The point is, as before, that the reputational mechanism fails to operate if the detection and the collective memory of deviant behavior is imperfect.[12]

If reputation is an inadequate mechanism, however, one may ask why a *multilateral* institution such as a credit bureau is a better precommitment device than a contracting arrangement at the *individual* bank's level, for instance by hiring an external auditor to monitor and publicly certify its credit policy. The answer is that a multilateral institution is likely to be both cheaper and more credible than a bank-level contract with an auditor. First, a credit bureau is likely to entail lower resource costs, its fixed outlays being spread over many participating banks. Second, it should have better incentives to police and sanction deviations than an auditor, since by serving many banks it would be less easily captured by any individual lender.

Finally, one may wonder if banks at different locations could entrust the task to enforce their precommitments to some *other multilateral institution*, for instance a trade association, rather than to a credit bureau. Though in principle equivalent, in practice this solution would run into greater problems than a credit bureau. Detecting deviations would require collecting information about the pricing strategies of individual banks, which is strictly forbidden by the antitrust laws of most developed countries.[13]

---

[12] Sharpe (1990) was first to propose the simple solution of precommitment to a sequence of interest rates in a banking model related to ours. In his model, entrepreneurial incentives are not a problem, but still inefficiencies in the credit market may arise because of distortions in the borrowers' optimal investment choices due to ex post monopoly power. However, Sharpe himself emphasized that the effectiveness of a decentralized reputation mechanism 'depends upon the bank's valuation of future transactions and *the existence of informal mechanisms for transmitting information about a bank's behavior.*' [Sharpe (1990, p. 1084); italics added by the authors.]

[13] Information agreements involving communication to competitors about details of a company's pricing policy, price lists, discount structures, and the dates when prices would be increased are not lawful under, for instance, Article 85 of the Treaty of Rome (which regulates anticompetitive agreements within the European Union), the U.K. Restrictive Trade Practices Act 1976, and section 1 of the U.S. Sherman Act 1890. On the contrary, information agreements as to descriptions of persons to whom goods are to be supplied are not prohibited unless they plainly distort competition. [See Singleton (1992) for further discussion.]

2. EXTENDING THE BASIC MODEL

Proposition 1 shows that, under simple assumptions on the returns to entrepreneurs' projects and on the elasticity of the demand for credit, banks strictly prefer to share information about the quality of their borrowers. Indeed, in the absence of such informational exchange, the credit market fails to operate. In this section we show that when some of these assumptions are relaxed, the credit market can operate even without information sharing. Banks can also operate when they choose not to communicate, but in some cases their expected profits are higher if they do communicate. The focus thus shifts to the parameters that determine the profitability of information sharing and to the effects of information sharing on default rates, interest rates, and lending volume. This enables us to draw several empirical predictions from the model.

We consider three extensions. First, we relax the assumption that, absent information sharing, the inside bank has an unchecked monopoly over its customers and can therefore wholly expropriate the surplus produced by them. Despite the inside bank's informational advantage, outside banks may in fact exert some pressure on its pricing policy. Second, we analyze what happens if there are more than two classes of potential borrowers, by introducing a third class of 'medium-type' entrepreneurs, whose projects are less profitable than those of high-ability entrepreneurs but nevertheless are 'creditworthy', in the sense that they have positive net present value if financed at the actuarially fair interest rate. Third, we relax the assumption that the size of the investment projects is fixed and construct an example featuring an elastic demand for loans at the individual level.

One extension that we abstain from modeling explicitly is the endogenous production of information by banks. All the versions of the model analyzed here assume that initially each bank has private information about the ability of the local entrepreneurs. In each case, one could instead assume that the bank must produce such information at a cost, thus adding a period 0 decision about information production. Then it is easy to see that whenever information sharing is shown to increase the bank's expected profits, the bank would be more willing to produce the information in the first place: communication among banks, rather than depressing the incentives to produce private information, can stimulate its production.

2.1. Limited Informational Monopoly by the Inside Bank

In Section 1.2 the inside bank was assumed to have such a large informational advantage that, absent information sharing, it was a complete monopolist. Outside banks would make losses in lending to the local bank's clients, even if the safe clients exerted the first-best level of effort $\hat{p}$, since the return on successful projects R^* would not cover the break-even pooling rate of uninformed banks: $R^* < \bar{R}/\gamma\hat{p}$. Here we instead consider what happens when, absent information sharing, outside competition 'bites' in the local bank's customer pool. This requires the return to successful projects to exceed the break-even pooling rate offered by uninformed banks: $R^* > \bar{R}/\gamma p_0 \equiv R_0$, where p_0 is the effort of high-ability entrepreneurs consistent with the break-even rate R_0.[14]

Consider first what happens if banks do not share information. Neglecting corner solutions, the optimal effort level of a high-ability entrepreneur i who borrows from bank h is given by the first-order condition

$$(R^* - R_{h1}) + \beta(R^* - E(R_{h2})) = V'(p(i)). \tag{6}$$

By symmetry the equilibrium effort choice is obtained by setting $p(i) = p$ for all i. The lowest rate that outside competitors can offer to the local customers in either period is the break-even rate

$$R_0 = \frac{\bar{R}}{\gamma p_0}, \tag{7}$$

where p_0 is the effort level corresponding to the break-even rate, that is, solves

$$(1 + \beta)\left(R^* - \frac{\bar{R}}{\gamma p_0}\right) = V'(p_0). \tag{8}$$

There can be several positive values of p_0 (and corresponding values of R_0) that solve this equation, but for the purpose of our argument it suffices that there is at least one such value of p_0. Clearly this requires our initial assumption that $R^* > R_0$: the effort level is positive if a surplus is left to the entrepreneurs.

We now turn to determine the equilibrium of this game. To ensure the existence of a pure-strategy equilibrium, we assume that the two banks move sequentially: first, the inside bank offers its menu of rates to local entrepreneurs, then the outside competitors make their bid (while the results about equilibrium interest rates do not depend on the order of moves, no pure-strategy equilibrium exists with simultaneous moves). We also assume that, if offered the same rate by the inside bank and its competitors, entrepreneurs borrow from the inside bank.

The optimal policy for the inside bank is to offer the rate R_0 to the high-ability entrepreneurs in both periods and refuse lending to the low-ability ones. To avoid losing money, competitors can at most match this offer and will attract no customers. But their potential competition erodes the informational monopoly of the inside bank, forcing it to leave a fraction of the surplus to the entrepreneurs. As a result, even without information sharing, entrepreneurial effort is positive: $p^{ns} = p_0$ and the credit market does not collapse—or to be more precise, there is at least one SPE in which this is true.

Consider now what happens if in period 2 banks share their information. The period 2 equilibrium interest rate offered to high-quality entrepreneurs will then

---

[14] This is a more stringent condition than $\gamma \hat{p} R^* > \bar{R}$, since the level of effort elicited by the break-even rate R_0 will generally be less than the first-information level of effort: $p_0 \leq \hat{p}$.

be their actuarially fair rate $\bar{R}/p^{is}$: period 2 informational rents will be wiped out. In period 1, when the inside bank still has superior information, its optimal policy is to offer the rate $\bar{R}/\gamma p^{is}$ to the high-ability entrepreneurs—which cannot be undercut by outside competitors—and refuse lending to the low-ability ones. The equilibrium effort level will be given by

$$\left(R^* - \frac{\bar{R}}{\gamma p^{is}}\right) + \beta\left(R^* - \frac{\bar{R}}{p^{is}}\right) = V'(p^{is}). \tag{9}$$

Information sharing raises the equilibrium effort level, because it leaves a larger surplus to the entrepreneur. To see this, note that when evaluated at $p^{is} = p^{ns} = p_0$ the function on the left-hand side of Equation (9) exceeds that on the left-hand side of Equation (8). But the right-hand side of both equations, $V'(p)$ is increasing in p. So it must be $p^{is} > p^{ns} = p_0$.

Will information sharing also raise the profits of the inside bank h? In this case, it will not. The difference between its profits in the two regimes is

$$\Pi_h^{is} - \Pi_h^{ns} = -\beta(1 - \gamma)\bar{R} < 0.$$

In this case the loss of the period 2 informational rents is not compensated by greater profits in period 1, because the fall in the pooling rate charged to high-ability entrepreneurs, $\bar{R}/\gamma p$, fully offsets the effect of their increased effort level. The entrepreneurs appropriate all the increase in surplus, also in the first period. So the inside bank will not want to share its information if, absent information sharing, it already experiences limit pricing competition by outside banks.

To summarize, the results in this section and in Section 1.2, taken together, show that in an economy with two types of potential borrowers, information sharing is privately profitable only if there is no limit pricing competition for the better type. Only in that case, inside banks can effectively appropriate some of the rents resulting from the extra effort exerted by entrepreneurs when information is shared. But this extreme result only holds if there are two types of entrepreneurs. With more than two types, we can have cases in which the inside bank wants to share information *and* still the credit market would not collapse without information sharing.

2.2. More than Two Types of Entrepreneurs

The results of the model are considerably richer if one introduces an additional type of entrepreneur in addition to the two already present in the basic model. The new type of entrepreneur features a medium level of entrepreneurial ability, and their type is indexed by M. In fact, the payoff to their projects is $\tilde{R} < R^*$, that is, less than that obtained by H types. However, they are creditworthy, in the sense that the expected return of their projects exceeds the cost of capital $\bar{R}$ rather than being zero as for L types.

In this more general setting, one can show that [see Padilla and Pangano (1996a)]:

1. Credit markets can function in the absence of information sharing, as in Section 2.1 and in contrast with Section 1. This occurs when inside banks face limit competition for M-type and H-type entrepreneurs. In this case, creditworthy entrepreneurs enjoy some surplus, and hence exert positive effort, even when information is not shared.
2. There are parameter configurations for which information sharing is privately profitable, although not needed to avoid market collapse. If inside banks face limit pricing competition for the two creditworthy market segments, but outside banks cannot distinguish between M-type and H-type entrepreneurs, then inside banks still retain some monopoly power over H-type entrepreneurs. Hence, in contrast to Section 2.1, the impact of higher effort by H-type entrepreneurs on the inside bank's period 1 profits is not fully offset by the fall in the period 1 interest rate charged on them. If the increase in period 1 profits is sufficiently large, information sharing becomes privately profitable.
3. When information is not shared, credit is expensive and may be affordable only for top-notch borrowers, whereas if information is shared, interest rates are on average lower and loans may be extended to lower-grade borrowers.
4. The time profile of interest rates extended to individual entrepreneurs is flat if information is not shared and declines over time if it is shared.

Moreover, one obtains some predictions that specifically pertain to the cases where information sharing produces an expansion in credit market participation: in these cases, information sharing is more likely the greater the profitability of the projects of the potential borrowers (as measured against the benchmark of the banks' cost of capital), the lower the discount factor of banks, and the higher that of entrepreneurs (in a slightly more general version of the model where these two factors are allowed to differ).

Finally, the welfare implications are the same as in the basic model: in all the instances in which information sharing is profitable for banks, it is also welfare increasing for borrowers. This is true whether information sharing draws new borrowers into the market or merely reduces the interest rates faced by existing borrowers.

2.3. Elastic Individual Demand for Credit

In this section we revert to the initial assumption that there are only two types of entrepreneurs—high- and low-ability ones—but extend the model in a different direction: we assume that the scale of investment projects is endogenous and therefore that the demand for loans by each entrepreneur is elastic with respect to the interest rate. Note that if the demand for loans is elastic, the inside bank's ability to appropriate the surplus produced by its customers is reduced: as borrowers can scale down the project in response to higher interest rates, the monopolistic bank will have less scope for 'squeezing' its clientele. Since the incentive problem is less severe, one would expect that information sharing will be less needed. Indeed, there are instances in which banks will optimally refrain from communicating. Nevertheless, we show below that in this case the rationale for information sharing can survive: there are values of the parameters for which banks want to communicate their private information.

To illustrate these points, consider the following example where the only production technology available to high-ability entrepreneurs features decreasing returns to scale, the future is undiscounted ($\beta = 1$), and the total disutility of effort is given by $V(p) = hp^2/2 - dp$, where $h > 2d > 0$ (otherwise effort is always positively valued). Let us denote the number of units of capital invested by l and assume that the average product per unit invested is given by $f(l) = l^{-1/2}$, so that total output $F(l) = f(l)l$ is a concave and isoelastic function of l.[15] Then the optimal scale of an investment project undertaken at time t (once effort is sunk), given the interest rate R_t, is $l(R_t) = 1/4R_t^2$, and the associated return per unit (or average product) is $R_t^* = 2R_t > R_t \forall t$. Hence, the total discounted utility for a high-ability entrepreneur who chooses an effort level $p(i)$ is

$$U_H(p(i)) = p(i)[(R_{h1}l(R_{hi})) + (E(R_{h2})l(E(R_{h2})))] \\ - bp(i)^2/2 + dp(i), \qquad (10)$$

and, given the ex ante average probability of success p, the profits of bank h are

$$\Pi_h(p) = \gamma[(pR_{h1} - \bar{R})l(R_{h1}) + (pR_{h2} - \bar{R})l(R_{h2})]. \qquad (11)$$

Assuming that a condition analogous to Equation (2) holds, so that without information sharing banks have full monopoly power over the entrepreneurs at their respective locations, one can show that (1) when banks do not communicate the characteristics of their local clientele to rivals, p^{ns} is equal to 1 if $b < (1/4\bar{R}) + d$ and equal to $4\bar{R}d/(4\bar{R}b - 1)$ if $b > (1/4\bar{R}) + d$; $R_1^{ns} = R_2^{ns} = 2\bar{R}/p^{ns}$; (2) when banks inform their rivals, p^{is} is equal to 1 if $b < (3/8\bar{R}) + d$ and equal to $8\bar{R}d/(8\bar{R}b - 3)$ if $b > (3/8\bar{R}) + d$; $R_1^{is} = 2\bar{R}/p^{is}$, $R_2^{is} = \bar{R}/p^{is}$. So in equilibrium, $p^{is} \geq p^{ns}$, and they are both positive since $V'(0) = -d < 0$. Thus information sharing leads to lower interest rates and to an increased demand for loans.

From (1) and (2), it follows that.

1. For relatively low values of the marginal disutility of effort (low b and/or high d), effort is set at the maximum level in both regimes: if $b < (1/4\bar{R}) + d$,

---

[15] Consider the more general case where the average product per unit invested is $f(l) = l^{-1/\varepsilon}, \varepsilon > 1$ and the total disutility of effort is given by $V(p) = Ap^\alpha$, where $A > 0$ and $\alpha > 1$. In this more general case, existence of an interior solution requires $\alpha > \varepsilon$. In this section, instead, we have assumed $\alpha = \varepsilon = 2$ to keep the algebra tractable, but in exchange we had to introduce a linear term $-dp$ in function $V(\cdot)$ to ensure existence (which introduces an additional, albeit minor, departure from the assumptions of the basic model in Section 1.1).

then $p^{is} = p^{ns} = 1$. In this case, banks' profits are greater if information is not shared because information sharing dissipates informational rents without any countervailing effect on entrepreneurial effort: if $b < (1/4\bar{R}) + d$, then $\Pi^{ns}(1) > \Pi^{is}(1)$.

2. For intermediate values of the marginal disutility of effort, information sharing raises effort and banks' profits: if $(1/4\bar{R}) + d < b < 1/2\bar{R}$, then $p^{ns} < p^{is} \leq 1$ and $\Pi^{ns}(p^{ns}) < \Pi^{is}(p^{is})$.

3. Finally, for relatively large values of the marginal disutility of effort, information sharing raises effort but fails to raise banks' profits. This is because the increase in first-period profits stemming from increased effort does not outweigh the loss of informational rents in the second period: if $\max\{3/8\bar{R} + d, 1/2\bar{R}\} < b$, then $p^{ns} < p^{is} < 1$ and $\Pi^{ns}(p^{ns}) > \Pi^{is}(p^{is})$.

3. CONCLUSIONS

When banks have an informational monopoly about their borrowers, the latter's incentives can be thwarted by the fear that the return to their effort will be partly appropriated by their banks via high future interest rates. Banks can correct this incentive problem by committing to share with other lenders their private information about the quality of their customers. The resulting competitive pressure forces them to forgo opportunistic behavior in the future and encourages borrowers to perform better. As a result, information sharing among banks has two opposite effects on their profits: the borrowers' higher effort levels raise current profits (when each bank retains an informational advantage), but the fiercer competition triggered by information sharing lowers future profits. The trade-off between these two effects determines the banks' choice to sign an information sharing agreement.

At the outset of this article we focused on a setting in which this trade-off is carried to the extreme, since without communication among banks lending cannot even get off the ground: lacking the competition induced by information sharing, the inside banks' informational monopoly destroys all entrepreneurial incentives. Clearly in this case information sharing is profitable and socially efficient. Moreover, we show that it can be sustained as the equilibrium of a repeated game between long-lived banks and short-lived borrowers, provided banks have a sufficiently low discount rate and the costs of verifying private information are not too large. In this context we also formally explain why information sharing agreements are easier to sustain ex post than precommitment to low interest rates, even if they both have the same efficiency properties ex ante.

We then extend the model and show that in general the trade-off is less stark than in the basic model: the credit market can operate even if banks do not agree to communicate, and there are instances in which banks will indeed refrain from communicating. We also find that if they share information, interest rates and default rates are lower on average, and interest rates decrease over the course of the relationship between each client and his bank. In addition, the volume of lending may increase when we drop the assumption of only two types of borrowers and introduce a class of medium-quality entrepreneurs, we find that information sharing may expand the customer base; similarly, when we extend the model to the case of elastic individual demands for credit, we find that information sharing tends to increase the demand for loans. But in both these extensions the welfare implications of information sharing are the same as in the basic model: whenever banks choose to communicate, they bring about a Pareto improvement, since they raise the customers' welfare along with their own profits.

Finally, an interesting direction for further research is to investigate when banks will prefer to restrain their informational exchange to a subset of the relevant variables—for instance, providing only 'coarse' information about the quality of their customers or exchanging only data about their past defaults rather than about their quality. In a related model, Padilla and Pagano (1996b) show that partial information sharing can have stronger effects on entrepreneurial incentives than full disclosure. It remains to be shown if, in a model like that examined in this article, partial information sharing can be more profitable for banks than complete information sharing, which may explain why lenders often confine their informational exchange to 'black lists' of insolvent borrowers.

Appendix A. Proofs

Proof of Lemma 1. Under information sharing, the total discounted utility of a high-ability entrepreneur i, with a probability of success $p(i) \in [0, 1]$, denoted by $U_H(p(i)|p^{is})$, is equal to $p(i)\beta(R^* - \bar{R}/p^{is}) - V(p(i))$ if $p^{is} \geq \underline{p}$ (where p^{is} is the ex ante average repayment probability for high-ability entrepreneurs under information sharing), and is equal to 0 if $p^{is} < \underline{p}$. Hence, (1) if $p^{is} > \underline{p}$ and $\beta(R^* - \bar{R}/p^{is}) \geq V'(1)$, then $p(i) = 1$, provided that $U_H(1|p^{is}) = 0$, otherwise $p(i) = 0$; and (2) if $p^{is} \geq \underline{p}$ and $0 = V'(0) < \beta(R^* - \bar{R}/p^{is}) < V'(1)$, then there exists a unique interior optimal choice $p(i) \in (0, 1)$ such that $\beta(R^* - \bar{R}/p^{is}) = V'(p(i))$, provided that $U_H(p(i)|p^{is}) > U_H(0|p^{is}) = 0$, otherwise $p(i) = 0$. (Note that in both cases, (1) and (2), uniqueness of the optimal choice $p(i)$ follows from the global concavity of $U_H(p(i)|p^{is})$ in the relevant subspace.)

From (1) and (2) above and since in equilibrium $p(i) = p^{is} \; \forall \; i$, $R_1^{is} = R^*$, and $R_2^{is} = \bar{R}/p^{is}$, it is immediate that there may be multiple SPE for our game, which can be exhaustively characterized according to p^{is} as follows:

I $p^{is} = 0$ is always an equilibrium for our game.
II $p^{is} = 1$ provided that $\beta(R^* - \bar{R}) \geq \max\{V'(1), V(1)\}$.
III $p^{is} \in (0, 1) \,|\, \beta(R^* - \bar{R}/p^{is}) = V'(p^{is}) > 0$. (There may be several values of $p \in (0, 1)$ satisfying these conditions, which further increases the number of possible SPEs for our game.)

Equilibria of type II and type III both strictly Pareto dominate the type I equilibrium, which thus can only originate as a result of a coordination failure.

Furthermore, if an equilibrium of type II exists, then there also exists an equilibrium of type III.

To show the second part of this lemma, it is enough to find one such functional form for $V(\cdot)$. Take, for instance, $V(p) = Ap^2/2$, where $0 < A < \beta(R^* - \bar{R})$. Then, (i) $\beta(R^* - \bar{R}) > V'(1) > V(1)$ and (ii) if p^{is} solves $\beta(R^* - \bar{R}/p^{is}) = V'(p^{is}) = Ap^{is}$, then $p^{is} > \underline{p}$ and $U_H(p^{is} \mid p^{is}) > U_H(0 \mid p^{is}) = 0$ (since in equilibrium $U_H(p \mid p) = pV'(p) - V(p)$ and our functional form for $V(\cdot)$ is such that $V'(p)p > V(p)$). Hence, we have *three* SPE for our game:

I $\quad p^{is} = 0$ and the credit market collapses.
II $\quad p^{is} = 1$, $R_1^{is} = R^*$, $R_2^{is} = \bar{R}$.
III $\quad p^{is} = \frac{1}{2A}\left(\beta R^* - \sqrt{\beta^2 R^2 - 4\beta A\bar{R}}\right)$, $R_1^{is} = R^*$, $R_2^{is} = \bar{R}/p^{is}$.

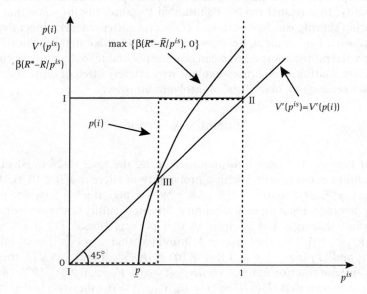

Figure 2. *Example with three equilibria*

The figure shows the choice of the probability of repayment by the individual borrower i, $p(i)$, as a function of the ex ante average probability of repayment in the regime with information sharing, p^{is}, in the basic model. The dotted line depicts individual i's best-reply function in his choice of $p(i)$. The solid 45-degree line shows the locus in which $p(i) = p^{is}$ and therefore it corresponds to the condition that the marginal disutility of effort of individual i, $V'(p(i))$, equals that of the average borrower, p^{is}. Subgame perfect equilibria correspond to points where the best-reply function and the 45-degree line intersect. In the figure, three equilibria arise: equilibrium I, which corresponds to a zero probability of repayment; equilibrium II, where repayment is certain; and equilibrium III, where the probability of repayment takes an intermediate value. In equilibrium III, borrower i is at an interior maximum in his choice of $p(i)$: in that point his marginal return from effort, shown as the curved locus $\max\{\beta(R^* - \bar{R}/p^{is}), 0\}$, equals his marginal disutility of effort, $V'(p(i))$. In the other two equilibria, the borrower is at a corner solution.

These three cases are illustrated in Figure 2, where for simplicity we set $A = 1$, so that the marginal disutility of effort $V'(p) = p$.

If, instead, $\beta(R^* - \bar{R}) < A$, then there cannot be an equilibrium involving $p^{is} = 1$. Whether there is an equilibrium with $p^{is} > 0$ or not depends on the sign of $(A - \tilde{A})$, where $\tilde{A} = \beta R^2 - 4\bar{R}$. If $A < \tilde{A}$, then there are two SPE of type III with $p_1^{is}, P_2^{is} \in (\underline{p}, 1)$ (see Figure 3a); if $A = \tilde{A}$ then there is a unique type III SPE with $p^{is} \in (\underline{p}, 1)$ (see Figure 3b); and, lastly, if $A > \tilde{A}$, then there is no SPE involving $p^{is} > 0$ (see Figure 3c). An equilibrium of type I with $p^{is} = 0$ always exists.

In conclusion, this example shows that there are functional forms for $V(\cdot)$ such that there exists at least an SPE involving $p^{is} > \underline{p} > p^{ns} = 0$ and active credit markets. The same proof goes through if $V(\cdot)$ is any power function $V(p) - Ap^\alpha$, with $\alpha > 1$ and $A > 0$ not too large (i.e., $A < \beta(R^* - R)/\alpha$). □

Proof of Proposition 2. Suppose that there was such an equilibrium, and consider the payoff to a bank that deviates from the equilibrium strategy at the end of the first period by refusing to release information on its old customers to other banks and charging the predatory rate R^* on their loans, but then reverts to the equilibrium strategy. The gains from deviating are equal to the additional profits that the bank earns on its old customers: $\gamma(p^{is}R^* - \bar{R}) > 0$. The informational assumptions of the model imply that the play of future generations is unaffected. So the bank's total payoff from deviating in the first period and then adhering to the purported equilibrium is equal to $\gamma(p^{is}R^* - \bar{R}) > 0$. Thus, the specified behavior is not consistent with Nash equilibrium. □

Proof of Proposition 3. Consider the following strategies:

1. At time t, each bank reports honestly to its competitors, and lends to the current old at its location at rate $\bar{R}/P^{is}$ and to the local entrepreneurs born at t at rate R^*, if and only if it has done so in all past periods. Otherwise it misreports the types of its current customers, lends at the monopoly rate R^* to the old local entrepreneurs of generation $t - 1$ and to the entrepreneurs of generation t in both periods of their life, and does not lend to any generation born after t.
2. Each entrepreneur born at t borrows from the local bank in both periods of his life and chooses a positive effort level $p^{is} > 0$ if and only if he has no knowledge of dishonest behavior by the bank. Otherwise he sets effort to zero and does not borrow.

The entrepreneurs' strategies are optimal because each of them cares only about payoffs in his own lifetime and thus is willing to exert positive effort if and only if the bank is expected to share its information honestly. If the bank ever refuses to report or misreports the true types of the local entrepreneurs, then local borrowers will choose to exert no effort in all subsequent generations (except for the generation whose effort is sunk when the bank deviates). Hence, the best pricing strategy of a deviant bank is to charge R^* to the current old at t, set (R^*, R^*)

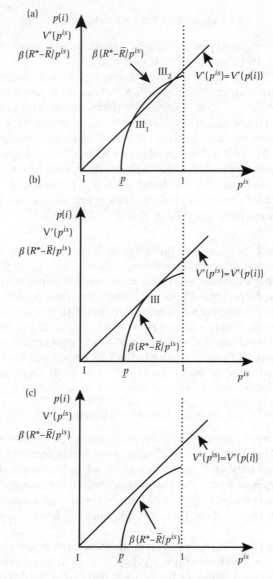

Figure 3. *Other potential equilibria configurations*

This figure shows that the basic model illustrated in Figure 2 can generate other equilibria configurations, under alternative parameter values. The interpretation of the curves in this figure is the same as in Figure 2. Panel 3a shows the situation in which there is an equilibrium where the probability of repayment is zero (point I) and two equilibria where it is positive but below unity (points III$_1$, and III$_2$). Panel 3b illustrates the case in which there are only two equilibria, one where the probability of repayment is zero (point I) and one where it is positive but below unity (point III). Finally, panel 3c depicts the case in which the only equilibrium is that corresponding to zero probability of repayment and credit market collapse (point I).

to the local entrepreneurs born at t, and then stop lending. The short-run gains from such deviation are equal to the profits made on the current old, $\gamma(P^{is}R^* - \bar{R})$, plus the extra profits to be made from the current young in the second period of their lives, $\beta\gamma(p^{is}R^* - \bar{R})$. The long-run cost incurred after a deviation is equal to the forgone profits on all generations born after the deviation, $\beta\gamma(p^{is}R^* - \bar{R})/(1 - \beta)$. Hence, the strategies (1) and (2) constitute an SPE for game 2, and information sharing is sustained in equilibrium if and only if $\beta - (1 - \beta^2) > 0$, that is, iff $\beta > \underline{\beta} \simeq 0.62$. $\quad\square$

Proof of Proposition 4. Consider the following strategies:

1. At time t, each bank reports honestly to the credit bureau and pays its membership fee c, and lends to the current old at its location at rate $\bar{R}/p^{is}$ and to the local entrepreneurs born at t at rate R^*, if and only if it has done so in all past periods. Otherwise it fails to report to the bureau and saves the membership fee c, lends to old entrepreneurs at rate R^*, lends also to the local entrepreneurs of generation t during the two periods of their life charging them the monopoly rate R^* in both periods, and stops lending to any generation born after t.
2. Each entrepreneur born at t borrows from the local bank in both periods of his life and chooses a positive effort level $p^{is} > 0$ if and only if he has no knowledge of dishonest behavior by the bank. Otherwise he sets effort to zero and does not borrow.

As in Proposition 3, the entrepreneurs' strategies are optimal given the strategies of banks. Hence we just need to consider the optimality of the banks' strategies and, in particular, their incentives to deviate, taking the entrepreneurs' strategies as given. Since membership is costly and misreporting is always detected, a deviant bank at t will save c and will not report to the credit bureau. Given that the statutes of the bureau make exclusion upon deviation automatic and readmission impossible, the threat of excluding the deviant bank from the exchange of information is credible unless a member, or a group of members, of the existing bureau quits it and forms a new bureau together with the deviator. However, the deviator has no incentive to create a new bureau. Strategy (2) implies that a deviating bank is not trusted by any future generation of entrepreneurs, who are informed of its misbehavior by the existing bureau. Hence its local customers would choose to exert no effort and the deviator would not raise any rents from lending to them. Moreover, no bank subscribing to the existing credit bureau has an incentive to create a new bureau with the deviator. First, the deviator's information has no marginal value for the remaining $N - 1$ banks, who can still reap the benefits of information sharing by exchanging it among themselves (and, due to competition, would make no profits from the information of the deviant bank). Second, creating a new bureau involves an additional fixed cost $K > 0$.

Hence, as in Proposition 3, the best pricing strategy of a deviant bank is to charge R^* to the current old at t, set (R^*, R^*) to the local entrepreneurs born at t, and then stop lending. The gains from this deviation are equal to the extra profits made on the current old, $\gamma(p^{is}R^* - \bar{R})$, plus the discounted profits to be made from the current young when old, $\beta\gamma(p^{is}R^* - \bar{R})$, *plus* the savings of all current and future membership fees, $c/(1 - \beta)$. The long-run cost incurred after a deviation equals $\beta\gamma(p^{is}R^* - \bar{R})/(1 - \beta)$, as in Proposition 3. Therefore strategies (1) and (2) constitute an SPE for game 3 and, thus, information sharing will be sustained as an equilibrium outcome of this game if and only if

$$\chi(\beta, c) = \gamma(p^{is}R^* - \bar{R})(\beta - (1 - \beta^2)) - c \geq 0.$$

Note that $\chi(\beta, c)$ is a continuous function, strictly decreasing in c and strictly increasing in β. Let c^* be such that $\chi(1, c^*) = 0$ (i.e., $c^* = \gamma(p^{is}R^* - \bar{R}) \in (0, \infty)$). For all $0 \leq c \leq c^*$, (1) there exists a value of β, $\underline{\beta}(c) \in [0, 1]$, such that $\chi(\underline{\beta}(c), c) = 0$ (since for all $0 \leq c \leq c^*$, $\chi(0, c) < 0$ and $\chi(1, c) > 0$); (2) for all $\beta \geq \underline{\beta}(c)$, $\chi(\beta, c) \geq 0$; and (3)$\underline{\beta}(0) \simeq 0.62$.   □

Appendix B. Unlimited Liability

In this appendix we extend our model to analyze the case of unlimited liability, formally proving the results stated at the end of Section 1.2. We distinguish two alternative scenarios, depending on whether failed entrepreneurs can elude past liabilities by switching banks or not. A failed entrepreneur can elude his unpaid debts by switching banks if the profitability of his project can only be observed by the current lender and cannot be verified by a third party, such as a court. We shall refer to this scenario as case 1. If instead a third party can verify the profitability of the current project at the request of a previous unpaid creditor, then switching banks does not eliminate the consequence of past defaults. We shall refer to this scenario as case 2.

Suppose that $\gamma(\hat{p}R^* + \hat{p}(1 - \hat{p})R^*) < \bar{R} < \hat{p}R^*$, so that in the absence of information sharing, in both cases the local bank enjoys monopoly power at its own town in both periods and there are effort levels for which such a monopoly power is profitable.

Case 1. Consider first the total discounted utility for a high-ability entrepreneur who chooses a success probability $p(i)$ and borrows from the inside lender I in both periods. This is equal to

$$U_H(p(i)) = p(i)\{(R^* - R_{I1}) + \beta[R^* - p(i)E(R_{I2}^{nd})$$
$$- (1 - p(i))\min(E(R_{I2}^d) + R_{I1}, R^*)]\} - V(p(i)), \tag{12}$$

where R_{I1} represents the period 1 rate charged by I, R_{I2}^{nd} is the period 2 rate charged on borrowers who repaid their period 1 loans [which occurs with probability $p(i)$], and R_{I2}^d is the period 2 rate charged on entrepreneurs who defaulted in period 1 [which occurs with probability $(1 - p(i))$]. If, instead, he borrows from the outside competitor O in period 2 at a rate R_{O2}, his utility is

$$U_H(p(i)) = p(i)[(R^* - R_{I1}) + \beta(R^* - E(R_{O2}))] - V(p(i)). \tag{13}$$

Under no information sharing, the inside bank's second-period profits are equal to $\gamma[p(pR_{I2}^{nd} + (1-p)\min(R_{I2}^d + R_{I1}, R^*)) - \bar{R}]$ and, thus, it sets R_{I2}^d such that $R_{I2}^d + R_{I1} = R^*$ for those borrowers that defaulted in period 1 and $R_{I2}^{nd} = R^*$ for those who repaid the period 1 loan. Consequently, the inside bank's second-period profits are $\gamma(pR^* - \bar{R})$. In period 1, the inside bank sets R_{I1} to maximize its total discounted profits $\gamma[(pR_{h1} - \bar{R}) + \beta(pR^* - \bar{R})]$, implying that $R_{I1} = R^*$. Given these rates, $U_H(P(i)) = -V(p(i))$ for all $p(i)$ and, therefore, $p(i) = p^{ns} = 0 \ \forall \ i$.

Under information sharing, the inside bank competes with all outside lenders. The former's period 2 profits are given above while the latter's are equal to $\gamma(pR_{O2} - \bar{R})$. Bertrand competition ensures that $R_{I2}^{nd} = R_{I2}^d + R_{I1} = R_{O2} = \bar{R}/p$ so that period 2 profits are zero. Hence outside competition effectively prevents the inside lender from recovering unpaid period 1 interest rates. In period 1, the inside bank sets R_{I1} to maximize its total discounted profits $\gamma[pR_{h1} - \bar{R}]$ so that $R_{I1} = R^*$. Given these rates, $U_H(p(i)) = p(i)[\beta(R^* - \bar{R}/p)] - V(p(i))$ so that $p(i) = p^{is} \ \forall \ i$ as characterized in Lemma 1. Hence, the level of effort, banks' profits, and borrowers utility are exactly the same as those obtained under the assumption of limited liability.

Case 2. In this case, the total discounted utility for a high-ability entrepreneur who chooses a success probability $p(i)$ is given by Equation (12) if he borrows from the inside lender in both periods. If, instead, the entrepreneur borrows from the outside competitor O in period 2, his utility is equal to

$$U_H(p(i)) = p(i)[(R^* - R_{I1}) + \beta\{R^* - p(i)E(R_{O2})$$
$$- (1 - p(i))\min(E(R_{O2}) + R_{I1}, R^*)\}] - V(p(i)). \tag{14}$$

The analysis is identical to case 1 for the no information sharing regime. Under information sharing, however, the analysis is now slightly different. Now an entrepreneur can no longer elude his previous debts by switching banks, so that $R_{I2}^{nd} = R_{I2}^d = R_{O2} = \bar{R}/p$. Hence period 2 profits are simply equal to the interest payments that are recovered from defaulting entrepreneurs: $\gamma(1-p)p \max(R_{I1}, R^* - \bar{R}/p)$. In period 1, R_{I1} maximizes its total discounted profits $\gamma[(pR_{I1} - \bar{R}) + \beta(1-p)p \max(R_{I1}, R^* - \bar{R}/p)]$ so that $R_{I1} = R^*$. Given these rates, $U_H(p(i)) = p(i)[\beta(p(i)R^* - \bar{R}/p)] - V(p(i))$. Following the same steps as in the proof of Lemma 1, we can show that there are functional forms of $V(\cdot)$ for which there exists a (Pareto nondominated) SPE such that $p^{is} > p^{ns}$, and hence, $\Pi^{is}(p^{is}) > \Pi^{is}(p^{ns}) = 0$. Note that in this case p^{is} does not coincide with that derived in Lemma 1 because there are additional incentive effects due to the unlimited liability: a negative effect, since the entrepreneur appropriates a smaller share of the investment's expected proceeds, and a positive 'disciplinary' effect, since unlimited liability makes default more costly for the entrepreneur.

REFERENCES

Allen, F., 1984, 'Reputation and Product Quality,' *Rand Journal of Economics*, 15, 311–327.

Dewatripont, M., and J. Tirole, 1994, *The Prudential Regulation of Banks*, MIT Press, Cambridge, Massachusetts.

Farrell, J., and N. T. Gallini, 1998, 'Second-sourcing as a Commitment: Monopoly Incentives to Attract Competition,' *Quarterly Journal of Economics*, 103, 673–694.

Greif, A., P. Milgrom, and B. Weingast, 1994, 'Coordination, Commitment, and Enforcement: The Case of the Merchant Guild,' *Journal of Political Economy*, 102, 742–776.

Hannan, T., 1991, 'Bank Commercial Loan Markets and the Role of Market Structure: Evidence from Surveys of Commercial Lending,' *Journal of Banking and Finance*, 15, 133–149.

Klein, B., and K. B. Leffler, 1981, 'The Role of Market Forces in Assuring Contractual Performance,' *Journal of Political Economy*, 89, 615–641.

Milgrom, P. R., D. C. North, and B. R. Weingast, 1990, 'The Role of Institutions in the Revival of Trade: The Law Merchant, Private Judges, and the Champagne Fairs,' *Economics and Politics*, 2, 1–23.

——, and J. Roberts, 1992, *Economics, Organization and Management*, Prentice-Hall, Englewood Cliffs, New Jersey.

Padilla, A. J., and M. Pagano, 1996a, 'Endogenous Communication among Lenders and Entrepreneurial Incentives,' Discussion Paper No. 1295, CEPR, January.

——, and ——, 1996b, 'Sharing Default Information as a Borrower Discipline Device,' Discussion Paper No. 73, Industry Studies Program, Department of Economics, Boston University, October.

Pagano, M., and T. Jappelli, 1993, 'Information Sharing in Credit Markets,' *Journal of Finance*, 48, 1693–1718.

Petersen, M. A., and R. G. Rajan, 1995, 'The Effect of Credit Market Competition on Lending Relationships,' *Quarterly Journal of Economics*, 110, 407–445.

Rajan, R. G., 1992, 'Insiders and Outsiders: The Choice between Informed and Arm's–Length Debt,' *Journal of Finance*, 47, 1367–1400.

Shapiro, C., 1983, 'Premiums for High-Quality Products as Returns to Reputations,' *Quarterly Journal of Economics*, 98, 559–579.

Sharpe, S., 1990, 'Asymmetric Information, Bank Lending and Implicit Contracts: A Stylized Model of Customer Relationships,' *Journal of Finance*, 45, 1069–1087.

Shepard, A., 1988, 'Licensing to Enhance Demand for New Technologies,' *Rand Journal of Economics*, 18, 360–368.

Singleton, E. S., 1992, *Introduction to Competition Law*, Pitman, London.

Van Cayseele, P., J. Bouckaert, and H. Degryse, 1994, 'Credit Market Structure and Information Sharing Mechanisms,' working paper no. 14, Katholieke Universiteit Leuven, CES.

von Thadden, E.-L., 1992, 'The Commitment of Finance, Duplicated Monitoring, and the Investment Horizon,' working paper no. 27, CEPR-ESF Network in Financial Markets.

PART IV

CREDIT MARKET IMPERFECTIONS
AND ECONOMIC ACTIVITY

11

Survival of the Fittest or the Fattest? Exit and Financing in the Trucking Industry

LUIGI ZINGALES

Most economic theories are either implicitly or explicitly based on an evolutionary argument: Competition and exit assure that only the most efficient firms survive. This argument implicitly relies on the existence of perfect capital markets. In the presence of capital market imperfections, efficient firms may be forced to exit due to lack of funds. Although this argument is well understood in theory (Telser (1966) and Bolton and Scharfstein (1990)), its empirical relevance is much less clear.

The crucial issue in trying to assess the effects of financing choices on the survival of firms and, thus, on the product market competition is the endogeneity of capital structure choices to the industry structure. If leverage affects a firm's competitive position, then the firm's financing decisions will take this into account. As a result, in the absence of a structural model we cannot determine whether it is the product market competition that affects capital structure choices or a firm's capital structure that affects its competitive position and its survival.

This paper attempts to address the endogeneity problem by looking at the effects of leverage on the survival of trucking firms after the Carter deregulation. Deregulation was an exogenous shock that unexpectedly changed both the competitive environment in which firms operate and the leverage of firms, driving the effective leverage far away from the desired one. By decreasing the value of firms' operating certificates, a sort of monopoly license, deregulation sharply increased leverage above the desired level. Also, because deregulation increased the risk in

I wish to thank Abhay Pande for interesting me in the trucking industry, and Judy Chevalier, Kent Daniel, Colin Mayer, Antonio Merlo, Marzio Galeotti, Austan Goolsbee, Charlie Himmelberg, Vojislav Maksimovic, Steve Kaplan, Anil Kashyap, Sam Peltzman, Raghu Rajan, Fabio Schiantarelli, Per Stromberg, Sheridan Titman, Rob Vishny, an anonymous referee, René Stulz (the editor), and participants at seminars at a CEPR conference on "International Perspectives on the Macroeconomic and Microeconomic Implications of Financing Constraints," in Bergamo, the University of Chicago, the London Business School, the NBER, the WFA meetings, and the AEA meetings for useful comments. Andy Pruitt provided excellent research assistance. Research expenses have been supported by the Center for the Study of the Economy and the State. The author also acknowledges financial support from the Center for Research in Security Prices and NSF grant #SBR-9423645.

the industry and made predation possible, it is likely that the target leverage decreased at the same time that firms' real leverage increased dramatically.

I study the survival of trucking companies during the eight years following the beginning of deregulation as a function of their economic efficiency (fitness) and their financial resources (fatness). I find evidence that more efficient firms are more likely to survive after deregulation, but I also find evidence that their leverage at the beginning of the deregulation period has an impact on the probability of survival eight years later. Therefore, not only the 'fittest' but also the 'fattest' firms survive.

This result might appear obvious. It is well known that firms in a weak financial position are more likely to go bankrupt; this may be true independent of any effects of financing on a firm's competitive position. To address this issue, I try to control for the ex ante risk of default by using Altman's (1973) Z-score method. Even after controlling for the ex ante probability of default, leverage still has a negative and statistically significant impact on survival. I also show that this effect is not present in the early years after deregulation, but is concentrated in the 1980 to 1985 period, when the industry shakeout was more dramatic. Interestingly, this effect is not homogeneous across different segments of the industry. It is most pronounced in the segment that remains imperfectly competitive even after deregulation, and it is zero in the segment that becomes fully competitive.

I also try to probe deeper into the reasons why debt may jeopardize survival. In particular, I look at the investments undertaken by motor carriers after deregulation and their pricing policy as a function of their initial level of leverage.

I find that the initial level of leverage has a negative impact on the ability of a motor carrier to invest in the years following deregulation. The effect is particularly pronounced in those companies that are eventually forced to exit, suggesting that the underinvestment problem caused by the high debt level might have forced these firms out of the market.

I also find evidence that the prederegulation level of leverage negatively impacts the price per ton-mile that a carrier charged during the price war that followed deregulation. This effect is entirely concentrated in the less competitive segment of the industry.

This paper is part of a growing literature on the interaction between capital structure and product market competition. Besides a very early article by Spence (1985), the pioneer works in this area are Phillips (1995) and Chevalier (1995a, 1995b). They study the effects of leverage on price competition and exit in industries that experienced a large number of leveraged buyouts (LBOs). Both find significant effects of the LBOs on the competitive environment, under the form of increased prices and increased exit. Similarly, Kovenock and Phillips (1997) use plant-level data to analyze the impact of a company's leverage on its plant closing decisions in industries where at least one of the major players undertook an LBO. They find that debt affects plant closing and investment decisions only in highly concentrated industries.

The interpretation of all these results, however, is made controversial by the fact that the decision to undertake an LBO is not necessarily exogenous with respect to the competitive environment in which a prospective LBO firm operates. If the managers of LBO firms anticipated the ultimate outcome of their actions, it would be impossible to distinguish whether these outcomes are the desired effects that LBOs tried to achieve in the first place or their unwanted side effects.

A step forward in addressing the endogeneity problem is represented by Chevalier and Scharfstein (1996). They look at supermarkets' profit margins during recessions in regional markets differentially affected by LBOs. To the extent that some major recessions (like the Texas oil shock) are unexpected or very unlikely ex ante and that these recessions change the very nature of the competitive environment, it is possible to interpret the results in a causal sense. A related paper by Holtz-Eakin, Jouflaian, and Rosen (1994) studies the effects of liquidity constraint on survival by using an exogenous shock. They study the impact of inheritance on the probability of survival of small entrepreneurial firms.

The rest of the paper proceeds as follows. Section I provides some back-ground information on the characteristics of the trucking industry before and after deregulation. Section II describes the competing hypotheses on the effects of financial variables on the survival of firms and explains why the natural experiment represented by trucking deregulation helps identify these effects. Section III introduces the reader to the new dataset used in this paper. Section IV presents the results on the determinants of survival and Section V discusses the possible sources of this effect. Finally, Section VI concludes.

I. THE TRUCKING INDUSTRY

Interstate motor carriers were brought under federal regulation by the Motor Carrier Act of 1935, designed 'to protect the public interest by maintaining an orderly and reliable transportation system, by minimizing duplications of services, and by reducing financial instability.' The act exempted the trucking industry from the antitrust law and required all interstate motor carriers to file their rates with the Interstate Commerce Commission (ICC), which had the authority to set minimum rates and suspend rate cuts. Similarly, the ICC had the power to regulate entry into the industry through the concession of operating certificates. The ICC followed a policy of not granting authority to serve a route already being served if the existing carriers provided adequate service.

As a result of this regulation, rates were above marginal costs, as shown by the fact that the operating certificates were priced at 15 to 20 percent of carrier annual revenue (Breen (1977)). Besides the holders of the operating certificates, the other big beneficiaries of regulation were the unionized employees (International Brotherhood of Teamsters) who, according to Moore (1978), earned 30 percent more than similar workers in unregulated carriers.

The deregulation process began as a change in policy at the ICC level and was sanctioned by the passage of the Motor Carrier Act of 1980. The appointment of

Daniel O'Neal as a chairman of the ICC in 1977 was instrumental in this change. A detailed chronology of the events and their impacts on the stock prices of publicly traded carriers is contained in Rose (1985) and Schipper, Thompson, and Weil (1987). In sum, between 1978 and 1979 the ICC reversed its policy toward entry, accepting well over 90 percent of new service applications and beginning to liberalize rate settings. The effect was a substantial drop in the stock market value of trucking companies and a reduction in the premium of unionized workers in the trucking industry (Rose (1987)).

The deregulation effects on the entire industry were devastating. Carriers started to compete on price. As the president of a Teamsters local viewed it, 'the rate cutting is horrible. The shippers are pitting one trucking company against the other. I heard that one cut the rate 47 percent.'[1] As a result of this new intense price competition, between 1980 and 1985 a total of 4,589 trucking companies across the nation shut down, compared to 1,050 that closed between 1975 and 1980.[2] At the same time the industry experienced a huge wave of new entries. The number of carriers at the end of 1983 was about 40 percent higher than the number that existed when the Motor Carrier Act went into effect.[3] In many cases unionized trucking companies were closing to leave room for new, nonunionized companies.

There is no question, then, that the regulatory reform of the late 1970s changed the competitive environment of the trucking industry (see also Winston (1993)). However, there might be some question about how expected this event was when it took place. Had this event been perfectly anticipated, its effects would have already been reflected in the financing policy of trucking firms. Rose (1985) mentions that some initial steps for industry reform were taken by the ICC as early as 1975, with the main activity taking place in the 1978 to 1979 period. In a subsequent paper, Rose (1987) adopts the convention of dating deregulation from 1979. From an analysis of the S&P Industry Outlook of those years, I conclude that it is probably safe to take 1977 as the watershed. In that year, the industry report stated: 'The industry will continue to be faced with the threat of regulatory reform.... However, given the strong opposition of the Teamsters' union, the successful lobbying campaign by the industry, and the opposition of the ICC, the materialization of any serious threat over the near term remains unlikely.' The large decline in stock prices during the 1978 to 1980 period (see Rose (1985) and Schipper et al. (1987)) confirms that deregulation was largely unanticipated, and that deregulation hit the industry during that period.

In studying the trucking industry, it is important to keep in mind its division into two fairly different segments: the truckload (TL), with shipments of 10,000 pounds or more, and the less-than-truckload (LTL), with shipments of less than 10,000 pounds. The TL segment is characterized by easy-to-finance capital investment and facility of market entry (in the absence of regulation). The LTL segment

---

[1] United Press International, January 19, 1986.   [2] Ibid.
[3] *The New York Times*, December 13, 1983.

requires large capital investments to create hubs and generate a network able to distribute loads across different trucks, minimizing empty backhaul mileage.[4]

The competitive pressure was experienced differently in the two segments. According to Moore (1986), rates in the TL sector fell 25 percent from 1977 to 1982. During the same period the LTL rates fell only 12 percent. The source of competition was also different. The TL segment suffered from both the entry of new carriers and the expansion of private carriers (businesses that haul their own products). By contrast, the LTL segment quickly became crowded with existing carriers that expanded in the LTL market as a way to refocus their operating strategy in the face of entry by nonunionized carriers in the TL market.

II. THE COMPETING HYPOTHESES

A. The Theoretical Predictions

This paper addresses two related questions. First, how does leverage affect a firm's ability to respond to unexpected changes in the competitive environment? Second, what are the sources of these effects? In this section, I briefly summarize what theory has to say about these two questions and how my 'natural experiment' helps test these predictions.

If a firm's financial structure is irrelevant, then I should find no effects of the initial leverage on a firm's ability to survive, provided I can properly control for a firm's efficiency level. Otherwise, there are three main reasons why the prederegulation level of leverage may negatively impact a motor carrier's survival during deregulation.

First, the initial level of debt may negatively affect survival because highly indebted firms may be unable to finance large new investments (Myers (1977)). This debt overhang might force leveraged firms to pass up profitable growth opportunities and, in the most extreme cases, even force them out of the market. As Myers (1977) points out, this problem is more likely to arise when investments cannot be collateralized easily. Therefore, debt overhang should not in general be a very serious problem for TL trucking companies, which have easy-to-collateralize assets. LTL carriers, however, might suffer more, because a larger fraction of their assets is intangible.

Second, the initial level of debt may negatively affect survival because it directly affects a firm's ability to compete. For example, in Bolton and Scharfstein (1990), shallow-pocket firms are prone to predation by deep-pocket competitors. This predation may force highly leveraged firms to lose their market share or even

[4] As Glaskowsky (1986) points out, while the TL segment of the industry is fairly close to the textbook definition of a competitive market, with no significant economies of scale, very low barriers to entry and many atomistic players, "the LTL carrier segment is *not* atomistic in any sense of the word. A small and still shrinking group of increasingly large firms dominates this traffic nationally. LTL operations *do* have significant economies of scale. The established large national LTL carriers are beneficiaries of an almost insurmountable financial barrier to entry: their large and widespread terminal networks." The emphasis is in the original text.

exit the industry. This effect should be present only in less competitive industries, because only in the presence of some barriers to entry can the predator recover the short-run costs of preying in the long run. Alternatively, a high level of leverage may affect a firm's competitiveness because customers avoid dealing with a company that is likely to go bankrupt (Titman (1984)), or because the leverage affects a firm's incentive to maintain its reputation for producing a high-quality product (Maksimovic and Titman (1991)). All of these effects should be unimportant for TL carriers, which provide a standardized service, but they may be relevant for LTL companies.

Finally, the initial level of debt may negatively affect survival, because it forces inefficient firms to liquidate (Harris and Raviv (1990) and Stulz (1990)). Note that here, unlike in the two previous examples, a negative correlation between survival and leverage is not evidence of a cost, but of a benefit of debt. The costs of liquidating a TL versus an LTL carrier are likely to be very different. Most of TL carriers' assets are represented by trucks, which can be liquidated at no significant cost. By contrast, part of the value of an LTL carrier comes from its terminal network and its sales organization, which are more costly to liquidate. As a result, it is plausible that the reduction in profitability produced by deregulation makes it optimal to liquidate more TL carriers than LTL ones. It follows, then, that debt should have a stronger negative impact on survival of TL carriers, rather than LTL ones.

On the other hand, there are two main reasons why the preregulation level of leverage may positively impact a motor carrier's survival during deregulation.

First, debt might force firms into restructuring sooner (Jensen (1989)), maximizing their chances of survival. This might be particularly true in the trucking industry, where one of the biggest problems of existing firms was to convince unionized workers to accept wage cuts. For example, Perotti and Spier (1993) have modeled the benefits of debt in extracting wage concessions from unions. If this is the case, then highly indebted carriers should be able to address their wage bargaining problems sooner and more effectively and, by so doing, should be more likely to survive. Because the TL market is more likely to be nonunion and to pay competitive wages (through purchased transportation agreements), this effect is likely to be more pronounced in the LTL sector.

Second, a highly leveraged firm may compete more aggressively because of the option-like payoff of leveraged equity (Brander and Lewis (1986)). If ex post an aggressive expansion turned out to be the winning strategy, then I should find that more highly leveraged firms are more likely to survive in the post deregulation period. This argument should apply mainly to the LTL segment of the industry because of its less competitive structure.

B. The Nature of the Experiment

As it is well known, any attempt to investigate the effects of financial variables on real variables is affected by two econometrics problems. First, capital structure choices are endogenous and, in the absence of an accepted structural model, we cannot determine whether, for instance, it is the product market competition that affects capital structure choices or rather the firms' capital structure that affects their competitive position and, eventually, their survival. Second, an econometrician can only observe imperfect proxies of the firm's characteristics that determine its capital structure and its performance. As a result, a correlation between the initial financial position and the probability of exit may arise even if there is no causal relationship between the two, simply because both a company's debt level and its survival are affected by the same company's characteristics that are unobservable to the econometrician.

The 'natural experiment' provided by trucking deregulation helps address the first problem in several ways. First, motor carrier deregulation brought a major and unexpected change in the competitive structure of the trucking industry. During the regulated period firms had been barred from price competition and isolated from new entry, but beginning in 1979 they suddenly faced intense price competition and massive new entry. This change in the competitive environment is exogenous with respect to trucking firms' leverage and their performance.[5] Because this exogenous change in the competitive environment was largely unexpected, it is difficult to argue that the capital structure was optimally chosen beforehand to deal with it. As a result, I can try to separate the undesired effects of debt from the desired ones by estimating the effect of debt on exit after controlling for the expected defaults under the preexisting conditions.

Second, not only did deregulation change the product market environment, but it directly affected firms' capital structure. In fact, a significant portion of a motor carrier's assets was represented by the value of the operating certificates. In many cases, these were also used as a collateral for bank loans. I have estimated that in the 1977 to 1980 period the market-to-book value ratio of assets of publicly traded trucking firms dropped by 20 percent. This translates into a sudden and unwanted increase in the effective level of leverage. As a result, it is likely that motor carriers found themselves excessively leveraged. This is especially true if one considers the increased uncertainty that followed deregulation.

Third, the nature of the sample makes it very unlikely that companies could promptly adjust their capital structure to the deregulation shock. In fact, most of the firms in my sample are small, privately held firms with little or no access to the public equity or bond markets. This makes it harder for them to quickly readjust the leverage after a negative shock such as the loss of the operating rights value and the change in the competitive environment.

The natural experiment of deregulation, though, does not resolve by itself the second problem: the possibility of spurious correlation due to unobservable characteristics. I address this problem in three ways. First, I address it directly, by

---

[5] One could claim that regulatory actions are not independent of the economic performance. Although this argument is generally valid, it does not seem to fit well the trucking deregulation. For instance, Rothenberg, as cited in Rose (1987), argues that motor carrier deregulation was largely independent of interest lobbying activity. In fact, both the American Trucking Association and the Teamsters Union aggressively opposed deregulation.

using a wide variety of control variables that should help capture all firms' characteristics. Second, I look for evidence of the mechanism by which an excessive amount of debt forces exit. In particular, I focus on its effect on investment and on pricing. Third, I divide the sample according to a carrier's percentage of LTL revenues and estimate the impact of debt across different groups. Because the theories discussed above suggest that debt has different impacts for high and low LTL carriers, in a linear probability model I can use this splitting as an instrumental variable.[6] In this way, my estimate of the differential effect of debt on survival across groups is consistent even if there are unobservable firm characteristics correlated with leverage.

III. THE DATA

As a consequence of the Motor Carrier Act of 1935, each regulated motor carrier holding interstate operating authority is required to file a calendar year report. In this report, trucking companies have to disclose not only financial variables but also operating statistics, like the number of shipments made, the total number of ton-miles hauled, etc. The level of disclosure depends on the size of the carrier. Before 1980, carriers with gross revenue above $500,000 (Class I and Class II) filed comprehensive reports, including operating statistics. Carriers with gross annual revenues above $100,000 but below $500,000 (Class III) had to file brief statements. In 1980, the minimum threshold for Class II carriers was increased to $1,000,000 and Class III carriers were released from filing. The data used for this paper come from the American Trucking Association, which has been collecting and reclassifying ICC filings since 1976.

To determine the survival after deregulation, I have to establish when the deregulation shock hit the industry, and when the transition to a more competitive industry can be considered to be accomplished. On the basis of the stock price evidence and of the industry report I identify three periods: the pre-1978

---

[6] Assume that, after partialing out the observable measures of qualities, the true relationship between survival and leverage is given by $y = x\beta + z\gamma + \epsilon$, where x is leverage and z is an unobservable measure of quality. The concern is that $\text{cov}(z, x) \neq 0$ so that $\hat{\beta}$ is inconsistent. In particular, I am concerned that $\text{cov}(z, x) < 0$; that is, worse quality firms are more highly leveraged. This is the case in a pecking order theory à la Myers (1984), where firms become highly leveraged because they are unprofitable. In this case, however, $\text{cov}(z, x)$ will be the same across different market segments. I can, then, divide the sample in high LTL carriers and high TL carriers. In a linear probability model the estimate of the impact of leverage on survival in the two groups is given by

$$\hat{\beta}_{LTL} = \beta_{LTL} + \frac{\text{cov}(z, x)}{\text{var}(x)} \gamma_{LTL} + \frac{\text{cov}(z, x)}{\text{var}(x)} \epsilon_{LTL}$$

and

$$\hat{\beta}_{TL} = \beta_{TL} + \frac{\text{cov}(z, x)}{\text{var}(x)} \gamma_{TL} + \frac{\text{cov}(z, x)}{\text{var}(x)} \epsilon_{TL}.$$

If the impact of quality on survival is similar between the two groups (i.e., $\gamma_{TL} = \gamma_{LTL}$), then it is easy to see that the difference between the two estimated coefficients is a consistent estimate of the true difference between the two coefficients.

years can be considered a fully regulated period, 1978 to 1980 represents a transition period, and the post-1980 years represent the deregulation period. By reviewing the S&P Industry Outlooks for every year since 1977, I decided that the industry transition was complete by 1985. The 1982 to 1983 recession hit the trucking industry particularly hard and caused enormous exits. However, by 1984 to 1985 profits and rates in the industry became more stable. This can be considered as the first period in which the industry returned to normal.

Thus, my dataset consists of all ICC filings collected by the ATA for the period 1976 to 1985. As a result of the higher threshold for disclosure and the reduction in Class I and Class II carriers following deregulation, the number of carriers in the dataset drops from 2,897 in 1976 to 1,922 in 1985.

The ICC divides carriers into 13 categories as a function of the goods hauled: from general freight to household goods, from package (courier) to bulk commodities, etc. These categories can be thought of as different market segments. Specialized commodity carriers, for example, use different trucks, which cannot be easily adapted to carry general freight. As Table I shows, general freight carriers are by far the largest group (41 percent of the carriers). They are required to disclose more detailed information than specialized carriers. For both of these

Table I. *Industry segments in 1977*

Commodity	Frequency	Percent
General freight	1,300	41.27
Household goods	248	7.87
Heavy machinery	80	2.54
Petroleum products	162	5.14
Refrigerated liquids	12	0.38
Refrigerated solids	143	4.54
Dump trucking	84	2.67
Agricultural commodity	97	3.08
Motor vehicles	49	1.56
Armored truck service	2	0.06
Building materials	135	4.29
Films & Associated commodities	5	0.16
Forest products	22	0.70
Mine ores not including coal	5	0.16
Retail store delivery service	26	0.83
Dangerous and hazardous materials	7	0.22
Other commodities not elsewhere classified	773	24.54
Total	3,150	100.00

Note: This table reports the distribution by main activity (types of goods hauled) of the 3,150 carriers reporting to the Interstate Commerce Commission (ICC) in 1977. These categories can be thought of as different market segments. The data used come from the American Trucking Association, which has been collecting and reclassifying ICC filings since 1976. In the rest of the paper, I focus only on general freight carriers.

L. Zingales

reasons, I restrict my analysis to this segment of the market. This guarantees greater homogeneity within the sample used and greater availability of data.

A. Definition of Exit

For the purpose of this study it is important to understand how I measure exit. I consider that a firm exits when it disappears from the ATA dataset. Trucking firms keep reporting to the ICC even if they are acquired, as long as they are separately operated. Each one has its own identification number, so name changes should have no impact. As a result, firms disappear from the dataset if they are liquidated (both voluntary liquidation and bankruptcy) or if they are acquired and merged with the acquiring firm. Therefore, by using the disappearance from the ATA dataset as an indication of exit, I measure the survival of a trucking company as a separate organization.

During the postderegulation period exit took place not only through bankruptcy, but also through voluntary liquidation. ICC reports show that, during the 1979 to 1985 period, 1,328 Class I, II, and III interstate motor carriers ceased operations for 'legal, personal, economic or labor reasons,' not involving bankruptcy.[7] Although the different ways in which firms exit from a market are also an interesting subject, the objective of this paper is to test whether the most efficient organizations survived, regardless of the way they were financed. The measure I obtained seems appropriate for this scope.

Firms exit from my dataset also because they fall below the minimum level of revenues that mandates disclosure ($500,000 up to 1979, $1 million afterward). Although a significant drop in revenues can be regarded as an indication of failure in the marketplace, I do not want to consider as exited those firms that have a temporary drop in sales. For this reason, I classify a carrier as exited in year t only if it is not present in the dataset in that year and does not appear in any subsequent year, up to and including 1985.

Furthermore, to reduce this problem and to try to eliminate the bias induced by the change in disclosure requirements during the sample period, I restrict my analysis to companies having at least $1 million in revenues in 1977. Note that, given the high level of inflation in those years, a carrier with $1 million in revenues in 1977 will easily qualify as a Class II carrier in 1980 even with a significant drop in real revenues.[8]

B. Summary Statistics

Table II presents summary statistics for Class I and II general freight carriers with more than $1 million in revenues in 1977. In that year there were 941 firms satisfying these criteria.

---

[7] Cited in Glaskowsky (1986).

[8] The results are not sensitive to the level of this cutoff. In fact, the pre-1980 exits appear to be uncorrelated with leverage.

Table II. *Summary statistics*

Variable	Definition
Panel A: Variable Definitions	
Average load	Ton-miles/Total miles
Average haul	Ton-miles hauled/Tons of revenue freight
Cost per ton-mile	Operating expenses/Ton-miles hauled
Coverage	EBITDA/Interest expenses
Debt	Short term + Long term debt + Advance payables
Debt-to-capital	Debt/(Debt + Equity)
Intangibles	Intangibles/Total assets
Labor cost	(Wages + Benefits)/Operating costs
Net debt-to-capital	(Debt − Cash reserves)/(Debt + Equity)
Market share	Operating revenues/Total operating revenues of carriers in the same state
Proportion LTL revenues	Freight revenues up to 10,000 pounds/Freight revenues
Return on assets	EBITDA/Total assets
Return on sales	EBITDA/Operating revenues
Revenue per ton-mile	Operating revenues/Ton-miles hauled

Variable	Mean	Median	Std. Dev.	Min.	Max.	Diff.	p-value	Obs.
Panel B: Summary Statistics								
Revenues ($ million)	15.0	3.25	47.52	0.90	684	6.33	0.041	941
Assets ($ million)	6.88	1.22	2.41	0.05	355	4.08	0.009	941
Debt-to-capital	0.40	0.35	0.30	0.00	1.00	−0.10	0.000	940
Net debt-to-capital	0.22	0.20	0.38	−0.97	1.00	−0.13	0.000	910
Coverage	27.33	9.78	33.42	0.00	100	10.96	0.000	923
Return on assets	0.18	0.18	0.13	−0.45	0.88	0.07	0.000	939
Return on sales	0.08	0.07	0.06	−0.43	0.52	0.04	0.000	941
Intangibles	0.06	0.03	0.08	0.00	0.64	−0.01	0.005	930
Labor cost	0.48	0.54	0.18	0.01	0.88	−0.03	0.005	939
Revenue per ton-mile	0.32	0.21	0.42	0.02	6.9	−0.03	0.405	773
Cost per ton-mile	0.41	0.21	0.70	0.00	6.87	−0.09	0.059	768
Proportion LTL revenues	0.58	0.66	0.27	0.00	1.00	0.00	0.949	649
Average load	10.32	10.04	5.33	0.47	36.54	0.26	0.502	772
Average haul	227.15	169.40	209.92	6.93	1713	−27.70	0.105	606
Market share	0.05	0.01	0.12	0.00	1.00	0.02	0.016	941
Number of employees	418.46	86.25	1405.37	2.00	26,035	184.36	0.048	906

Note: Data are presented for the population of 941 general freight carriers with more than $1 million in operating revenues in 1977. Variables are defined in Panel A and are averages of the 1976 and 1977 values. Advance payables include any notes payable. Negative book values of equity are set equal to zero. Coverage is set equal to zero when earnings before interest, taxes, and depreciation (EBITDA) are less than or equal to zero and is set equal to 100 when coverage is greater than or equal to 100. Observations with a return on assets larger than 1 or smaller than −1 are set equal to missing. The difference column (Diff.) reports the difference in means between carriers that were still alive in 1985 and carriers that were not alive at that date. The p-values refer to the null hypothesis that the difference between the two means is equal to zero.

A particularly detailed level of disclosure is requested of the so-called Instruction 27 carriers. These are carriers that derive on average 75 percent or more of their revenues from the intercity transportation of general commodities (approximately 60 percent of general freight carriers). Information for total ton-miles hauled, number of shipments made, and percentage of shipments of more or less than 10,000 pounds tends to be present only for these carriers. Therefore, whenever I use this information, I lose 20 to 30 percent of the observations.

As the preregulation level of all the variables I use the average of the 1976 and 1977 values. The extremely high return on assets (ROA), equal to 18 percent, can be viewed as a sign of the rents enjoyed by trucking companies during the regulation era. Similarly, return on sales (ROS) is 8 percent. Another effect of regulation is the high value of intangibles as a fraction of assets (6 percent). Operating certificates bought from other carriers are included under this category. This is simply a rough estimate of the true value of operating certificates, because only the certificates recently acquired (through a direct purchase or a merger) are valued fully.

Leverage measured as total debt divided by total debt plus book equity is 40 percent (median 35 percent). By subtracting cash reserves from the total debt, the mean leverage becomes 22 percent (median 20 percent). It is difficult to judge whether these are high or low levels of leverage, because very little is known about the capital structure of privately held companies (as most of these are). What makes the comparison even harder is that firms are required to file with the ICC on a nonconsolidated basis. As a benchmark, I collected data for the 66 trucking firms present in COMPUSTAT in 1977 (SIC codes 4210 to 4213). For these firms the ratio of debt to capital is 44 percent, not very different from the ICC sample.

The book value of leverage probably overestimates the actual leverage before deregulation, because the book value of equity does not include the market value of monopoly profits (except for the recently traded operating certificates). A more appropriate measure of actual leverage before deregulation is provided by the level of coverage (earnings before interest, taxes, and depreciation over interest expenses).[9] A median coverage of 9.8 gives a sense of the rather healthy financial conditions of the trucking industry before deregulation. The book leverage, however, is probably a good estimate of the market leverage after deregulation, when operating certificates became worthless.

During the 1977 to 1985 period 57 percent of general freight carriers with more than $1 million in revenues exited the industry. Of those, 22 percent exited in the 1977 to 1980 period, and 35 percent exited between 1980 and 1985.

Although the trucking industry did not grow very much during the period, surviving trucking companies experienced substantial growth during both sub-periods. For carriers surviving up to 1980 the average rate of nominal growth in revenues during the 1977 to 1980 period is 40 percent. The same rate during the 1980 to 1985 period for carriers surviving up to 1985 is 92 percent.

---

[9] Whenever EBITDA is negative I put the value of coverage to zero. If coverage exceeds 100 or the interest expenses are zero I artificially equate coverage to 100.

C. The TL versus LTL Distinction

In the following analysis, an important role is played by the distinction between TL carriers and LTL carriers. Ideally, we would like to compare 'pure' TL carriers with 'pure' LTL carriers. As the summary statistics indicate, however, there is no such clear-cut distinction. In 1977, most carriers hauled both truck loads and less-than-truck loads, and on average 58 per cent of general-freight carrier revenues came from LTL shipments.

To try to disentangle the differential effects of leverage in these two different segments of the market, I create three groups: carriers with less than 30 percent of their revenues in LTL, carriers with 30 to 70 percent in LTL, and carriers with more than 70 percent in LTL. In 1977, among those carriers that reported information about their revenues per class of weight, there are 113 carriers in the first group, 266 in the second, and 270 in the third. The attrition rate is identical in the two extreme groups (59 percent), it is slightly higher in the middle one (67 percent).

D. Ex Ante Differences between Survivors and Non-Survivors

Before turning to a multivariate analysis, it is interesting to analyze the ex ante differences in financial and operating characteristics of carriers as a function of their fate in 1985. This is done in the sixth and seventh columns of Table II, Panel B.

Survivors tend to be larger firms, with higher profitability and lower leverage. In particular, the 1977 return on sales of future survivors is 4 percentage points higher, while ROA is 7 percentage points higher. This result suggests that deregulation did, on average, select more efficient firms. This finding is confirmed by cost per mile (9 cents per ton-mile lower for survivors), although this difference is not statistically significant at conventional levels. Quite surprisingly, survivors tend to have lower revenues (3 cents) per ton-mile. This might be an effect of the fact that carriers who used to enjoy large monopoly rents are less likely to survive. The same effect is observed in the fraction of intangibles: survivors have on average 1 percent fewer assets represented by intangibles. If the value of operating certificates reflected in intangibles is an indication of the degree of monopoly enjoyed by a certain carrier in its routes, this fact suggests that survivors are firms that enjoyed lower monopoly rents during the regulation era. It is remarkable how much lower was the 1977 level of leverage of firms that survived. The median ratio of debt over debt plus equity for survivors is 0.30, while for nonsurvivors it is 0.41. The difference is similar when I subtract cash reserves: 0.13 versus 0.27.[10]

---

[10] One might wonder whether these differences in leverage simply reflect differences in the investment opportunities across firms (for example, see Smith and Watts (1992)). However, Rajan and Zingales (1995) show that the negative relation between investment opportunities (measured as Tobin's q) and leverage appears to be mainly driven by equity issuers. Because almost all the firms in this sample are privately held (and thus cannot issue equity at wish), this negative correlation is not likely to be a major source of concern.

Motor carriers can differ substantially in their cost structures. Some carriers rely mostly on employees for their shipments, others contract out a significant amount of transportation services. Contracting out transportation services was often used to prevent the unionization of the workforce.

The proportion of wage and benefits over total operating expenses captures these differences in cost and degree of unionization, because transportation services contracted out are recorded as purchased transportation and, thus, they reduce the fraction of reported labor cost over operating expenses. Interestingly, survivors have a significantly smaller percentage of their operating costs accounted for by wages.

By contrast, there is no statistically significant difference between the average haul and the average load of survivors versus nonsurvivors. Similarly, the percentage of LTL revenue is not significantly different for survivors.

IV. THE EFFECT OF LEVERAGE ON SURVIVAL

The first question I want to answer empirically is whether initial leverage has any effect on a firm's probability of surviving, beyond what efficiency considerations would suggest. In a perfect capital market world the survival and the growth of a firm should be entirely determined by its efficiency characteristics. Therefore, the null hypothesis is

$$Pr\{\text{survival in } 1985\}_i = f(X_i^{1985}) + v_i, \tag{1}$$

where X_i is a measure of firm i's efficiency. Unfortunately, X_i^{1985} is not observable for the firms that exited. Even if it was, I would not necessarily want to use it because the observed level of efficiency might be affected by the preexisting level of leverage. However, I can use some ex ante efficiency measures as a proxy for a motor carrier level of expected efficiency in the absence of any real impact of financial variables. In other words, I use X_i^{1977} as a proxy for X_i^{1985}.

This substitution corresponds to the assumption that the prederegulation level of efficiency is linked to the postderegulation one. As long as surviving companies are concerned, this assumption is supported by the data (for instance, the level of return on sales (ROS) in 1985 is statistically and economically significantly related to the level of ROS in 1977). Nevertheless, one potential concern is that the preexisting level of leverage is correlated to some unobservable characteristics that determine future efficiency. In what follows, I present a series of proxies designed to address this concern.

In sum, the basic regression relates a firm's status in 1985 to financial and operating variables in 1977, or

$$Pr\{\text{survival in } 1985\}_i = f(X_i^{1977}, Lev_i^{1977}) + \epsilon_i, \tag{2}$$

where Lev_i is a measure of financial leverage.

Table III presents the results of estimating equation (2) through a probit model. For ease of interpretation, I report the coefficients as the derivative of the probability of survival with respect to the corresponding right-hand-side variable computed at the mean of the dependent variable. This represents the marginal impact of a change in the explanatory variable.

In the basic specification the explanatory variables, besides leverage, are: return on sales, a company's size (logarithm of the level of the average sales in 1976 and 1977), the level of intangibles (as a fraction of total assets), the proportion of wages over total costs, and nine regional dummies.

Return on sales is chosen as a main measure of efficiency for two reasons. It is directly related to the operating ratio (operating expenses over operating revenues), which is the leading efficiency index used in the trucking industry. Second, it is less sensitive than return on assets to misvaluation of assets or to the extent to which some transportation is done with 'for hire' trucks.

Table III. *Effect of initial leverage on the probability of survival*

Independent variables	I	II	III
Net debt-to-capital	−0.180***	−0.180***	
	(0.049)	(0.048)	
log(1 + Coverage)			0.042***
			(0.016)
Return on sales	2.878***		2.584***
	(0.347)		(0.363)
Return on assets		0.925***	
		(0.134)	
log(Revenues)	0.048***	0.044***	0.043***
	(0.014)	(0.014)	(0.014)
Intangibles			
	−0.299	−0.583**	−0.355
	(0.249)	(0.245)	(0.245)
Labor cost			
	−0.324***	−0.233**	−0.319***
	(0.103)	(0.103)	(0.102)
Pseudo-R^2	0.12	0.09	0.11
N	889	887	902

***, **, * Significantly different from zero at the 1 percent level or less, at the 5 percent level, or at the 10 percent level, respectively.

Note: The dependent variable is the probability that a general freight motor carrier with more than $1 million in revenues in 1977 survives until 1985. The reported coefficients are probit estimates of the effect of a marginal change in the corresponding regressor on the probability of survival, computed at the average of the dependent variable. All the independent variables are measured as of 1977 (average of the 1976 and 1977 values). Net debt-to-capital is total debt minus cash reserves divided by total debt plus equity. Intangibles is the ratio of intangible assets to total assets. Labor cost is the ratio of the wages and benefits to operating costs. Among the independent variables there are also nine regional dummies (not reported). Standard errors are reported in parentheses.

A measure of size is inserted for various reasons. Size might be a proxy for efficiency, because only efficient firms become big.[11] Larger firms may also have more bargaining power on the product market and/or have easier access to financing. Finally, size may matter for spurious reasons, because small firms are more likely to fall below the threshold that requires them to file with the ICC. All these explanations predict a positive impact of size on the chances of survival.

I insert the level of intangible assets as a proxy for the extent to which a carrier enjoyed monopoly rents before deregulation. This is admittedly a poor proxy, because only recently acquired operating certificates appear in the balance sheet.[12] It is important, though, to attempt to control for monopoly rents before deregulation because the measure of efficiency used (ROS) is distorted by the presence of monopoly rents. For a given level of profitability, a higher degree of monopoly indicates that a firm is less efficient. The level of intangibles, then, is expected to have a negative effect on survival.

A high proportion of wage and benefits over total operating expenses reflects a limited role of purchased transportation and/or a more expensive labor force. Because both these phenomena are generally associated with unionization, a high proportion of wage and benefits can also be interpreted as a proxy for unionization. All these factors are likely to have a negative impact on a firm's ability to survive in a deregulated environment.

Finally, regional dummies are inserted to control for possible heterogeneity across different areas. Carriers are attributed to one of the nine geographical groups established by the ICC on the basis of a carrier's main location.

As expected, more profitable firms are more likely to survive, and so are larger firms. By contrast, firms with a higher proportion of labor cost over total cost are less likely to survive. All these effects are statistically significant at the 5 percent level or less. Even after controlling for these variables the initial level of debt seems to jeopardize a firm's chances of survival. The effect is statistically significant at the 1 percent level and is also economically relevant, although not huge. An increase in leverage of one standard deviation reduces the probability of survival by 8 percent.

An alternative way to measure the economic importance of this effect is by answering the following question: How much more efficient (i.e., profitable) must a company be to offset the negative impact on survival produced by an increase in leverage from 0.2 (the average) to 0.3? By using the probit estimates, I obtain that a trucking company needs to have a return on sales 0.7 percentage points higher (i.e., 10 percent higher with respect to the median ROS of 7 percent)

---

[11] This argument, although standard, is not necessarily appropriate to this case because the industry was regulated until 1977, and thus the size of a firm may be influenced more by regulation than by efficiency.

[12] These intangibles might also appear in the balance sheet in case of a merger, if the acquiring company used the purchased method of accounting. In such case, the potential impact of intangibles is ambiguous.

in order to offset 10 percent more capital financed by debt. The effect, thus, is small but not trivial.

The impact of leverage remains unchanged when I use return on assets (ROA) rather than return on sales as a measure of a firm's efficiency (see column II). Similarly, results are not substantially changed if other measures of leverage are used. For example, specification III uses coverage instead of net debt-to-capital, with similar results.

A. Alternative Measures of Efficiency

Using return on sales (or on assets) as a measure of efficiency can pose some problems. First, given that in 1977 the trucking industry was regulated, a high return on sales may just indicate the presence of large monopoly rents, not a high degree of efficiency. Second, high return on sales is also associated with a greater availability of cash flow from operations, and ROS may also capture this additional effect.

In order to test the robustness of my findings, I try some alternative measures of efficiency. The first is an estimate of the distance of each motor carrier from the production possibility frontier. This is a measure of technical inefficiency, which does not rely on any assumption on the market in which a firm operates. As described in the Appendix, I estimate this by following the technique suggested by Schmidt and Sickles (1984).

The results are reported in the first column of Table IV. The degree of inefficiency has a *positive* (and not negative) effect on the probability of survival, and this effect is borderline statistically significant.[13] However, it is interesting to notice that the impact of leverage on the probability of survival remains unchanged after this additional measure of efficiency is introduced.

Another measure of efficiency is the cost of operations. For the carriers that disclose the number of ton-miles hauled, I can obtain a measure of the cost per ton-mile. This measure has the advantage of being independent of the market structure in which a carrier operates. Regardless of the size of monopoly rents, a trucking company should always minimize costs. This measure has the drawback that it improperly accounts for a firm's cost of capital. In fact, operating expenses include depreciation (accounting, not economic, depreciation) and do not include the opportunity cost of capital. Another disadvantage is the fact that cost per ton-miles does not control for differences in the traffic mix (i.e., different average hauls and different average length of hauls).

The second column of Table IV reports the results of the previous probit model, when cost per ton-mile is inserted as an additional measure of efficiency. Notice that, because of data limitation, the number of observations available drops by 25 percent with respect to Table III. Higher-cost carriers are not at all less likely to

---

[13] In their original article Schmidt and Sickles (1984) apply their technique to the airline industry and find that there is no link between estimated inefficiency and survival of airline carriers.

Table IV. *Robustness to different measures of efficiency*

Independent variables	I	II	III
Net debt-to-capital	−0.245***	−0.226***	−0.277***
	(0.066)	(0.057)	(0.058)
Return on sales	3.142***	3.101***	1.131**
	(0.481)	(0.410)	(0.512)
log(Revenues)	0.030*	0.029*	0.022
	(0.017)	(0.016)	(0.015)
Intangibles	−0.045	−0.234	−0.066
	(0.303)	(0.274)	(0.280)
Labor cost	−0.332**	−0.436***	−0.187
	(0.152)	(0.124)	(0.119)
Estimated inefficiency	0.504*		
	(0.266)		
Cost per ton-mile		−0.019	
		(0.032)	
Return on sales in 1980			2.450***
			(0.452)
Pseudo-R^2	0.13	0.14	0.14
N	574	723	670

***, **, * Significantly different from zero at the 1 percent level or less, at the 5 percent level, or at the 10 percent level, respectively.

Note: The dependent variable is the probability that a general freight motor carrier with more than $1 million in revenues in 1977 survives until 1985. The reported coefficients are probit estimates of the effect of a marginal change in the corresponding regressor on the probability of survival, computed at the average of the dependent variable. Net debt-to-capital is total debt minus cash reserves divided by total debt plus equity. Intangibles is the ratio of intangible assets to total assets. Labor cost is the ratio of the wages and benefits to operating costs. All the independent variables are measured as of 1977 (average of the 1976 and 1977 values) except the 1980 return on sales in the last column. Column I uses the estimated inefficiency of a carrier as additional proxy for a carrier's efficiency. This is computed as the distance of its output from the production frontier, estimated using a translog function (see the Appendix). Column II uses as additional proxy for efficiency the cost per ton-mile. Cost per ton-mile is the ratio of operating expenses to ton-miles hauled. Column III uses the ex post value of efficiency as of 1980 as a proxy for efficiency. In such case the dependent variable is the probability of survival after 1980. All regressions contain nine regional dummies (not reported). Standard errors are reported in parentheses.

survive after deregulation than low-cost carriers. Again, the impact of leverage is still present and statistically significant.

Finally, a last attempt to control for the expected efficiency of motor carriers after deregulation is done in column III, by using the return on sales in 1980. I use 1980 because it is a watershed year. The major changes in the trucking industry took place in the 1980 to 1985 period, following the ICC deregulation started in 1978. Therefore, the 1980 ROS should at least partially capture the after-deregulation efficiency level, while leaving enough observations of exit.

Column III in Table IV shows that the results are not substantially changed when I disregard 1978 to 1980 exits and insert the 1980 ROS as an additional explanatory variable. This suggests that 1977 leverage is not simply a proxy for an unobserved efficiency factor.[14]

B. Controlling for the Ex Ante Risk of Default

It is possible that the most highly leveraged firms in 1977 were also the most inefficient and, thus, the most likely to exit the industry independent of any negative effect of debt. In the event that my measures of efficiency do not fully capture a firm's quality, the observed effect of leverage may simply be a spurious one.

To address this problem I try to control for the ex ante probability of default. I do that by using Altman's Z-score method. Altman (1968) is the first to develop a discriminant analysis method to forecast the probability of a firm's default using accounting information. One of the many applications of Altman's method is to the railroad industry (Altman (1973)). Given the similarities of the regulatory environment and of the accounting disclosure between the railroad and trucking industries, I choose to use the estimates of the Z-score model derived in this context.[15] Each firm is assigned a score according to the following formula in Altman (1973):

$$Z = 0.2003X_1 - 0.2070X_2 + 0.0059X_3 + 0.1040X_4 + 0.0885X_6 \\ + 0.0688X_7, \tag{3}$$

where X_1 is cash flow over fixed charges, X_2 is transportation expenses over operating revenues, X_3 is earned surplus over total assets, X_4 is the 1-year growth rate in operating revenues,[16] X_5 is earnings after taxes over operating revenues, X_6 is operating expenses over operating revenues, and X_7 is income before interest and taxes over total assets. The higher the Z-score, the lower the probability of default is.

Table V, column I, reports the estimates of the basic regression after having inserted a carrier Z-score as a proxy for the ex ante probability of exit. As expected, companies with a higher Z-score are more likely to survive. Nevertheless, the initial leverage still has a negative and statistically significant impact on the chances of survival, and its magnitude is substantially unchanged.

I can also use the Z-score to separate the desired effect of debt on exit from the undesired one. Suppose that the preregulation level of leverage was chosen to induce the optimal liquidation policy of motor carriers in the preregulation

---

[14] It also implies that the 1977 level of leverage has some predictive power on the probability of a firm's survival between three and eight years after. This rejects the hypothesis that the impact of leverage on survival is simply driven by firms on the verge of bankruptcy in 1977.

[15] A preferable alternative would be to estimate the Z-score model with trucking data. Unfortunately, the ATA dataset starts in 1976, making it impossible to estimate the Z-score model for trucking firms in the preregulation period.

[16] Altman (1973) uses a three-year growth rate, but I use the one-year growth because I have just one year of accounting data for the pre-1977 period.

Table V. *Effect of leverage controlling for the ex ante risk of default*

Independent variables		Predicted survivors	Predicted defaults
Net debt-to-capital	−0.150**	−0.199**	−0.183**
	(0.064)	(0.078)	(0.083)
Return on sales	2.344***	2.930***	2.1385***
	(0.397)	(0.563)	(0.526)
Log-revenues	0.0395***	0.078***	0.017
	(0.015)	(0.023)	(0.019)
Intangibles	−0.372	−0.639*	0.107
	(0.262)	(0.350)	(0.371)
Labor cost	−0.149	−0.331**	−0.298
	(0.150)	(0.163)	(0.320)
Z-score	0.012**		
	(0.005)		
Pseudo-R^2	0.12	0.15	0.07
N	778	369	409

***, **, * Significantly different from zero at the 1 percent level or less, at the 5 percent level, or at the 10 percent level, respectively.

Note: The dependent variable is the probability that a general freight motor carrier with more than $1 million in revenues in 1977 survives until 1985. The reported coefficients are probit estimates of the effect of a marginal change in the corresponding regressor on the probability of survival, computed at the average of the dependent variable. Net debt-to-capital is total debt minus cash reserves divided by total debt plus equity. Intangibles is the ratio of intangible assets to total assets. Labor cost is the ratio of the wages and benefits to operating costs. The first column reports the results of the basic regression of the probability of survival when the Altman Z-score is used as an additional explanatory variable. The Altman Z-score is an index, based on accounting information, of the risk of default. The higher the Z-score, the lower the probability of default is. The second regression reports results of the basic regression of the probability of survival conditioned on the fact the Z-score model predicted survival. The third regression reports the results of the basic regression of the probability of survival conditioned on the fact the Z-score model predicted default. All regressions contain nine regional dummies (not reported). Standard errors are reported in parentheses.

environment. Then, the preregulation Z-score should capture the desired effect of debt on exit and any residual effect can be interpreted as the undesired effect. Therefore, I want to estimate the effect of debt conditioned on the fact that the Z-score method predicted survival.

To transform the Z-score into a prediction on a firm's default I need to choose a cutoff point. If I use Altman's cutoff point, I obtain very few defaults and the results are substantially identical to that reported in Table III. Therefore, I choose the cutoff point so that the number of predicted defaults corresponds to the number of actual exits from my sample. Note that by doing so I bias the results against finding any effect of debt. In fact, ex ante people did not expect such a large exit from the trucking industry.

Table V, column II, reports the estimates of the basic regression restricted to the firms that the Z-score method predicts would survive. The initial level of leverage still has a negative impact on survival, and this impact is statistically significant at the 1 percent level. Profitability and size have coefficients similar to the basic estimates and are both statistically significant at the 1 percent level. This negative effect of debt can be interpreted as the undesired effect of debt on survival.

For completeness, I also report the estimates conditioned on the Z-score model predicting a default (column III). Again leverage has a negative impact on the probability of survival, statistically significant at the 5 percent level. All the other variables have the same sign, and all except the ratio of intangible assets are significant at the 10 percent level or better.

C. Comparison of Leverage and Its Effects in the TL and LTL Segment

Table VI, Panels A, B, and C, report summary statistics for carriers in the different segments of the market. LTL carriers tend to be larger, in terms both of sales and of assets, and to be less highly levered. Interestingly, there is no difference in the initial level of debt between survivors and nonsurvivors among TL carriers, but

Table VI. *Summary statistics split according to the industry segment*

Variable	Mean	Median	Std. Dev.	Min.	Max.	Diff.	p-value	Obs
Panel A: Carriers with less than 30 percent of revenues from LTL								
Revenues ($ millions)	5.35	2.45	7.85	0.92	46.60	3.61	0.014	113
Assets ($ millions)	2.06	0.90	3.32	0.16	23.70	1.86	0.003	113
Debt-to-capital	0.45	0.38	0.32	0.00	1.00	−0.03	0.575	113
Net debt-to-capital	0.27	0.25	0.43	−0.88	0.99	0.00	0.984	109
Coverage	22.27	7.52	30.10	0.00	100.00	3.52	0.538	112
Return on assets	0.19	0.19	0.13	−0.19	0.73	0.05	0.033	113
Return on sales	0.08	0.07	0.07	−0.03	0.42	0.02	0.059	113
Intangibles	0.07	0.03	0.08	0.00	0.44	−0.01	0.740	111
Labor cost	0.28	0.30	0.18	0.02	0.64	−0.04	0.198	112
Revenues per ton-mile	0.11	0.07	0.10	0.03	0.62	−0.01	0.625	90
Cost per ton-mile	0.19	0.07	0.41	0.03	3.68	−0.12	0.170	90
Average load	13.55	13.45	5.75	1.00	31.10	0.96	0.432	90
Average haul	252.51	217.64	196.32	6.93	1164.46	74.62	0.077	87
Market share	0.05	0.01	0.13	0.00	1.00	0.03	0.156	113
Number of employees	88.89	47.25	114.28	2.00	596.50	23.60	0.290	106
Panel B: Carriers with 30 to 70 percent of revenues from LTL								
Revenues ($ millions)	28.80	6.79	56.60	0.95	508.00	4.42	0.530	266
Assets ($ millions)	13.80	2.48	32.00	0.05	309.00	5.06	0.203	266
Debt-to-capital	0.42	0.36	0.29	0.00	1.00	−0.13	0.000	265
Net debt-to-capital	0.25	0.26	0.36	−0.86	1.00	−0.20	0.000	257
Coverage	24.55	8.67	31.66	0.00	100.00	12.72	0.001	261
Return on assets	0.17	0.17	0.14	−0.30	0.88	0.08	0.000	264
Return on sales	0.07	0.07	0.07	−0.43	0.52	0.05	0.000	266
Intangibles	0.07	0.04	0.09	0.00	0.64	−0.01	0.293	265
Labor cost	0.52	0.55	0.13	0.01	0.76	−0.00	0.942	266

Table VI. *(Continued)*

Variable	Mean	Median	Std. Dev.	Min.	Max.	Diff.	p-value	Obs
Revenues per ton-mile	0.24	0.18	0.21	0.06	1.86	0.03	0.230	259
Cost per ton-mile	0.26	0.18	0.32	0.06	2.46	0.04	0.286	259
Average load	10.90	11.45	4.21	0.80	29.54	0.35	0.504	259
Average haul	278.45	207.31	261.05	12.52	1713	−61.39	0.062	258
Market share	0.08	0.02	0.14	0.00	0.94	0.02	0.273	261
Number of employees	760.90	199.25	1421.08	2.00	13157	148.26	0.401	266
Panel C: Carriers with more than 70 percent of revenues from LTL								
Revenues ($ millions)	14.70	3.70	55.70	0.93	684.00	11.70	0.083	270
Assets ($ millions)	6.73	1.45	28.50	0.23	355.00	6.83	0.048	270
Debt-to-capital	0.34	0.29	0.28	0.00	1.00	−0.15	0.000	270
Net debt-to-capital	0.14	0.09	0.37	−0.97	1.00	−0.20	0.000	261
Coverage	33.10	13.35	36.05	0.00	100.00	19.66	0.000	264
Return on assets	0.19	0.18	0.12	−0.33	0.56	0.06	0.000	270
Return on sales	0.08	0.07	0.05	−0.07	0.30	0.04	0.000	270
Intangibles	0.06	0.04	0.07	0.00	0.47	−0.02	0.007	268
Labor cost	0.56	0.59	0.11	0.02	0.78	0.00	0.923	269
Revenues per ton-mile	0.44	0.32	0.37	0.12	3.46	0.04	0.402	261
Cost per ton-mile	0.44	0.31	0.39	0.11	3.20	0.01	0.861	261
Average load	8.25	8.47	3.99	0.81	24.06	−0.35	0.477	261
Average haul	167.98	134.76	126.86	17.45	788.00	−11.60	0.461	261
Market share	0.05	0.01	0.12	0.00	0.90	0.02	0.204	270
Number of employees	426.64	114.25	1398.94	6.00	18015	310.07	0.072	264

Note: General freight carriers with more than $1 million in operating revenues in 1977 are divided in three groups according to the fraction of their revenues coming from less-than-truckload (LTL) shipments as of 1977. Net debt-to-capital is total debt minus cash reserves divided by total debt plus equity. Intangibles is the ratio of intangible assets to total assets. Labor cost is the ratio of the wages and benefits to operating costs. Revenues per ton-mile is the ratio of operating revenues to ton-miles hauled. Average load is the ratio of ton-miles hauled to total miles traveled. Average haul is the ratio of ton-miles hauled to tons of revenues freight. Market share is the ratio between carriers' operating revenues and the sum of the operating revenues of all the carriers located in the same state. The Diff. column reports the difference in means between carriers that still existed in 1985 and carriers that did not exist at that date. The *p*-values refer to the null that the difference is equal to zero.

this difference is large and statistically significant for carriers with at least 30 percent of revenues in LTL and for carriers with more than 70 percent of revenues in LTL (see the last two columns of Table VI).

This differential impact of leverage, however, does not control for the different characteristics of the carriers in the three segments. This is done in Table VII, which reports the estimates of equation (2) for the three segments. Interestingly, the initial level of debt has no impact on the probability of survival of motor carriers with less than 30 percent of their revenues in LTL. The point estimate is actually positive (0.02), albeit not statistically significant. By contrast, the initial level of debt has a strong and statistically significant negative effect on survival in the other two groups, more heavily involved in LTL. In particular, the impact of

Table VII. *Differential impact of the initial leverage on survival in different segments of the trucking industry*

Independent Variables	LTL < 0.3	0.3 < LTL < 0.7	LTL > 0.7
Net debt-to-capital	0.021	−0.224**	−0.277***
	(0.127)	(0.102)	(0.101)
Return on sales	1.481*	3.520***	3.247***
	(0.829)	(0.730)	(0.821)
log(Revenues)	0.125*	−0.010	0.063**
	(0.064)	(0.025)	(0.031)
Intangibles	0.151	0.089	−0.591
	(0.687)	(0.464)	(0.512)
Labor cost	−0.417	0.086	−0.320
	(0.341)	(0.300)	(0.341)
Pseudo-R^2	0.09	0.17	0.15
N	100	249	259

***, **, *, Significantly different from zero at the 1 percent level or less, at the 5 percent level, or at the 10 percent level, respectively.

Note: The dependent variable is the probability that a general freight motor carrier with more than $1 million in revenues in 1977 survives until 1985. The reported coefficients are probit estimates of the effect of a marginal change in the corresponding regressor on the probability of survival, computed at the average of the dependent variable. Net debt-to-capital is total debt minus cash reserves divided by total debt plus equity. Intangibles is the ratio of intangible assets to total assets. Labor cost is the ratio of the wages and benefits to operating costs. All the independent variables are measured as of 1977 (average of the 1976 and 1977 values). Among the independent variables there are also nine regional dummies (not reported). General freight carriers are divided into three groups according to the fraction of their revenues coming from less-than-truckload shipments as of 1977. The first column reports the estimates for motor carriers with less than 30 percent of revenues from less than truckload (LTL) shipments. Estimates in the second column are for motor carriers with more than 30 percent but less than 70 percent of their revenues in LTL shipments. Estimates in the third column are for motor carriers with more than 70 percent of their revenues in LTL shipments. Standard errors are reported in parentheses.

debt on survival of the carriers most concentrated in LTL is statistically different (at the 10 percent level) from the impact of debt on survival of the carriers least concentrated in LTL.

In an unreported regression, I also estimate the effect of debt on survival across the three groups using a linear probability model. As discussed in Section II.B, in a linear framework the estimated difference in the impact of debt in the high LTL carriers and in the low LTL carriers is a consistent estimate of the true difference. The estimated difference is −0.26, which is statistically different from zero at the 10 percent level. Thus, consistent with the theories predicting a negative effect of debt, this effect is larger (in absolute value) for predominantly LTL carriers. This finding also supports the view that the impact of debt on survival is not simply an effect of unobserved quality differences.

It is important to notice that these results arise in spite of the fact that the percentage of exits in the two extreme groups is the same. This fact makes implausible the assumption that these results are driven by a difference in an unobserved firm characteristic that affects both leverage and exit.

V. WHY DOES DEBT AFFECT SURVIVAL?

The findings thus far suggest that the initial level of debt might have some consequences on the ability of a motor carrier to survive during deregulation. In this section, I try to uncover the sources of this observed relationship.

A. Investment

If highly leveraged motor carriers are weeded out because they cannot success-fully finance new investment, then I should be able to find some effects of initial leverage on the amount of investment undertaken by each firm during the post-deregulation period.

Because the ATA data set does not contain flow of funds data, I measure the total amount of capital expenditures in the postderegulation period as the dif-ference in gross operating property over the period 1977 to 1985 divided by the 1977 level of net operating property. I then estimate a reduced form equation in which investments are a function of a company's profitability, its size, the level of intangibles, and the proportion of labor cost.

Table VIII reports the OLS estimates of this equation. After controlling for the likely determinants of investments, the initial level of leverage seems to have no impact on the amount of investment actually made during the postderegulation period.

One caveat, however, is warranted. If debt affects a firm's investment policy, the negative efficiency consequences of this underinvestment are likely to jeo-pardize a firm's ability to survive. We can observe the investment over a certain period only for the firms that survived until the end of the period; therefore, by estimating the investment over the entire postderegulation period I may miss the most important effect. To overcome this problem, I estimate the same investment equation considering only the investments that took place up to 1980. By that time the deregulation shock on leverage has already occurred, but the large exodus from the industry has not.

The results are reported in the second column of Table VIII. In this case we do observe a negative effect of leverage on investment. An increase of one standard deviation in the initial level of leverage decreases the total investment in the three years following deregulation by 10 percent, and this effect is statistically sig-nificant at the 5 percent level.

If the proposed explanation is indeed the source of these ambivalent results, then I should find that the effect of debt on investments is mostly concentrated among firms that eventually exit the industry. The last two columns of Table VIII show that this is indeed the case. The investment policy of firms that eventually survive is not very much affected by debt. By contrast, this effect is very strong (both economically and statistically) among firms that exit the industry.

Table VIII. *Investments*

Independent variables	Investment period			
	1977–1985	1977–1980	1977–1980 of survivors	1977–1980 of nonsurvivors
Net debt-to-capital	−0.092	−0.224**	−0.068	−0.379**
	(0.203)	(0.106)	(0.131)	(0.180)
Return on sales	2.249*	2.208***	1.840***	1.619
	(1.173)	(0.693)	(0.796)	(1.493)
log(Revenues)	−0.125**	−0.063***	−0.057***	−0.034
	(0.052)	(0.028)	(0.033)	(0.053)
Intangibles	−0.697	0.645	0.504	0.556
	(1.137)	(0.518)	(0.733)	(0.761)
Labor cost	−1.081***	−0.087	−0.005	−1.438***
	(0.393)	(0.084)	(0.082)	(0.400)
R^2	0.09	0.05	0.05	0.11
N	420	669	412	257

***, **, * Significantly different from zero at the 1 percent level or less, at the 5 percent level, or at the 10 percent level, respectively.

Note: This table reports the OLS estimates obtained by regressing capital investments of general freight motor carriers with more than $1 million in revenues in 1977 on some predetermined explanatory variables. Investments are computed as differences in carriers' gross operating properties over the period divided by the 1977 level of net operating properties. Net debt-to-capital is total debt minus cash reserves divided by total debt plus equity. Intangibles is the ratio of intangible assets to total assets. Labor cost is the ratio of the wages and benefits to operating costs. All the independent variables are measured as of 1977 (average of the 1976 and 1977 values). The period 1977–1980 is also considered with the sample restricted to the motor carriers that survived until 1985 and with the sample restricted to motor carriers that exited between 1980 and 1985. All the regressions also contain nine regional dummies (not reported). Standard errors are reported in parentheses.

Why is the effect of debt mostly limited to firms that eventually exited? One possible explanation is that the market had different perceptions of the long-term viability of highly leveraged carriers. Some were perceived as viable, obtained financing, invested as much as the low leveraged carriers, and survived. Others, which were not perceived as viable, were forced to curtail their investments and eventually left the industry. This explanation is consistent with Lang, Ofek, and Stulz (1996), who find that debt reduces the growth of firms with a low Tobin's q, but not of firms with a high Tobin's q. In fact, if one interprets survival ex post as a proxy for the ex ante Tobin's q (which I cannot observe because the firms are privately held), my results are analogous to Lang et al. (1996). This interpretation is consistent with some unobserved heterogeneity, but it does not necessarily imply that the nonsurviving carriers were of inferior quality. As Lang et al. (1996) point out, it might just be that they were perceived by the market as such.

Another (related) possibility, which does not rely on the surviving carriers being of a higher quality, is that highly leveraged firms differ in the resources available to their owners. Some firms may be owned by deep-pocket investors, ready to support the necessary financing. These highly leveraged carriers, then, invest as the low leveraged ones and survive. By contrast, highly leveraged carriers without a deep-pocket investor cannot keep up the investment level and, as a result, are forced to exit eventually.

In sum, the evidence suggests that the firms that exited the industry have suffered from an underinvestment problem linked to their initial level of debt. Yet, I cannot rule out the possibility that this effect is caused by unobserved heterogeneity in carriers' quality.

B. Pricing

Leverage may affect survival also by weakening a firm's competitive position. As reviewed in Section II, several models suggest that a high leverage may force firms into cutting their prices. These models, however, differ substantially in the nature of their predictions. Bolton and Scharfstein's (1990) model of predation makes predictions on the equilibrium price prevailing in a certain market as a function of the incentive of deep-pocket firms to prey on their shallow-pocket competitors. By contrast, Titman (1984) and Maksimovic and Titman (1991) do not make any prediction on the market equilibrium price but only on the price differential between a firm and its competitors.

B.1. *Price Data*
General freight carriers are required to disclose the amount of ton-miles transported in a calendar year. By dividing a carrier's operating revenues by the number of ton-miles reported, I obtain a proxy of the actual price per ton-mile charged by each carrier. This measure is noisy because the price changes not only as a function of the segment of the market a carrier is in (TL versus LTL), but also as a function of the average haul of a carrier because there is a fixed cost for loading and unloading each shipment.

However, if the composition of shipments of each individual carrier is fairly stable over time (a nontrivial assumption during deregulation), I can eliminate some of the noise by considering the changes in the prices charged by the same carriers over a certain period. Therefore, I will use these estimated price changes over different time intervals to analyze the effects of the initial level of leverage on a carrier's pricing policy.

B.2. *Estimates of the Impact of Leverage on Prices*
To test the predation hypothesis I would need to identify many separate markets. Unfortunately, I lack a clear way to do that. If I use the nine geographical regions identified by the ICC, I will have too few observations to estimate a cross-market regression. Using state boundaries would give me more observations, but it is highly unsatisfactory from an economic point of view as there is no reason why the effective market in which a carrier competes is limited to the state in which its headquarters is located. To make things worse, the results would be very sensitive to

the way a market is defined (and, thus, to who the main competitors in this market are). Therefore, I cannot test the predation hypothesis with the available data.

By contrast, I am better positioned to test the effect of leverage on the prices of individual carriers. Although it would certainly be better to be able to control for factors that affect prices at a local-market level, the lack of a precise definition of market only weakens the power of the test.

For this reason, I try to explain changes in the prices charged by individual carriers as a function of some real variables and the initial level of leverage. The control variables are: first, state dummies, which absorb any regional effect; second, the proportion of labor cost over total cost at the beginning of the period, as a proxy of the cost structure of each carrier and, indirectly, of its degree of unionization; third, the size of the carrier vis-à-vis its state competitors in 1977 (which I improperly refer to as market share), fourth, the percentage of revenues obtained through LTL shipments.

Table IX reports OLS estimates obtained from regressing the changes in the price charged by each carrier on these controlling variables and the initial leverage. I estimate separate equations for every year from 1980 to 1985. The rate setting was liberalized in 1980, so that year marks the beginning of price

Table IX. *Firm-level prices and leverage*

Independent variables	1980	1981	1982	1983	1984	1985
Net debt-to-capital in 1977	0.046	−0.037	−0.138***	−0.126**	−0.120**	−0.103
	(0.031)	(0.040)	(0.051)	(0.050)	(0.058)	(0.073)
Labor cost in 1977	0.092	0.088	0.087	0.249	0.328*	0.201
	(0.090)	(0.124)	(0.159)	(0.157)	(0.193)	(0.240)
Market share in 1977	0.063	0.121	0.058	0.138	0.101	0.102
	(0.100)	(0.122)	(0.157)	(0.164)	(0.184)	(0.216)
Medium LTL revenues in 1977	0.054	0.089*	0.063	−0.008	−0.015	−0.023
	(0.039)	(0.052)	(0.064)	(0.065)	(0.080)	(0.101)
High LTL revenues in 1977	0.107**	0.141**	0.119*	0.080	0.034	0.066
	(0.042)	(0.055)	(0.068)	(0.069)	(0.082)	(0.106)
R^2	0.14	0.17	0.16	0.20	0.22	0.22
N	428	376	354	333	302	264

***, **, * Significantly different from zero at the 1 percent level or less, at the 5 percent level, or at the 10 percent level, respectively.

Note: This table reports OLS coefficient estimates for a sample of general freight motor carriers with more than $1 million in revenues in 1977 that disclose data on the volume of their shipments (Instruction 27 carriers). The dependent variable is the difference between the price per ton-mile charged by a carrier in the year of reference and the price charged in 1977. Net debt-to-capital in 1977 is debt minus cash reserves divided by debt plus equity. Labor cost in 1977 equals wages plus benefits over operating costs. A carrier market share in 1977 is the ratio between carriers' operating revenues and the sum of the operating revenues of all the carriers located in the same state. Medium less-than-truckload (LTL) carriers are carriers with more than 30 percent but less than 70 percent of their revenues in LTL shipments. High LTL carriers are carriers with more than 70 percent of their revenues in LTL shipments. All the regressions contain state fixed effects (not reported). Standard errors are reported in parentheses.

competition. On the other hand, 1985 can be considered the year when the postderegulation industry equilibrium was reached. In between, 1982 represents the trough of a recession when, according to industry sources, price cuts were most aggressive.

Interestingly, in 1980 the price changes are unaffected by the initial level of debt; the coefficient is actually positive, but is economically and statistically indistinguishable from zero. It is only beginning in 1982 that carriers entering the deregulation period with more leverage start to charge significantly lower prices than their direct competitors. This effect is both economically and statistically significant. One standard deviation increase in the initial level of leverage decreases a carrier's prices by 7 cents per ton-mile. This represents approximately a 22 percent discount with respect to the average price per ton-mile. This effect persists in 1983 and 1984, then in 1985 it is economically weaker and not statistically significant.

These results seem to support the idea that more highly leveraged firms are forced to discount their products, especially during recessions. It is less clear, though, what the ultimate reason for this discount is. It might be the fact that highly leveraged carriers are desperate for cash, or that consumers require compensation for the risk of dealing with a company that might go bankrupt (Titman (1984)). The first effect should hold indifferently across TL and LTL carriers, but the second one is more likely to be important in LTL carriers that deliver a nonstandardized product, where service is more important. It is worth noting that at the time there was much discussion in the press about the potential cost a less-than-truckload shipper might incur if its carrier defaulted in the middle of an important shipment.

For this reason, I explore the differences in the impact of debt across industry segments. To present these results in a concise form, I pool the price changes over the six-year period and estimate a separate coefficient of the initial level of debt for every year (the results are substantially identical if I estimate six separate regressions). Year dummies (not reported) are also inserted. Table X reports the results. Interestingly the initial level of debt has no effect in the price changes of 'pure' TL carriers. By contrast, the effect is very pronounced for the 'pure' LTL carriers. It starts to manifest itself in 1981 and is particularly pronounced in 1982 and 1983. This finding is consistent with the hypothesis that leveraged carriers discount their services to compensate consumers for the risk associated with the probability of default of the carrier.

These results seem to contrast with Phillips (1995) and Chevalier (1995b), who find a positive relation between the increase in leverage caused by LBOs and increases in prices. The contrast, however, is more apparent than real. In fact, the industries studied by Phillips (gypsum, polyethylene, fiberglass insulation, and tractor trailer) and Chevalier (supermarkets) do not involve much specific investment by the customers. Thus, the need to discount the goods in order to compensate the customers from the risk of bankruptcy, which is present for LTL carriers, is not likely to arise for their firms.

Table X. *Prices and leverage in different segments of the trucking industry*

Independent variables	LTL < 0.3	0.3 < LTL < 0.7	LTL > 0.7
Net debt-to-capital in 1977	0.087	0.027	0.017
*1980 dummy	(0.056)	(0.054)	(0.069)
Net debt-to-capital in 1977	0.108	−0.053	−0.080
*1981 dummy	(0.063)	(0.056)	(0.079)
Net debt-to-capital in 1977	0.080	−0.090	−0.239***
*1982 dummy	(0.062)	(0.058)	(0.079)
Net debt-to-capital in 1977	0.037	−0.064	−0.222***
*1983 dummy	(0.066)	(0.061)	(0.084)
Net debt-to-capital in 1977	0.002	−0.054	−0.212**
*1984 dummy	(0.076)	(0.062)	(0.083)*
Net debt-to-capital in 1977	0.074	−0.130**	−0.091
*1985 dummy	(0.079)	(0.066)	(0.091)
Labor cost	0.086	0.281***	0.185
	(0.083)	(0.083)	(0.144)
Market share	−0.078	0.189**	−0.112
	(0.514)	(0.076)	(0.134)
R^2	0.19	0.24	0.12
N	300	831	927

***, **, * Significantly different from zero at the 1 percent level or less, at the 5 percent level, or at the 10 percent level, respectively.

Note: This table reports OLS coefficient estimates for a sample of general freight motor carriers with more than $1 million in revenues in 1977 that disclose data on the volume of their shipments (Instruction 27 carriers). The dependent variable is the vector of the differences between the price per ton-mile charged by a carrier in any year from 1980 to 1985 and the price charged in 1977. Net debt-to-capital in 1977 is debt minus cash reserves divided by debt plus equity. Labor cost in 1977 equals wages plus benefits over operating costs. A carrier market share in 1977 is the ratio between carriers' operating revenues and the sum of the operating revenues of all the carriers located in the same state. The first column reports the estimates for motor carriers with less than 30 percent of revenues from less than truckload (LTL) shipments. Estimates in the second column are for motor carriers with more than 30 percent but less than 70 percent of their revenues in LTL shipments. Estimates in the third column are for motor carriers with more than 70 percent of their revenues in LTL shipments. All the regressions contain state fixed effects and yearly dummies (not reported). Standard errors are reported in parentheses.

Moreover, neither paper finds that prices always increase. Phillips (1995) finds that, in one of the four industries he analyzes, prices drop after the LBOs. Similarly, Chevalier (1995b) finds that, in some local markets, supermarket prices drop after the LBO wave. In both cases, the authors point out that this phenomenon occurs in markets where there are some competitors with deep pockets. This is certainly the case in the trucking industry, if I consider that carriers are competing throughout the nation. In sum, the relation between prices and leverage seems to be very dependent on the nature of the goods and the financial position of competitors.

VI. CONCLUSIONS

This paper studies the impact of capital market imperfections on the survival of firms. In general, the feasibility of such a study is seriously impaired by an endogeneity problem. It is impossible to determine whether firms perform poorly and exit because they are highly leveraged, or vice versa, that they are highly leveraged because they perform poorly and should be induced to leave. Deregulation in the trucking industry provides a unique natural experiment that may overcome this problem.

I study the effect of the prederegulation level of leverage on the subsequent survival of trucking firms during deregulation. I find that firms that happened to be highly leveraged at the beginning of deregulation are less likely to survive afterward, even when controlling for some measures of efficiency and for the ex ante probability of default.

I find that the initial level of leverage has a negative impact on the ability of a motor carrier to invest in the years following deregulation. The effect is particularly pronounced in those companies that are eventually forced to exit, suggesting that the underinvestment problem caused by the high debt level might have forced these firms out of the market.

I also find evidence that the prederegulation level of leverage negatively impacts the price that a carrier charges during the price war which follows deregulation. This effect is entirely concentrated in the LTL segment of the industry.

In general, my findings raise the possibility that sometimes natural selection leads to the survival of relatively inefficient firms, which happen (or choose) to have deep pockets. In industries with high barriers to entry (like LTL shipments), relatively inefficient firms that survive are not likely to be challenged by new entrants. Thus, in these industries, the selection 'mistakes' may have long-lasting effects. In other words, my findings challenge the commonly held assumption that competition will necessarily lead to the survival of the fittest. Only future research will be able to answer how generalizable these findings are.

Appendix. Technical Measure of Efficiency

The first step consists of estimating a production function with a panel of firms. The firm-specific effect represents the difference between a firm's output and the predicted level of output given the observed inputs. This difference can be used to assess the relative degree of inefficiency of each firm with respect to the most productive firm in the sample.

I use the period 1976 to 1978 to estimate the degree of relative inefficiency before deregulation started.[17] Following the literature on the subject, and

---

[17] The estimator of a firm's inefficiency is consistent for T (number of periods) going to infinity. Therefore, I decide to include 1978 as a prederegulation year to increase the precision of the estimates. I also try to estimate a model using data up to 1980 without significant changes in the results.

Table AI. *Production function estimate*

$\log K$	-0.432***
	(0.078)
$\log L$	0.832***
	(0.112)
$\log M$	-0.334**
	(0.147)
$\dfrac{(\log K)^2}{2}$	0.040***
	(0.007)
$\dfrac{(\log L)^2}{2}$	0.110***
	(0.016)
$\dfrac{(\log M)^2}{2}$	0.052***
	(0.017)
$\log K \log L$	-0.043***
	(0.008)
$\log K \log M$	0.015**
	(0.007)
$\log L \log M$	-0.045***
	(0.012)
Average load	0.049***
	(0.002)
Average haul	0.002***
	(0.000)
1977 dummy	0.014**
	(0.006)
1978 dummy	0.000
	(0.007)
R^2	0.60
N	1683

***, **, * Significantly different from zero at the 1 percent level or less, at the 5 percent level, or at the 10 percent level, respectively.

Note: This table reports a fixed effect estimate of a translog production function where capital (K), labor (L), and intermediate goods (M) are the three factors. The sample is an unbalanced panel of firms present for at least two years in the period 1976 to 1978. The dependent variable is the logarithm of ton-miles hauled each year. Capital is the book value of net carrier operating properties. Labor is the number of workers employed. Intermediate goods are deflated expenses in fuel and supplies. As a factor controlling for possible heterogeneity of the principal input categories, the average haul and the average load plus two yearly dummies are used. The average load is the ratio of ton-miles hauled to total miles traveled. The average haul is the ratio of ton-miles hauled to tons of revenues freight. Standard errors are reported in parentheses.

especially its application to the trucking industry (see Friedlaender and Spady (1981)), I estimate a translog production function of the form

$$\ln Y_{it} = \alpha_i + \sum_z^K \beta_z \ln X_{zit} + \sum_z^K \gamma_z \frac{\ln^2 X_{zit}}{2}$$

$$+ \sum_z^K \sum_j^K \delta_{zj} \ln X_{zit} \ln X_{jit} + \sum_l^L F_{lit} + \epsilon_{it}, \tag{A1}$$

where $\ln Y_{it}$ is the logarithm of firm i's output at time t, X_z are the K factors used in the production process, and F_l are L controlling factors to account for possible heterogeneity of the principal input categories.

In this context, the firm's specific factor α_i is the algebraic sum of a common intercept α and a firm-specific level of inefficiency u_i:

$$\alpha_i = \alpha - u_i. \tag{A2}$$

The output Y is the number of ton-miles transported by carrier i in year t. The factors used are capital (net carrier operating properties), labor (number of workers), and intermediate goods (deflated expenses in fuel and supplies). As controlling factor I use the size of the average haul and the average load, plus two yearly dummies. The within estimates of equation (3) are presented in Table AI.

The estimates look reasonable. The estimated elasticity of output with respect to capital is 0.09, with respect to labor 0.20, and the elasticity with respect to fuel and supplies is 0.32. The within regression can explain 60 percent of the variability.

Schmidt and Sickles's (1984) intuition is that the estimated firm-specific effect $\hat{\alpha}_i$ can be used to obtain an estimate of the production inefficiency of firm i ($\hat{u}_i$). This is obtained as

$$\hat{u}_i = \max\{\hat{\alpha}_i\} - \hat{\alpha}_i. \tag{A3}$$

I estimate the $\hat{u}_i$ by using regression (A1) and then use the estimated value as a measure of inefficiency in regression (2).

REFERENCES

Altman, Edward, 1968, Financial ratios, discriminant analysis, and the prediction of corporate bankruptcy, *Journal of Finance* 23, 589–609.

—, 1973, Predicting railroad bankruptcies in America, *Bell Journal of Economics and Management* 4, 184–211.

Bolton, Patrick, and David Scharfstein, 1990, A theory of predation based on agency problems in financial contracting, *American Economic Review* 80, 93–106.

Brander, James, and Tracy Lewis, 1986, Oligopoly and financial structure, *American Economic Review* 76, 956–970.

Breen, Dennis A., 1977, The monopoly value of household-goods carrier operating certificates, *The Journal of Law and Economics* 20, 153–185.

Chevalier, Judith, 1995a, Capital structure and product market competition: Empirical evidence from the supermarket industry, *American Economic Review* 85, 206–256.

—, 1995b, Do LBO supermarkets charge more: An empirical analysis of the effects of LBOs on supermarket pricing, *Journal of Finance* 50, 1095–1113.

—, and David Scharfstein, 1996, Capital-market imperfections and countercyclical markups: Theory and evidence, *American Economic Review* 86, 703–725.

Friedlaender, Ann, and Richard H. Spady, 1981, *Freight Transport Regulation. Equity Efficiency, and Competition in the Rail and Trucking Industries* (The MIT Press, Cambridge, Mass.).

Glaskowsky, Nicholas A., 1986, *Effects of Deregulation on Motor Carriers* (Eno Foundation for Transportation Inc., Westport, Conn.).

Harris, Milton, and Artur Raviv, 1990, Capital structure and the informational role of debt, *Journal of Finance* 45, 321–350.

Holtz-Eakin, Douglas, David Jouflaian, and Harvey Rosen, 1994, Sticking it out: Entrepreneurial survival and liquidity constraint, *Journal of Political Economy* 102, 53–75.

Jensen, Michael C., 1986, Agency costs of free cash flow, corporate finance and takeovers, *American Economic Review* 76, 323–329.

—, Michael C., 1989, The eclipse of the public corporation, *Harvard Business Review* 67, 61–74.

Kovenock, Dan, and Gordon M. Phillips, 1997, Capital structure and product market behavior: An examination of plant exit and investment decisions, *Review of Financial Studies*, forthcoming.

Lang, Larry, Eli Ofek, and René Stulz, 1996, The leverage, investment, and firm growth, *Journal of Financial Economics* 40, 3–31.

Maksimovic, Vojislav, and Sheridan Titman, 1991, Financial policy and reputation for product quality, *Review of Financial Studies* 4, 175–200.

Moore, Thomas G., 1978, The beneficiaries of trucking regulation, *The Journal of Law and Economics* 21, 327–344.

—, 1986, Rail and trucking deregulation, in Leonard W. Weiss and Michael W. Klass, eds.: *Regulatory Reform. What Actually Happened* (Little Brown and Company, Boston, Mass.).

Myers, Stewart C., 1977, The determinants of corporate borrowing, *Journal of Financial Economics* 5, 146–175.

—, 1984, The capital structure puzzle, *Journal of Finance* 89, 575–592.

Perotti, Enrico, and Kathryn Spier, 1993, Capital structure as a bargaining tool: The role of leverage in contract renegotiation, *American Economic Review* 83, 1131–1141.

Phillips, Gordon, 1995, Increased debt and product-market competition, *Journal of Financial Economics* 37, 189–238.

Rajan, Raghuram, and Luigi Zingales, 1995, What do we know about capital structure? Some evidence from international data, *Journal of Finance* 50, 1421–1460.

Rose, Nancy, 1985, The incidence of regulatory rents in the motor carrier industry, *Rand Journal of Economics* 16, 299–318.

—, 1987, Labor rent sharing and regulation: Evidence from the trucking industry, *Journal of Political Economy* 95, 1146–1178.

Schipper, Katherine, Rex Thompson, and Roman L. Weil, 1987, Disentangling interrelated effects of regulatory changes on shareholder wealth: The case of motor carrier deregulation, *Journal of Law and Economics* 30, 67–100.

Schmidt, Peter, and Robin C. Sickles, 1984, Production frontiers and panel data, *Journal of Business and Economic Statistics* 2, 367–374.

Smith, Clifford W. Jr., and Ross L. Watts, 1992, The investment opportunity set and corporate financing, dividend, and compensation policies, *Journal of Financial Economics* 32, 263–292.

Spence, Michael, 1985, Capital structure and the corporation's product market environment, in Benjamin M. Friedman, ed.: *Corporate Capital Structures in the United States* (The University of Chicago Press, Chicago, Ill.).

Standard & Poors, various years, S&P Industry Outlook.

Stulz, René, 1990, Managerial discretion and optimal financing policies, *Journal of Financial Economics* 26, 3–28.

Telser, Lester G., 1966, Cutthroat competition and the long purse, *Journal of Law and Economics* 9, 259–277.

Titman, Sheridan, 1984, The effect of capital structure on a firm's liquidation decision, *Journal of Financial Economics* 13, 137–151.

Winston, Clifford, 1993, Economic deregulation: Days of reckoning for microeconomists, *Journal of Economic Literature* 31, 1263–1289.

12

Endogenous Cycles in a Stiglitz–Weiss Economy

JAVIER SUAREZ AND OREN SUSSMAN

1. INTRODUCTION

Economic research in recent years has revitalized the idea that financial factors should play a central role in business-cycle theory.[1] On the one hand, there exists a growing body of empirical work showing that financial imperfections affect real economic decisions[2] in a way which varies systematically along the business-cycle. On the other hand, theoretical work—Bernanke and Gertler [2] and more recently Kiyotaki and Moore [20]—shows how transitory shocks are *propagated* via imperfections in financial markets. The novel contribution of this paper is the modeling of an endogenous *reversion mechanism*, such that the economy may converge to a two-period equilibrium cycle. The model is kept deliberately simple so as to allow a transparent exposition of the mechanism. Indeed, the model is a dynamic extension of the well-known Stiglitz–Weiss [24] (henceforth SW) model of lending under moral hazard.[3]

Let it be clear that we view the reversion mechanism as a complement to the propagation mechanism. Obviously, it takes both to produce a complete theory of business fluctuations. But further, we use our model to clarify some theoretical issues. First, it is often argued that financial imperfection provides a crucial amplification effect that can solve the 'small shocks, large cycles' puzzle (see Bernanke et al. [3]). In our model the amplification effect is dramatic: the variance of external shocks is zero while output fluctuations may still be sizable.

This work was initiated during the 1994 European Summer Symposium in Financial Markets at the Gerzensee Studienzentrum. Earlier versions of this paper were presented at the CEPR Conference on Macroeconomics and Finance in Gerzensee, 16–20 January 1996, and the V 'Tor Vergata' Financial Conference in Rome, 28–29 November 1996. We thank Martin Hellwig, Bengt Holmstrom, and John Moore for extremely helpful comments and suggestions.

[1] Fisher [10] gives one of the first coherent statements; see King [19]. For many years, however, it was ignored: it is not quoted by Patinkin [22], the authoritative handbook of the 1950s and 1960s.

[2] Usually, this literature shows that liquidity affects economic decisions, in contrast to the prediction of the Modigliani–Miller theorem where only net-present value matters. See Bernanke et al. [3] for an up-to-date survey.

[3] SW also contains a, maybe better known, adverse-selection section.

Secondly, in both Bernanke and Gertler [2] and Kiyotaki and Moore [20] the external shock is not anticipated in advance. Hence, agents do not hedge in precaution. It seems, however, that agents who fail to foresee a repeated shock do not have rational expectations. That raises the concern that irrationality is an indispensable ingredient within such a theory. We show that this is not the case. In our model the whole sequence of future prices is rationally (and perfectly) foreseen. Moreover, contracts are 'complete' and all relevant information (future prices included) is internalized. To the best of our knowledge our example is the first clear-cut demonstration of a cycle generated solely by financial imperfections, without any modification of the rationality assumption.

More to the point, the issue at hand is that of 'indexation'. Consider, again, Kiyotaki and Moore [20].[4] The external shock operates *via* a price decline that decreases the value of collateral and, hence, borrowing capacity. It is well known that in that case insurance can easily be provided by price indexation.[5] Since such indexation is mutually beneficial, assuming it away is hard to justify.[6] In our model, the economy slumps due to endogenous reversion and that happens despite the fact that contracts are optimally designed on the basis of a perfect foresight of future prices. It follows that financial factors can affect business fluctuations even without assuming indexation away.

And finally, we use our model in order to clarify the role of a potential stabilizing policy: its existence and welfare evaluation. (Note that it is full rationality and completeness of contracts which open the way for the welfare analysis.) We start the analysis of this part by demonstrating that there exists a stabilizing policy, which can be interpreted as an ordinary demand policy. Then, we show that when costs and benefits are aggregated, the policy produces a net positive surplus. But, unfortunately, the surplus cannot be lump-sum redistributed so as to generate a Pareto-dominating allocation. The reason is that lump-sum transfers do not exist in our model: because rents and liquidity matter, any reallocation of wealth affects real economic decisions.

As noted, our model is, essentially, a dynamic extension of the SW model with overlapping two-period projects. Hence, external finance generates excessive risk taking (i.e., above first-best probability of failure).[7] Entrepreneurs face a

---

[4] The problem goes back to Fisher [10]. In his view, the Great Depression was a result of money-price deflation that increased the real value of corporate debt, drained capital out of the corporate sector, which caused an adverse supply effect. But the initial effect can be indexed away to the mutual benefit of lenders and borrowers. Note that Fisher's explanation has two ingredients: lack of indexation and financial imperfections (which create the link between corporate wealth and supply). We show that the second effect is sufficient for a business-cycle theory. Needless to say, the first ingredient is extremely problematic. It may have been one of the reasons that prevented a serious consideration of Fishers's theory for so long.

[5] Indexation is assumed away for the shock period only. All subsequent price dynamics is indexed.

[6] We believe our model can be used in order to defend the Kiyotaki–Moore model against such criticism: had their economy slumped due to endogenous reversion, there would have been no need to assume indexation away.

[7] After SW, the words risk and probability of failure are used interchangeably.

downward sloping demand schedule so that prices fall when quantities boom. So here our story follows:[8] boom production leads to low prices, which generates low liquidity and increases external finance. That leads to excessive risk taking and a high rate of failure—a bust. When quantities decrease, prices increase, liquidity flows in and the moral-hazard problem is mitigated. Low levels of risk taking will expand the industry, and it all starts over again.[9]

It is important to stress that our model is 'clean' in the sense that it contains no unusual ingredient that drives the result. As mentioned above, contracts are fully endogenized. The asymmetric information structure is a simple textbook moral-hazard problem. The basic story about the relation between external finance and risk taking comes from SW. The extension of project duration to more than one period is just an ordinary (and realistic) feature of capital theory. Preferences are standard and display risk neutrality in the *numeraire* good. In addition, we take a precautionary measure in order to assure that our result is properly interpreted: we prove formally (in Appendix A), that output quickly converges to a stationary level once the moral hazard is removed. Hence, the cycle results from the financial imperfection.

We have already made clear that the primary goal of this paper is theoretical. Obviously, it does not produce realistic time series. Yet, it is not without empirical value. A salient feature of the business cycle is that it is usually accompanied by a 'credit cycle:' profits tend to decline towards the peak of the cycle, and the 'liquidity crunch' leads the economy into the bust.[10] The essence of this story is captured in our model: it is the high quantities of the boom which depress prices and create the liquidity shortage that increases the propensity to default that ends in a bust.

It is also noteworthy that our model can, in principle, be calibrated. The main behavioral relationship—the inverse relation between liquidity and default risk—is observable and can be estimated. Indeed, Holtz-Eakin et al. [17] examine the wealth effect of an 'exogenous' windfall (bequest) on the probability of survival of individual entrepreneurs. They find a significant positive effect which is consistent with our modeling. Needless to say there is, still, much work to be done before the model is ripe for calibration.

There are two other branches of the literature which deserve to be mentioned. Boldrin and Woodford [6] survey the general equilibrium theory on endogenous fluctuations (*a la* Day [8] or Grandmont [12]). They argue that although endogenous cycles are compatible with complete markets, some 'friction' (financial or other) is probably needed in order to get empirically relevant results. A step in that direction is taken by Woodford [26] (see also Bewley [4] and Scheinkman and Weiss [23]). In his model equilibrium dynamics may be chaotic, but financial

---

[8] Some elements of this story can be found in Sussman [25].

[9] There is some similarity with the cobweb model, but, with differences in two major respects: first, rationality of expectations, and second, the cobweb model is a partial equilibrium model. Nevertheless, the general equilibrium characteristics of our model are too primitive to be emphasized.

[10] See Gertler and Gilchrist [11], Kashyap et al. [18] and Bernanke et al. [3].

structure is crude and exogenously determined. Secondly, there is a growing literature, mostly of a static nature, on more realistic features of financial structure and aggregate economic activity. Many emphasize the role of the banking system, and describe mechanisms by which aggregate economic activity may be affected by changes in the cost of financial intermediation or by the level of banks' capitalization.[11] Some authors have stressed the role of bankruptcy costs (Greenwald and Stiglitz [14]). Others still have remarked on the role different financial instruments (i.e., debt and equity) play in the 'transmission mechanism' (see [14] or King [19]).

The paper is organized as follows. Section 2 presents the model. Section 3 analyzes the contract problem and shows the relationship between liquidity and risk taking. Section 4 derives the aggregate supply and defines a market equilibrium. Section 5 discusses the existence and stability of equilibrium cycles. A welfare analysis of the stabilizing policy is provided in Section 6. Section 7 contains some concluding remarks.

2. THE MODEL

Consider an infinite horizon, discrete time ($t = 0, 1, \dots$) economy with two goods. One is a *numeraire* good which is used for both consumption and investment, the other is a perishable staple good which is used for consumption only. We call it *coffee*.[12] At each date there is a perfectly competitive spot market in which coffee is exchanged for the numeraire good at a price p_t.

There are two types of agents in our economy: entrepreneurs (who grow coffee) and consumers-lenders (who consume coffee and provide external finance to the entrepreneurs). Consumers are identical and live forever. They consume both the numeraire and coffee and they are risk-neutral in terms of the numeraire good:

$$E_t \left\{ \sum_{s=0}^{\infty} \left(\frac{1}{1+r} \right)^s [x_{t+s} + u(c_{t+s})] \right\}. \tag{1}$$

x_{t+s} and c_{t+s} are the consumption of the numeraire and coffee, respectively, at date $t + s$; $u(c)$ is an increasing and concave utility function; the constant $r > 0$ is the rate of time preference; E_t denotes expectations formed at date t. Let a_t denote the amount of (period t) external finance they supply; and let $\tilde{R}_t$ be the gross (random) rate of return per unit of finance extended at period t (to be determined by the contract problem below). Then, the consumers' budget constraint is

$$x_t + p_t c_t + a_t = e + \tilde{R}_{t-1} a_{t-1}. \tag{2}$$

---

[11] See Bernanke [1], Bolton and Freixas [7], Blum and Hellwig [5], Holmstrom and Tirole [16].

[12] We use this name to hint that the coffee sector may be interpreted as a small open economy which is highly dependent on the production of a single staple good.

Suppose that consumers' endowments are such that the solution to their problem is always interior.[13] Their behavior is characterized by two simple behavioral functions: (i) a time-invariant perfectly elastic supply of lending at the expected gross rate of return $1 + r$ (namely, r is the riskless rate), and (ii) a time-invariant downward sloping demand for coffee, $D(p_t)$, which will only depend on the spot price of coffee at each period. The one-period indirect utility function of the consumers can be written as

$$U(p_t),$$

where, by Roy's Identity,

$$U'(p_t) = -D(p_t). \tag{3}$$

At each period a measure one continuum of entrepreneurs is born, each of which lives for three periods. They consume no coffee themselves, and have linear preferences in the numeraire good; their rate of time preference, r, is the same as the consumers'. (Hence, given that r is the riskless rate, entrepreneurs are indifferent about the timing of consumption.) Entrepreneurs have exclusive access to the production technology of coffee: each is endowed with a single, indivisible, project that can be activated by investing one unit of the *numeraire* good. Once invested, this amount is sunk.

Once activated (at the entrepreneurs' first period of life), a project has two production periods. In the first period it yields $Y > 0$ units of coffee deterministically. In the second period it yields Y units of coffee in case of 'success' and zero in case of 'failure.' The probability of success is π. Returns in the second period of production are independent across projects, which means that there is no aggregate uncertainty in the economy. Both the entrepreneur, his project and the capital invested perish, simultaneously, after the second production period. It may be useful to think of failure as a random event which destroys capital after the first production period.

An entrepreneur can affect the probability of 'success,' π, through the amount of 'effort' he puts into the project. We denote the disutility of effort (evaluated at the second production period, in terms of the numeraire) by $\psi(\pi)$, and assume

$$\psi(0) = 0, \ \psi' \geq 0, \ \psi'' > 0, \ \psi''' = 0, \ \psi'(0) = 0, \ \psi'1 = +\infty. \tag{4}$$

Hence, increasing the probability of success entails a sacrifice of entrepreneurial utility (at an increasing rate). The last two assumptions are made to guarantee that the entrepreneurs' problem has an interior solution. The assumption about the third derivative guarantees that the solution is a continuous function of the relevant prices (see below).

---

[13] It is sufficient to assume that the endowment e is large enough to cover the entrepreneurs' financing requirements at each date.

Entrepreneurs are born penniless, and have to borrow in order to activate their projects. Note, however, that the $t - 1$ born entrepreneur has a deterministic cash flow of $p_t Y$, in the first production period, which is not affected by the agency problem. This source of 'liquidity' plays a crucial role in the analysis below.

We assume that effort is not observable by the consumers. It is therefore impossible to write contracts contingent upon the amount of effort the entrepreneur puts into his project. A certain level of effort can be implemented only by making it incentive compatible with the entrepreneur's self interest. Crucially, we impose no other constraint on the problem, and allow entrepreneurs and financiers to use any observable information they wish so as to minimize the agency problem.

It is worth mentioning that our story is, in essence, the same as in SW.[14] The crucial assumption is that the $(t - 1$ born) entrepreneur may increase his second-period income (net of the disutility of effort), $p_{t+1} Y - \psi(\pi)$, by increasing the risk of failure. As we show below, the outcome is the same as in SW: when investment is externally financed, entrepreneurs tend to take an excess risk of failure. We differ from SW in that we split net income into an observable (pecuniary) part and a non-observable (non-pecuniary) part. That is done in order to make effort unobservable *ex post*, so that the contract is resilient to a De Meza and Webb [9] sort of criticism. Also, we have a continuum of failure probabilities rather than two ('risky' and 'safe' in SW), but that is done, mainly, for analytical convenience.

3. THE CONTRACT PROBLEM

In this section we solve the contract problem. It is convenient to consider the problem of the generation born at $t - 1$ so that t is the first production period and $t + 1$ the second production period.

To establish a benchmark, consider the first-best, full-information problem. In that case, the interests of the entrepreneur and the financier are aligned: to maximize the project's net present value and to activate it if such value is positive. Hence

$$\text{Maximize}_{\pi} -1 + \left(\frac{1}{1+r}\right) \cdot p_t Y + \left(\frac{1}{1+r}\right)^2 [\pi p_{t+1} Y - \psi(\pi)]. \tag{5}$$

The first order condition of this problem is

$$p_{t+1} Y = \psi'(\pi), \tag{6}$$

which has an ordinary production-theory interpretation. Effort is an input; to find its optimal amount one should equate the value of its marginal product to its marginal cost.

---

[14] In the moral-hazard section of their paper.

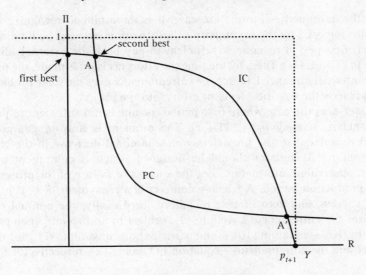

Figure 1. *The contract problem*

We plot, in Figure 1, a rotated (by 90°, counter clock-wise) ψ' curve with its origin at the point $(p_{t+1}Y, 0)$. For reasons to become clear below, we call it the IC curve.[15] It follows from Eq. (6) that the first-best level of effort is at the intersection of the IC curve with the vertical axis (see Figure 1). Obviously, when the price of second-period output increases, the value of the marginal product of effort increases as well and the input of effort should be increased. We refer to this as the *profitability* effect.

To check whether activating the project is profitable at all, denote the solution of (5) by the function

$$\pi = \bar{\Pi}(p_{t+1}), \quad \text{where} \quad \bar{\Pi}' > 0, \tag{7}$$

and the value of the project by

$$\bar{v}(p_t, p_{t+1}) \equiv -1\left(\frac{1}{1+r}\right) \cdot p_t Y$$

$$+ \left(\frac{1}{1+r}\right)^2 \{\bar{\Pi}(p_{t+1})p_{t+1}Y - \psi[\bar{\Pi}(p_{t+1})]\}, \tag{8}$$

which is increasing in both prices. Then the project is activated if and only if its value is positive. Note that p_t has a pure rent effect on profits (and the activation decision), but it does not interfere with the optimal allocation of effort. The reason is that effort is an input in the production of second-period output; hence, it is not affected by first-period prices.

[15] The shape of the IC curve is determined by the assumptions in (4).

Now the asymmetric-information case. It is important to recognize that the constraint imposed by the asymmetry of information may not be binding. Suppose that first-period revenue is sufficient to pay back the external financiers, namely $p_t Y \geq (1 + r)$. Then, by the time the effort decision is made, the project is already internally financed. Hence the entrepreneur solves the same problem as in (5) and inserts the first-best level of effort into the project.

Consider next the case where first-period income is not sufficient to pay back the financiers, namely $p_t Y < (1 + r)$. The problem is how to guarantee the required repayment to the financiers with a minimal decrease in the entrepreneur's welfare. A contract should be designed which is contingent upon all relevant, observable information, i.e., the success or failure of the project in the second production period. A feasible contract is a repayment, $R \in [0, p_{t+1} Y]$ in case of success, and zero in case of failure. Technically, the optimal contract maximizes the entrepreneur's welfare (9), subject to an incentive compatibility constraint (IC)—equation (10)—and participation constraints (PC) for both the financier and the entrepreneur—equation (11) and (12), respectively:

$$\underset{\pi, R}{\text{Maximize}} \left(\frac{1}{1+r} \right)^2 [\pi(p_{t+1} Y - R) - \psi(\pi)] \tag{9}$$

subject to:

$$\pi \in \arg\max_{\pi} \left(\frac{1}{1+r} \right)^2 [\pi(p_{t+1} Y - R) - \psi(\pi)], \tag{10}$$

$$\left(\frac{1}{1+r} \right) \cdot p_t Y + \left(\frac{1}{1+r} \right)^2 \pi R \geq 1, \tag{11}$$

$$\left(\frac{1}{1+r} \right)^2 [\pi(p_{t+1} Y - R) - \psi(\pi)] \geq 0. \tag{12}$$

By standard considerations one can show that the constraint in (12) is not binding. It follows that the feasibility set is defined by Eq. (10) and (11) only. First, consider the first-order condition of equation (10):

$$p_{t+1} Y - R = \psi'(\pi). \tag{13}$$

Hence, for any repayment R, the incentive-compatible level of effort can be found with the aid of the IC curve of Figure 1: just measure R on the horizontal axis and find π on the curve. Next, consider the financier's participation constraint (11). The (R, π) combinations that satisfy this constraint lie above the PC curve, which is given by

$$\left(\frac{1}{1+r}\right) \cdot p_t Y + \left(\frac{1}{1+r}\right)^2 \pi R = 1. \tag{14}$$

That is the rectangular hyperbola in Figure 1. Hence, the feasibility set is defined by the arc of the IC curve between points A and A'. It is easy to see that moving leftwards, and closer to the first-best point, would increase the value of the objective (9).[16] Hence, point A, where (11) holds with equality, is the second-best, optimal contract.

It is obvious that the IC and PC curves may not intersect at all, in which case the feasibility set defined by constraints (10)–(12) is empty. In that case no funds can be obtained by the entrepreneur. Let the boundary of the set of activation prices be given by the $p_{t+1} = f(p_t)$ function, defined by the tangency of the IC and PC curves. Then, the project is activated if prices are above f, and is not activated if prices fall below f. It is easy to see that f is downward sloping.

Hence, the optimal contract is characterized by three 'regimes:' internal finance, external finance and no activation as follows:

$$\begin{aligned}
\pi_1 &= \Pi(p_t, p_{t+1}) \\
&= \begin{cases} \bar{\Pi}(p_{t+1}) & \text{if } p_t > (r+1)/Y \\ \text{'point } A\text{'} & \text{if } p_t < (1+r)/Y \text{ and } p_{t+1} > f(p_t). \\ 0 & \text{if } p_{t+1} < f(p_t) \end{cases}
\end{aligned} \tag{15}$$

Let us summarize the solution with the aid of Figure 2, where the three regimes are clearly visible.

(i) Internal finance: this regime is effective when p_t is sufficiently high for the project to be financed out of the first-period deterministic income. Higher first-period prices will increase rents but will have no effect on the allocation of effort as it is already at the first-best level. Hence, the Π function is flat with respect to p_t (see Figure 2).

(ii) External finance: this regime is effective for interim p_t's such that the project cannot be internally financed, but is still activated. It is clear from Figure 1 that effort is *below* the first-best level. Further, $\Pi_1 > 0$: as p_t increases, effort increases *continuously*[17] and approaches its first-best level. The reason is straightforward: p_t is a source of liquidity which allows the entrepreneur to mitigate the distortionary effect of external finance. Hence, the Π function is upward sloping with respect to p_t (see Figure 2). The crucial difference between this regime and the one above is in the presence of this *liquidity*

---

[16] To prove this claim diagrammatically notice that the area below the IC and right of R represents the value of the objective multiplied by $(1+r)^2$.

[17] Within the external finance regime continuity is guaranteed by $\psi''' > 0$ (see Figure 1); continuity is preserved at the switch from the external to the internal finance regime: as p_t approaches $(1+r)/Y$ (from below) the PC curve collapses to the axes and effort approaches the first-best level.

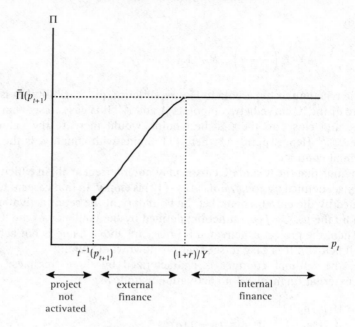

Figure 2. *The three regimes*

effect: whether first-period income has a pure-rent or an allocational effect. Note also that $\Pi_2 > 0$ (see Figure 1), thus, since $\bar{\Pi}' > 0$ as well, the whole curve in Figure 2 shifts upwards when p_{t+1} increases.

(iii) No activation: this regime is effective when p_t is very low. Financial requirements are so high that incentive-compatible effort falls to a level at which financiers cannot get the market return on their funds. Finance is not supplied, the project is not activated, and effort jumps *discontinuously* to zero.[18]

For the sake of the welfare analysis in Section 6, we define

$$v(p_t, p_{t+1}) \equiv -1 + \left(\frac{1}{1+r}\right) p_t Y$$
$$+ \left(\frac{1}{1+r}\right)^2 \{\Pi(p_t, p_{t+1}) p_{t+1} Y - \psi[\Pi(p_t, p_{t+1})]\}, \tag{16}$$

which represents the present value of entrepreneurial profits, provided the project is activated at all.[19] It is easy to check that the two partial derivatives of (16) are positive.

[18] When the IC and the PC curves are tangent π is still strictly positive.

[19] Equation (14) is obviously valid for the internal finance regime, but also for the external finance regime. To see the latter, one can use the fact that the financier's participation constraint (11) is binding to rewrite (9).

4. AGGREGATE SUPPLY AND MARKET EQUILIBRIUM

Credit rationing is a possibility in our model. Intuitively, suppose that prices are p_t and $p_{t+1} = f(p_t)$ such that the IC and the PC curves are just tangent. These prices are demand determined and some $(t-1$ born) entrepreneurs do not participate in the market. Now what would happen if they participated? Prices would fall further below, which would drive *all* entrepreneurs into the no activation regime. Hence the credit rationing. We focus, below, on no-rationing equilibria because they are simpler to analyze and sufficient to illustrate the functioning of the reversion mechanism in which we are interested.

Suppose there exist an equilibrium with no rationing at any point on the equilibrium path. (We provide a condition that guarantees the existence of such an equilibrium at the end of this section.) Hence all entrepreneurs participate in the market, and the market-clearing condition in period $t+1$ is simply

$$[1 + \Pi(p_t, p_{t+1})]Y = D(p_{t+1}). \tag{17}$$

Note that the $t+1$ supply is made up of the output of all the t born entrepreneurs who are producing for the first time, and the successful $t-1$ born entrepreneurs who are producing for the second time.

Equation (17) defines a first-order difference equation in prices. Denote it by

$$p_{t+1} = g(p_t).$$

The function g has two properties which are essential to our analysis. First, if projects are internally financed, i.e., $p_t \geq (1+r)/Y$, then the market-clearing condition is

$$[1 + \bar{\Pi}(p_{t+1})]Y = D(p_{t+1}). \tag{18}$$

The solution of (18) in terms of p_{t+1} is unique. Denote it by $\bar{p}$. It follows that, for $p_t \geq (1+r)/Y$, p_{t+1} equals $\bar{p}$ as Figure 3 shows. Intuitively, projects are internally financed, so that higher period t prices create additional rents, but rents do not affect effort, so the next period price does not change in response.

On the other hand, if $p_t < (1+r)/Y$, g is downward sloping

$$g'(p_t) = -\frac{\Pi_1}{\Pi_2 - D'} < 0. \tag{19}$$

Notice that g is continuous at point $(1+r)/Y$ (see Figure 3 again) due to the corresponding continuity of Π. As for the magnitude of g' (to the left of $(1+r)/Y$), note that the more responsive demand is to changes in prices, the flatter the curve is. It is useful to describe two limiting cases:

(i) Inelastic demand. As $D' \to 0$, g approaches the level set defined by $\Pi(p_t, p_{t+1}) = \bar{\Pi}(\bar{p})$. Using (13) and (14) one can verify that this level set is linear with a (downward) slope of $-(1+r)/\pi < -1$.
(ii) Perfectly elastic demand. If $D' \to -\infty$, g will be flat and equal to $\bar{p}$.

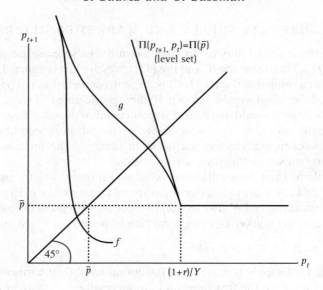

Figure 3. *The difference equation.*

Thus, for intermediate values of D', the g function lies anywhere in the triangle below the above mentioned level set, and the horizontal line $p_{t+1} = \bar{p}$. So, it turns out, the slope of g may be greater than one (in absolute value).

Having discussed the law of motion, let us look at the initial conditions. Suppose that at $t = 0$ there is a measure one continuum of entrepreneurs (born at $t = -1$) who have only one production period left. Given their wealth, they choose an effort level π_0 such that the initial price, p_1, is determined by

$$(1 + \pi_0)Y = D(p_1).$$

Since there exist a one-to-one mapping from the wealth of the initial generation to p_1,[20] we consider the initial price p_1 as a given data for our economy.

We can now state a sufficient condition for a no-rationing equilibrium. Obviously, any pair of consecutive prices (p_t, p_{t+1}) should lie above the graph of the f function. So consider the case where g and f intersect like in Figure 3; if the point $(\bar{p}, \bar{p})$ lies above f, then whenever p_t exceeds $(1 + r)/Y$, the following p_{t+1} and the whole continuation equilibrium sequence will be above f; if, in addition, the initial point is above f the equilibrium path will have no rationing at any point. Hence, a sufficient condition for a no-rationing equilibrium is

$$\bar{p} > f(\bar{p}), \quad \text{and} \quad p_1 \geq \bar{p}. \tag{20}$$

---

[20] Namely: for any initial price p_1 there exists a level of initial wealth, $g^{-1}(p_1)Y$, such that π_0 is a rational choice for a perfectly-foreseen p_1.

That condition (20) can be satisfied at all is clear from the fact that if the demand D became larger the graph of g would shift upwards and to the right, whereas the graph of f would remain unchanged. Hence, for some demand schedules this sufficient condition can be satisfied.

Before we continue, let us just point out that the downward sloping segment of g captures the basic intuition of our model. When the period t price of coffee increases, entrepreneurs are more liquid. They are thus less dependent on external finance, which gives them an incentive to increase π. That increases the quantity supplied next period and decreases prices. So next period entrepreneurs would be less liquid. Hence, a cobweb sort of dynamics appears and cycles may be generated.

5. DYNAMICS, STEADY STATES AND CYCLES

Denote the stationary point of g by p^*. Then, given an initial price p_1, three types of equilibria can emerge

(i) If the point $[(1+r)/Y, \bar{p}]$ lies to the left of the 45° line then $p^* = \bar{p}$. The system would converge to its stationary point at $t = 3$, the latest.

(ii) If the point $[(1+r)/Y, \bar{p}]$ lies to the right of the 45° line then $p^* > \bar{p}$. If $|g'(p^*)| < 1$, the system would converge[21] to p^* with short run oscillations which would die out, eventually.

(iii) If $p^* > \bar{p}$ (like in the previous case), but the system cannot converge to its stationary point (say) because $|g'(p^*)| > 1$, then the system would converge (after a finite number of periods) to a (two-period) periodic equilibrium as in Figure 4. The only exception is when the initial price happens to equal p^*. Since the high price is associated with a contraction of supply we call it the 'bust price.' By the same logic, we call the other price the 'boom price.' Note that entrepreneurs live through both a boom and a bust, but they face different sequences of the two prices depending on whether they start to produce in a boom ('boom start-ups') or in a bust ('bust start-ups').

A few points are in place here. The stationary cycle may not be unique. But all stationary cycles have a periodicity of two.[22] Further, the whole equilibrium path is uniquely determined by the g function and the initial condition. If there are many stationary cycles, the initial price will determine to which of these the system will converge. Our story involves no element of multiplicity of equilibria. Note also that the system cannot 'jump' to p^* by means of saddle path convergence because of the tight correspondence between initial prices and initial wealth as discussed above.

---

[21] At least from a neighborhood of p^*.

[22] It is well-known that it takes a non-monotonic (first-order) difference equation to produce higher order cycles, see Grandmont [13].

It is obvious that without the informational problem, the system would quickly converge to the stationary price $\bar{p}$.[23] That reflects some fundamental differences in the way a moral-hazard economy operates, relative to the full-information one. As already emphasized, rents have no allocational role in the full-information economy. In that case p_{t+1} is not affected at all by p_t, and can 'freely' jump to $\bar{p}$. The whole dynamic relation between p_t and p_{t+1} results from the mechanics of the contract and the agency problem. Without that mechanism cycles are not generated. In fact one should be more careful about that argument: the discussion above already assumes (*via* the restriction on the location of f) that the demand for coffee is high enough so that all entrepreneurs get sufficiently high rents and participate in the market. What would happen in the full information case if demand is not high enough to assure positive net present value under full participation? Can the dynamics of partial entry generate cyclical prices? The answer is no. In Appendix A we explore partial entry dynamics with a binding 'zero profit' condition $\bar{v}(p_t, p_{t+1}) = 0$, and prove that this equilibrium has a unique saddle path convergence to a stationary point. (Note that in this case, unlike in the asymmetric information case entrepreneurs are indifferent between participating in the market and staying out of it.) Hence, a full-information economy will not oscillate even without the restrictions imposed on the location of the demand schedule. This property gives extra power to our claim that moral hazard is the very ingredient that generates cycles in our model.

It is obvious that the economy is more cyclical the steeper is the g function. Looking again at equation (18) we can relate its slope to the liquidity and the profitability effects mentioned above (in relation to Figure 2). g is steeper the stronger is the liquidity effect Π_1, and the weaker is the profitability effect Π_2. That a strong liquidity effect contributes to cyclicality is in line with the main thrust of the paper: entrepreneurs depend more on external finance, and effort is reduced further away from the first best. Note, however, that a weak profitability effect contributes to cyclicality. To understand why, consider an entrepreneur who starts to produce in the bust (see Figure 4). Obviously he is little liquid and may be tempted to choose a low level of effort. But then, he anticipates that other entrepreneurs will do the same, generating high second period prices which will bring about high profits. This will push him in the direction of a higher level of effort. The more effort he puts, the lower are next period prices, the flatter is the g function, and the smaller is the magnitude of output fluctuations.

So flows of wealth in and out of the entrepreneurial sector keep on fueling the cycle. A boom leads to a bust and the bust to a boom. Importantly, no constraints on rationality, either via expectations formation or suboptimal contracting are imposed. In particularly, we do not assume indexation away: all contracts written from period one onwards make use of all available information, including the future price of coffee. But this sort of indexation does not provide insurance and it

---

[23] As indicated, a non-negative net present value condition should be satisfied. It is easy to see that condition (20) ensures that.

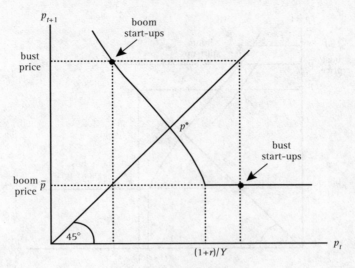

Figure 4. *Endogenous cycles*

does not smooth entrepreneurs' income. We may think about it in the following way: since the state of the world (i.e., the initial p_1) is already realized when an entrepreneur is born, insurance markets are closed by a standard Hirshleifer [15] argument. On the other hand, our theory depends on some initial, maybe just a little deviation, from the stationary price p^*. We build no theory to explain the initial discrepancy, but we show that the cycle can persist even as we get arbitrarily further away from period one.[24]

6. STABILIZATION: WELFARE ANALYSIS

Now to the policy issue: can a stabilizing policy be implemented, and could such a policy be justified on the basis of some welfare accounting? We focus on the case in which the economy is at the periodic equilibrium as in Figure 4, with alternating 'boom' (low) and 'bust' (high) prices, $\bar{p}$ and $\hat{p}$ respectively (see Figure 5). Obviously, entrepreneurs who start up production in the bust (when prices are high) put the first-best amount of effort into their projects. Hence, there is no point in trying to improve on them. But those who start up in the boom (when prices are low) are excessive risk-takers. Getting them closer to the first-best level of effort would require enhancing the liquidity or the profitability of their projects by means of a subsidy. Suppose that is done by an expansionary demand policy in the bust, just like in an old-fashioned macroeconomics textbook.

---

[24] Unlike in Kiyotaki and Moore [20] where the cycle dies out, eventually, and it takes an additional 'unanticipated' shock to start it all over again.

J. Suarez and O. Sussman

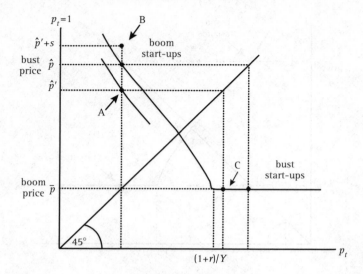

Figure 5. *Stabilization policy*

Consider a perfectly foreseeable policy that allocates a subsidy s per unit of output to old boom start-up entrepreneurs, in a bust period.[25] Note that the policy is discriminating: entrepreneurs who start producing in the bust do not get the subsidy. To see the effect of the subsidy, use the implicit function theorem on the market-clearing condition for the bust price

$$[1 + \Pi(\bar{p}, \hat{p} + s)]Y - D(\hat{p}) = 0,$$

in order to set

$$-1 < \frac{\partial \hat{p}}{\partial s} = -\frac{\Pi_2 Y}{\Pi_2 Y - D'(\hat{p})} < 0. \tag{21}$$

Consider the boom start-ups and assume, for the moment, that they face the same boom price, $\bar{p}$, as before. The subsidy drives these entrepreneurs closer to the first-best level of effort. Hence, bust quantities are expanded (see the broken line in Figure 5); the market-price of coffee—as seen by coffee buyers and bust start-ups (who do not get the subsidy)—falls to $\hat{p}'$. Since the price falls by less than the subsidy (see (21)), the price, as seen by the boom start-ups increases to $\hat{p}' + s$. Note that if the subsidy is not too big, the lower bust price will not affect the effort of the bust start-ups, who are already at the first best. Hence, the boom price, $\hat{p}$, is indeed unaffected. It follows that the price combination observed by the boom start-ups is given by point B, while the price combination observed by the bust

---

[25] A policy giving a subsidy per unit of first period output or per investment project to each generation of boom start-ups has an identical impact.

start-ups is given by point C. But then, the market (i.e., buyers) price combination is given by point A. Obviously, the amplitude of boom-bust market prices is decreased by the policy: from $(\bar{p}, \hat{p})$ to $(\bar{p}, \hat{p}')$. Since market prices are monotonic in quantities the policy is, indeed, unambiguously stabilizing.

It is obvious that the bust start-ups are hurt by the policy: they face a lower price when starting-up and the same price when old. Obviously, boom start-ups gain by the policy. Also, coffee buyers gain by facing a lower price in the bust. To see whether the benefits exceed the losses, let us add-up both (they are easy to evaluate in terms of the numeraire); the whole computation is done for a bust period

$$W = (1+r)^2 \cdot v(\bar{p}, \hat{p}+s) + (1+r) \cdot \bar{v}(\hat{p}, \bar{p}) + U(\hat{p}) - s\Pi(\bar{p}, \hat{p}+s)Y.$$

W adds up the (properly capitalized) values of the projects of the boom and bust start-ups, the utility of the consumers, and the cost of the subsidy to the tax-payers.

Differentiating W with respect to s and evaluating at $s = 0$, we get

$$\frac{\partial W}{\partial s} = (1+r)^2 \cdot \frac{\partial v}{\partial \hat{p}}\left(1 + \frac{\partial \hat{p}}{\partial s}\right) + (1+r) \cdot \frac{\partial \bar{v}}{\partial \hat{p}} \cdot \frac{\partial \hat{p}}{\partial s} + U'(\hat{p}) \cdot \frac{\partial \hat{p}}{\partial s} - \Pi(\bar{p}, \hat{p})Y.$$

(See Appendix B for the derivatives in this and the next equation.) For brevity, denote $\partial \hat{p}/\partial s$ by $-\lambda$ (recalling that $0 < \lambda < 1$ by equation (21)), $\Pi(\bar{p}, \hat{p})$ by $\hat{\pi}$, and the repayment obligation of the boom start-ups by $\hat{R}$. Then, using Eq. (3), (8), (16), and $D(\hat{p}) = (1 + \hat{\pi})Y$, we can write

$$\frac{\partial W}{\partial s} = \hat{\pi}\left(Y - \frac{\partial \hat{R}}{\partial \hat{p}}\right)(1 - \lambda) - Y\lambda + (1 + \hat{\pi})Y\lambda - \hat{\pi}Y = -\hat{\pi}\frac{\partial \hat{R}}{\partial \hat{p}}(1 - \lambda),$$

where $\partial \hat{R}/\partial \hat{p}$ can be computed using (13) and (14). Note that if $\hat{R}$ were zero (as it is for the bust start-ups), the above derivative would equal zero; this confirms our intuition that there is no room for a subsidy like s in a boom. If $\hat{R}$ is positive (as it is for the boom born generation), then $\partial \hat{R}/\partial \hat{p} < 0$ and the aggregate welfare measure can be improved by choosing a positive s. Intuitively, unlike other agents, the marginal value of income for the entrepreneurs who start to produce in a boom is higher than one, since, in addition to the direct distributive effect, increasing their income has an allocational effect, that pushes them closer to the first best. Thus, when they obtain additional rents by means of the subsidy, they generate added value in excess of the taxpayers' loss.

From this result, it is tempting to say that Pareto improvements could be achieved by compensating the losers by lump-sum taxation. But this is not true. In a world where rents have a role in providing incentives, lump-sum taxes are not neutral. Consumers and bust start-ups could be lump-sum taxed without affecting their marginal decisions.[26] But if the boom start-up entrepreneurs were lump-sum taxed for compensation purposes (say, out of their first-period revenue) that would undo the allocational effect of the subsidy.[27]

Hence, the question of whether cycles as those described in this model should be stabilized has no clear answer. Stabilization policies are desirable according to a policy criterion which is weaker than Pareto optimality.

7. CONCLUDING REMARKS

As noted above, our modeling gives priority to analytical transparency rather than to realism. Since we model a pure reversion mechanism the system (while in a stationary cycle) reverts each period to its previous state: from boom to bust and vice versa, one period after another. Of course, this is an incomplete description of the fluctuations observed in the real world, as captured by macroeconomic time series.

There is no reason why the reversion and the propagation mechanisms cannot be combined, within a single model, in order to generate equilibria with realistic time-series properties. Namely, after a reversion period the propagation mechanism takes over for several periods and the system grows out of the recession. At a certain point it reverts back to a bust and it all starts over again. It is unlikely, however, that such a combined model can preserve the simplicity and transparency that characterizes the current one. Our experience with related models (work in progress) shows that important properties may vanish: the equilibrium path may not be unique, the dynamic system may be of a higher order, numerical procedures may have to replace analytical arguments. Also, getting a more realistic financial structure may require to depart from complete contracts, thus undermining one of the main points we make. We have thus chosen, in this paper, to put down the bare bones of the theoretical skeleton and prove some basic results. Hopefully, that would provide better foundations for future, more empirically motivated, work.

Meanwhile, it is useful to point out that even in its crude form our model can provide some insight into an important policy question. It is sometimes argued that insufficient indexation, especially in the banking sector is the source of financial instability. The remedy would be to make banks' assets and liabilities more responsive to market conditions, either through indexation or via securitization. It is argued that by the mere replacement of banks by mutual funds, much of the problem can be resolved.[28] Our analysis does not support that sort of

---

[26] It is immediate to check that the consumers' gain from the subsidy does not suffice to compensate for both its direct cost to the taxpayers and the losses caused to the bust start-ups.

[27] Strictly speaking, entrepreneurs cannot be lump-sum taxed in the second period. Since they have zero wealth in case of failure, any tax is necessarily state contingent, and can be avoided in probability by excessive risk taking. Hence, it is not neutral.

[28] See Mankiw [21] for an argument along these lines, though more in the context of liquidity provision and bank-runs.

an argument. Rather, it shows that even after contracts are made responsive to any relevant market price, 'financial instability' is still a basic fact of life: an inherent feature of a competitive market economy subject to moral hazard.

Appendix A

Existence and Uniqueness of a Saddle-Path in the Full-Information Economy

This Appendix analyzes first-best full-information dynamics. We prove that the system converges, within at most one period, to an equilibrium with stationary prices and stationary *total* output. It has been shown in the text that the optimal choice of π by the entrepreneurs facing prices (p_t, p_{t+1}) is $\bar{\Pi}(p_{t+1})$ and the associated net present value of the project is $\bar{v}(p_t, p_{t+1})$. Investment is feasible if and only if $\bar{v}(p_t, p_{t+1}) \geq 0$. In fact, when $\bar{v}(p_t, p_{t+1}) = 0$ entrepreneurs are indifferent between investing and not investing, and we may have a situation where only a fraction $q_t < 1$ of the entrepreneurs who can start up production at t activate their projects at $t - 1$. Allowing for that possibility, the dynamics of the system can be described by the market-clearing condition

$$[q_{t+1} + q_t \bar{\Pi}(p_{t+1})] Y = D(p_{t+1}), \tag{A1}$$

and the free-entry condition

$$\bar{v}(p_t, p_{t+1}) \begin{cases} > 0 & \text{and} \quad q_t = 1 \\ = 0 & \text{and} \quad q_t \in [0, 1] \\ < 0 & \text{and} \quad q_t = 0. \end{cases} \tag{A2}$$

Notice that $\bar{v}(p_t, p_{t+1}) = 0$ defines a first-order difference equation in p_t, with

$$dp_{t+1}/dp_t = (1 + r)/\bar{\Pi}(p_{t+1}) < -1. \tag{A3}$$

It intersects with the horizontal axis at $p_t = (1 + r)/Y$. Denote the stationary point of this difference equation by $\tilde{p}$ and recall that $\bar{p}$ was defined by $[1 + \bar{\Pi}(\bar{p})] Y = D(\bar{p})$. Clearly, if $\bar{p} \geq \tilde{p}$ then $\bar{p}$ is the stationary equilibrium with $q_t = 1$ for all t and, as shown in the text, the system converges to this steady state immediately.[29] If $\bar{p} < \tilde{p}$ the stationary price is $\tilde{p}$ and the stationary q_t is the value $\tilde{q}$ which satisfies $[1 + \bar{\Pi}(\tilde{p})]\tilde{q}Y = D(\tilde{p})$. We now show that convergence to the stationary price $\tilde{p}$ (within, at most, one period) is the unique equilibrium in the system. The proof is done in two steps.

---

[29] Actually, the demonstration in the text is for an initial value of $q_0 = 1$. But it extends immediately to other initial values, only that convergence will then take one period.

Step 1. *Existence of an equilibrium convergent to* $\tilde{p}$. Let q_0 and π_0 represent the initial conditions of the system in terms of the fraction and effort decision of the entrepreneurs who start up production at $t=0$ and whose projects are activated. Consider the following two cases:

(i) $q_0\pi_0 \in [0, [1+\bar{\Pi}(\tilde{p})]\tilde{q}]$. Then $p_t = \tilde{p}$ and $q_t = [1+\bar{\Pi}(\tilde{p})]\tilde{q} - \bar{\Pi}(\tilde{p})q_{t-1}$ for $t=1,2,\ldots$ is an equilibrium of the system given by (A1) and (A2).

(ii) $q_0\pi_0 \in ([1+\bar{\Pi}(\tilde{p})]\tilde{q}, 1]$. Then $p_1 < \tilde{p}$ and $p_t = \tilde{p}$ for $t=2, 3,\ldots$ and $q_1 = 0$ and $q_t = [1+\bar{\Pi}(\tilde{p})]\tilde{q} - \bar{\Pi}(\tilde{p})q_{t-1}$ for $t=2, 3,\ldots$, where p_1 solves $q_0\pi_0 Y = D(p_1)$, is an equilibrium of the system given by (A1) and (A2).

Checking the previous assertions is immediate. Notice that in (ii) $\bar{v}(p_1, p_2) < \bar{v}(\tilde{p}, \tilde{p}) = 0$, since $p_1 < \tilde{p}$. Note also that in both (i) and (ii) the convergence of q_t to $\tilde{q}$ is asymptotic and non-monotonic. Note also that no agent cares about these oscillations in q, least of all entrepreneurs themselves who are on the zero profit condition (A1) along the whole process.

Step 2. *Uniqueness.* We now show that there are no oscillations in prices after $t=2$. Suppose that there exists an equilibrium with such oscillations. Notice, first, that we can rule out the possibility of having oscillations with $\bar{v}(p_t, p_{t+1}) = 0$ for all t since that dynamics is explosive according to (A3); two consecutive $\bar{v} > 0$ or $\bar{v} < 0$ periods can be also excluded. Thus, oscillations must involve either (a) periods of $\bar{v} > 0$ between periods of $\bar{v} \leq 0$ or (b) periods of $\bar{v} < 0$ between periods of $\bar{v} \geq 0$. Further, some of these *switching* periods must dampen the otherwise explosive oscillations. Suppose (a): the cycle is dampened at $t=s$ with $\bar{v}(p_s, p_{s+1}) > 0$, hence $q_s = 1$. Then, $p_{s-1} \leq p_{s+1} < p_s$. Using (A1), $D(p_{s+1}) > D(p_s)$ implies

$$q_{s+1} - q_{s-1}\bar{\Pi}(p_s) > 1 - \bar{\Pi}(p_{s+1}). \tag{A4}$$

Similarly, as $D(p_{s-1}) \geq D(p_{s+1})$ and $\bar{\Pi}$ is increasing, $q_{s-1} - q_{s+1} \geq \bar{\Pi}(p_{s+1}) - q_{s-2}\bar{\Pi}(p_{s-1}) > 0$. Then,

$$q_{s+1} - q_{s-1}\bar{\Pi}(p_s) \leq q_{s+1} - q_{s+1}\bar{\Pi}(p_s). \tag{A5}$$

Using the property of $\bar{\Pi}$ again, we get

$$q_{s+1}[1 - \bar{\Pi}(p_s)] < 1 - \bar{\Pi}(p_{s+1}). \tag{A6}$$

Combining (A5) and (A6) we contradict (A4). A similar contradiction can be obtained for (b) where $\bar{v}(p_s, p_{s+1}) < 0$ and $p_s < p_{s+1} \leq p_{s-1}$.

From here we deduce that the saddle-path convergence to the stationary price described in Step 1 is the unique equilibrium of the system given by (A1) and (A2).

Appendix B

Derivatives Used in the Welfare Analysis

The partial derivatives of the solution of the contract problem for the external finance regime are

$$\frac{\partial \pi}{\partial p_t} = \frac{(1+r)Y}{\pi \psi''(\pi) - R},$$

$$\frac{\partial \pi}{\partial p_{t+1}} = \frac{\pi Y}{\pi \psi''(\pi) - R},$$

$$\frac{\partial R}{\partial p_t} = \frac{\psi''(\pi)(1+r)Y}{\pi \psi''(\pi) - R},$$

$$\frac{\partial R}{\partial p_{t+1}} = \frac{RY}{\pi \psi''(\pi) - R}.$$

Notice that $\pi \psi''(\pi) - R > 0$ because of the relative slopes of the IC and PC curves at the optimum. The partial derivatives of equation (16) for the external finance regime are

$$\frac{\partial v}{\partial p_t} = -\frac{\Pi(p_t, p_{t+1})}{1+r} \frac{\partial R}{\partial p_t},$$

$$\partial v_{t+1} = \frac{\Pi(p_t, p_{t+1})}{1+r} \left(Y - \frac{\partial R}{\partial p_{t+1}} \right).$$

REFERENCES

1. B. Bernanke, Non-monetary effects in the propagation of the Great Depression, *Amer. Econ. Rev.* **73** (1983), 257–276.
2. B. Bernanke and M. Gertler, Agency costs, net worth, and business fluctuations, *Amer. Econ. Rev.* **79** (1989), 14–31.
3. B. Bernanke, M. Gertler, and S. Gilchrist, The financial accelerator and the flight to quality, *Rev. Econ. Statist.* **78** (1996), 1–15.
4. T. Bewley, Dynamic implications of the form of the budget constraint, *in* 'Models of Economic Dynamics' (H. Sonnenschein, Ed.), Springer-Verlag, New York, 1983.
5. J. Blum and M. Hellwig, 'The Macroeconomic Implications of Capital Adequacy Requirements for Banks,' WWZ Discussion Paper No. 9416 University of Basel, 1994.
6. M. Boldrin and M. Woodford, Equilibrium models displaying endogenous fluctuations and chaos, *J. Monet. Econ.* **25** (1990), 189–222.
7. P. Bolton and X. Freixas, Direct bond financing, financial intermediation and investment: an incomplete contract perspective, unpublished manuscript, ECARE, Brussels, 1994.
8. R. Day, Irregular growth cycles, *Amer. Econ. Rev.* **72** (1982), 406–414.

9. D. De Meza and D. C. Webb, Too much investment: a problem of asymmetric information, *Quart. J. Econ.* **102** (1987), 281–292.

10. I. Fisher, The debt-deflation theory of Great Depressions, *Econometrica* **1** (1933), 337–357.

11. M. Gertler and S. Gilchrist, Monetary policy, business cycles, and the behavior of small manufacturing firms, *Quart. J. Econ.* **109** (1994), 309–340.

12. J. M. Grandmont, On endogenous competitive business cycles, *Econometrica* **53** (1985), 995–1046.

13. J. M. Grandmont, Periodic and aperiodic behavior in discrete, one-dimensional, dynamical systems, *in* 'Contributions to Mathematical Economics' (W. Hildenbrand and A. Mas-Collel, Eds.), North-Holland, New York, 1986.

14. B. C. Greenwald and J. E. Stiglitz, Financial market imperfections and business cycles, *Quart. J. Econ.* **108** (1993), 77–114.

15. J. Hirshleifer, The private and social value of information and the reward to inventive activity, *Amer. Econ. Rev.* **61** (1971), 561–574.

16. B. Holmstrom and J. Tirole, Financial intermediation, loanable funds and the real sector, unpublished manuscript, Massachusetts Institute of Technology, 1994.

17. D. Holtz-Eakin, D. Joulfaian, and H. Rosen, Sticking it out: Entrepreneurial survival and liquidity constraints, *J. Polit. Economy* **102** (1994), 53–75.

18. A. K. Kashyap, J. C. Stein, and D. W. Wilcox, Monetary policy and credit conditions: Evidence from the composition of external finance, *Amer. Econ. Rev.* **83** (1993), 78–98.

19. M. King, Debt deflation: Theory and evidence, *Eur. Econ. Rev.* **38** (1994), 419–445.

20. N. Kiyotaki and J. H. Moore, Credit cycles, *J. Pout. Economy* **105** (1997), 211–248.

21. N. G. Mankiw, Discussion of 'Looting: The economic underworld of bankruptcy for profit' by G. Akerlof and P. Romer, *Brookings Pap. Econ. Act.* **2** (1993), 64–67.

22. D. Patinkin, 'Money, Interest, and Prices', Harper and Row, New York, 1965.

23. J. Scheinkman and L. Weiss, Borrowing constraints and aggregate economic activity, *Econometrica* **54** (1986), 23–45.

24. J. Stiglitz and A. Weiss, Credit rationing in markets with imperfect information, *Amer. Econ. Rev.* **71** (1981), 393–410.

25. O. Sussman, On moral hazard and spontaneous fluctuations, unpublished manuscript, Ben-Gurion University of the Negev, 1993.

26. M. Woodford, Imperfect financial intermediation and complex dynamics, *in* 'Economic Complexity: Chaos, Sunspot, Bubbles, and Nonlinearity' (W. A. Barnett, J. Geweke, and K. Shell, Eds.), Cambridge Univ. Press, Cambridge, 1989.

Index

Index